Hugh Walker

The greater Victorian poets

Hugh Walker

The greater Victorian poets

ISBN/EAN: 9783743658127

Printed in Europe, USA, Canada, Australia, Japan

Cover: Foto ©Thomas Meinert / pixelio.de

More available books at **www.hansebooks.com**

THE GREATER
VICTORIAN POETS

BY

HUGH WALKER, M.A.

PROFESSOR OF ENGLISH IN ST. DAVID'S COLLEGE, LAMPETER
AUTHOR OF "THREE CENTURIES OF SCOTTISH LITERATURE"

LONDON
SWAN SONNENSCHEIN & CO.
NEW YORK: MACMILLAN & CO.
1895

TO MY WIFE.

CONTENTS.

CHAPTER		PAGE
I.	INTRODUCTION	1
II.	TENNYSON: THE FIRST PERIOD OF AUTHORSHIP	16
III.	BROWNING: 1833 TO 1846	35
IV.	THE SECOND PERIOD OF TENNYSON'S WORK	70
V.	BROWNING'S INTERMEDIATE PERIOD, 1850-1869	91
VI.	MATTHEW ARNOLD	122
VII.	TENNYSON AND BROWNING: THE CLOSING PERIOD	150
VIII.	THE DRAMAS	171
IX.	THE POETRY OF NATURE	201
X.	THE INFLUENCE OF SCIENCE	231
XI.	THE SOCIAL AND POLITICAL ASPECTS OF THE POETS	258
XII.	FAITH AND DOUBT	292
	INDEX	329

THE GREATER VICTORIAN POETS.

CHAPTER I.

INTRODUCTION.

It is impossible to define precisely, and often difficult to define at all, a period of literature. The political divisions commonly adopted are approximations, in many cases of the roughest kind. When we begin to ask what are the limits of the Elizabethan period, or of the period of Queen Anne, we find that the divisions which criticism can establish in literature by no means synchronise with the time covered by the reigns of those sovereigns. Nevertheless, it requires but little reflection to show that expressions of this kind, though never exact, generally convey a substantial truth. The movement of time is an abstract expression which means the movement of the human spirit in all its manifestations; and the movement of time is best marked by political events. Thus, when, with reference to literature, we speak of the age of Pericles or of Elizabeth, or of the period of the French Revolution, we mean that there was in those ages a movement in literature bearing conspicuously the impress of its connexion with the history of the time. No one can doubt that the marvellous literary activity of Athens in the fifth century B.C. was intimately connected with the events which made the city politically so prominent and so powerful; nor is it possible to deny that the great outburst of poetic genius in England in the end of the sixteenth and the beginning of the seventeenth centuries was an expression of a heightened and intensified national life. Naturally therefore, and not inappropriately, those periods of literature have been associated with the most prominent names of the time in politics. It is equally clear that the greatest historical event since the Reformation had a profound influence upon literature, and that, for a period of at least seventy years, what men wrote, outside France only less than within it, was coloured by the French Revolution. Even before the Revolution was accomplished, we see its shadow projected over the thoughts, aspirations and artistic conceptions of men. A good defence might be made on these lines of the traditional association between the political revolution and the literature produced about the same time. The tendency of late has been to insist too much upon the almost inevitable divergence between the chronological limits of a literary movement and of a political period. The literary "age of Elizabeth" extends far beyond the reign of Elizabeth. The name, therefore, is not wholly satisfactory; but it is better to have even an inaccurate name which implies the connexion of literature with the widest human life than one which tends to confine the view to the contents of books alone.

In a similar way posterity will probably justify the name of the Victorian period as applied to the English literature of some two-thirds or three-quarters of the nineteenth century. The connexion of the literature of this time with history is no doubt less obvious than it was during the two preceding generations, and perhaps it does not go so deep; but it too is real. The great movement to democracy, the progress of physical science, and the advance in material comfort have all left their mark both upon the poetry and the prose of recent times. And a new name is necessary. We must recognise that sometime between 1825 and 1835 the period of the Revolution came to an end. If any particular year is to be fixed upon, perhaps 1832, the date of the death of Goethe in Germany and of Scott in England, is the best. A glance at the death-roll of men of letters about that date shows what a startling clearance had been made for the new generation. In a poem dated November, 1835, Wordsworth laments how swiftly brother has followed brother "from sunrise to the sunless land". Hogg, the immediate subject of the verses, Scott, Coleridge, Lamb, Crabbe, and—an addition characteristic of the time—Mrs. Hemans had all passed away within little more than three years. If we look a little farther back the catalogue becomes still more striking. Keats died in 1821, Shelley in the following year, Byron in 1824, and Blake in 1827. The one great survivor, Wordsworth himself, had already done his work; and what Arnold mourned in 1850 as "the last poetic voice" was practically dumb long before the grave closed over him. Landor, Southey, Campbell and Moore were lesser men, and they too were nearly exhausted. Like Wordsworth and Coleridge, they betrayed, years before their death, the exhaustion of the great poetic "motif" of their youth. If we consider poetry alone we may say that, for England, the period closes with the death of Byron. It was not without reason that to so many there was an almost immeasurable significance in the removal of that stormful personality.

> He taught us little ; but our soul
> Had *felt* him like the thunder's roll.

To Mrs. Carlyle it seemed as if "the sun had fallen from the heavens". The young Tennyson felt that "the whole world was at an end," "that everything was over and finished for every one—that nothing else mattered," and stole away in secret to carve on the stone the words, "Byron is dead". Whoever has studied the *Poems by Two Brothers* will easily believe that these expressions came from the heart. The youthful authors certainly paid to Byron the homage of imitation. And in the poetry which immediately followed his death there is some excuse for such expressions, exaggerated as they seem now. It is marked by a feebleness and triviality in striking contrast to the abundant if not always well-directed energy of the period which was just coming to a close.

But the end of an old period is a different matter from the beginning of a new one. For the latter event it is not essential that the old leaders should die off, but it is essential that younger men, animated by a different spirit, should arise. And they did arise, in numbers and of power quite sufficient to stamp the new generation with their own characteristics. During those years Carlyle, Macaulay, Elizabeth Barrett, afterwards Mrs. Browning, Edward Bulwer, afterwards Lord Lytton, Tennyson, and Robert Browning made their first appearance.

Two of these writers, Tennyson and Browning, have indelibly impressed the poetry of their era. To them attaches not only the interest of extraordinarily great work, but of exceptionally long careers. Running a literary course, the one of more than sixty years, the other of fifty-six, they cannot fail to betray, in the very changes through which they pass, some of the most potent influences at work in their time. Their greatness, however highly it may be appraised, did not alter the fact that what they thought and what they wrote were in large measure determined for them by the circumstances and ideas of the time in which they lived. This fact, which ought to be evident, has to some extent been obscured by the indiscriminating way in which it has become customary to speak of the greatest authors, Shakespeare in particular, as "not of an age, but for all time". It is true that poets, philosophers, artists, statesmen, and great men of all sorts, if they are only great *enough*, are for all time; but it is equally true that even the greatest of them are of their own age first of all. We need ask no better illustration of the fact than is found in Shakespeare. His literary form, the atmosphere of his poetry, many of his characteristic interests, are Elizabethan. It was customary with poets in his day to write sonnets in series; and he has left a series of sonnets. The drama was the most popular form of literature; and he wrote mainly dramas. Subjects from English history possessed a special interest for his audience and had a special fascination for writers of the time; and he wrote English historical plays. The fact, therefore, that Shakespeare is "for all time," does not prevent his being, in a very real sense, "of an age". It will be strange indeed if Tennyson and Browning do not prove to be of their age as well as Shakespeare; and it will be no derogation from their greatness to inquire how far they are so.

There will be general agreement that those two, Tennyson and Browning, represent at its best the poetry of the period just closed or closing. Some, perhaps, would add that they are not only the greatest, but that there is no rival or third to them. When however we remember that only a short time ago not a few would have demurred to assigning to Browning so lofty a position, we may reasonably hesitate before we put even those men on an eminence so solitary. There may be others who have been misjudged, as Browning was, or inadequately appreciated. To me it seems that there is among the Victorians one other, and only one, so emphatically great that whether or not he be judged equal to those two, he must be named along with them. I allude to Matthew Arnold, who, though inferior to Browning and Tennyson in compass, and perhaps in some respects in power, is so exquisite within his range that he can be placed nowhere except in the first rank. He was younger than the others, he died earlier, and he had practically ceased to write poetry many years before his death. The period of his activity is therefore brief. The other two stretch beyond him at both ends, and in the bulk of their work far surpass him. The interest of their development is also necessarily greater. But if a poet is to be judged by what he has done best, Arnold must stand very high.

Those three, then, I take to be the greatest and best representatives of Victorian poetry. I propose to attempt a critical estimate of them. In doing so I shall in the first place follow the chronological sequence of their works. Frequently the best possible comparison is between a man in his youth and the same man in his maturity or in old age; and in any case it is not easy to miss instruction in following the succession of a man's works. As regards Browning and Tennyson, the chronological method is, on account of the length of time between their first and last publications, unusually promising. In the case of Arnold it may be expected to yield less valuable results. This chronological study will occupy the first part of the book. In the concluding chapters I propose to lay special emphasis on the relation of the poets to the spirit and thought of the time. It is only thus, by careful reference, first to their own development, and secondly to the time in which they lived, that I can hope to understand them. The world is greater than its greatest man. It reflects from a thousand angles a thousand rays back upon him, and in their light enables the ordinary observer, with patience and industry, to comprehend much that would otherwise baffle him. I neither purpose to make, nor am I capable of making, excursions into all the fields of human activity. My object is rather to use the general results of politics, philosophy, religion and science, as clues to the underlying thought of the poets, or as points of view from which to regard them.

The years immediately succeeding the close of the terrible struggle with Napoleon were marked all over Europe by weariness, want and depression. The first exultation of victory was succeeded everywhere by a sense of failure. The revolutionary republic and the empire that had sprung from it were crushed; but the old order in politics was by no means restored or capable of being restored. On the other hand, those who had looked to the Revolution for the regeneration of society were forced to recognise that what they had expected could not be, or at least could not be fully and as they had expected it. It has been the task of two generations to work out that portion of their expectations which could be realised; but the work has been done with little of the buoyant hope which characterised the men of the Revolution. The limits of the possible, which seemed then to fade into an almost invisible distance, have proved to be somewhat narrow. The legislator has been forced to recognise (if he is not again forgetting) that it is only to a slight extent and by slow degrees that he can mend the condition of humanity; though, as has been said with a somewhat cynical truth, he may console himself with the thought that his power to mar it is almost unbounded. Nevertheless, the real work done has been very great. The impossible democracy of the Revolution, founded on an unreal and unrealisable equality, has been perforce abandoned; but a democracy, less attractive perhaps, because less lavish of promises, has, whether for good or evil, established itself in some of the principal countries of Europe, and is obviously on the way to establishment in others. The "rascal multitude" of Shakespeare is rascal no longer, because it is master. Within the period under review we have learnt to comprehend, if not fully, at least better than men did before, the significance of the change. It is no longer possible for an intelligent man, as it was for one so able and so learned as Grote, to draw direct lessons from an ancient to a modern democracy. Young as it is, the vast force of the new democracy is already showing itself. We have pretty nearly done with tinkering the machinery of government. We have nearly done also with the negative work of removing obstructions, which for so long was thought to be the be-all and end-all of English Liberalism; and, though the fact has been obscured in recent years, the great problems of the future are labour problems and social problems.

Our task is to discover how changes such as these, politically vital, have affected literature, and especially the three men with whom we are directly concerned. It is hardly possible that they can have remained uninfluenced by forces so great, working at first beneath the surface, but afterwards in the open. Consciously or unconsciously their thoughts must have taken a bias and their feelings a colour from the aspirations and struggles of their fellow-men.

During the past sixty years far less trust has been put in politics than during the previous sixty. But it seems to be almost a law of human life that large and unreasoning faith must be put in something or other. At different times and for long periods the faith has been placed upon various forms of religion. During the period in question those immeasured hopes which a generation earlier were centred in politics have been transferred to science. The advance of physical knowledge has thrown the mind of the present and the last generations to some extent off its balance. It has been imagined, by the smaller rather than by the greater men of science, that the instrument which has done so much can do everything; and science has seemed at times to threaten the existence of everything else. This spirit, it must be added, has been fostered by an unwise dread of inquiry, which means a distrust of truth, on the part of those who, hesitating to accept some of the conclusions put forward in the name of science, have failed to see that the only way of meeting reason is by reason. The hesitation was justifiable enough. Though the broad and stable foundation on which physical science rests precludes all danger of any such nemesis as has in recent years overtaken political economy, the radical error of the latter, that of proclaiming conclusions too wide for the premises, has been committed in the name of the former also.

To the general mind perhaps science has been most conspicuous and most interesting for the material results to which it has conduced. Not so however either to its own professors or to the best minds in literature. The faith that man liveth by steam-engines alone is not a faith that has ever been held by any great poet. Nevertheless, such great material changes as the last sixty or seventy years have witnessed could not come to pass without in some way or other affecting the spiritual elements of human nature. Man is a creature that moves altogether if he move at all. Criticism has rightly concluded that the discovery of America was an event which had much to do with the production of Shakespeare's plays, remote as it seems from them. So it is with the railways and the expanding commerce of recent times. They have altered the outward conditions of life; and modern science has taught us in what unexpected forms the effects of environment may exhibit themselves. Changes of this sort are not primarily spiritual; but the unity of nature assures us that they will, somehow or other, get themselves translated into terms of spirit. In poetry we may expect that theirs will be an underground and hidden influence. We do not look for poems on mechanical inventions, but we do look for an influence from such inventions, if they are great enough to alter the customary mode of life of a people. A negative influence is none the less an influence; and the not inconsiderable portion of Ruskin's work devoted to protests against railways and similar "abominations" proves how they affected him.

But it is rather to the fundamental ideas of science than to any practical and intellectually subordinate developments of them that we must look. The idea of a universal reign of law, grasped, before the present century, only by a few choice minds, but now the property of all who can think; the idea of the ultimate oneness of the great forces of nature; above all the idea of evolution, the master-thought of the century;— these appeal to the imagination; they alter our whole conception of the relation of man to the universe; and they not only may but must have left their mark upon poetry. It was once thought that the advance of science must sooner or later prove prejudicial to poetry, because it was believed to mean the gradual disappearance of mystery. Whether this opinion is sound or not, whether the effect of the advance of science is not rather to substitute great mysteries for little ones, is a question which must be examined hereafter.

The wider problems of science impinge upon the sphere of philosophy; and some of those which have just been mentioned are at least as much philosophical as scientific. Philosophy too, though it can boast no such triumphs as science, has moved even in England within this century. The dominance of utilitarianism in the early and middle periods was significant and characteristic. The rise of an idealistic school somewhat later, and its coexistence along with the philosophy of evolution, are facts to be noted. It is worthy of remark that Oxford, the home of the most influential religious movement of the century, has been also, more than any other single place, the home of the philosophy which has looked to Germany for its inspiration. The two are in fact different manifestations of the same tendency. A mind which cannot rest in materialism either seeks refuge from it, like Newman, in some authority not to be disputed; or it tries to turn criticism by a new appeal to reason, as did Jowett, and after him T. H. Green and the present Master of Balliol. Ignorance of German, as has been acutely remarked, had much to do with the course pursued by the first; a knowledge of German not a little influenced the others.

The English however are a practical people, practical even in their speculation. They have spent probably more energy in the discussion of political economy, which promises some not too distant material result, than in any other branch of philosophy. The period under discussion has been marked by the rise and decline of this science, and some might add by its fall. Taking shape towards the end of last century, it became widely and deeply influential in the early and middle periods of the present, and it has gradually sunk in power and credit since. There can be no doubt as to the importance of political economy as a factor in the life of the century; and even though its day should prove to have passed as completely as is sometimes asserted, it has still to be reckoned with historically. It has coloured social speculation, politics, and, through Malthus, even science. It goaded to anger the two prose writers, Carlyle and Ruskin, who have had most of the poetic spirit: it may well have influenced poetry itself.

But the most purely spiritual of all the forces that play upon human nature is religion. We may therefore anticipate that its direct influence upon poetry will be greater than that of any of the other forces mentioned. Religion too has moved and changed within the present century. To inquire into the precise nature of the change would open far too wide a question. It is enough for the purpose to recognise that it has not been quite of the kind supposed by those who confine their view to a few years, or at most to a single generation. To many such the present time seems to be marked by the decay of faith. And so in a certain sense and within certain limits it is. Doubtless a spirit of distrust of outworn theological dogmas has spread to classes which, a century ago, such a spirit never penetrated and hardly even touched. But among the intellectual leaders of the time there is far less of the spirit of absolute negation than there was a century ago, probably there is less than there was even thirty years ago. This certainly was Browning's view; at least it seems tolerably safe to ascribe to him, on this particular point, the opinions which he puts into the mouth of Bishop Blougram. The Bishop supposes a jury of twelve men, chosen for their intelligence, to examine the question whether his profession of faith is a reality or a sham :—

> Had I been born three hundred years ago,
> They'd say, " What's strange ? Blougram of course believes,"
> And, seventy years since, " disbelieves, of course ".
> But now, " He may believe, and yet, and yet
> How can he ? "

Thus, the question which, seventy years before the poem was written, was closed to education and intelligence, is regarded as open once more. And in this Browning has clearly read the thought of the time aright. Scientific writers have never within the last forty years been as negative in their attitude as the French encyclopædists were; and they are now less negative than they were a generation ago. Apart then from any movement within what are commonly regarded as religious circles, there has been, among the thoughtful who are not committed by position or profession to any particular view, a reversion to an open attitude of mind on questions of this kind. In such circumstances we might expect that religion would claim an exceptionally prominent place in the poets of the time; for it is just questions which are undecided either way that are intellectually absorbing. We should expect moreover that the kind of interest manifested would be not that of the convinced devotee, like George Herbert, not that of the man who has found, but of him who seeks truth. There ought to be more of aspiration than attainment, more questions asked than answered. Many or most of the questions may even be answered in the negative; but as the face long exposed to the storms of sea or mountain bears permanent traces of conflicts past, so the spirit which has constantly fronted these difficulties will carry the marks through life. They may be deeply scarred or furrowed, or only marked with soft and peaceful lines; the one thing impossible is that there should be no effect.

This movement outside specifically religious circles has been coincident with a similar change within them. For the present purpose the latter is far less important than the former, but the coincidence is too curious to be passed over unnoticed. The Oxford movement, that narrow and unphilosophical revolt against a " liberalism " (in Newman's sense of the word) equally narrow and unphilosophical, is interesting as a sign of the times, and as a proof that the forces at work in any age show themselves in many ways. It was closely contemporaneous with a very remarkable influx of the spirit of religion into poetry. But its direct influence on the poets was slight. It influenced Arnold negatively, and moved Browning to an occasional expression of contempt; but it did little more.

The many centuries which have turned with steady loyalty to Homer and Sophocles and Virgil and Horace, prove that of none are the words *homo sum* more emphatically true than of the great poet. The minor verse-writer skims the surface of life; nothing human is alien from his greater brother. This is our guarantee for asking of the poets some response to almost every question that can be put, provided only it has a human interest.

Poets ought to "deal in meanings". Their special function is indeed to be priests of the beautiful. But the beautiful must "clothe itself in circumstances," and can only be seen, known and represented in this garb. Besides, the most perfect beauty, the most satisfying for the purposes of art, in the end the only beauty, is beauty of thought. One of the most poetic of modern poets, in one of his best-known lines, identified beauty with truth; and Browning exclaims,

> Oh! world as God has made it! Truth is beauty,
> And knowing this is love, and love is duty.

It is therefore impossible for the poet to escape from his connexion with the current of contemporary life on the plea that he serves the eternal beautiful. Whatever men think, do, suffer, hope, is his theme. For this reason, and perhaps for this alone, he can evade the charge that he is "the idle singer of an empty day," the believer in a "creed outworn," the practitioner of an art which can do nothing but dress up anew the thoughts of better men long since dead. Poetry changes with life and grows with thought, nor will it die from dearth of matter till the waves of life and thought themselves are frozen into stillness. The goal of thought recedes, like

> That untravell'd world, whose margin fades
> For ever and for ever when I move.

But the poet for whom such a plea is to be advanced, who would be regarded as the real teacher, and would set the beautiful on the securest basis by proving that it is *also* the useful, must establish his right. He must be a teacher to his generation. He must offer some solution, or some fragment of a solution, of "the riddle of the painful earth". He must understand the life of his time, he must be in sympathy with it, and must clothe it in the vesture of beauty. If he does so much he deserves his modicum of praise. But to earn the highest praise he must do more. Not only must he detect the beauty here and now around him, and make it visible to whoever among his contemporaries has eyes to see; he must view it also *sub specie æternitatis*, bring out its permanent element, and so appeal to all the future. It is in this sense that great men, not poets alone, but all great men, are "for all time," and it is for this reason that it is so hard to gauge them. The appraisement of their value and meaning to their contemporaries is hard enough; to estimate their worth to future ages is much more difficult. One who stands near them in time must attempt the latter task with the greatest diffidence, and can only hope for very limited success. Nevertheless, it is in this way alone, and by the more or less satisfactory solution of both problems, that the value of a man's work can be measured.

It will be observed that the principle of criticism here adopted is practically the same as that which Matthew Arnold laid down, and which can be quite easily dissociated from his questionable definition of poetry. Though poets do not, properly speaking, criticise life, their principal function is to reveal its meaning. "The proper study of mankind is man". Even if the poet turns his eye upon inanimate nature or upon the lower animal creation, it generally proves that he does so, in part at least, for the sake of the light it reflects back upon humanity. Few would care much for nature but for the dim sense that nature is somehow akin to humanity. It was not by mere accident that the poetry of nature arose almost simultaneously with the philosophy which taught that nature is comprehensible to reason only in the degree in which reason finds itself in nature. Burns's lines *To a Mouse*, Shelley's *Skylark*, Keats's *Ode to a Nightingale*, and Wordsworth everywhere, all bear witness how near the surface, in modern nature-poetry, lies the reference to man. This reference may be direct, immediate and obvious, as it will be found to be in Browning, or it may be only indirect and implicit, as it often is in Tennyson, but in either case it is always present and generally important.

Many however disbelieve that poets seriously concern themselves with the facts of life or the meaning of life. They think the love of the beautiful implies little or nothing of this. But all the three great Victorians are against them. Arnold's view has been already referred to. Tennyson says of the poet :—

> He saw thro' life and death, thro' good and ill,
>   He saw thro' his own soul.
> The marvel of the everlasting will,
>   An open scroll,
> Before him lay.

To Browning again the poet was—

> The town's true master if the town but knew !
> We merely kept a governor for form,
> While this man walked about and took account
> Of all thought, said and acted, then went home
> And wrote it fully to our Lord the King.

The question however cannot be settled by authority; it must be determined rather by an examination of the great poets to discover what they actually contain. The Greece of Homer is practically unknown except from the poems of Homer himself, from scraps of archæological and linguistic evidence, and from inferences back from a later condition of things. Yet historians have not hesitated to paint the life of the time, and to set down in outline its social features and its political condition—chiefly from Homer. The other available evidence confirms him; and there is no reason to doubt that the Greece so restored is in the main a correct representation of the reality. It may be objected that those are comparatively external matters; but if we turn aside from social organisation and political institutions the result is still the same. The whole story of the aspirations, toils and wanderings of Odysseus is just a great storehouse of ideas upon life, with its hopes and fears, and impulses and aspirations, a storehouse so rich that it has furnished material for half the great modern poets from Dante to Tennyson. What was the view of the later Greeks themselves may be gathered by any one who notes how the philosophers use quotations, not from Homer alone, but from all the poets, as authorities on all manner of questions, religious, ethical, social and political. There is indeed to the modern mind something naïve in many of those quotations; but they at least show what was the habitual feeling of this race with its unique gift of criticism. And if there is some suggestion of the youth of the world in the simple trust with which those appeals to poetic authority are made, there is far more of vital truth in the view implied than there is in the dull and unintelligent view that poetry is something no way related to the serious business of life,—which is all contained in ledgers and day-books.

If we go farther back still, what are the books of Job and Isaiah but great poems filled with ideas of the profoundest kind about life and human destiny? If we come farther down, what are the writings of Shakespeare and Goethe but treasuries of ideas applied to life? Who can doubt that Milton, much as he moves in regions of the supernatural, is all the while drawing into light great ideas implied in the life of his age, but not quite consciously grasped by it? He, a Puritan and yet much more than a Puritan, illustrates almost to perfection the ideal relation of a great man to his own time. If he had been greater even than he was the illustration might have been less perfect, or at any rate more obscure; for then that element of the temporary and evanescent, which we see in his crude theology, would have been absent. Milton saw in the Puritans the most strenuous upholders of truth and right, soul and conscience. They had little outwardly to commend them to the artist. They neither felt nor professed any love for the beautiful. Their intellectual reach was limited, their spirit intolerant. They strangled the free, varied, human Elizabethan spirit. But, as Milton perceived, the heart of the matter was in them. When the path of truth and goodness seemed to diverge from the path of beauty, they rightly chose the former. They suspected that there was something wrong about the beautiful. Many of them condemned it altogether, and denounced it as a device of the devil. Milton knew better; but he knew also that unless it could be shown that the divergence of the paths was mere seeming, beauty was justly doomed. Accordingly, the true work of his life was to transform the hard, narrow and unattractive Puritan ideal into an ideal of beauty. In carrying out this work he necessarily soared above commonplace Puritanism; but he never ceased to be one of the Puritans, he was only the greatest of them all, greatest because unshackled by their most cramping fetters.

If Milton illustrates the fact that the great poet is at all points in touch with the spirit of his time, we can by comparing him with his contemporaries show what is lost by losing in any part this relation to the whole of life. Milton, who recognised beauty as one of the aspects of truth, rose above the lesser Puritans, who did not. The still greater loss which follows from the neglect of what we call, in the narrower sense, the good or the true itself, is seen if we compare Milton with the Cavalier poets. These men practically adopted the more limited view of poetry, as something concerned only with the beautiful, only meant to titillate the æsthetic sense and to amuse. The consequence is that, graceful and pretty as their work is, they bear nevertheless the brand of triviality. They have elements of high character, a splendid chivalry and a noble loyalty, and these are stamped here and there upon their work; but they are not filled, as are the Puritans, with a sense of the grandeur of goodness and of the inexorable rigour of its law. Consequently, though their opinions and their life were in many respects more favourable to art than those of the Puritans, they have produced no works which can be placed beside the works of Milton and Bunyan.

I propose, then, to apply to Tennyson, Browning and Arnold the kind of tests here indicated, in the confidence that if they are really great poets the result will be important, as it is in the case of Milton; while if they are smaller men than I suppose its importance will be proportionately diminished, as it is in the case of the Cavalier poets. The method promises results which might be unattainable otherwise. Plato, for reasons which apply still more forcibly to men of moderate powers than to men of genius, preferred to investigate the individual through the State rather than in himself; and it seems reasonable to believe that the diligent study of a great life in the light of all life may partly reveal its secret.

CHAPTER II.

TENNYSON: THE FIRST PERIOD OF AUTHORSHIP.

In 1827 Alfred Tennyson, at the age of eighteen, made, in conjunction with his brother Charles, his first venture in literature. The *Poems by Two Brothers*, as was natural in the case of authors so young, were essentially imitative. There is little to be discovered from them of the native spirit of Tennyson; they are interesting chiefly as evidence of the food on which his growing mind was nourished. A certain catholicity of taste is indicated by the variety of echoes from the poets of the generation just closing. But while the two boys were ready to admire all, it is evident that their worship was reserved for Byron. This is the more remarkable because in the later poetry of Tennyson there is very little of the Byronic touch; and in the light of our knowledge of his mature character, it would hardly be supposed that the panegyrist of order, of steady progress, and of "sober-suited freedom" would ever have been much attracted by a spirit so essentially revolutionary. The fleeting nature of the influence is a proof that there was little real harmony between the two minds; and the force of Byron's personality sufficiently explains his temporary sway over the boyish authors of the *Poems by Two Brothers*. The volume contains little or nothing of value. Tennyson was, as yet, no poet, and he was not even a very precocious writer of verse.

Neither can the prize poem, *Timbuctoo*, be regarded as showing much of the author himself. He was still only twenty, and the subject was dictated to him, not chosen by him. There have been prize poems at least as good written by lesser men. Tennyson had however made great progress in the two years which had passed since the appearance of his first work. He showed a wider sweep of imagination, greater command of language, and more independence of thought. But it was with the *Poems, chiefly Lyrical*, of 1830, that he made his real entrance into literature; and the pieces it contained, with those in the subsequent volume of *Poems*, published in 1833, may be regarded as constituting a group marked off from the rest of his poetry by characteristics of its own. Those two volumes are separated by an interval of nine years from his next publication. The long silence was probably due in the beginning to the shock of the death of Arthur Henry Hallam, which occurred in 1833; afterwards, no doubt, it was due to the poet's desire to mature his powers and perfect his art before he again ventured upon publication. In the *Poems* of 1842 we see the process of transition far advanced; but they are still linked, in form and character, with the early poems rather than with the series of long works of which *The Princess* was the first.

Robert Browning, three years younger than Tennyson, published his first work, *Pauline*, in 1833. In his maturity he would fain have suppressed it; but, for great men, the published word is eternal: he had to submit to the inevitable, and, to avoid at least the misprints and inaccuracies of pirated editions, he reprinted the piece in his collected works. In this instance we owe something to the pirates. *Pauline* certainly is immature; and there was a time, not long gone by, when Browning's reputation could ill afford to be burdened with the weight of an immature work. Now however it can easily bear that weight; and the fact that the "particular *dramatis persona*" which *Pauline* "would fain have reproduced" has many of the features of Browning himself, is reason sufficient for refusing to give up this early work. Moreover, though *Pauline* is not satisfactory as a whole, though, as Browning says in the preface, "good draughtsmanship and right handling were far beyond the artist at the time," it contains so many beauties that it may easily be defended on its own merits.

After *Pauline* Browning poured forth a rapid and unbroken succession of works. In his whole career indeed the only long interval was from 1855, when *Men and Women* appeared, to 1864, when it was followed by *Dramatis Personæ*. However, after *Luria* and *A Soul's Tragedy* in 1846, the intervals became longer, and the works when they appeared indicated a change in the author's view as to his function in poetry and the form which suited his genius. It will therefore be necessary to trace the development, in the case of Browning, from 1833 to 1846, alongside of that between 1830 and 1842 in the case of Tennyson.

When those two poets began to write Europe still felt the exhaustion of the long contest with Napoleon, and the recollection of it contributed to prolong an international rest unusually profound. Even England continued to feel the strain. The condition of the poor has seldom been worse than it was in the years immediately following the conclusion of the war; and the first generation of the century was drawing to a close before any real improvement could be seen. It is true the politicians were busy; but the measures which chiefly interested them were measures which did not directly or immediately affect the principal sufferers. The disputes of Whig and Tory were first and fundamentally disputes between the champions of the middle classes and the champions of the landed gentry. The new heaven and the new earth which had glittered before the eyes of the revolutionists had given place to the sad realities of an earth rather old and worn and a heaven by no means brighter than that which had bent above man from Adam downwards. Indeed, by contrast with the imaginary glow of fifty years before, it seemed abnormally dark. Even the sober Wordsworth found it bliss to be alive in the dawn of that earlier time, while "to be young was very heaven". Less balanced spirits blazed out in schemes of Pantisocracy, to be realised in the virgin lands beyond the Atlantic. But after the lapse of years the human spirit, mocked by many a will-o'-the-wisp, ceased to yield its faith so readily. We find no Pantisocrats when the century has passed its majority, none whose hopes make youth a heaven. Arnold, the critic of his time in verse as well as in prose, better represents the prevailing spirit. From the distance of two generations he looks back and asks sadly which of all those high promises has been realised, what harvest has been reaped from the tears and blood shed so plentifully at the Revolution? The disappointment leads him to question other ideals which have promised the regeneration of humanity; and in all cases he finds them, if not fruitless, at any rate much less potent for good than they have claimed to be. The lesson is, not indeed one of despair, but of severely chastened and strictly limited hope. There is no sure and easy road to happiness. By toil through many generations, and with much suffering, if at all, mankind must work out their salvation.

Carlyle did not act in accordance with his faith that silence is golden. Arnold too, fortunately for the world, was better than his creed. Literary genius, by its very nature, is not of the silent kind; and as it needs only pen, ink and paper for its apparatus, it is probable that there have been few "mute, inglorious Miltons". A Cromwell is another matter, as he requires a nation in convulsion to call him forth. There was therefore little danger that the poets would refrain from writing because the lavish promises of the Revolution could not be met. But it might be expected that, if Arnold's view of the time was at all true, the spirit which he found in it would influence them. And it did, all the more remarkably because neither of the two men with whom we have to deal had any tendency to pessimism while one of them, Browning, was among the most steadfast of optimists.

Both betray this influence in the manner in which, in their early poems, they conceive and handle the problems of life suggested by their subjects; Tennyson betrays it frequently in the *absence* of any such problem. Reference has already been made to the triviality which characterises the poetry of the years immediately following the death of Byron. A good deal of Tennyson's early work is chargeable with this fault. Occasionally, as in the case of the once too famous "darling room," he even lapsed into the namby-pamby style. Here is the secret of the frequently severe criticisms with which Tennyson was at first received. Nor was it only hostile critics who detected the flaw. Carlyle, who admired Tennyson, complained, not without reason, of the "lollipops," superlative though their quality was, which he offered to the world for food. The criticism was made with reference to the earlier *Idylls of the King;* it might have been made with far more point of the volumes of 1830 and 1833. For not only are the "lollipops" there, but they are the most prominent feature of those volumes. Probably the majority of readers would agree that what in them most strongly marks the individuality of the writer is the gallery of female portraits, so gracefully and so delicately touched. "Airy, fairy Lilian," "ever varying Madeline," "shadowy, dreaming Adeline," "rare, pale Margaret," and the rest, are kindred figures, unmistakably the offspring of one mind, and perennially popular for their sentimental charm. They carried captive the French taste of Taine; and to this day they are unsurpassed for dainty beauty. Yet there is a sense of something unsatisfactory about them. They are the work of a dilettante. There is no fervour, no passion in the verse, such as flames in Marlowe's lines on Helen, in Shakespeare's descriptions of female beauty, and in the lyrics of Burns. Exquisite as the portraits are, we can understand the fear which might have possessed the most discerning of contemporary critics that this feminine fineness of touch might be cultivated to the detriment, and ultimately even to the destruction, of all more masculine properties of mind. For, while Tennyson did much besides in his first volumes, it was this type of portrait that he executed best. Most of the other pieces which he reprinted have been freely revised, and some of them have been almost rewritten; but the female portraits remain substantially as they were when they were first published. They emerged from the author's mind at once perfect, so that his mature skill could add nothing and take away nothing. Minute changes were indeed subsequently made, but they did not alter the pictures. A critic might well have argued that it was a dangerous thing for a young poet to be perfect at once in one particular style of writing, unless that style had in it all the elements of greatness. The style in question had not; it was the perfection of grace, but it lacked strength.

Now, dilettantism such as this may proceed either from the inherent weakness of the writer, or from the fact that nothing has ever stirred him up to think thoughts and to write verse worthy of himself. The former is an incurable defect. If it had been the cause at work in Tennyson's case there would have been no *In Memoriam*, no *Idylls of the King*, no *Becket*, none of the later ballads with their magnificent force and their heroic elevation. The fault was rather that the time presented the young poet with no subject which fired blood and brain. Not that the time afforded nothing great to say, if only it could be discovered. Carlyle found plenty in it; but Carlyle had felt the throes of Europe in her death struggle. Browning too, only a little later, found great subjects and handled them greatly. But the point is, not that subjects could not be discovered sufficient to task the highest powers, but rather that those subjects were not imperatively thrust forward nor those powers called into action. In the periods of the great movements of humanity the impulse has been irresistible and has been felt universally. At the Renaissance and at the Reformation all Europe seemed to feel the thrill. It was so in the age of Elizabeth, and it was so in the period of the Revolution. The poet in those times was never in want of a subject, and unless he was by nature little he never gave the impression of trifling. Of course poets in all ages have written light and playful pieces; but the greater poets of those periods never published whole volumes remarkable chiefly for dainty flimsiness, and capable of being stigmatised by a friendly critic as "lollipops".[1]

Another indication that the author of the *Poems* of 1830 and 1833 was as yet only groping for a subject may be found in the great and indeed excessive variety they present. Apart from the female portraits, it does not appear that Tennyson had any particular preference as to his subject-matter. He wandered everywhere, there was no compulsion laid upon him, nothing was of absorbing interest. If it be permissible to employ again an expression which has been much misused, he showed as yet no indication of having any 'message' for his generation; or, what is just the other side of the same thing, of its having delivered any message to him.

A discerning critic might then very pardonably have been misled by those volumes as to the force of Tennyson. It is true that a very careful examination ought to have made him pause before pronouncing the young poet a weakling and a trifler. The evidence is easy to read in the light of Tennyson's later writings, but its significance might have been more readily missed then. Matthew Arnold insisted that a sound subject-matter, contact with the real, substantiality, was essential to poetry of the highest class; and it was because he thought Shelley wanted it that he described that fascinating poet as "a beautiful and ineffectual angel, beating in the void his luminous wings in vain". Whether he was right or wrong as to Shelley, Arnold was right in his general proposition. No visions of cloud-land, however entrancing, will atone for the absence of reality. Now, it is just this contact with reality which is comparatively rare in Tennyson's earlier work, and the existence of which it is therefore peculiarly important to point out.

[1] In the beginning of the Elizabethan period, however, before the great poetic outburst which may be dated about the year 1590, there is a similar tendency to trifling. Then too the poets seem at first to be groping for subjects, and it is only after they get into the stream of life that they write greatly.

Setting aside the portraits, the most remarkable poems in the two early volumes were the *Supposed Confessions of a Second-rate Sensitive Mind not in Unity with Itself, The Lady of Shalott, The Miller's Daughter, The Palace of Art, The Lotos-Eaters,* and *A Dream of Fair Women.* On the threshold it must be observed that it is dangerous to argue from the present shape of these poems to their original form. Only the *Supposed Confessions* and *The Lotos-Eaters* remain substantially what they were; and even *The Lotos-Eaters* has had one section added, while the conclusion has been unsparingly revised and much improved. In the case of Tennyson's revisions change may be taken as almost equivalent to improvement. He was wonderfully sure of touch, and he had in the long run great power of self-criticism.[1] That he was not exceptionally gifted with the power to judge his own work when it was fresh from his hand, is shown by his publishing from time to time a number of pieces quite unworthy of him. That his final judgment was singularly correct is proved by the fact that he almost invariably either eliminated those pieces or so changed them as to remove their most conspicuous blemishes. This fact may be taken as one indication of that steady growth which will be found to be the most conspicuous feature in Tennyson's literary history. He could criticise himself successfully because he was constantly outgrowing himself. But the need of a subsequent self-criticism was never afterwards as great as it was with respect to the volumes of 1830 and 1833. Of the poems just named, all, with those two exceptions, have been greatly, and one or two of them almost vitally, changed.

Turning then to the original versions of them, while the reader misses, and not very reasonably resents missing, many beauties with which he has been long familiar, he still finds a considerable body of poetry calculated to set at rest the doubts which, as has been already said, a perfectly fair critic might have felt, not so much with regard to the author's poetic faculty as with regard to the use he was likely to make of it. Among those poems, *The Lady of Shalott* is important, in the first

[1] Tennyson lost some of this sureness of touch in his old age. The changes made between the first and the final versions of *The Charge of the Heavy Brigade* do not on the whole improve it. This may be taken to indicate that while his imagination was as powerful as ever and his intellect at least as far-reaching, there was a certain stiffening in the artist's hand.

place, because it shows that Tennyson's mind was already brooding over, or perhaps as yet only dallying with, the Arthurian legends, in which he was destined to find a larger theme than any he had hitherto handled. For the present purpose it may even be thought that this is the sole importance of the poem. Its shadowy mystical charm is of the kind which still, to some minds, might leave possible a doubt as to the nature and extent of the writer's powers. Such a doubt, however, would be altogether unjust to the precision and sobriety, if I may use the word, of the descriptions of nature. These are perfectly clear cut and definite, and they betray the close observation of a man who could probably be as keen and practical as those who are most innocent of visions.

All the other poems mentioned have, in an even superior degree, the required contact with reality. *The Lotos-Eaters* has it, purposely dreamy as the poem is. The desire to be free from pain, to escape the weary sea and weary oar, is deeply human. This piece alone, with its wonderful charm of verse, its exquisite harmony of sound and sense, was enough to stamp its author as a poet of the rarest quality; and it was also, though this might be less obvious, a guarantee that he was more than a mere dreamer. The artist has himself always well in hand : he knows exactly the effect he wishes to produce, and he produces it. This is the solitary piece among Tennyson's early productions which, even in its first shape, can be ranked unreservedly along with his greatest work.

Probably no one will deny that *The Miller's Daughter* has a sound subject-matter. It is the poem which, among those enumerated, seems outwardly to have most in common with the female portraits already spoken of. But it is really very different. The canvas is broader, the interest deeper, it has the breath of genuine human life. Those other maidens are not to be taken too seriously, or else they are to be worshipped from afar; they are far too ethereal " for human nature's daily food ". It is not of such materials that wives and mothers are made. Tennyson himself seems to have been dimly conscious of this, for it is Isabel whom he makes " the queen of marriage, a most perfect wife "; and the portrait of Isabel has a force and dignity not to be found in the others. But the miller's daughter was and is a living English girl. Since its first appearance in 1833, this poem has been much changed and greatly improved; some blemishes have been expunged, and many beauties added. The first meeting between Alice and the youth's mother, with the beautifully natural touch which draws them together through the recognition of a common love, is an addition. The song, "It is the Miller's Daughter," has been re-written. Yet even in the first version there was enough to prove that the young poet had looked with shrewdness and penetration upon the actual world around him. It contained, for example, the masterly picture of the old miller, portly, double-chinned, shrewd, practical, but full of jest and kindliness.

In the remaining three poems, the *Supposed Confessions, A Dream of Fair Women* and *The Palace of Art*, we have likewise, though in diverse ways, contact with the real. They are not realistic poems—Tennyson wrote none such—but they have what Arnold meant by substantiality. The first has been little changed, the second greatly, the third vitally. In *A Dream of Fair Women* we see the poet's mind playing upon concrete facts of history and legend. In the *Supposed Confessions* (the excessively clumsy title of which may be looked upon as an evidence of immaturity) he handles the familiar, but inexhaustible and intensely real, modern problem of doubt and the decay of faith. It is not one of the best even of the early poems, but it is one of the most instructive. *The Palace of Art* is, as the poet himself explains it, an allegory of a soul which loves beauty only, and knowledge and good merely for their beauty. This soul builds herself "a lordly pleasure-house," in order to dwell there in solitary ease. But it proves that neither the solitude nor the exclusive devotion to beauty can be maintained. "The riddle of the painful earth" demands solution, and the claims of other souls assert themselves. The conclusion is worthy of notice :—

> So when four years were wholly finished,
> She threw her royal robes away.
> "Make me a cottage in a vale," she said,
> "Where I may mourn and pray.
>
> "Yet pull not down my palace towers, which are
> So lightly, beautifully built:
> Perchance I may return with others there
> When I have purged my guilt."

Thus the solution the poet suggests is that the love of beauty is legitimate, but the sense of good must go along with it, and it must be shared. There are two conditions to the soul's return to her pleasure-house. She may return *with others* there, and only *after* she has purged her guilt. It is clear that this, though a dream, is fast anchored in reality. The limits of self-indulgence, and the moderation to be observed in the satisfaction of desires in themselves innocent and even good, are very practical questions. It is important to observe that Tennyson was in this poem approaching from the opposite side a problem closely similar to that which occupied Browning in *Paracelsus*, and which indeed never ceased to occupy him.

It appears then that in the poems just spoken of, we have evidence of that strength and substance which the bulk of the two volumes did not, at any rate so conspicuously, exhibit. The new poet was not all nerves, he had thews and sinews as well. Yet in the first place, with a view to a judgment on Tennyson individually, we must keep in mind the proportion which such poems bore to the whole; and in the second place, we must remember that in later editions the more delicate pieces, as a rule, escaped with little or no alteration, while the weightier ones were sometimes almost re-written. This seems to show that in the poet's own mature judgment he was at that time less master of the strong than of the graceful style. It was in strength that development might be hoped for: if it came the result could hardly fail to be poetry of the first rank. It may be added that had *The Two Voices* and the three fine political poems, "You ask me why, tho' ill at ease," "Of old sat Freedom on the heights," and "Love thou thy land with love far brought," been published, as we are told they had been written, in 1833, there would have been less reason to doubt whether the development would come. Those four poems, though they could not enter into the contemporary judgment of what he was in 1833, enter fairly into the final judgment of him.

It remains to inquire, just so far as is necessary in order to comprehend Tennyson's early standpoint, to what extent this class of poems evince, as we have seen that the more dilettante poems evince, the spirit of the time. To expect to find traces of that spirit in every piece would be unreasonable, and to profess to find them would be most probably evidence merely of the ingenious spinning of a theory. *The Miller's Daughter*, though it certainly contains notes of time and place, is in essence a poem which might have been written at many different periods. The accent of the style indicates the date, but it seems impossible to lay the finger upon anything in the thought which belongs to one generation more than another. In the *Supposed Confessions* and in *The Palace of Art*, on the contrary, we have definable evidences of the working of the Zeitgeist. The very title of the former, as it runs in the original version, is instructive. The confessions are those of a mind not at unity with itself; and this sense of the want of unity is, not indeed peculiar to, but specially characteristic of, the present century. We see it in Browning as well as in Tennyson, and in Arnold it is all-pervading. In *The Palace of Art* the same division of the man against himself is visible. There, as we have just seen, reflection will not permit a single-minded pursuit of the object of desire ; and though an ultimate solution of the difficulty is suggested, it is not given. Hesitancy therefore, a facing both ways, towards the evil that attracts the lower nature and towards the good that appeals to the higher, a conflict between conscience and desire, resulting, not in the establishment of a new harmony, but in the paralysis of action,—these characteristics of the time have impressed themselves on Tennyson's early verse. The Elizabethan dramatists make their characters sin boldly and with singleness of heart. They see their goal clearly, and drive right at it through all obstacles. A Hamlet is quite exceptional, and is one of the most conspicuous instances of his creator's power to overleap the limits of his age. But in the nineteenth century Hamlet's " pale cast of thought " is not the exception but the rule.

In the political poems already referred to, which ought to be included among those of 1833, we have another note of the time. It is remarkable that pride in the great achievements of the British arms is a feature rather of the period under discussion than of the years when the triumphs were won. A few, like Scott, whose opinions were in harmony with the policy of the Government, did indeed feel in all its force the natural exultation of spirit over the victories of their countrymen. Wordsworth too, though swept away at first by the current of the Revolution, afterwards sang the praises of the moderate and safe English freedom, and looked to the men of Kent as

the "vanguard of liberty" against that very France which
a few years before had promised universal freedom. But in
most cases the poets never quite forgot that at the beginning
they had "hung their heads and wept at Britain's name". The
younger men, like Byron and Shelley, were still more lukewarm
patriots. Byron, it is true, admired Nelson and the fleet, but
he was always a hostile critic of Wellington and the army. Or
else, like Keats, they cared for none of these things, and wrote
verse in which there was no political note whatsoever. And
there is little reason to wonder that this was the attitude
assumed by the poets. Poetry is necessarily fervid; and the
fire of the Revolution had a natural attraction for the fervour of
the poets. They were captivated by the magnificent promise
of liberty, fraternity and equality, and the vision of a future in
which the downtrodden should have been raised, the weak
made strong, and all should be working harmoniously towards
an ideal almost too dazzling for fallen humanity. And it is
only just to say that while there was gross exaggeration in
such promises, there was also a sufficient groundwork of truth
to justify the poets. Europe at the present day owes a great
debt to the Revolution.

But when Tennyson began to write the failure of the
Revolution was far more conspicuous than its real though
partial success. That it had unsettled Europe was plain to
every one; but in order to detect the good it was necessary to
dive beneath the surface. Moreover, Tennyson was by nature
disinclined to sympathise with revolution. He drew his blood
from a district the inhabitants of which are English of the
English. It might have been better for him if he had had an
infusion of Celtic blood in his veins; and probably his birth and
upbringing in a region so Teutonic as Lincolnshire had something to do with his excessive detestation of "the blind hysterics
of the Celt".

Partly because of this inborn tendency of the man, and
partly through the natural drift of events, we find Tennyson, in
the three political poems, an eager and enthusiastic eulogist of
those English institutions and English forms of freedom which
Byron and Shelley regarded with such discontent and even disdain. It will be shown hereafter that the spirit manifested in
these poems inspired their author to the end.

After 1833 there was, as has been already mentioned, an

interval of nine years in the series of Tennyson's publications. Then, in 1842, came two volumes entitled simply *Poems*. An interval which changed the youth of twenty-four into the man of thirty-three was certain to produce notable results; all the more when the beginning of it was marked by an event so powerfully affecting him as the death of his friend Hallam.

Of those two volumes the first is filled almost entirely with pieces which had been already printed: but even in it there is more new work than is apparent from the table of contents. Mention has been already made of the unsparing revision of some of the old pieces; and alterations almost everywhere throughout the volume show that the poet had carefully examined all his former work. Hardly less important are the omissions. The presence of a number of weak, unworthy or commonplace pieces in a volume of poetry will go far to conceal the merit of even beautiful verse; and few qualities are better worth preserving than that openness of mind which enables a man to convince himself, or suffers him to be convinced by others, that certain parts of his work fall beneath his own level. Thanks to this openness of mind, in 1842 we have for the first time what was beautiful in the earlier volumes not only made more perfect, but freed from the alloy of pieces which it is impossible to praise.

But it is mainly to the second volume that we must look in order to discover the quality of the new work; and in it the drift of the change may be speedily detected. The volume contains only twenty-nine pieces, and not all of them are successful. Probably a majority of the admirers of Tennyson would wish away *Will Waterproof's Lyrical Monologue;*[1] for it is remarkable that while in character-sketches he afterwards proved himself to be, within certain limits, a master of humour, in pieces where he deliberately sets out in his own person to be humorous he is pretty certain to fail. Most of the poems however are fine, and nearly all of them have tangible subjects, and these are handled with vigour. The most noticeable among them are *Morte d'Arthur, The Gardener's Daughter, Dora, Ulysses, Locksley Hall, The Vision of Sin*, and the exquisite song,

[1] There are exceptions however,—the *Monologue* has been highly praised, for reasons which the writer could never understand. At the best it is pleasing verse: at the worst we have lines like these:—

    Is there some magic in the place?
    Or do my peptics differ?

"Break, break, break". There is sufficient variety here, but above all there is sufficient substance: every one of these poems is, in its own way, in intimate contact with the real. The poet has gained immensely in depth: we see it in the weightier matter of his pieces. He has gained also in sureness of touch: we see it in the fact that there was only one of the poems in this volume which his later taste rejected as unworthy of reprinting, and also in the fact that the changes he subsequently thought necessary were comparatively few and unimportant. Yet Tennyson was still far from being master of all the force and energy of his later years. Every one of the poems named has indeed the attribute of reality; but some of them are graceful rather than strong, and in others the strength is misapplied. Grace is the characteristic of *The Gardener's Daughter* and *Dora*; and kindred examples might easily be added from the same volume. *The Gardener's Daughter* continues the idyllic strain of *The Miller's Daughter*. It is in every way less exquisite than that beautiful poem; but what it was at first it still remains. The poet could now give at once such beauty as the subject was susceptible of. *Dora* betrays the influence of Wordsworth and the Bible. It is rich in knowledge of rural life and full of sympathy with the feelings of the rural population. The tenderness and pathos of the story have made it a favourite from the beginning; but, wanting as it does force and grandeur, it cannot be classed high in Tennyson's poetry.

Locksley Hall illustrates what seems to me the other defect of the poems of 1842. It is strength misapplied. Though complete in itself, this poem has since received in *Locksley Hall Sixty Years After* a supplement so grand and so strong with a strength well applied, that it must perforce be mentioned at a later stage. In *Locksley Hall* there is no trace of dilettantism: it is full of passion; but its defect is that the passion is somewhat shrill.[1] The natural defence is that the shrillness is not personal to the poet because the piece is dramatic. But the argument is not convincing. After all, Tennyson had the making of the hero; and there seems to be no sufficient reason why he should not have made him a somewhat worthier mouthpiece of the feelings and aspirations, the

---

[1] It has been wittily said of the hero that probably he "found his 'sorrow's crown of sorrows' in remembering sixty years after some of the speeches he was so proud of".

disappointments and revolts of youth. There are obvious reasons why the Northern Farmer is what he is with all his limitations, moral and intellectual. The limitations help the picture. Not so the hysterics of the hero of *Locksley Hall*. He exists in order to express certain feelings about "social wants that sin against the strength of youth," and "sickly forms that swerve from honest Nature's rule". The feelings are to a great extent worthy of sympathy, and it can hardly be doubted that Tennyson meant the reader to sympathise with them. In other words, though the hero is not Tennyson himself he is in some respects Tennyson's mouthpiece. For this reason it was the poet's clear duty, though it is not the duty of the dramatic writer as such, to win respect for the character in which he embodied such views and sentiments. This Tennyson fails to do, and therefore *Locksley Hall* falls short of greatness. We must recognise the energy of purpose of the poem ; but it is an energy not yet under the guidance of perfect wisdom. It is instructive to notice that when in *Maud* Tennyson had once more to depict a man in revolt against society, he fell into a similar error. *Maud* too would be improved if the hero had a little self-restraint and dignity. The truth seems to be that Tennyson was sometimes, especially in his early life, prone to mistake loudness for energy. It is his misfortune that the public followed him in the error. Not once nor twice has the popular preference been given to poems not in his best manner, because they filled the ear more than purer specimens of poetry.

A similar energy is manifest in *A Vision of Sin*. The name reveals its purpose. It is charged with a bitterness rare in Tennyson. The grim figure summoned up is one not to be forgotten, yet hardly to be remembered without a shudder. In the verses which the author puts into its lips he approaches from another side that defiance of law, order, respectability, morality, everything, which gives such a wild charm to the songs of Burns's *Jolly Beggars*. Perhaps this is, of all the poems of 1842, the most striking illustration of the change which was passing over Tennyson. It is almost impossible to imagine the poet of 1833 writing thus :—

> Fill the cup, and fill the can :
> Have a rouse before the morn :
> Every moment dies a man,
> Every moment one is born.

> We are men of ruin'd blood ;
> Therefore comes it we are wise.
> Fish are we that love the mud,
> Rising to no fancy-flies.
>
> Name and fame! to fly sublime
> Thro' the courts, the camps, the schools,
> Is to be the ball of Time,
> Bandied by the hands of fools.
>
> Friendship!—to be two in one—
> Let the canting liar pack!
> Well I know, when I am gone,
> How she mouths behind my back.
>
> Virtue!—to be good and just—
> Every heart, when sifted well,
> Is a clot of warmer dust,
> Mix'd with cunning sparks of hell.
>
> O! we two as well can look
> Whited thought and cleanly life
> As the priest, above his book
> Leering at his neighbour's wife.
>
> Fill the cup, and fill the can:
> Have a rouse before the morn:
> Every moment dies a man,
> Every moment one is born.

I have reserved to the end the three pieces which seem to me best of all,—*Morte d'Arthur*, *Ulysses*, and "Break, break, break". *Morte d'Arthur*, which, though not published till 1842, had been written at least as early as 1837, is substantially the latter part of *The Passing of Arthur*, of that great collection, which is also a great though loosely strung whole, the *Idylls of the King;* and it can hardly therefore be criticised now apart from the context in which it has been placed. The high position generally assigned to *The Passing of Arthur* in what many consider the greatest of all Tennyson's works, is evidence that in the *Morte d'Arthur* he had touched very nearly his high-water mark. And it, along with *Ulysses*, gave the first decisive proof of Tennyson's skill in the use of blank verse, a measure in the management of which he has had no superior since Milton, and certainly had no equal at that time. Coleridge, who occasionally used it with splendid effect, was dead ; and Wordsworth, who, though much of his blank verse was loaded with the weight of unhappy theories unhappily followed out, could also at times write in it magnificently, had produced all his great work. Arnold, whose blank verse will bear comparison with that of any of them, had not yet begun to write, unless we insist upon counting his Rugby prize poem.

"Break, break, break," contains only sixteen lines. It is a song, the expression of an emotion. The direct utterance of thought would be out of place in it; but surely the pathos of life has seldom been more touchingly expressed. The little lyric is human to the core.[1] *Ulysses*, again, is a noble picture of the heart hungering for truth, of the

> Grey spirit yearning in desire
> To follow knowledge like a sinking star,
> Beyond the utmost bound of human thought.

The ancient hero with his restless longing gives voice to an aspiration modern even more than ancient; for the emphasis thus laid on the desire for *knowledge* is clearly a nineteenth century adaptation of the Homeric tale. In a somewhat similar spirit Tennyson has modernised the Arthurian legends; for it is a feature of his work that however far he may dive into the past, he applies what he finds there to the present. This has been sometimes said of him by way of reproach, it is in reality only an answer to praise ill-judged. If it be said that Tennyson in the *Idylls* painted a true picture of the ancient Britons, or that in *Ulysses* he reproduced a Greek of the age of Homer, then indeed it is to the point to answer that the whole atmosphere of these poems is that of the nineteenth century. But they are not necessarily less perfect as poems because such is the fact, they may be even in some respects more interesting.

It may be questioned if the poet ever rose higher than he rises in *Ulysses*. Its heroism is magnificent, and it helps whoever reads it to take "with a frolic welcome," like the mariners, "the thunder and the sunshine" of life. The style too is admirable; not a word is wasted, yet there is nowhere any suggestion of harshness or abruptness. The personal emotion under which it is said to have been written seems to glow through the perfect lines.

[1] One of the most refined of critics, Dr. John Brown, says of "Break, break, break": "Out of these few simple words, deep and melancholy, and sounding as the sea, flows forth all *In Memoriam*, as a stream flows out of its spring, all is here." (*Horae Subsecivae*.)

In the two volumes of 1842 there is evidence, in the first place, of great progress on the part of the poet towards technical perfection. The verse is more finished, the imagery at once richer and in more perfect taste. It is true that there still remain some marks of youth. Any one who compares *Morte d'Arthur* with those parts of the *Idylls of the King* written in the poet's maturity, must be struck with the frequency of the echoes of Homer in the former. It was always Tennyson's method, as it has been the method of many great poets, Virgil and Milton for example, to weave the thoughts and expressions of his predecessors into his verse. But there is a difference between his earlier and his later manner of doing so. In the earlier period we find direct imitation: over and over again we meet with expressions which at once strike the ear as more or less foreign to the context, and so suggest the original. It is so with the Byronic echoes of the *Poems by Two Brothers*, and with the Homeric echoes of *Morte d'Arthur*. No doubt the imitation in the latter case at least is conscious and purposed; but the matter borrowed is not so handled as to become, as similar borrowings do in Tennyson's later work, part of the very fabric of the poem in which it is placed. The Wordsworthian and Biblical echoes of *Dora* are another example of the same kind of immaturity. But on the other hand it must be admitted that Tennyson never used the hints he borrowed more skilfully, or more perfectly fused them with the contributions of his own mind, than in *Ulysses*.

More important still, however, is the gain which nine years of life had brought to the poet in the substance of his poetry. We see this in the greater bulk of the more serious poetry. In the earlier volumes a search was necessary to discover anything besides elegance and prettiness: in the volumes of 1842 there are many things besides—wealth of imagination, depth of feeling, reach of thought—which at once rivet the attention. This is the truth which justifies the assertion frequently made, that it was with the poems of 1842 that Tennyson made his decisive appearance in literature. A poet's "decisive" appearance in literature is not to be determined by any temporary vogue, but by the permanent qualities of his work. It is because the poems of 1842 had, and the earlier poems had not, in sufficient quantity, elements of lasting value, that the name of Tennyson must from that date onwards, and not earlier, be considered a fixed name in the records of poetry. Though he continued to write only short pieces, he had found a place in them for nearly all the thoughts and aspirations of the complex time in which he lived. Religion, the desires that lie beneath science and philosophy, and social problems, like marriage and the question of the value of life itself, had all occupied his mind. It may indeed be said, as it has been said of the earlier volumes, that there is a tendency to excessive discursiveness. Concentration and treatment on the great scale were still things for the future.

CHAPTER III.

BROWNING: 1833 TO 1846.

WHILE Tennyson was slowly perfecting himself and spending his strength as much in the revision of his youthful work as in the production of new pieces, Browning was producing verse with that rapidity which always distinguished him. The whole of Tennyson's verse between 1830 and 1842 (all, that is, which he permanently retained) in Macmillan's edition of 1888 fills only part of two very moderate-sized volumes. But between 1833 and 1846 Browning published eleven long poems and over forty shorter pieces. This ratio of productiveness was characteristic of the two men, though the difference in later years was not so great. It is also characteristic that while Tennyson laboriously revised and touched up his poems, Browning made few changes. He seems indeed—to judge from the preface to *Pauline*—to have held peculiar notions as to the ethics of the relation between an author and his readers. In the first reprint he corrected only errors of the press, holding it "the honest course" to "leave mere literary errors unaltered".

Pauline bears throughout the marks of youth, but it is a youth of splendid promise. It is all the more imperative to recognise its merits because of Browning's own exaggerated, though doubtless quite sincere, depreciation. The poem is defective in construction and hazy in outline. It shows little of that intimate and masterly knowledge of human passion which the author's mature works display. He seems to be labouring at a work too great for him, while he shows by strokes here and there that he may some day be great enough for any work. But though its defects are grave they are redeemed by many fine passages, some of them beautiful with a luxuriant beauty not common in Browning's subsequent works. It is moreover always instructive to trace an author's early tastes, and particularly so in the case of one who has pursued a course so independent as Browning's. He is known to have long admired, and in his youth to have almost worshipped Shelley; but in most of his works, even those of the first period, it is difficult to detect the influence of Shelley. The style of *Pauline* however is much more rich and glowing than Browning's later style; and Mrs. Sutherland Orr is doubtless right in pointing to Shelley as the source of the "profusion of natural imagery" which *Pauline* presents, and of the "touches of naturalistic emotion, not at all in keeping with Mr. Browning's picturesque, but habitually human genius."[1] The ring of Shelley is distinctly audible in the following lines:—

> There were bright troops of undiscovered suns,
> Each equal in their radiant course ; there were
> Clusters of far fair isles which ocean kept
> For his own joy, and his waves broke on them
> Without a choice ; and there was a dim crowd
> Of visions, each a part of some grand whole :
> And one star left his peers and came with peace
> Upon a storm, and all eyes pined for him ;
> And one isle harboured a sea-beaten ship,
> And the crew wandered in its boughs and plucked
> Its fruits and gave up all their hopes of home :
> And one dream came to a pale poet's sleep,
> And he said, "I am singled out by God,
> No sin must touch me."[2]

But as Byron was too foreign to the genius of Tennyson to influence him permanently, so was Shelley too foreign to that of Browning. Shelley's home was in the clouds, Browning's was, if I may say so with no depreciatory meaning, on earth. Browning himself, in the well-known invocation to the "Sun-treader" in *Pauline*, speaks of Shelley's "dim creations gathered round like mountains"; and in doing so lays emphasis upon the difference between them and the strongly conceived and clearly outlined figures of his own imagination.

Reference has already been made to the fact that Browning himself is, to some extent at least, "the *dramatis persona*" of *Pauline*. The poem is indeed in some passages, and particularly in the invocation just mentioned, almost without disguise auto-

---

[1] *Handbook to the Works to Robert Browning*, p. 21.

[2] I., 40-41. The references in the case of Browning are to the seventeen-volume edition of his works.

biographic. But probably exaggerated views have been taken of the amount of truth it contains : the Wahrheit is very much mingled with Dichtung. And it is one of the marks of youth in the poem that while some of the features are those of Browning himself, others are such as not only do not but cannot possibly fit in with his character. The poem is fragmentary, and the fragments do not harmonise with one another.

Never, perhaps, was there such progress as there was from *Pauline* to *Paracelsus*, published two years after it, in 1835 ; and never surely did there issue from the head of a youth of twenty-three a poem so great. Had Browning subsequently advanced as Shakespeare did between the apprentice period when he touched up the plays of older dramatists, or produced his own first works, and the years when he wrote the great tragedies, it is not too much to say that the author of *Paracelsus* might have ranked as the first poet of all time. But he certainly made no such progress. There are some parts of his later work which may be put higher than *Paracelsus ;* but that wonderful poem is so near the front of its author's writings, that we may almost say he appears in it complete and perfect. The change we detect in his later work is not invariably improvement. In this respect Browning contrasts strikingly with Tennyson. The latter grew in force, in richness, and in depth of meaning almost to the close of his long life ; while Browning rarely wrote with greater force, and hardly ever, at least in his long pieces, with more perfect artistic balance, than in the first poem which he willingly acknowledged. Professor Jones, in his profound and fascinating criticism of Browning, has justly pointed out that in this opening poem the place of knowledge beside love is much more fairly stated than in the poet's later works.[1]

What we have here however to notice with regard to *Paracelsus* is, in the first place, as to its form, that it is a poem " dramatic in principle," yet not a drama. There are several interlocutors, but there is not that rapid march of events, nor is there to any considerable degree that influence of mind upon mind, that development of the catastrophe out of the words

---

[1] In a private note to the writer Professor Jones asks : " Was Browning ever whole-hearted after *Paracelsus ?* or did not some scepticism, that he never thought out into reasoned conviction, *sprain* him ? " There is much to be said for this view, and it would explain a great deal that needs explanation in the subsequent works of Browning.

and actions of the *dramatis personæ*, which is vital to the real drama. In essence *Paracelsus* is a monodrama. It is the development of the man who gives his name to the poem that is alone of importance in it; and that development is brought about mainly from within. In other words, *Paracelsus* is what may be called a psychological drama. If the soliloquy, instead of being an occasional device, held the chief place in Shakespeare's works, then we might have in them something such as we find in *Paracelsus*.

If *Paracelsus* stood alone, its characteristics would be of comparatively slight importance. But we have to view it, first in the light of the subsequent work of Browning, and secondly in connexion with the whole literature of the time. Now, one of the most prominent features of Browning's work is the prevalence of dramatic studies not placed in the context of the regular drama. His interest centred in character, but he did not conceive character as Shakespeare did, in the complex entanglement of its relations with the world. He is more at home in reflection and meditation than either in action or in dialogue. Even in his regular dramas there is little action; and after a number of experiments he gave up the attempt to write plays. Again, with regard to the literature of the time, it has passed almost into a common-place that the century, rich as it has been in poetic talent, has somehow proved itself incapable of producing great dramas. The questions opened up by these considerations are too wide for discussion in the present chapter; and moreover, Browning's dramas are best grouped with those of Tennyson written long after. It must therefore suffice to point out here that in *Paracelsus*, where, without attempting the construction of a play, he had full scope for his great dramatic gifts, Browning had struck upon the form of poetry which long experience proved to be best suited to his genius. Moreover, in his divergence from the regular dramatic form he was in accord with the genius of the time, which, for reasons to be discussed hereafter, was inimical to the drama.

Paracelsus to a certain degree varies from the form which Browning afterwards made specially his own: it is not a pure dramatic monologue. But Festus and Michal are only foils to set off the principal character; and Aprile is the contrast necessitated by the scheme of the poem, the other half of the "dissevered world". A more important difference is that the interest is not so intensely dramatic as it is in some of the later monologues. Great as is the character of *Paracelsus*, we are not absorbed in it as we are in Guido and Caponsacchi, in the Bishop of St. Praxed's and Andrea del Sarto. In these we sometimes seem to lose the thought in the dramatic vividness of the character, in *Paracelsus* we more frequently lose the character in the thought. This is one of the few indications of youthfulness which the poem affords. Browning could already think profoundly, but he had not yet that accumulated wealth of experience which went to the creation of the characters in *Men and Women* and in *The Ring and the Book*. *Paracelsus* therefore has much the nature of a poetised philosophy. The conception and the method are indeed truly artistic; the ideas here applied to life are of the poetic order, and they are displayed in the garb of beauty. But at the same time there is an underlying matter which it is perfectly easy to translate into the language of exact thought. Or perhaps it is a mistake to call it an *underlying* matter, for the thought is so conspicuously brought forward that it is impossible to miss its significance. Browning recognises two principles, Love and Knowledge. The first is embodied in the poet Aprile, the second in the devotee of science, Paracelsus. The pursuit of either of these principles alone is, in Browning's view, a fatal error. Paracelsus suffers shipwreck from his one-sided devotion to knowledge; Aprile falls short of the fulness of the stature of the perfect man because his desire is for love solely to the exclusion of knowledge. The harmonious development of humanity demands both. Even thus early however Browning showed the tendency, afterwards so strong in him, to give the first place to love. Paracelsus fails because he has chosen a part instead of the whole; but his failure is all the more complete because what he has chosen is not even the better part. Further, success such as he sought would have been worse than failure. It is a significant dramatic touch that Festus after a long discussion ceases to oppose the daring scheme of Paracelsus, and owns him one of higher order; but Michal, the woman, even then beseeches him to stay, dreading, not failure, but complete success. "You will find all you seek, and perish so." And on the final appeal of Paracelsus whether they believe he will accomplish his end, Festus replies, "I do believe"; Michal, "I ever did believe".

Thus, sanctioned at last in the hope he cherishes by conquered reason, sanctioned too by instinct, which nevertheless whispers that the hope is not the highest, Paracelsus sets out. The purpose of the poem is to follow the course of a spirit which loves knowledge only, as the soul in Tennyson's *Palace of Art* loves beauty. Knowledge, again, is but the gateway to power. In the end Paracelsus himself says: "I gazed on power till I grew blind". In this he found "the sign and note and character of man". The plan was vast,—to follow one of the richest of human spirits all through the course of a life devoted to a great, though, as it proves, a mistaken ideal. The execution could not fail to reveal the poet's deepest conceptions of life.

On the threshold it must be noticed that Browning has with true insight conceived in Paracelsus a character sensitive to all human impulses. Paracelsus fixes his eye on knowledge, which he believes may be translated into power, but he does so with clear consciousness of what he is relinquishing. To point out to him "the value of repose and love" is as superfluous as were the offerings of the embassy to the Eastern king:—

> The gifts they offered proved but dazzling dust
> Shed from the ore-beds native to his clime.

The error then of Paracelsus does not spring from an undeveloped and one-sided nature, it is the result of an intellectual conviction. Hence he is capable of learning, and when he finds the grounds of the conviction giving way he can acknowledge and in part repair his error. That there *is* error we are prepared from the first to discover. The instinct of Michal and the pleadings of Festus, though subdued, are not wholly crushed. The greater nature is going astray, and the lesser natures cannot set him right, only experience which is greater still. Nine years pass, and Paracelsus, worn, and touched already with doubt, needs but the impulse given by the poor crazed poet Aprile to turn him from the course he has pursued so long. The human feelings, long remorselessly crushed out, rush back and drive him from his solitary path to mix once more with men. The death of Aprile, says Paracelsus,

> Summoned me,
> As I would shun the ghastly fate I saw,
> To serve my race at once; to wait no longer
> That God should interfere on my behalf,
> But to mistrust myself, put pride away,
> And give my gains, imperfect as they were,
> To men (ii., p. 90).

There were two conceivable courses. One was to follow the path Aprile had trodden and live for love only. But for this the nature of Paracelsus was now "too warped and twisted and deformed". The other, which in reality was the only one possible, was to follow knowledge, no longer alone, but as a man among men. It was this pursuit which brought Paracelsus to Basil. It was partly the narrowness and ignorance of men, but partly also his own imperfections, that led to disaster there. Before the overthrow comes, even in the full blaze of his apparent success, there is a pathetic strain of failure in the conversation of Paracelsus with Festus.

> Love, hope, fear, faith,—these make humanity;
> These are its sign and note and character,
> And these I have lost! (ii., p. 109.)

This, it will be noticed, is a complete reversal of his original view, when he found in knowledge that "sign and note and character". The fault then lay partly in Paracelsus, and it must be "burnt and purged away" in the fires of adversity. Symmetry of nature, destroyed by long pursuit of a partial aim, could be restored only by a moral cataclysm.

In the two closing parts we see Paracelsus starting anew upon his greater quest. He has hitherto been content to be but half a man, to foster one side of his nature at the expense of the other. He is now determined to be just to both, to follow knowledge as before, but in the pursuit to welcome all the joy and all the beauty fortune or Providence may offer. The end is death, but not defeat. There are few passages in poetry more profound and more moving than the closing speech of Paracelsus which sums up the lesson of the whole, and teaches the secret he had wrung from life. Perhaps only in *The Pope*, the culminating point in *The Ring and the Book*, are Browning's deepest thoughts more finely expressed. Experience has taught Paracelsus the cause of his own failure. Even after his awakening by Aprile he failed at Basil, because, as he says:—

> In my own heart love had not been made wise
> To trace love's faint beginnings in mankind,
> To know even hate is but a mask of love's,
> To see a good in evil and a hope
> In ill-success (ii., p. 175).

This was the truth which had in the end to be added to the two half-truths already learnt. Paracelsus himself was from the beginning partly right, and Aprile even more so,—"love preceding power, and with much power, always much more love";—but there was a third truth which had to be added to both, the deepest and most difficult, the recognition of the good inherent in evil itself. This is no chance thought in Browning: it runs through all his works from *Paracelsus* to *Rephan*, and it is one of his weightiest and most original contributions to poetic thought. It springs from his combination of deep religious feeling with great speculative power and clearness of mind. He saw that "religious pessimism is a contradiction in terms," and that the idea of the absolute character of evil logically leads to religious pessimism, or to a pessimism which is not religious. He might have derived the hint from German philosophy, but "he was emphatic in his assurance that he knew neither the German philosophers nor their reflection in Coleridge".[1] We must therefore account for this and for many other striking points of contact between him and them on the ground suggested by Miss Martineau,—"that he had no need to study German thought, since his mind was German enough already".[2] No doubt it is likewise true that both he and they thought these thoughts because, as the phrase goes, they were "in the air". They are notes of time.

Thus *Paracelsus* exhibits the struggles of a great spirit to blend ever more and more colours in the varied web of life. The hero starts with the crude belief that there is one colour the most beautiful of all, and that the whole web should consist of it: like the Eastern artist, he ends with the conviction that every colour has its place and will be beautiful there, the business of life being just to find what that place is.

The thoughtful weight and the philosophic power of this poem will not be disputed. The question asked with regard to Browning is rather whether his matter is of the poetic cast and whether his method is artistic. The answer in the case of *Paracelsus* is clear. History has been defined as "philosophy teaching by examples". The definition might be transferred to dramatic poetry. Browning has embodied his philosophy in a great character. It is true, as has been already admitted, that the grandeur of the thought sometimes draws the attention away from the character, and that the author's experience is less mature than

---

[1] Mrs. Sutherland Orr's *Life*, p. 108.   [2] *Ibid*.

his intellect. But when we examine closely we always find that the thought is in keeping with the man as he is conceived, or in other words that the poet is " teaching by examples," not giving utterance to abstract arguments. Further, there is a fervour about *Paracelsus* which is the accent of poetry, not of philosophy. We breathe throughout an atmosphere of emotion. The departure of Paracelsus on his quest, his meeting with Aprile, the hilarity which veils his anguish after the failure at Basil, and his death, all exhibit him " touched with emotion ". It is the duty as well as the right of poetry to break the white light of intellect into the prismatic splendour of the affections, and Browning has done so in this poem. It would be impossible, for example, to state in prose, without an incalculable loss of power, the original aim of Paracelsus and his assurance of success :—

> I go to prove my soul!
> I see my way as birds their trackless way.
> I shall arrive! what time, what circuit first,
> I ask not: but unless God send his hail
> Or blinding fireballs, sleet or stifling snow,
> In some time, his good time, I shall arrive:
> He guides me and the bird. In his good time (ii., p. 27).

The strong impressive metaphors and similes scattered through the poem bear likewise the stamp of a poet's mind :—

> The wroth sea's waves are edged
> With foam, white as the bitten lip of hate (ii., p. 167).

And few pictures in six lines surpass the picture of Constantinople which opens part ii. :—

> Over the waters in the vaporous West
> The sun goes down as in a sphere of gold
> Behind the arm of the city, which between,
> With all that length of domes and minarets,
> Athwart the splendour, black and crooked runs
> Like a Turk verse along a scimitar (ii., p. 39).

In some of his later works, Browning undeniably overstepped the line which divides poetry from philosophy; but in *Paracelsus* he is poetic both in conception and in execution.

It is to be regretted that Browning did not remain faithful to the poetic form he had fashioned for himself in *Paracelsus*. That he was fully conscious of the meaning and merits of the form, and also of what would probably be said against it, is proved by the interesting preface to the first edition, quoted in

Mrs. Sutherland Orr's *Life of Browning*. But unfortunately the poem did not win the success it deserved. "*Paracelsus, Sordello,* and the whole of *Bells and Pomegranates* were published at his father's expense, and, incredible as it appears, brought no return to him".[1] We may reasonably conclude that a feeling of disappointment at the reception of *Paracelsus* had an influence in inducing him to try other forms of poetry. He had put his soul into the work, he could not hope soon to surpass it, and he must have felt that if the world would not have it there was little "return" to be looked for from any similar effort. He was young too, and probably as yet uncertain where his real strength lay. Less of the artist than Tennyson, Browning lacked that half-instinctive guidance which often preserves the artist from error. Hence it comes that the years after the publication of *Paracelsus* seem to have been years of experiment. Browning tried the drama, he tried narrative, and he reverted to dramatic monologue; but he showed the strongest inclination to abide in the regular drama. Not before the year 1846 does he seem to have convinced himself that this was not his proper sphere. Thus Browning's first period gives no such impression of sure and steady growth as Tennyson's does. As surely as, in *Paracelsus*, Browning had incomparably the advantage over Tennyson in scope and depth and grandeur of thought, and in all that goes to make the great rather than the elegant poet, so surely, in the years which immediately followed, had Tennyson the advantage in development. Like his own Paracelsus, Browning went forth in the confidence that sooner or later he would reach his goal; but, again like Paracelsus, he must try the wrong way before he found the right. What has been lost through the fact that for those eleven years the poet was simply groping his way, can never be known; but, comparing the *Dramatic Lyrics* and *Dramatic Romances* of the period with *Strafford* and the other plays, we may infer that the loss has been great. The regret must be all the keener because the years in question were just those in which the poet's mind was artistically most flexible. He had already given ample proof of capacity for thought, he was every year growing richer in experience, and he did not yet, as he did in later days, suffer his thought to usurp the place of his sense of beauty.

[1] *Life*, p. 53.

The list of Browning's works (omitting stray pieces published separately) from *Strafford*, published and acted in 1837, to *A Soul's Tragedy*, published in 1846, when the period of experiment ended, shows both his prevailing interests and the character of the mistake he made. *Strafford* was followed in 1840 by *Sordello*. Then came in rapid succession the works originally published under the fanciful title of *Bells and Pomegranates*.[1] These were *Pippa Passes, King Victor and King Charles, Dramatic Lyrics, The Return of the Druses, A Blot in the 'Scutcheon, Colombe's Birthday, Dramatic Romances and Lyrics, Luria,* and *A Soul's Tragedy*. In all of these the poet was studying the soul's development: "Little else," he says significantly, "is worth study".[2] In most of them however he was studying it in a way in which it had not been granted to him to excel.

I have already stated the reasons why it seems to me desirable to reserve for the future the discussion of the dramas. It is necessary however for the sake of chronological connexion to summarise here my principal conclusions. In the first place, then, I think it will be found that Browning's plays generally resolve themselves into studies of single characters. *Strafford* is the only one of them that has anything approaching an average number of *dramatis personæ*. But not only is the stage half empty, the actors who are brought upon it are, to a degree unexampled in Shakespeare or Goethe or probably any acknowledged master of the drama, subordinate to the one central character. Secondly, the plays are deficient in action, and the impression is conveyed that the action does not matter. Another

---

[1] This title is a good example of one source of the difficulty so many readers (and all in some degree) find in getting at Browning's meaning. He explains that he only "meant by that title to indicate an endeavour towards something like an alternation, or mixture, of music with discoursing, sound with sense, poetry with thought". He adds: "It is little to the purpose, that such is actually one of the most familiar of the many Rabbinical (and Patristic) acceptations of the phrase; because I confess that, letting authority alone, I supposed the bare words, in such juxtaposition, would sufficiently convey the desired meaning". (Note to the last number of *Bells and Pomegranates*, quoted in Mrs. Sutherland Orr's *Life*, p. 114.) What percentage of Browning's readers have possessed the Rabbinical clue, or have, without it, been able independently to fathom the meaning? Undue confidence in the knowledge, and undue confidence in the imagination of his reader, were among Browning's errors.

[2] *Dedication of Sordello.*

way of stating the same thing would be to say that the study of character is internal or psychological, rather than external or through the medium of events. And thirdly, the study of even the one character fully developed is, in comparison with the standard Browning attains elsewhere, deficient in subtlety. It is strange to find Browning complaining of the necessity of chalking " broadly on each vesture's hem the wearer's quality," when we observe that one of the great defects of his dramas is just that he is apt to chalk it too broadly. If these conclusions are sound it will be admitted that Browning's proper vocation was not to write for the stage.

But while it is necessary to point out that in all the works of those years, except the *Dramatic Romances* and *Dramatic Lyrics*, Browning deviated from the form in which he wrote best, it is equally necessary to insist that in the matter and essence of his poems he remained throughout faithful to the true bent of his genius. All the works of the period were studies of the human soul. *Sordello* is so as well as the rest, though the narrative form modifies the dramatic presentation. It appears from the opening that in choosing narrative Browning was conforming to what he conceived to be a popular preference. From the tone of this opening it may be inferred that the reception of *Strafford* had not a little to do with the poet's opinion and the choice it determined. Narrative, he thinks, is " if not the worst yet not the best expedient". For him this was certainly true. He would rather and he could better make Sordello speak, keeping himself out of view. Nevertheless, in deference to public prejudice, he determines to take his stand, " motley on back and pointing pole in hand," beside his character. It may be observed that it is difficult to reconcile this with the dedication, dated 1863, to J. Milsand. " I wrote it," says the poet there, " twenty-five years ago for only a few, counting even in these on somewhat more care about its subject than they really had." A poem written for the few has no need to conform to the prejudices of the many. Doubtless Browning wrote, as a great poet may legitimately write, and perhaps ought to write, in the hope that he would interest the many; and when he found that he had in that respect so entirely failed, he forgot that he had ever cherished the hope.

In the last resort it is vain to appeal from the many to the few; on the contrary, the ultimate court of appeal in matters critical is from the few to the many. It no doubt may and does happen that a great poet may be unappreciated in his own generation. Yet even this is exceptional. The great Attic dramatists, Virgil, Shakespeare and Goethe were all known to their own age as giants. That their stature was accurately measured it would be too much to say; but they were known for men who overtopped their fellows, and they were "popular" in the sense that they had won the suffrage of the great majority of those who were interested in literature. In any wider sense there is perhaps only one poet of real power who ever has been in modern times popular,—Robert Burns. But while this is the rule it is likewise true that in some cases greatness misses immediate recognition. There is no instance more conspicuous than Browning himself. When this happens however we look to the future to redress the present, not to the steady love of the select few to redress the lasting indifference of the many. There are indeed some authors who possess a permanent interest for a small circle, but who are never likely to be read by many. It would seem that there is such a thing as literary, as we are assured there is such a thing as theological, "election". Only the elect can enter within the heaven where these exclusive spirits reign. There can be little doubt that Landor is a case in point. In such cases the reason for the limited audience is not that the men are too great, but that they are not great *enough*. The love of the select few may rest on sound critical grounds, but if it does not expand into the love of the many the cause is some failure in catholicity, the want of some quality profoundly human. The need of "election" is never felt in the case of the very greatest men of all. There is no esoteric school of Shakespeare or of Homer. In the end there is no way to measure greatness half as sure as the general judgment of humanity. Even Milton, who asked for "fit audience though few," and who if any might be regarded as an exception, shows the certainty of the rule. He is frequently spoken of as a great poet who is not popular. It is true; but, as has been already pointed out, "popular" is a misleading word. Milton has been acknowledged by nearly all, not in England alone but wherever European civilisation has spread, as a great poet. There is no doubt about his position, no such wide variation of critical opinion as there is with regard to the lesser men referred to. Experience then seems to point to the conclusion that the poet's true audience is a wide one. It should consist, if not of all humanity, at least of all who have intelligence and education enough to take interest in poetry. And if such is the ultimate audience, it cannot be wrong but rather a virtue to attempt to address as wide an audience immediately. To lower the quality of the work because that audience was for the time unappreciative would be a very different thing. A great man may have to trust his fame "to foreign nations and to future ages".

If however Browning in *Sordello* chose the narrative form in the hope of making his poem more popular, legitimate as the desire was, the choice was most unfortunate. Not that success in narration was beyond his reach: the ride from Ghent to Aix and *The Pied Piper of Hamelin* are universally known examples of the rapidity, vigour and point with which he could on occasion tell a story. But it is strange he should have thought there was any virtue in the narrative *form* as such. It could increase his popularity only if it lessened the difficulty readers felt in understanding him; but used as he uses it in *Sordello*, far from diminishing difficulties, it only adds a new one. In a narrative the reason must be strong indeed which justifies an author in abandoning the chronological sequence of events. But Browning does so. The first scene is taken from the close of Sordello's life; and there are only enigmatical hints of the course the poet is pursuing. Nearly every reader probably has felt himself perplexed by this eccentric opening; and most have been left helplessly asking what gain there is to justify this violent departure from all ordinary rule. Thus it would seem impossible to acquit Browning of waywardness and of quite unnecessary obscurity in his manner of telling the story. If the difficulty lay wholly in the nature of the subject or of the thought we could only acquiesce; but the fact that *Sordello* is the greatest of all stumbling-blocks to the readers of Browning is due largely to the poet himself.

Two reasons, besides that already given, may be assigned to account for the difficulty felt in understanding *Sordello*. One is the manner in which Browning uses the obscure names and facts of history on which the poem is founded. In this we detect, if not a perverse pleasure in mystification, at any rate an indifference to the ease and convenience of the reader. The names were familiar enough to him, but to the great majority of readers they are quite unknown. Browning sometimes forgot the gulf between his own immense learning and the knowledge of ordinary men; sometimes, it is to be feared, he put the thought of it behind him. Many of his poems, and *Sordello* above all others, are overloaded with a learning not only recondite, but seemingly useless for the illustration of the subject. The allusive manner in which this learning is introduced adds to the evil. The attention is constantly on the strain because, in the middle of a line perhaps, the poet breaks off with some abrupt sidereference. It is a great misfortune that "he prepared himself for writing *Sordello* by studying all the chronicles of that period of Italian history which the British Museum supplied".[1] It is a misfortune, because, although such conscientious thoroughness is in itself admirable, unless the historical knowledge so acquired be rigidly subordinated to the purposes of art, it can only lead the artist into error. And Browning did not so subordinate it. Who would not prefer to his method the lordly way of Shakespeare in dealing with English history? A little of the spirit of the famous saying, "so much the worse for the facts," is occasionally a good thing. Browning's mind, when he wrote *Sordello*, was teeming with facts which clogged his imagination. Over and over again some incident or phase of character occurs to him, and he cannot make up his mind to let it go. But *Sordello* would have been much improved had such excrescences been severely pruned away. A plain straightforward statement of the facts so far as they were strictly relevant would have been far more instructive to the ordinary reader, and not less so to the few whose knowledge of Italian history makes the allusions clear.

This leads to a more vital objection. The deepest faults of *Sordello* spring from the fact that Browning having adopted the narrative form does not keep true to the narrative spirit. He fails in two ways to do so. Movement is vital to a narrative. Reflection is admissible and legitimate, but it must be subordinated to the movement of events. This is not done in *Sordello:* Browning follows the train of his own reflection without law or rule. Again, narrative will bear a certain admixture of the dramatic spirit, and is usually enriched by it. Probably it would not be possible to define the limit of this admixture more exactly than by saying that it must not reduce the events to a secondary position. So much seems almost to follow from the name,

[1] Mrs. Sutherland Orr's *Handbook*, p. 82.

narrative. But Browning has overstepped this limit. His conception of the character of Sordello is throughout dramatic. It is true he says in the dedication, already quoted, that his stress "lay on the *incidents* in the development of a soul"; but practically, in the poem, the emphasis falls, not on the word "incidents," but on the words "development" and "soul". A rough test may be made by any one who merely runs his eye down the pages of *Sordello* and observes the great proportion put into the mouth of one or other of the characters; and a closer examination would deepen the impression thus conveyed. For in the first place the speeches are not, like those in Milton's Pandemonium, devoted to helping forward some one great event in the narrative, their object is rather to delineate character; and in the second place, the narrative parts themselves are often dramatic in conception. For example :—

> Lo, the past is hurled
> In twain : up-thrust, out-staggering on the world,
> Subsiding into shape, a darkness rears
> Its outline, kindles at the core, appears
> Verona (i., p. 54).

The result is that *Sordello* is a chaotic and disjointed poem, neither epic nor dramatic nor any proper union of the two. It stands at the opposite pole from that perfection of form which characterises Greek poetry; because it exhibits none of that restraint on the part of the author which the Greek poet never forgot to impose upon himself. Many things worthy to be said must remain unsaid because there is no place for them. Browning hardly ever in *Sordello*, and too rarely elsewhere, seems to restrain himself in this way. Consequently the poem by its very defects preaches loud the need of self-restraint and regard for form. It is difficult, partly indeed because the thought is profound, but still more because it is shapeless. The thought of *Sordello* is not greater than, and it may be questioned if it is as great as, the perfectly clear and intelligible thought of *Paracelsus*. The rules of art are not meaningless. They are the outcome of the thought of many generations, they apply to the delineation of the soul as well as to all other subjects which can be treated by art, and even the greatest must pay a heavy penalty for ignoring them. The suggestion in the dedication of *Sordello* in 1863, that the fault in connexion with the poem lay with the readers, was at the utmost only half the truth. The writer too was seriously to blame ; and the more readily and frankly those who admire Browning acknowledge this, the better in the end for his reputation. He, like Wordsworth, has to be set free from the load of his own mistakes, and to be judged by what he was, not by reason of but in spite of them,—in spite of wilfulness, of lawlessness, and of native artistic defects. Browning in part, but never completely, outgrew those defects.

The faults of *Sordello*, marring and almost ruining as they do the poem as a whole, are the more to be regretted because it contains many singular beauties of expression and imagery, and is rich in striking and original thought. Much the same may indeed be said of nearly all Browning's poems; but *Sordello* contains perhaps more than most of his later works of the kind of beauty generally associated with the adjective " poetic " ; and it is the more important to insist upon this because it is this kind of beauty in which Browning is commonly supposed to be deficient; and also because *Sordello* is probably the last place to which those who have been repelled by its harsh and crabbed thought would turn for poetry. Yet happy metaphors, phrases that brand themselves upon the memory, single lines charged with overflowing wealth of imagination, and vivid fragments of description are flung down with a careless profusion in the midst of the perplexed and puzzling narrative. Such are—

> The blind night seas without a saving star (i., p. 137),

and

> Some insane rose that burnt heart out in sweets,
> A spendthrift in the spring, no summer greets (*Ibid*, p. 262).

Of a similar character is the picture of the outburst of spring :—

> As in the slumbrous heart o' the woods
> Our buried year, a witch, grew young again
> To placid incantations, and that stain
> About were from her cauldron, green smoke blent
> With those dark pines (*Ibid*, p. 91).

Even more admirable because less fanciful is the comparison of the autumn sunset burning in the woods to a torch-flame :—

> That autumn eve was stilled :
> A last remains of sunset dimly burned
> O'er the far forest, like a torch-flame turned
> By the wind back upon its bearer's hand
> In one long flame of crimson ; as a brand,
> The woods beneath lay black (*Ibid*, p. 54).

In another style, but also excellent, is this :—

> Shrinking Caryatides
> Of just tinged marble like Eve's lilied flesh
> Beneath her Maker's finger when the fresh
> First pulse of life shot brightening the snow (i., p. 67),

where it may be remarked that Browning possibly borrowed a hint from his favourite artist, Michael Angelo, whose vigorous bold method had so much in common with his own.

On the other hand, there are examples only too numerous of all the faults which indifference to rule can make possible and perverse ingenuity commit. Thus, within the space of a page or two we have a specimen of the misuse of hyphens in "linden-flower-time-long", a needless and ungainly coinage in *mollitious* alcoves, and a harsh inversion such as—

> The Troubadour who sung
> Hundreds of songs, forgot, its trick his tongue,
> Its craft his brain (*Ibid*, p. 135).

Shakespeare wrote "the courtier's, scholar's, soldier's, eye, tongue, sword," which is even worse; but his faults are no justification for cognate faults in his successors. The man who wrote as Browning wrote in these passages had still, not perhaps to learn, but to be convinced of some of the fundamental rules of the art. Browning always acted upon the principle that poetry must be true, but he sometimes forgot that it is equally bound to be beautiful.

In the thought of *Sordello*, so far as it is possible to penetrate it (and the writer is far from professing to have done so completely), we have Browning's familiar view of life and of the world. A large tolerance, a steady optimism, the faith that in spite of the evil men do each proves, by the fact that he contrives to live, the presence in him of good,—these are the unvarying ground-work of Browning's philosophy. They are present in *Sordello*—as they were in *Paracelsus*. But in *Sordello* there is the added interest that all is seen in the light of a poetic soul, who must be taken to be Browning himself rather than the nominal hero. It is interesting to notice that in each of his three first poems Browning brings forward the figure of a poet. In *Paracelsus*, it is true, Aprile is little more than the necessary contrast to the principal character. He is as one-sided as Paracelsus himself, and he does not live even to attempt to correct his error as Paracelsus does. Hence the latter afterwards refers to him as crazed. We cannot therefore look to him for a theory of poetic art: he is rather a warning beacon to mark the rock on which the man must founder who gives full sail to his emotional nature and leaves it unballasted by intellect. But in *Pauline* there are hints towards a theory of poetry, and in *Sordello* the theory, as embodied in the man Sordello, is complete. Browning returned to the subject long afterwards, and in *Fifine at the Fair* gave what we must take as his mature and final view. This interest in the principles underlying his art is characteristic of the man. Tennyson is the artist without much troubling himself to ask why. To take the artistic view of life is as natural to him as it is to breathe. His two poems, *The Poet* and *The Poet's Mind*, do not investigate principles; they as much presuppose and leave unexplained the artistic view as the songs do. The one tells us that

> The poet in a golden clime was born,
>   With golden stars above;
> Dower'd with the hate of hate, the scorn of scorn,
>   The love of love.

The other warns off the "dark-brow'd sophist," with his "hollow smile and frozen sneer," because "all the place is holy ground".

Browning's method was different—I do not say, nor do I mean to imply, better. His "poet's mind" is not an abstraction. He must embody it in a man, with "hands, organs, dimensions, senses, affections, passions". He must imagine it working upon these, making the hands dexterous, sharpening the senses, nourishing the affections, kindling the passions. We get the poet therefore in his relation to life, not in a golden clime and under golden stars, but in a work-a-day world. His actions bear their natural fruit, and the actions of others have their natural effect upon him. If he is pricked he bleeds, if he is wronged he is apt to seek revenge. It follows from this that we may look, in Browning's pictures of the artist, for something which will reveal his conception of the actual working of the artistic nature in contact with the world. The effects will be different according as the artistic powers are differently embodied, and allowance must be made for this personal element; but if we find common elements running through several dramatic presentations, we may reasonably infer that in the author's view they are necessary parts of the artistic nature. And there is one very striking feature common to all the characters in which Browning has embodied the artistic nature. It is an intense concentration, in the earlier stages, upon self. Even Aprile, though his watchword is love, is no exception; for it is to be observed that his love is a love which, so to speak, absorbs all beauty in itself, not that which allows itself to be absorbed in the object loved. In his ideal there is sympathy, but the end of the sympathy is to enable him to make everything his own. It is by virtue of it that he hopes to draw the whole world into himself. He knows that to conquer nature he must understand nature, or rather, because the word "understand" is inappropriate, must *feel* it. This is the end and object of his sympathy. Contrast for a moment the "other way of love" Browning comprehended so fully:—

> Teach me, only teach, Love!
>   As I ought
> I will speak thy speech, Love,
>   Think thy thought—
>
> Meet, if thou require it,
>   Both demands,
> Laying flesh and spirit
>   In thy hands.
>
> *Dramatic Lyrics: A Woman's Last Word.*

Still less, if we cast the eye forward, is the Don Juan of *Fifine at the Fair* an exception. But it would be misleading to insist upon him, for the theory of art put into his lips is not his, and indeed he can hardly be regarded as a true instance of the embodiment of the artistic spirit. He has certain sympathies with art, and a certain comprehension of it; but his life is not ruled by it. On the other hand, in the case both of Sordello and of the speaker in *Pauline* this initial concentration on self (it is only an *initial* concentration) is almost too obvious to need demonstration. The speaker in *Pauline* says of himself:—

> I am made up of an intensest life,
> Of a most clear idea of consciousness
> Of self, distinct from all its qualities,
> From all affections, passions, feelings, powers;
> And thus far it exists, if tracked, in all:
> But linked, in me, to self-supremacy,
> Existing as a centre of all things,
> Most potent to create and rule and call
> Upon all things to minister to it;

> And to a principle of restlessness
> Which would be all, have, see, know, taste, feel all—
> This is myself; and I should thus have been
> Though gifted lower than the meanest soul (i., p. 14).

So in *Sordello* the sense of self is to begin with limitless, and half the poem is occupied in tracing the development of the soul through this phase. Sordello in his youthful fancy idealises himself as the Apollo whom all nature and all men must worship. He goes into the world to conquer for himself what he thinks his right, universal homage. He does not propose to win this homage by giving himself in any sense to the world. He is simply going to live his own life, and the homage is to come as his natural reward for being what he is.

To this extent *Sordello* is in agreement with the other poems which deal with the same subject. But *Pauline* is fragmentary, and Aprile is from the necessities of the design a one-sided nature. Of the poet-souls Browning has depicted Sordello alone is complete; and it is in his completeness that we discover both the limits Browning would set to this view, and the reason why he holds it true within those limits.

Sensitiveness, keenness of perception, a quick response to pleasure and pain, are features of the artist-nature. Just because they are so, that nature must begin by being more egoistic than ordinary humanity. High-strung nerves must necessarily seek to protect themselves from excitements destructive to them, and will inevitably seek pleasurable excitements. The invertebrate creature is less self-centred than the vertebrate just because it is less nervous, and the development of nerves through every grade of life means in the first place a demand for a Self growing more and more imperious. For the same reason poets have been through all ages known as a *genus irritabile*. But this high nervous organisation means not only a great *demand* for pleasure, but great *power* to use and to enjoy. Consequently the demand is, at least in part, founded in reason, for power is one of the principal elements in right.

In Browning the moralist is never far from the surface; and he never forgets the complexity of human nature. If the artist might rest in egoism, the moral man will not suffer him. It is likewise true that the artistic nature itself must be warped and stunted if the moral nature is not developed along with it; nay more, it is true that the artistic nature itself, even if it could be severed from morality, would remain imperfect if it did not pass beyond the egoistic stage. Browning at least held so, though minor poets have frequently denied both propositions. Egoism is only a stage, and the high organisation which at first shows itself in the will to absorb everything, afterwards passes on to the capacity and the will to give everything. Hence Sordello's egoism vanishes at the touch of experience. It has been nourished on his own fancy, and it fades away when he learns what the world really is. He intends to use the whole world for his own purposes; but he finds that the mass of men are not what he has imagined. He becomes acquainted with their misery, and knowledge awakens sympathy. Hence, instead of seeking to use them for his own, ends, he turns round to dedicate his life to their service. This is the completed poet. He is in the first place a being "made up of an intensest life," and his demands are infinite. But in the second place contact with other life makes him conscious of the rights even of others, and of the fact that, for the full development even of his own nature, giving may be more blessed than receiving. *Noblesse oblige;* the loftier his endowments the greater his duty to his inferiors. It is true that in the case of Sordello a great temptation comes after his resolution to dedicate himself to the people's cause. He finds suddenly placed within his grasp the sovereignty and the love his early fancy had conceived. There is just the one condition attached, that he must abandon the cause to which he has vowed himself. The close of the poem depicts the struggle in Sordello's mind, and the sophistries with which he tries to persuade himself that it is possible to serve the mammon of power as well as the God in his own nature. Death comes before the struggle is ended; but Browning clearly indicates what the end would have been. The origin of the struggle had been the investing Sordello with the badge which marks him as successor of Eccelino. He is discovered dead,

> Under his foot the badge: still, Palma said,
> A triumph lingering in the wide eyes,
> Wider than some spent swimmer's if he spies
> Help from above in his extreme despair [1] (i., p. 279).

Sordello was followed in 1841 by *Pippa Passes*. It has even more of the dramatic spirit than Browning's poems generally have, yet it is not a drama. It is rather a series of dramatic

---

[1] I am indebted for some hints in this paragraph to Mr. J. T. Nettleship's valuable essay on *Sordello* in *Robert Browning: Essays and Thoughts*.

sketches loosely strung together by the movements of Pippa.
The plan suited Browning and set him free from some of the
difficulties which prevented him from ever attaining complete
success in the regular drama. Each sketch represents one
dramatic situation, and depicts a person or a group at a crisis of
life. There is no need to follow them through various developments. The critical method, which Browning seems to have
followed, suffices. The poet knows from the start just what his
characters are going to do, he is not compelled to track them,
as the true dramatist must, through mazes where he cannot see
his way. Moreover, all the sketches subserve a purpose outside
themselves. They are meant to throw a light upon Pippa, as
she in her turn throws light upon and indeed controls them; for
the turning-point in each of the sketches is her song heard without. Thus in the picture of Ottima and Sebald, by far the most
powerful and finished of them, this turning-point is reached at
the words of Pippa heard as she passes:—

> God's in his heaven—
> All's right with the world!

Ottima and Sebald are among the most marvellous of all
pictures of guilty love. They are represented with the influence
of their crime strong upon them. It is Sebald who first speaks
of the blood they have shed, the blood of the young wife's aged
husband. Ottima tries to win him away from the subject, but
he returns to it again and again, fascinated by its horrors.
Sebald has eaten Luca's bread, worn his clothes, and lived
upon his money. The meanness and ingratitude sting
him. "Do lovers in romances sin that way?" he asks. The
reproaches of Luca have been deserved. Ottima meets his
heart-sinkings with the question whether he could give up the
past, pleasure and crime together. She loves him better for the
crime, she is glad that the silence is broken, that "this simulated
ignorance, this affectation of simplicity" has fallen off it, and
that the naked crime may be looked over and looked down.
Her magnificent picture of the past wins Sebald over.

> *Ottima.* Buried in woods we lay, you recollect;
> Swift ran the searching tempest overhead;
> And ever and anon some bright white shaft
> Burned through the pine-tree roof, here burned and there,
> As if God's messenger thro' the close wood screen
> Plunged and replunged his weapon at a venture,

  Feeling for guilty thee and me: then broke
The thunder like a whole sea overhead—
  Sebald. Yes!
  Ottima.—While I stretched myself upon you, hands
To hands, my mouth to your hot mouth, and shook
All my locks loose, and covered you with them—
You, Sebald, the same you!
  Sebald.   Slower, Ottima!
  Ottima. And as we lay—
  Sebald.   Less vehemently! Love me!
Forgive me! Take not words, mere words, to heart!
Your breath is worse than wine! Breathe slow, speak slow!
Do not lean on me!
  Ottima.   Sebald as we lay,
Rising and falling only with our pants;
Who said, " Let death come now! 'Tis right to die!
Right to be punished! Nought completes such bliss
But woe!" Who said that?
  Sebald.   How did we ever rise?
Was't that we slept? Why did it end?
  Ottima.   I felt you
Taper into a point the ruffled ends
Of my loose locks 'twixt both your humid lips.
My hair is fallen now: knot it again!
  Sebald. I kiss you now, dear Ottima, now and now!
This way? Will you forgive me—be once more
My great queen?
  Ottima.   Bind it thrice about my brow;
Crown me your queen, your spirit's arbitress,
Magnificent in sin. Say that!
  Sebald.   I crown you
My great white queen, my spirit's arbitress,
Magnificent . . . (iii., pp. 23-24).

And here the whole fabric, laboriously reared by a woman splendid for beauty, for fervour of passion, for force of character, for intellect, "magnificent in sin," crumbles into ruin at the voice of an insignificant mill-girl—

> God's in his heaven—
> All's right with the world!

  This is great. Browning has never surpassed it, perhaps no one has ever surpassed it. Every word and touch is powerfully dramatic. The woman is the stronger nature, she leads the man, and he throbs and pants at her words. But there is something stronger still, the eternal law of right and wrong. It is because Pippa embodies here the principle of good that she can undo in a moment all that Ottima has done. The little peasant's voice leaves Sebald in wonder how he could ever have dreamed " guilt from its excess superior to innocence."

In more respects than one this grand sketch challenges comparison with the play of *Macbeth*. The relation of the man to the woman is similar. It is true Ottima is a different character from Lady Macbeth; but Browning agrees with Shakespeare in representing the woman as less remorseful after the crime than the man. It is evident from their works that both looked upon women as far less likely to commit crime than men; and in this experience bears them out. But both thought that once the fatal step was taken over the line which divides guilt from innocence, they were less likely to be troubled with remorseful visitings, to be divided against themselves by recollections of former stainlessness, and to be always pondering fruitlessly the circumstances of the crime. This arises from the fact that women are, more than men, the creatures of impulse and the slaves of passion. Lady Macbeth for a great ambition and Ottima for a great love determine upon crime. The whole being of each is absorbed in the one idea. There is no other way but crime to the end, or none which headlong impatience will consider. The end they have determined upon they must have, and they accept the means to it. All else but the one object of desire is blotted out. Not that they do not feel the crime: Lady Macbeth's sleep-walking scene proves how deeply she felt it. But while her mind retains its balance she resolutely turns her face away from the crime, and in the case of Ottima there is never a hint that she wishes the past undone. The crime is the necessary price to pay, it is paid, and there is an end. Yet there is an instructive difference between the two. Love is more the woman's passion than ambition. In love rather than in high position may she reasonably hope to find the full satisfaction of her nature. Consequently we see that while the one great master pictures his criminal's mind unhinged by her crime, the other does not breathe a hint of remorse. Ottima loves Sebald better for the crime, she justifies it, she is quite unmoved by the song of Pippa. Notice the careless words with which she answers Sebald's startled question:—

> Oh—that little ragged girl!
> She must have rested on the step: we give them
> But this one holiday the whole year round.

> Did you ever see our silk-mills—their inside ?
> There are ten silk-mills now belong to you.
> She stoops to pick my double heartsease . . . Sh !
> She does not hear : call you out louder ! (iii., p. 25.)

What does stir her is not the crime but the sense to which she soon awakes that Sebald's love is gone. "You hate me then ? You hate me then ?" is her helpless and hopeless exclamation.

On the men, Macbeth and Sebald, the effect of their crime is quite different. They too have willed crime, but not with such singleness of purpose as the women. Macbeth is a more complex character than Lady Macbeth. Probably Sebald is less complex, as he is certainly far less powerful, than Ottima; but at any rate he differs from her in that he cannot silence reason. He has only succumbed to passion, he is not absorbed in it. The remorse of the men is not all due to infirmity of purpose, as in the case of Macbeth at least it has been frequently said to be. Lady Macbeth, it is true, says so; but she knows better. Macbeth is more imaginative than she, and he takes from the first a wider and a deeper view. His ambition is only part, not as in her case all. He is conscious of the position of trust in which he stands towards Duncan, and of Duncan's virtues which will plead " trumpet-tongued against the deep damnation of his taking off". Lady Macbeth's only scruple springs from an accidental resemblance between the sleeping Duncan and her father, not from anything reasoned out beforehand and fully grasped by her mind. Sebald is a weaker character than Macbeth, and he is only a sketch, whereas Macbeth is a finished picture. Nevertheless it is plain that the same principle is at work in both cases. Sebald's whole nature is not immersed in the crime : it has only stained, not drenched his mind. Nor does he, like Ottima, find in his passion the full satisfaction of his entire being. She contemplates the crime willingly, for is not the end sufficient recompense for the means taken to attain it ? But it is by compulsion that he looks " before and after,"—after, to the deed itself with its degrading surroundings of ingratitude and treachery ; before, to the price which has to be paid for it, and which is so completely natural that he welcomes it :—

> I see what I have done
> Entirely now ! Oh I am proud to feel
> Such torments—let the world take credit thence—
> I, having done my deed, pay too its price ! (iii., p. 26.)

One other point of resemblance between *Macbeth* and the scene of Ottima and Sebald must be noticed. De Quincey, in a wonderfully suggestive fragment of criticism, pointed out the effect of the knocking at the gate in *Macbeth*. His view is that to mark the character of the crime the murderers have been removed into a world not human, and the knocking at the gate calls them back. "The retiring of the human heart, and the entrance of the fiendish heart, was to be expressed and made sensible. Another world has stept in; and the murderers are taken out of the region of human things, human purposes, human desires. They are transfigured: Lady Macbeth is 'unsexed'; Macbeth has forgot that he was born of woman; both are conformed to the image of devils; and the world of devils is suddenly revealed. But how shall this be conveyed and made palpable? In order that a new world may step in, this world must for a time disappear. The murderers and the murder must be insulated—cut off by an immeasurable gulf from the ordinary tide and succession of human affairs—locked up and sequestered in some deep recess; we must be made sensible that the world of ordinary life is suddenly arrested—laid asleep—tranced—racked into a dread armistice; time must be annihilated; relation to things without abolished: and all must pass self-withdrawn into a deep syncope and suspension of earthly passion. Hence it is, that when the deed is done, when the work of darkness is perfect, then the world of darkness passes away like a pageantry in the clouds: the knocking at the gate is heard; and it makes known audibly that the reaction has commenced; the human has made its reflux upon the fiendish; the pulses of life are beginning to beat again; and the re-establishment of the goings-on of the world in which we live, first makes us profoundly sensible of the awful parenthesis that had suspended them."

Probably Browning had not *Macbeth* consciously in mind when he wrote the scene of Ottima and Sebald; but it is plain that in it he has in his own way applied the same principle. Not indeed when they are as fresh as Macbeth from the crime, but when they have been worked up again to the same intensity of feeling from which the crime had birth, when they too in their glorification of a guilty love, in their defiance of law human and divine, are removed from the world of men to a world of devils, comes, in the song of the little mill-girl, the knock which summons them back to common earth. It is characteristic that in

Shakespeare's hands the most commonplace of everyday incidents serves the purpose. In Browning it is not the mere sound of Pippa's voice, but the meaning of her words, that awakens Sebald from his dream that "guilt from its excess" may show itself "superior to innocence". Artistically, the elder poet has the advantage: he has produced his effect less obtrusively and by simpler means. The difference goes deep. It is a difference not at this point only, but in the general method of the two poets, and it is felt all through their works. Browning is a moralist. He made the scene of Ottima and Sebald with a moral purpose, and with a moral purpose he brought Pippa in contact with them just at this special point. The purpose is written on the face of the poem. Shakespeare is a moralist too; but he is an artist first. The moral is not revealed at any one point, it gradually unfolds itself in the development of the characters and in the play of circumstances upon them. The knocking at the gate is no sermon audible to every ear; nor does it produce any sudden change in the hearts of the murderous pair. Silently and slowly that change takes place, the work of years, not of one supreme moment. But Browning's works may almost be described as a collection of such supreme moments. He does not and cannot trace the insignificant steps which lead to great results, but he does present the great results themselves with matchless force.

It is much to be regretted that the succeeding parts of *Pippa Passes* sink below this high level. The same general idea is however preserved throughout. At each movement of the drama the issue of a moral crisis is determined by the song of the girl passing without; and as it happens she is in each case in her girlish fancy personating the individual the course of whose life she thus turns. By way too of illustrating the irony of life, Browning has made her fix for personation, as "Asolo's four happiest ones," upon just the four who are either most deeply stained with crime, or in the shadow of crime projected, or on the rack of a great trouble. The repetition of the device, and the externality of the relation between Pippa and the other characters, stamp the work as a phantasy, and deprive it of all right to compete, as a whole, with the great triumphs of art; though, as a detached passage, the one scene of Ottima and Sebald will bear comparison with any. For though these realms of pure fancy are quite within the demand of the poet, in his more kingly moods he will cross the border into his other province of imagination.

Two of Browning's works, in the years immediately following, were exactly adapted to his genius. These were the *Dramatic Lyrics* of 1842 and the *Dramatic Romances and Lyrics* of 1845. A few of the pieces included under these titles had been printed before, but the great majority of them were new. They are dramatic just in the sense and in the degree which the poet liked. As a rule one character speaks, and exhibits its relations to others in monologue, not dialogue; at most, as in the fine poem, *In a Gondola*, there are two interlocutors; and there the lyric form helps to remove it from the ordinary dramatic category. Another respect in which the general design is a happy one for Browning is that it leaves him free to choose just what incident he pleases. He does not take up the *dramatis persona* a moment before the point in which his interest centres, nor does he follow its development after his interest wanes. The popularity which these collections have enjoyed, for they, with perhaps *Men and Women*, have been more widely read than any other of Browning's works, is one proof of the felicity of the design. But he was not yet himself convinced that it was the best for him. It should be noticed that during those years only his short poems took this form; in his more sustained works he preferred the regular drama. If we set aside *Pippa Passes*, *Bells and Pomegranates* began with two dramas, and the series likewise ended with two. Browning may have been influenced in this preference not entirely by the consideration of what was the best means of expression for his poetic talent. Mrs. Sutherland Orr evidently believes that he was moved by a natural and legitimate, and in his circumstances laudable, desire for the solid rewards which a successful drama, more than any other form of poetry, would bring. But he did not reap those rewards, and the world lost through this diversion of his mind. The short poems of those years are more valuable than the longer and more ambitious ones. In the latter there is always some blot, a defect or an excrescence, or some unevenness in the execution which mars the effect of the whole. Among the former there are many which leave nothing to be desired, and no criticism to be offered except such as attempts to point out and explain their beauty.

Perhaps the most prominent characteristic of the *Dramatic*

Lyrics and *Dramatic Romances* is the suddenness and surprise with which they frequently strike the mind. They are often as rapid as the lightning-flash; and this quality, which clung to Browning always, helps to explain at once the charm he exercises over some, and the dislike felt for him by others. *Porphyria's Lover* has this startling suddenness. It is especially evident in the wonderful close, the murderer sitting with the murdered girl's head upon his shoulder. "The smiling rosy little head, so glad to have its utmost will":—

> And all night long we have not stirred,
> And yet God has not said a word!

Equally sudden is that marvellously rich and glowing "dramatic romance," *In a Gondola*. The lover, stabbed on the breast of her he loves, wastes not one word of regret upon his own fate, hardly even a word of scorn on the cowards who killed him. It is best for him to die beneath her eyes and upon her breast. His only care is that she should put aside the beautiful hair his blood will soil. "I have lived indeed and so—(yet one more kiss)—can die." To the same order belongs *Parting at Morning*, a mere fragment of four lines, but inexhaustibly rich; and a similar spirit is present in the second part of *Earth's Immortalities* and in portions of *The Flight of the Duchess*. There is much of the "inevitable" in the poetry of which these pieces form part.

Browning carried this abruptness and rapidity to excess. It is one source of the difficulty commonly felt in understanding him, and it frequently makes his style harsh; but it is not a mere trick. In the first place, it comes to him naturally, and therefore cannot be so stigmatised. And secondly, it is often the best means of securing the effect he wishes. In the instances quoted, it is the very suddenness of the turn that impresses the reader and rouses him to think and reveals to him the poet's meaning as no connectives or introductions could possibly do. It is therefore a natural feature of the situation, and as such is justified from the point of view of the artist. As a rule, smoothness and orderly articulation are merits; but in certain modes of conception abruptness and the very absence of such orderly articulation may be so too.

The excellence of the characters in these collections, where character can be said to be delineated, is generally recognised; and it is remarkable that in the great majority of cases where Browning has succeeded perfectly in the presentation of character, he has adopted what is in essence the same method. There are two vital points in that method. It deals with human beings singly, and it deals with them at some supreme moment in their moral history. Those who desire to illustrate Browning's mastery of character turn as a rule to *Men and Women* or to *The Ring and the Book;* both poems proceed upon this method. The scope of the latter is indeed considerably wider than that of the single figures of *Men and Women*; but the points raised are really few, and all are lit by the lurid light of the murder. Still more in *Dramatic Lyrics* and *Dramatic Romances* is the attention concentrated upon one illuminating instant. The character is fixed at the moment, as the movement of life is fixed by instantaneous photography. Thus, in *The Lost Mistress* and in *The Bishop Orders His Tomb at St. Praxed's Church*, it is a mere glimpse of a character that is given, but it is a glimpse that lays it bare to the innermost recess. The curtain is so skilfully lifted at just the right moment that everything seems to be revealed. Such is the case too in *My Last Duchess*, in *The Flight of the Duchess*, and in the *Soliloquy of the Spanish Cloister*. The first mentioned is a perfect picture, drawn by himself, of a man without heart. Doubtless it would be an exceptional character that would be so confidential to a stranger; but granting that (and the poet cannot move unless it be granted), all is irreproachable. The cold matter-of-fact tone of the speaker, the careless transitions as in an ordinary conversation, the off-hand reference to Neptune, "taming a sea-horse, thought a rarity," are all excellent. *The Flight of the Duchess* is more elaborate and more varied. The wild hot gipsy blood is widely different from that of the speaker in *My Last Duchess*, cooled in its transmission through nine hundred years of ancestry lifted above ordinary human contact; yet its mysterious sympathies, its impulses, and the acts in which they issue, are given almost equally well; and if in this respect the balance is on the whole in favour of *My Last Duchess*, it is restored by the rapidity, the rich glow, and the admirable similes of the other piece.

Wholly different from either again is the *Soliloquy of the Spanish Cloister*. Part of its value lies just in the contrast, for it helps to show the extraordinary range of Browning in the painting of character. He no doubt had preferences. By far the greater number of these sketches deal with some phase of love. Within this range itself there is sufficient room for variety. But in the *Soliloquy* Browning goes to its opposite, hate (which he declares elsewhere, but does not show here, to be "but a mask of love"). The monk who utters the soliloquy is a man of vigorous mind and fiery passions, fanned to flame by the asceticism, the quiet tastes, the vapid conversation, and the feeble intellect of Brother Lawrence. Not a little of Browning's own sympathy goes with the speaker of the soliloquy.

The difficulty generally felt in understanding Browning is associated, in the minds of most, probably, with the longer rather than with the shorter poems; and perhaps the superior popularity of *Dramatic Romances* and *Dramatic Lyrics* is partly due to the greater simplicity ensured, in some instances at least, by their shortness. The lyrical and semi-lyrical measures too have had some effect in holding in check the eccentricities of Browning's style. Yet even among those poems there are traces of what can only be regarded as wilful eccentricity. But for the best, and worst, example of this fault we have to look beyond the limits of the present period to *Holy-Cross Day*, first published in *Men and Women*. This piece sinks to offensive vulgarity. Browning clearly lacked on this side the power of self-criticism, and he had apparently no one who could and would tell him when he was going wrong, or no one with sufficient influence to persuade him. The fact is much to be regretted. Pieces of this kind, with enigmas like *Childe Roland to the Dark Tower came*, have helped to make Browning repellent to many, and have stood, perhaps more than anything else, in the way of his popularity. They are only one side of his work and not an important one, but still one which it is necessary to recognise. Such pieces, which after all are not numerous, might be ignored, though the tendency of readers is probably rather to insist upon them. But unfortunately the spirit they indicate is apt to insinuate itself into greater works, where the prevailing tone is very different. Thus, even in Browning's masterpiece, *The Ring and the Book*, the parts devoted to the two lawyers are much of this description. These parts are happily detachable, and so do less harm than they might have done. Still, the fact remains that the work as the poet conceived it included them. It needs a robust faith to believe that he judged well, or that what they add to the effect of the whole is not more than counterbalanced by the jar to the feelings in passing from Pompilia to Dominus Hyacinthus de Archangelis.

Browning, it has been well said, had a Gothic mind. Artistic order in construction and classical finish in execution were alike foreign to him. Like the Gothic architects, he poured out the farrago of his imagination on whatever work he had in hand; and as they admitted the grotesque freely into their cathedrals, so did he into his most serious poems. But there are points of difference. The grotesque in Gothic architecture is only one element in many, and its effect is softened by its surroundings. In the poems of Browning just referred to it stands out too prominent, or else it is not prominent enough. The alternative would seem to be either that it should stand alone, or, if introduced into a serious poem, that it should be quite subordinated. Thus Browning's own *Soliloquy of the Spanish Cloister* is a purely grotesque conception thoroughly well executed. But in the other cases the grotesque is not properly subordinated. There is in such cases a vital difference between architecture and literature. In architecture the eye takes in a great deal at a glance; and the effect of the fantastic ornamentation of the corbels and gargoyles is diminished and softened by the other parts of the building along with which they are seen. Language on the other hand produces its effect by successive impressions. The reader must indeed carry the whole in his mind, but at each point the sentence before him predominates over the rest. It follows from this that a grotesque element in literature takes a prominence it has not in architecture. It follows also that the use of the grotesque must in the former case be more carefully circumscribed. Browning seems sometimes to have forgotten this. He employs the grotesque with the utmost freedom; and unfortunately it does not always blend with the whole, but stands out distinct and incongruous.

It may be said, with some degree of truth, that Shakespeare in his mingling of comedy with tragedy has done the same thing. The question is one of manner and circumstance: what is good in one case need not necessarily be good in another. In Shakespeare's plays as they have been handed down to us, reasonable criticism must conclude that there are cases of such mingling for which no higher reason can be assigned than a desire to please the pit. This is true of the porter's speech in *Macbeth*, which the fine taste of Coleridge rejected as spurious. When the intermixture of comedy with tragedy has been critically approved it is because, as in the grave-digging scene in *Hamlet*, the comedy intensifies the tragedy, rather than disturbs the effect. Further, it should be noticed that the Elizabethan method, which in this respect is not Browning's method, almost necessitated the intermixture. The Elizabethan drama is a miniature picture of life, not of one phase or moment of life. Browning, on the contrary, habitually chooses some turning point or crisis. The very concentration of his method excludes the grotesque: except in very rare cases there can be no room for it. It is condemned, not for being *what* it is, but for being *where* it is.

At the close of the period under discussion Browning was only thirty-four; yet he had already produced a body of work greater than many poets have written in an average life. His range is at least as remarkable. The variety even of form in his poetry is considerable, and the variety of substance is still greater. The poet had wide knowledge and was catholic in his interest. The mere geographical distribution of his subjects is worthy of notice. *Strafford* and *A Blot in the 'Scutcheon* are English, *Paracelsus* and *Colombe's Birthday* are German, *The Return of the Druses* is Eastern in more than the sense merely of locality; for the key to the character of Djabal, and therefore to the whole, is the mingling of a European or Western training with an Eastern heart and disposition. Djabal is, as he himself says in the end, spoilt by the equipoise of these two elements: "As a Frank schemer or an Arab mystic I had been something". But the one destroys the other. The equipoise however is not perfect. Rightly or wrongly, Browning paints the child of the East as conquering, so far as he does so, by the arts of the West. The mysticism becomes quite consciously part of the Frank scheming. But, like oil and water, the two never really mingle. Mr. Rudyard Kipling has since sung,

> Oh, East is East and West is West, and never the twain shall meet
> Till Earth and Sky stand presently at God's great judgment seat;

and Browning in *The Return of the Druses* takes the same view. But it is to Italy that by far the largest share of his attention is given. *King Victor and King Charles*, *Luria*, and *A Soul's Tragedy* all have their scene laid in Italy. So have the earlier works, *Sordello* and *Pippa Passes;* and so have many of the *Dramatic Lyrics* and *Dramatic Romances*. Browning said that as Queen

Mary believed that the word "Calais" would be found written in her heart, so in his would be found "Italy"; and he proved the depth of his affection both by living in the country and by going to it again and again for his subjects. It has been thought that this partly explains his unpopularity in his own country; but we may doubt whether much if any of the unpopularity can be traced to that cause. Though Browning chose Italian subjects, the cast of his mind was not in the least Italian. Unfamiliarity with the history and the art amidst which he moves may have been felt at times as an obstacle to the full understanding of him, but rarely as the principal one. Very few of his poems are more generally liked than *Andrea del Sarto*, and it is at once Italian in scene and artistic in substance. The causes of the unpopularity are rather to be found in that perversity noticed above, and still more in the philosophic tone of his thought. These together left him in the year 1846, notwithstanding *Paracelsus* and the admirable dramatic monologues, a very weak competitor with Tennyson for fame.

CHAPTER IV.

THE SECOND PERIOD OF TENNYSON'S WORK.

THE middle of the century was an eventful period in its literary history. It was marked in the case of Tennyson by the advance to longer and more ambitious works than he had hitherto attempted; in the case of Browning by the final recognition of the limits to his dramatic genius and his consequent concentration on forms better suited to him; and most of all by the first appearance of Matthew Arnold in the field of poetry. It will be convenient in the first place to follow the course of the writings of the two elder poets.

The chronological list of Tennyson's principal poems, between the last of those already noticed and his new departure with *Queen Mary* in 1875, is as follows: *The Princess*, 1847; *In Memoriam*, 1850; *Maud*, 1855; *Enoch Arden*, 1864; and various parts of the *Idylls of the King* from 1859 onwards, the whole being still incomplete at the limit mentioned.

A glance at this list reveals two points of difference between it and Tennyson's earlier work. In the first place, we notice that it is a period of long poems; and in the second place, which is indeed only the other side of this fact, that the lyrical element is now in the background. Not that Tennyson by any means abandoned the writing of lyrics during this period. *Maud* is a lyrical poem, and the beautiful songs in *The Princess* prove that the writer never, either before or since, was a more perfect master of the lyric strain. But the proportion which the lyrics bear to the whole work of this period is very different from that which they bear to the work of the earlier years. It might seem that Tennyson, having already proved his capacity to write short pieces exquisitely, was devoting himself to the task of establishing a reputation for constructive power.

The view, if any one holds it, that no man can be a great poet who has not written a long poem, needs no refutation.

Horace and Burns have each built up an enduring reputation on poems all of which are short. It is however true that there are certain gifts the presence or absence of which can only be demonstrated in a long work. The happy snatch, the light lilt of song, or the brilliant sketch, is a thing different in its nature from the epic or the drama which moves in stately progress from book to book or from act to act. The powers which produce the one, when they are liberally bestowed, are generally accompanied by the powers which produce the other; but it need not be so always, and the history of literature presents us with cases in which it must remain doubtful whether the faculties were united or not. The Cavalier poets had a gift for light graceful pieces; but either the circumstances of the time, or the constitution of their minds, or both, confined them to short pieces. So too it is impossible to be certain that an epic from the pen of Burns would have had the vigour and fire of *Tam o' Shanter*, or that a drama by him would have been equal to the *Jolly Beggars*. A long poem therefore, if successful, adds to the reputation of a poet who has hitherto produced only short pieces, something which the most copious additions of similar short pieces could not give; and a special interest must always attach to a first effort of this kind. The interest will be all the greater when we observe how rarely in recent times long poems have been fully successful. Coleridge's deservedly great reputation rests exclusively on short pieces, for *Christabel* is a fragment. Wordsworth is valued principally for his odes, lyrics, sonnets, and shorter reflective poems. Shelley is most satisfactory as a lyrist. Keats in *Hyperion* gave promise of success almost as complete on the great as on the smaller scale, but he died too young to redeem the promise fully. Byron, it is true, wrote principally long works, but they are admired, by those who in the present day admire Byron at all, rather in parts than as wholes. *Childe Harold* has practically no construction, and *Don Juan* has just as little. Scott indeed wrote with easy and fluent energy in the romantic strain, but a comparison of his prose with his verse shows how his powers of construction were fettered in the metrical tales. Browning, who had already written a number of long poems, was in this respect as in many others an exception to the rule; but Tennyson himself seemed hitherto to have tacitly accepted the limitation. He had at any rate as yet published nothing of great length, though there is a hint in the introduction to the *Morte d'Arthur*, if it is to be taken seriously, that he had attempted an epic.

The Princess is the first poem of Tennyson's long enough to have tested seriously his powers of construction. But *The Princess* is described on the title-page as "a medley," and the description may be interpreted as a warning to the reader that he is not to expect such articulation of parts as he would otherwise look for. *The Princess* therefore for this purpose either falls, as it were, out of competition, and leaves the question of Tennyson's power of construction where it was; or it may be argued that the evasion of the difficulty is a kind of evidence of inability to surmount it. The horse which shies at a fence may be able to leap it, but he is at least doubtful of his own power to do so. The artist who omits to give unity to his work obviously does so because he cannot. The incapacity may proceed either from the character of his mind, or from the nature of the subject he has chosen, or from both causes combined. In Tennyson's case a consideration of the other works of the period will give countenance to the view that his powers of construction were not of a high order. There is perhaps among all his works only one clear triumph in this respect, the drama of *Becket*, unless we rank the drama of *Harold* as another. But it must be added that the subject of *The Princess* presented peculiar difficulties. There is a perspective to the poet as well as to the painter. If the latter wishes to paint a wide landscape, he must view it from a distance: his immediate surroundings he can take in only in fragments. So the poet finds in distance a relief to eye and brain. It is not indeed impossible for him to treat modern problems on the great scale, but it is difficult; and most poets have preferred to set such problems far off from them, to dress them up in the garb of an older life, and while preserving the essence to modify the form.

Now, *The Princess* illustrates, better perhaps than any other poem of the century, the peculiar difficulties which beset the path of the poet who chooses a purely modern subject and treats it in a purely modern spirit. Not that such choice and such treatment are wrong: on the contrary, much that is most admirable in all the three great Victorian poets is of this description. To take only one example from each, Browning's *Inn Album*, Tennyson's *Maud*, and Arnold's *Thyrsis* are all modern in subject and treatment. It is no doubt true of each of these poems, as it must always be true of all great poems, that the cardinal facts of human passion, the principal relations of men in society, and the principal problems of life which they present are common to all ages. But they are set in a modern setting, and their tone is indubitably modern. There is however a difference between them. With regard to two of the three, it is only upon reflection that we attach much importance to the question of when or where the scene is laid. Reflection does indeed show that the question is interesting, but we are not compelled to ask it. In *The Inn Album* the pulse of the magnificent heroine's life would have beat to the same measure in any age. She might have been an Antigone in the hands of Sophocles, as Antigone might have been a heroine of Browning's. Strip off the surface soil, the special form of deceit and trickery which wrecked her life, her husband's theology and the outward details of her dreary days and years, and we are down at the solid rock of human character. The same is true, though in a less degree, of *Maud*. Its passion is fundamentally the same as the passion which Sappho sang. Modern social distinctions, modern *bourgeois* wealth, and modern warfare are externals. In Arnold's poem, as is usual with him, the element of the time is more significant. In *Thyrsis* great part of his charm arises from the skill with which he throws the light of modern criticism upon modern forms of the great problems of life. We are always conscious, because the poet is always insisting, that it is of vital importance to comprehend the special difficulties and the special needs of the time. Thus in his case it is impossible to separate the jewel which is everlasting from the setting which belongs to his own age; and it is very difficult even to imagine them apart. Arnold would not be Arnold without that characteristic and most touching note which makes his voice emphatically the voice of his own generation.

The reason of the difference may become clearer if it be expressed in another way. In *The Inn Album* Browning's interest centres in character. It would be hardly fair to Tennyson to say that his interest centres in the somewhat contemptible hero of *Maud*: it centres rather in the greatest of all passions which go to make character. But in such matters time is of minor consequence. For the vital significance of these poems it makes little difference whether the scene be laid ten years or ten thousand years back. In the case of Arnold his position in time is essential. His poem deals neither with character as a whole nor with the great constituents of character, it is essentially reflective. Browning's object is to depict the spirit, but Arnold takes it for granted, for the spirit is his own. He is like some sailor pondering over a complex chart. It is all-important to him to thread his way through the tortuous channels, and it is this necessity which rivets his gaze to the chart. Above all, if he has reason to believe that any of the shoals are shifting, it is essential that he should make the proper allowance for the change. He must be on the watch for any indication of difference since the chart was made. Browning is rather the spectator of this struggle. To him the shoals marked on the map and the changes which may have occurred since are only of indirect importance. If the ship strikes, then the particular danger which destroys her stands out at once from the rest; but until then the interest is in the thoughts and calculations of the sailor. His mind is first, the external facts are important only in so far as they affect his mind.

The Princess is different from all those three works. In the fact that it is in essence a poem of the time, it comes nearer to Arnold's method than to that of Browning or even of Tennyson himself. But it does so only in this fact. It is widely different in spirit from anything of Arnold's; and we may doubt whether it has the undying value of some of Arnold's poetry. In the first place, the *kind* of problem is different from any that Arnold ever handled. It belongs to the order of the problems of current politics, while those which interested Arnold were more purely spiritual, or were larger and more enduring. The division, though by no means absolute, is practically useful. Whatever affects the permanent position of women must clearly go to the very heart of human life. But what is called " the woman question " was when Tennyson wrote, as it still is, in the stage of political controversy. The poet may be within his right in meddling with such subjects; but he must prove his right, and it is hard to see how he can do so except by translating the controversy into another tongue. The world would certainly not be enriched by political discussion served up in verse. It is necessary then to ask whether Tennyson in *The Princess* has been successful in lifting his " woman question " into the purer atmosphere of poetry.

Almost from the beginning the reader feels that the accent of *The Princess* is somehow wrong. The author had the choice of treating his subject either seriously or sportively. To do the latter, to any one possessing the necessary gifts, would have been easy; but the result would hardly have been a great poem. To do the former with effect it was necessary that the poet should see more clearly than his contemporaries, that he should have some light to throw upon the subject, and above all that the light should be poetical rather than political. Tennyson hesitated between the two alternatives, apparently because he lacked the power to treat the subject successfully in either way. On the one hand, as has been already remarked, his gift of humour was limited. Neither when he speaks in his own name, nor in the character of a member of his own class, is he successful. It may be doubted whether a purely humorous treatment of *The Princess* would have been truly successful, even if his gifts had been greater. If we may judge from the witticisms to which it has given rise, it is difficult, on "the woman question," to avoid some taint of vulgarity, and almost impossible to escape the commonplace. Hence perhaps the thinness of the lighter thread in *The Princess*. Unfortunately, that thread is woven in with it and mars the whole. To change the metaphor, the atmosphere of the picnic hangs permanently about the poem.

On the other hand, and this is still more important, the poet has really little or nothing new to say. Many had doubtless thought similar thoughts before, as far more have, independently, thought similar thoughts since. That there is some reason for the complaints, something amiss in the relations between men and women, and especially something wrong with the education of the latter, nearly all are agreed now. The fact that the subject lay ready made to Tennyson's hand is proof sufficient that not a few felt so before 1847; otherwise it would have been absurd to introduce it as a subject for discussion at the festival of a Mechanics' Institution. Again, that the something right is more vital than the something wrong, that motherhood is a greater education than school or college can give, and that one touch of nature is sufficient to bring down a cloud-built system, are important facts. But they are not very recondite: it needed no Tennyson to arise and tell us this. Yet this is in substance all that he does tell us. An impulsive and inexperienced girl, whose head is full of impossible though not ignoble ideas, and an amorous prince, are the raw material out of which *The Princess* is constructed. She has on her side unlimited means and plenty of followers to help her in setting up her woman's Utopia. On his side he has nature. The result cannot be for a moment doubtful; but when it comes it does not seem to bring us any nearer a conclusion on the question of the position of women. Even the fine poetry of the close helps little.

> The woman's cause is man's: they rise or sink
> Together, dwarf'd or godlike, bond or free:
> For she that out of Lethe scales with man
> The shining steps of Nature, shares with man
> His nights, his days, moves with him to one goal,
> Stays all the fair young planet in her hands—
> If she be small, slight-natured, miserable,
> How shall men grow?[1]

All this is true, and it is worthily said; but it is what might be said by both sides.

There is much beautiful verse in *The Princess*: the pity is that it should not rather be somewhere else; for as a whole the poem is written for the time and will perish with the time. The fact that it is Tennyson's will doubtless give it in some sense life as long as his other poems live; but the interest in it will soon be purely a reflected one. If indeed the exquisite songs interposed between the parts were indissolubly connected with it, this judgment would require to be modified; but they are easily detachable; and in fact *The Princess* was originally published without them. Their value therefore is not really an addition to the value of *The Princess*: they stand upon their own merits, for they are independent poems.

Tennyson's next work in order of time, *In Memoriam*, is incomparably richer than *The Princess*. In writing the latter he was only half in earnest, and half playing with a subject which moved him to a kind of scornful interest. But *In Memoriam* stirred his deepest feelings. Seventeen years had passed since the death of the friend to whose memory it is the most beautiful and the most lasting monument. Whether or not Tennyson had complied with the letter of the advice of Horace as to keeping the poem by him, he had more than complied with its spirit, for doubtless his mind had been during all that time brooding over

---

[1] *The Princess*, p. 134. The references in the case of Tennyson are to Macmillan's nine-volume edition.

the subject. Hence, we may presume, the profuse wealth of the poem in thought and imagery, and its wonderful polish and harmony of verse and style. Perhaps, on the other hand, we may set down to the same long brooding that over-elaboration and that oppressive breath of the tomb which many have felt in it. The effect upon Tennyson of this concentration of mind on a solemn subject was in the main most salutary. It made permanent in his verse that weight and seriousness in which, as we have seen, his early poems were somewhat deficient. Yet the good was not altogether unmixed. The length of *In Memoriam* is excessive, and it is not wholly free from a morbid strain. It has probably not been given to humanity to dwell so long on thoughts of death and preserve altogether the colour of health. Even Tennyson, whose disinterested love of beauty would have protected him, if anything could, has suffered in this way.

In Memoriam is of all the great English elegies the one which is most closely associated with the immediate subject. The connexion of Milton with Edward King and of Shelley with Keats was notoriously slight; and even *Thyrsis* shows far less absorption of friend in friend than *In Memoriam*. Of the four poems, the *Adonais*, in spite of its fire and enthusiasm, and the rich beauty of many passages, is probably that which has least permanent poetic value. *Lycidas* has all the fascination of Milton's wonderful style, with its grace not yet marred by twenty years of envenomed controversy and by a superabundance of Puritan theology. *Adonais* is less an elegy on an individual than an indignant protest against the injustice of the world, for which the death of Keats affords little more than the occasion. In *Lycidas* too the shepherd's pipe becomes a trumpet, and its blast sounds like a battle-call to the great forces of the time. Neither of the two later elegies lays such stress on social questions or shows such hope in social change as do the poems of Milton and Shelley. Doubtless the difference is partly due to the deeper personal feeling with which they are touched; but partly also it seems to show the influence of a time more weary and less hopeful. *In Memoriam* is a hopeful poem, but the hope is rather in the ultimate destiny of humanity beyond this life, than in any change which is to reform it; and in *Thyrsis* the hope is equally distant and much vaguer.

In Memoriam is far more than merely an elegy on an individual. The subject broadens out into the treatment of death and the unknown after. The poem traces with unwearying minuteness and close fidelity the various phases of emotion in the bereaved person from the moment when speech first becomes possible to sorrow, when he still holds it

> Half a sin
> To put in words the grief I feel,

to the softened close, when the clang of marriage bells makes no dissonance with the tone of the piece, when, he says,

> Regret is dead, but love is more
> Than in the summers that are flown,
> For I myself with these have grown
> To something greater than before.

But in this process the very softening of the personal feeling widens it. The sense of sympathy grows. The cause of the sorrow is the common lot of humanity; and if any cure is possible it too must be common. Thus the poet is led to ask what is the ultimate meaning of life and death; and the most widely known passages of *In Memoriam* are those which contain his answer to the question, or rather which without definite answer affirm his faith. Thus considerable if not quite sufficient relief is given to what must otherwise have been, in a poem of such length, a most unwholesome iteration of a gloomy train of thought.

Notwithstanding this, *In Memoriam* moves constantly within the circle of one brooding mind and its experience. It is among the most introspective of poems: there is in it no objective order of events at all. This is the secret why so many have found in it a certain heaviness, why it pleases best taken in bits, and why it is a relief to turn to some work, perhaps inferior, over which there breathes a fresher and stronger breath of life. In *In Memoriam* Tennyson is too much alone. Action is at a stand, "the pleasant human voices" are silent. It seems to be artistically a mistake to treat such a subject at so great length. *In Memoriam* is at once by far the longest of the great elegies, and the one which, from its more limited appeal to the sympathies of ordinary life, can least bear great length.

In this respect *Thyrsis* is widely different. It is not only shorter than *In Memoriam*, but even within its narrower compass it dwells far less on death, and appeals far more to common sympathies and a common life in the past. These in Tennyson are slightly touched upon, and appear chiefly in an indirect way as the cause of the passionate regret for the lost friend. But half of Arnold's poem is filled with the scenes around Oxford, and with recollections of the old life there which he and Clough had shared. He treads again their old haunts, turns to dwell upon the beauty of "that sweet city with her dreaming spires," recalls how trouble had entered into his own life, and so is led to reflect how Thyrsis had wandered away. In all this he merely alludes to his friend's death. When he is brought to the point he lightens the touch by classical references to Pluto and Proserpine and Orpheus, and escapes from it again to dwell upon "the wood which hides the daffodil," "the Fyfield tree," and the "sedged brooks" which "are Thames's tributaries". And so throughout the poem he refuses to linger over his dead friend. It is the past life which fills his mind, or the pathos of the thought that his own day is passing.

> Yes, thou art gone! and round me too the night
>   In ever-nearing circle weaves her shade.
>   I see her veil draw soft across the day,
>   I feel her slowly chilling breath invade
>   The cheek grown thin, the brown hair sprent with grey;
>   I feel her finger light
>   Laid pausefully upon life's headlong train;—
>   The foot less prompt to meet the morning dew,
>   The heart less bounding at emotion new,
>   And hope, once crush'd, less quick to spring again.

It seems safe to ascribe the difference in this respect between the two poems to two causes. In the first place, though *Thyrsis* is truly a poem written by a friend in memory of his friend, it does not appear that the friendship was of that absorbing kind which bound Tennyson to Hallam. If it had been, the tone of calm and measured regret in *Thyrsis* would have given place to that of passionate sorrow. Of the two, *In Memoriam* is unquestionably the poem which will most appeal to the man who has suffered a great loss. But in the second place, the creed of the two poets had much to do with the difference. Tennyson dwelt on death because he could point to a definite hope after it. Arnold on the contrary declined to dwell upon it, because his faith afforded him no such hope. To him therefore the subject would have been too gloomy, and he rightly laid his stress by preference on the life before. Here too there is to him a necessary loss of richness. There is at the same time something of gain. Partly by the comparative shortness of his poem, and partly by his concentration upon life rather than death, he entirely avoids that oppressiveness which characterises *In Memoriam*.

Maud, the next poem, was a new departure for Tennyson in plan and construction. It is described on the title-page as "a monodrama," and if the adjective "lyrical" be added, the description is complete. We may notice here an approach, though a distant one, to the dramatic form, and some evidence of interest in character. The interest is only slight. The hero of *Maud* counts for little; the lyrics may almost be described as the voice of so many disembodied passions; and the reader is sometimes tempted to wish that they did not profess to be anything else. The weakest point in the poem is the character which gives it such unity as it possesses.

Among all Tennyson's great gifts there was none greater than his exquisite lyric feeling and his mastery of lyric verse; and these we see at their best in *Maud*. In the gradual development of his genius he had now reached, in these respects, its perfect balance. The great quality of passion is more prominent in *Maud* than in any of the earlier poems. We are no longer tempted to think of the writer critically regarding his own work from a distance, adding a touch here and toning down an expression there, until the impression left is that of a painting on ivory, something altogether too smooth and delicate for real life. Not that Tennyson in *Maud* is a whit less careful as an artist than he had been twenty years before; but the superior energy of his thought gives to all this care and minute attention a totally different effect. The lyrics in *Maud* belong to the class of poems which seem to have "written themselves," and yet it would be difficult to find any more beautifully finished. This note of passion is the result partly of Tennyson's internal development, partly of the superior earnestness of the time. It is true, the lines from which *Maud* sprung, those beginning "O that 'twere possible," were published as far back as 1836; and there are none with a deeper tone of feeling in the whole poem. But we have already seen that Tennyson always had the power, on occasion, to touch this chord. In *Maud* it sounds not intermittently, but continuously.

In *Enoch Arden* there was no such change as in *Maud* from the poet's customary style and his favourite themes. It is a poem of homely English rural life, a longer and more ambitious *Dora*. The verse is beautiful, many of the descriptions are excellent, and it is full of sympathy with the life portrayed. But there is a want of clearness in the outline of the characters, the sentiment is not altogether healthy, and on the whole it gives little impression of power. The nature of the story has secured for it a degree of favour out of proportion to its real merits.

The *Idylls of the King* present many points of difficulty to the critic. What is their date? Where are they to be put in relation to the author's other works? How come they to be one work at all? They *are* one, perhaps the greatest that Tennyson has written; but surely no poem that claims to be a whole was ever so strangely given forth. The *Idylls* practically begin with *Morte d'Arthur* in 1842, and stretch on for over forty years after that, to the publication of *Balin and Balan* in 1885. Nor is any order preserved in the composition: beginning, end and middle are bewilderingly mingled in the sequence of production. The bulk however of this series of poems—which is also one great though loosely compacted poem—is the work of the twelve years onward from 1859, when four of the Idylls, *Geraint and Enid*, *Merlin and Vivien*, *Lancelot and Elaine*, and *Guinevere* were published. Moreover, it was during those years that the plan of the poem as a whole took shape. It will therefore be most convenient to treat them in connexion with the work of that time.

For variety, for harmony of verse, for a style at once subtle, graceful and strong, the *Idylls* take a high rank. They form one of the greatest additions to English poetry in a century of great additions. The original *Morte d'Arthur* is modestly alluded to as "faint Homeric echoes, nothing worth". But though there are plenty of imitations of Homer, conscious and perhaps unconscious too, and more in *The Passing of Arthur* than elsewhere, this is just what the *Idylls* are not. Neither are they reproductions of the fabled age of Arthur. He must have but a feeble comprehension of Tennyson who does not perceive that almost always and almost everywhere, after his first period, he has at heart some present human need. "Art for art's sake," if it means art divorced from such needs, or from all except the need of beauty, was no creed of his. As artist he would fail in his duty if he did not satisfy the craving for beauty; but in all his greater works he attempts to satisfy something else as well. The *Idylls* therefore do not merely represent the long-past struggles and ultimate failure of a visionary king. So long as the world produces men of high hopes and lofty conceptions who go out to battle with evil; who, if they are unable to impart to others their own purity of spirit, impart at least the desire for that purity; and who sink at last baffled, perhaps in appearance crushed and utterly defeated,—so long will the drama of the Round Table continue to be re-enacted. The *Idylls* have been severely censured for this modern air. If it is a flaw the poet sins deliberately. Under the image of the Round Table, its greatness, gradual degradation and final destruction, he means to represent at once the extent and the limitation of the influence of one conspicuously pure and noble spirit. He is profoundly conscious of the impossibility of embracing in one conception, however magnificent, all that human progress requires. Earthlier minds aspire to, but cannot attain, the height of Arthur's ideal, and by their failure they throw discredit upon the ideal itself. Evil enters, and, as is the nature of all things low in the scale of being, it proves to be more easily and more rapidly propagated than good. There is nothing sadder, yet there are few things more masterly, than the way in which the growth of the principle of evil is represented in *The Last Tournament*. Low desires, cynicism, mean thoughts and criminal passions are almost universal, and scarcely deign to pay to virtue the homage of wearing a disguise. Arthur on his return is greeted only by the fool.

Nevertheless, neither here nor elsewhere is Tennyson pessimistic. Arthur's attempt does not after all end in failure. Much has been accomplished, though not all that was aimed at, and Arthur's eclipse is only temporary.

> He passes to be King among the dead,
> And after healing of his grievous wound
> He comes again (*Idylls : The Passing of Arthur*, p. 417).

It is a necessary law that "the old order changeth, yielding place to new". Further, in the best human conception there lurks a germ of evil, so that it must become self-destructive, else it becomes destructive of everything.

> God fulfils himself in many ways
> Lest one *good* custom should corrupt the world.

It is significant that it is not evil alone that overthrows the Round Table. The quest for the Holy Grail itself plays a part, and

Arthur recognises the vision of the Grail as "a sign to maim this order which I made". It *was* such a sign, partly because of the many knights who entered upon the quest unworthily, but partly also because the quest itself indicated the existence of ideals not recognised in the constitution of the Round Table. Those who saw the Grail, as well as many who did not, were lost to the order. No single "custom," however good, suffices for all. Moreover, though the quest of the Grail is the pursuit of abstract spiritual purity, we are reminded in the course of it that even so high an end is not to be sought by every means. Duty may prevent the quest. The ideal of the Round Table was to live in the world and reform it, to be always ready on demand "to ride abroad redressing human wrongs"; but this could not be fulfilled by men intent only on their own salvation. The "blameless king" himself does not join the quest, and to those who thought that if he "had seen the sight he would have sworn the vow," he answers,

> Not easily, seeing that the King must guard
> That which he rules, and is but as the hind
> To whom a space of land is given to plow
>   (*Idylls: The Holy Grail*, p. 314).

Nowhere is the fine style of Tennyson seen to greater advantage than in the *Idylls*. Matured experience gives it a weight we miss in the early poems, and in the verse there is an almost perfect balance of strength and grace which is only once or twice rivalled in the poet's former writings. The judgment of Coleridge, qualified even then with words of praise, that Tennyson had begun "to write verses without very well understanding what metre is," would never have been pronounced with regard to the productions of his maturity. The growth of experience shows itself particularly in some of the fragments of portraiture. The characters of the *Idylls* are by general consent ranked among the weakest parts of the work; yet occasionally a figure is touched to perfection.

> Modred's narrow foxy face,
> Heart-hiding smile, and gray persistent eye
>   (*Idylls: Guinevere*, p. 873),

is a description not easily surpassed; and the picture of Lancelot, in which Tennyson seems to have had in mind Milton's "archangel ruined," is only less excellent:—

> The great and guilty love he bare the Queen,
> In battle with the love he bare his lord,
> Had marr'd his face, and mark'd it ere his time.
> Another sinning on such heights with one,
> The flower of all the west and all the world,
> Had been the sleeker for it: but in him
> His mood was often like a fiend, and rose
> And drove him into wastes and solitudes
> For agony, who was yet a living soul
> *(Idylls: Lancelot and Elaine*, pp. 230-231).

It is impossible to speak of the *Idylls of the King* without some reference to the question of its general character. Is the poem to be read as an allegory?[1] In face of Tennyson's declaration that it shadows "Sense at war with Soul," it is impossible to deny to it in some degree an allegorical character. But much depends upon the degree; and on the other hand it may be asked what unsophisticated reader ever, for himself, found the allegory to be the principal thing in it. The truth seems to be that the allegory was an afterthought, that it is a reality in some of the later parts in order of publication, like *The Coming of Arthur*, but that in the case of the earlier *Idylls* it has to be read in. We may suspect that Tennyson having begun to treat in a fragmentary way a story essentially fragmentary, found as he went on the need of some unifying principle, and invented the allegory. At any rate it remains throughout of subordinate importance, and in some of the *Idylls* the thread of it is almost invisible. It would be well for Tennyson's reputation if the theory of the allegory could be either quite forgotten, or reduced to the smallest dimensions. To treat it as the principal motive of the work is to court disastrous comparison with *The Pilgrim's Progress*, to say nothing of lesser allegories, which must still be ranked as superior to Tennyson's. Bunyan's work has the advantage over Tennyson's in every way in which an allegory can be judged. The allegorical meaning is clearer and better sustained; and at the same time the figures in which it is embodied are more real.

Though the period under review was a period of long poems, it may be doubted whether the question, already touched upon, of Tennyson's power of construction was fully settled in the

---

[1] This question has been admirably treated by Mr. Stopford Brooke, with whom I am in general agreement, and to whom I wish to acknowledge my indebtedness.

course of it. In all the poems there is either some peculiarity of subject or treatment which leaves doubt still possible as to the extent of his endowment, or there is some lack of the necessary weight. The latter is the case with *Enoch Arden*. It is a sufficiently coherent narrative; but in the first place its scope is rather that of a single one of the *Idylls* than of a great and complex poem; and secondly its reputation has been due, like that of *The May Queen*, to a strain of sentimentality not in the highest style of art. As to the *Idylls* again, while it is true that they form a unity, it is likewise true that it is rather that sort of unity which we see in a series of companion pictures, than the closer unity of one great work of art. Or we may compare it more nearly to the unity of a Greek trilogy. Different parts or phases of one great story, too large or too disjointed for treatment in a single work, are taken up successively and treated in a series of works distinct yet related. But there are gaps to be supplied by the imagination or from the common legend from which all are taken. So in the *Idylls of the King*, the several idylls are related to and throw light upon one another. In the course of the series we pass from the foundation of the Round Table through a stage when all is enthusiasm and hope, to other stages when the whispers of evil grow louder and louder, and when even the pursuit of another form of good threatens dissolution, and thence to the final ruin. But there are large gaps between the parts. The very order of publication of the several idylls betrays the character of their connexion. The author of a great poem which is vitally one does not publish the conclusion first and go on to work indifferently at the beginning or at any of the intermediate parts. It was not so that *Paradise Lost* or the *Æneid* was written; and even those who hold that the *Iliad* was produced much in this way would add that at some time or other it was edited and made one in the editing. But Tennyson did not edit his idylls in this fashion. He gathered them together and gave them a place in a collection into which they fitted, partly because he had made them so, but partly also because his predecessors in the treatment of the Arthurian story had given them a place in it. But he did not attack, and therefore could not overcome, the difficulty of welding the parts together. One idyll does not spring out of another in the way in which one book of a regular epic springs out of its predecessors. *Gareth and Lynette* does not lead up to *The Marriage of*

Geraint as the first book of *Paradise Lost*, which describes the gathering of the fallen angels to the infernal council, leads to the second, which recounts their deliberations. In some respects then the unit in the *Idylls of the King* remains the single idyll; and while these idylls are poems of considerable length, they are necessarily of far less complexity than a single poem equal in bulk to the whole of them united.

For different reasons *In Memoriam* and *Maud* similarly fail to settle the question of Tennyson's capacity for construction. The former is the most rounded whole among the poems of the period; but there is in it no objective order of events for the poet to follow. It is the musings of the mind on death and the problems suggested by it. The order is not arbitrary; doubtless it is as fixed and necessary as the order of events in time and space. We can see at any rate an irreversible progress from the state of a mind crushed for the time by the stroke of a great sorrow, to a state when regret is dead. But all the same it is at least difficult to demonstrate this order; and to a certain extent every mind is in such matters a law unto itself. If we ask why a particular section of the poem is here rather than there, the final answer is that such were its connexions in the poet's mind. It is true that every sane mind moves in the same general direction, but it is equally true that the threads of association are infinite in number, and that it is impossible to say in what order they may be taken up. Further, there is not in *In Memoriam* a variety of elements to be reduced to harmony and to be set in the proper relation to one another. The whole movement is not only within the sphere of mind, but of a single mind, and the difficulties which arise in bringing one character, or the events of one life, into connexion with others do not emerge.

In the latter respect *Maud* is similar. Here the poet does indeed look out into the world; but the part which events play is still very slight, and the influence which the actions and feelings of others exercise upon the hero is learnt at second hand. Everything takes the colour of his mind before it reaches the mind of the reader. Because it is a monodrama *Maud* escapes the necessity of portraying the interaction of life upon life, or at least simplifies the problem by keeping the point of view always the same; and because it is lyrical the poet is not only justified in giving, but compelled to give it, the aspect of a succession of emotions. Hence the feeling of discontinuity in passing from one part and even from one section to another. The reason of the change is revealed, but we do not see it taking place. The movement is like crossing a stream on stepping-stones, we leap from part to part as we spring from one stone to another. There is not the orderly development in the mind of the hero that there is of the seeds of evil in the mind of Othello. I repeat that Tennyson's plan did not require this, and it is therefore no reproach to him that we do not find it. We have only to recognise that he had not hitherto given indubitable proof of the possession of that power of construction which is usually involved in the composition of a long poem.

But while it may be granted that none of the poems is a triumph of construction, it is also true that they tested the poet's faculty for construction far more than any of his earlier pieces. Except in *The Princess* and possibly in the *Idylls of the King*, it may be added that so far as the demand was made it was met. In other respects too there is evidence of a continuance of that growth which was so conspicuous between 1833 and 1842. There can be no doubt as to the weight of thought in the poems of the second period. *In Memoriam* is thoughtful in its very essence. The artistic conditions are never forgotten, but neither is the philosophy of life far in the background. Without pressing the allegorical theory, the same may be said of the *Idylls of the King*. It is the work of a serious artist, of one who has more to do than simply to feed " on the roses " and lie " in the lilies of life," of one who has something to teach that is " worth the knowing ". It is equally true of *Maud*. The intense passion of that poem is at the opposite pole from dilettantism, and it serves to bring into prominence the poet's vivid interest in the actual course of events.

The lines inspired by the war which was raging when *Maud* was published have sometimes been the subject of blame. They take their place along with other utterances of the poet, both earlier and later, which have earned for him the reproach of Jingoism. And it must be admitted that some grander occasion than the Crimean War might be found to prove " we have hearts in a cause, we are noble still ". But variety of opinion on contemporary events is eminently pardonable; and it will be time to press the blame when universal peace, " the parliament of man and federation of the world," comes a little nearer realisation, and when peaceful industry seems a little more dissociated from the "cheating yard-wand". Meanwhile, it appears to be a virtue rather than a fault to have sympathised so deeply with one of the most strenuous phases of life. Probably opinion will always be divided as to the mental detachment of Goethe from the political events of his time. Some will see in it the elevation of a great spirit above the dust and turmoil of the petty lives of ordinary men; others will think that the best it is possible to say for him is that it indicated a nature on one side incomplete, because the true birth of German nationality had yet to come. It is significant that Scott, one of the most manly men of that generation, as well as Tennyson, one of the most manly men of his, felt very differently. Count Tolstoi has recently denounced patriotism in no measured terms, maintaining that to the peasant it matters far more what is the quality of the land he tills than what is the government under which he lives. Certainly, if man lives by bread alone; not so certainly if there are elements in his nature to which bread is no more food than a stone would be. All the races that have left their mark on the world have been patriotic races; all of them too have been fighting races. Until we see indications of a change in the nature of men, we may continue to respect him who respects these great human passions.

Another aspect of Tennyson's development during this period is seen in his growing interest in character. This may be looked upon as a step in the direction of the drama. But his presentation of character is still as a rule far from being dramatic, and few would at this time have anticipated that he would ever attempt the dramatic form of art. It is in separate pieces, like *The Grandmother* and *The Northern Farmer*, that he makes his nearest approach to its spirit; the dramatic element in the longer poems is always slight. Still, to portray character at all was a noticeable step on the part of a poet who had previously kept so far aloof from it. Were it not for one or two exceptions, the reader of the early poems would be inclined to say that Tennyson had no interest in character. Even where his pieces were associated with some historical or mythical name, his interest lay in a situation, a mood, or a moral problem, rather than in the figure of a man. This is partly true even of his Ulysses, who is pictured, not, like Homer's, acting and suffering, but moralising on the need to do so. Tennyson's inspiration in that poem came from the necessity he felt in himself of stoical endurance and of continuing in the face of all difficulties to discharge the ordinary duties of life. He did not realise the character objectively. Neither did he in *Tithonus*. The myth presented him with a problem, What is the use to man of eternal life without eternal youth? If we insist upon viewing it as a representation of character, we are forced to pronounce it radically false and inconsistent. Tithonus is endowed with feelings and desires which, under the hypothesis, ought to have long ago died out. To advance this as an objection to the poem would be the falsest of false criticism; but it shows how far the piece is removed from character-painting. Under the circumstances imagined Tithonus must have been reduced to the condition of the Struldbrugs. In all Tennyson's early poetry there is hardly a clear-cut and distinct figure of a man, or of a woman either. There are plenty of clever and dainty pictures in words; there are some, as in *A Dream of Fair Women*, of bolder outline and of greater power; and there is even a sketch or two, as in *The Miller's Daughter*, suggestive of dramatic talent; but there is no finished character. Even in pieces where, as in some of the *English Idylls*, we make approaches to character-drawing, it is remarkable how it is the verse, the story, the pictures of nature, anything rather than the character, that impresses us.

But after the turn of the century there is a marked change. Except *The Northern Farmer*, there is still indeed no figure which seems to live, no one we seem to know. It is wonderful, considering the nature of the subject, how slight is the interest roused in the personages of the *Idylls of the King*. Still, when full allowance is made for the bloodlessness of most of the figures and the limitations of all as pictures of character, it remains true that there is more human nature in Lancelot and Tristram and Sir Bors, in Enid and Elaine and Guinevere, than in any of the figures of the earlier period. It may be noticed that the sinners, and among the male characters they almost alone, to some extent excite this personal interest. It would seem to be almost a law of nature that the "unco guid" are uninteresting; perhaps it is a dispensation of Providence, which never heaps all its favours on one head. The blameless king himself, Galahad, and all the supernaturally stainless, are felt to be mere abstractions. Arthur is most interesting when, if not himself sinning, he is brought into contact with sin. The culminating point in his character and in the *Idylls*, if it be too much to say even in Tennyson's poetry, is in that great scene where he last meets and last parts from the fallen and repentant queen. Here if anywhere is the justification of her final judgment on him, that he is " the highest and most human too ". But to the very end his humanity is hidden from the reader as it had been from the queen.

CHAPTER V.

BROWNING'S INTERMEDIATE PERIOD, 1850-1869.

WE have seen that up to 1846 Browning was principally engaged on a series of dramas. There was no indication at that date that he had done with regular dramatic composition, but such was the case: he never afterwards wrote an original drama. *In a Balcony* is no exception, for it is only a single phase of a drama. Experience had shown that Browning's work was not likely to find its way to the stage; and if he could not have the advantage of representation he was not the man to fetter himself with restrictions only necessary with a view to secure it. Consequently, for the future to a greater degree than in the past, he devoted himself to poetry "dramatic in principle," but either monologue or cognate to monologue.

Between the earlier and the intermediate work however there stand a pair of companion pieces in some important respects different from all his previous works. These are *Christmas Eve* and *Easter Day*. Their first peculiarity is that they appear to drop, at least in great measure, that dramatic disguise which in most of his other works more or less conceals the poet. There is only one speaker in *Christmas Eve*, and it seems impossible to resist the conclusion that in large measure if not wholly he represents the poet himself. In *Easter Day*, where there are two interlocutors, it would be a mistake to identify Browning with either. He seems rather to let his opinions shine through both.

A second peculiarity is that these poems deal with religious questions more directly and specifically than any that Browning had as yet written. The question what really are the views they present will be subsequently discussed. It is within the scope of the present chapter to remark that what distinguishes them, both in form and substance, may be ascribed to two facts, one in the life of Browning himself, the other in the history of the country. Browning married in 1846; and in these two poems, if anywhere, we may trace the influence of his wife. He was himself sufficiently inclined to dwell upon such subjects, and the inclination was growing. But the spirit in which he approaches the question of religion here, and the bias, if it may be so expressed without invidiousness, in favour of orthodoxy, point to the woman's influence. It is instructive to compare these poems with *La Saisiaz*, written in a more boldly speculative spirit after that influence had been changed and rendered less immediate by death. In the comparison large allowance must be made for the change through the mere operation of time; but after it has been made there seems to remain something which justifies the conclusion just suggested.

But further, the years before the publication of *Christmas Eve and Easter Day* were years during which religious questions were discussed with unusual eagerness; and it is impossible to doubt that Browning was influenced by the movement going on around him. He was clearly impelled, by forces distant as well as near, to regard his favourite objects of thought in a new light. His references, in the poems in question, to the new ritualistic tendencies are the least part of the proof of this. Their whole spirit leads to the same conclusion; and it is worthy of notice that the three principal parts of *Christmas Eve* are connected with the three leading phases of religious controversy at the time,—evangelical nonconformity, Roman Catholicism (Browning does not think it worth while to stop short at the "surplice question," he makes the leap with Newman), and German criticism.

But it would be a mistake to regard these poems as theological arguments. They are lifted above that level in two ways, first by their beauty, and secondly by the spiritual fervour which inspires them. *Christmas Eve* especially for varied charm ranks high among its author's works. The opening sections, with their description of the gathering of the dissenting congregation, are rich with bold racy humour. The student is tempted to explain the vigour and truth of the picture by reference to Browning's dissenting up-bringing; but confidence in any such explanation is diminished when we observe that he is equally happy in depicting the German professor's lecture-room. In the first scene the speaker has been driven by the rain into the little chapel, and standing in "the sheepfold's lath-and-plaster entry," sees the congregation file past him :—

> Well, from the road, the lanes or the common,
> In came the flock: the fat weary woman,
> Panting and bewildered, down-clapping
>   Her umbrella with a mighty report,
> Grounded it by me, wry and flapping,
>   A wreck of whalebones; then, with a snort,
> Like a startled horse, at the interloper
> (Who humbly knew himself improper,
> But could not shrink up small enough)
> —Round to the door, and in,—the gruff
> Hinges invariably scold
> Making my very blood run cold.
> Prompt in the wake of her, up-pattered,
> On broken clogs, the many-tattered
> Little old-faced peaking sister-turned-mother
> Of the sickly babe she tried to smother
> Somehow up, with its spotted face,
> From the cold, on her breast, the one warm place;
> She too must stop, wring the poor ends dry
> Of her draggled shawl, and add thereby
> Her tribute to the door-mat, sopping
> Already from my own clothes' dropping,
> Which yet she seemed to grudge I should stand on:
>   Then, stooping down to take off her pattens,
> She bore them defiantly, in each hand one,
> Planted together before her breast
> And its babe, as good as a lance in rest (v., pp. 211-212).

Almost as fine, and almost as much in the style of one who is personally familiar with what he describes, is the picture of the professor. The one point in which the former passage has clearly the advantage is the external detail, the sopping mat, the flapping umbrella, and the pattens held like a lance in rest.

> All settle themselves, the while ascends
> By the creaking rail to the lecture-desk,
>   Step by step, deliberate,
>   Because of his cranium's over-freight,
> Three parts sublime to one grotesque,
> If I have proved an accurate guesser,
> The hawk-nosed high-cheek-boned professor.
> I felt at once as if there ran
> A shoot of love from my heart to the man—
> That sallow virgin-minded studious
>   Martyr to mild enthusiasm,
> As he uttered a kind of cough-preludious
>   That woke my sympathetic spasm
> (Besides some spitting that made me sorry)

> And stood, surveying his auditory
> With a wan pure look, well nigh celestial,—
> Those blue eyes had survived so much!
> While, under the foot they could not smutch,
> Lay all the fleshly and the bestial (v., pp. 241-242).

Easter Day is less varied than its companion piece. It has none of the humour which lights up the congregation of the little chapel, but it has a large share of another kind of beauty common to both poems, the beauty of apocalyptic visions. Probably not since the middle ages, when faith in the reality of such things strengthened the artist, has the Day of Judgment been pictured as Browning pictures it :—

> Sudden there went,
> Like horror and astonishment,
> A fierce vindictive scribble of red
> Quick flame across, as if one said
> (The angry scribe of Judgment) " There—
> Burn it!" And straight I was aware
> That the whole rib-work round, minute
> Cloud touching cloud beyond compute,
> Was tinted, each with its own spot
> Of burning at the core, till clot
> Jammed against clot, and spilt its fire
> Over all heaven, which 'gan suspire
> As fanned to measure equable,—
> Just so great conflagrations kill
> Night overhead, and rise and sink,
> Reflected. Now the fire would shrink
> And wither off the blasted face
> Of heaven, and I distinct might trace
> The sharp black ridgy outlines left
> Unburned like network—then, each cleft
> The fire had been sucked back into
> Regorged, and out it surging flew
> Furiously, and night writhed inflamed,
> Till, tolerating to be tamed
> No longer, certain rays world-wide
> Shot downwardly (v., pp. 285-286).

This clearness of vision with the spiritual eye is the most prominent characteristic of both poems, and it must be borne in mind in interpreting them. There is no doubt that they embody the truth, and it seems reasonably clear that Browning identifies himself, in the main, with the speakers. But it does not follow that he would have accepted, as literally translatable into prose, all the views he may seem in these visions to support. The temptation is to read far too much of a positive and dogmatic theology into them. Browning would probably have held that one of the advantages of the apocalyptic form is that it leaves open such a variety of interpretations. "Truth is this to me and that to thee"; and Browning was in the habit, especially in his later days, of advising students of his poetry to take as its meaning what they found in it. That might be not what he found, or had been conscious of, but the fact that others after genuine study discovered it, was a proof that in some sense it was there.

The publications of Browning in the two decades after the turn of the century were comparatively few in number, but they were as a whole rich beyond anything he ever did either before or after. Next in chronological succession to *Christmas Eve and Easter Day* came *Men and Women* in 1855. *Dramatis Personæ* followed in 1864, and *The Ring and the Book* in 1868-9. Nowhere else has Browning done work so great as the best of this; and in no other period has he kept on such a uniformly high level. In former years the dramas are poor beside *Paracelsus* and *Pippa Passes*; in later days there is in *Prince Hohenstiel-Schwangau*, *Jocoseria* and *Ferishtah's Fancies* a mixture of unsatisfactory verse quite sufficient to bring down the average value of the work of those years. In a double sense therefore the period between *Christmas Eve and Easter Day* and *The Ring and the Book* may be regarded as the culminating period of Browning's genius. In the first place, the latter poem is by general consent pronounced Browning's greatest work. In the second place, then, and then only, does he remain throughout worthy of himself. This assertion is made in spite of the fact that an analysis of the publications of those years reveals a good deal of the inequality which unfortunately marked him. With the possible exception of *Faust*, if we include the second part, I know no great poem so unequal as *The Ring and the Book*; and it is very doubtful if even *Faust* should be excepted. In *Men and Women* too, and in *Dramatis Personæ*, there are a few pieces, like *Holy-Cross Day*[1] in the one, and *Gold Hair* in the other which fall far below Browning's level. But these pieces are so exceptional that they hardly disturb the impression of the general excellence of the collections in which they occur. It must be remembered moreover that about half the pieces now called

---

[1] This is now printed among the *Dramatic Romances*.

Dramatic Romances and *Dramatic Lyrics*, including many of the best of them, were originally published under the title of *Men and Women*. All the inequality therefore does not alter the fact that during those years Browning published no poem or collection of poems which would not be classed among the greatest of his works.[1]

The superiority was doubtless due in part to the fact that the balance of Browning's faculties was more perfect then than at any other time. On the one hand, his thought had reached its full maturity. There is immaturity in *Pauline*, perhaps there are traces of it even in *Paracelsus*, and in all probability the greater mistakes of *Sordello* would not have been committed by an older man. He did in later days meditate recasting it, and desisted, not because he thought it could not be done, but because the labour would have been disproportionate to the results.[2] On the other hand, we are still free from the curse of argumentative verse. Even *Christmas Eve* and *Easter Day* keep, as we have seen, on the right side of the line. With regard to the other poems it is still more clear that we are always within the limits of artistic creation. They express a great deal of thought, they suggest far more, but except where for dramatic reasons it is necessary to be so, they are not argumentative. A comparison between them and some of the later poems, such as *La Saisiaz*, some of the *Parleyings*, and much of *Ferishtah's Fancies*, reveals at a glance the difference between the poet within his own sphere and the poet trespassing on the domain of philosophy.

It has been said, somewhat rashly, that no really great poem was ever written by a man under forty. The exaggeration is at any rate a useful corrective of the shallow view against which it was directed, that poetry is essentially an affair of the youthful mind. That certainly would not have been Browning's view. His conception of the poet, as expressed in *How it strikes a Contemporary*, presupposes large experience as well as varied powers. He is the spectator of all existence, and observes everything. But the accumulation of experience requires time. Browning was certainly richer in experience in the second period than he was in the first. His poems prove that he was, and prove also the

---

[1] A few short pieces were published separately in this period. The assertion has reference to the principal publications, which have been enumerated.

[2] Mrs. Sutherland Orr's *Handbook*, p. 85.

value of this accumulation of experience. It is principally in the wealth drawn from a more intimate acquaintance with life that the productions of the second period excel those of the first.

At the beginning of this period Browning was on the verge of forty; at the close of it he was nearing sixty. It needs no proof that as age comes on, even if there be no decay of the mental powers, there is a stiffening of the intellectual joints and a loss of some of the susceptibilities of youth. It may be thought therefore that the simple fact of his age is a sufficient reason why Browning was at his best just in those years. And no doubt it is great part of the reason. The change for the better, as compared with his earlier poems, is, as has just been said, exactly such a change as comes from the growth of experience. The change for the worse which we see in his later poems is just such a change as age might be expected to bring with it. Browning was very different from Tennyson, who in some important respects improved almost to the close of his life. The poet's work may be compared to the human frame. As man stands erect and moves, has substance, firmness and vigour, by reason of the bony substructure, so great work in poetry must rest upon a solid framework of thought. But again, as we neither see nor wish to see the grinning skeleton, so this framework must be clothed with the flesh and blood of imagery and emotion. In Browning's case it is as if the flesh and blood were not always sufficient, and were never more than sufficient, to hide the angularities beneath. He could spare none of it without detriment. Hence he suffered from that drying up of the processes of life inseparable from advancing years. The flesh shrank, the blood flowed more scantily. The truth which he always sought burst through the veil of the beauty with which, as artist, it was his duty to drape it. In Tennyson on the contrary there was to begin with a superfluity of the covering. The beauty which he lavished would have decently clothed a good deal more than the sometimes puny skeleton of thought underneath. In his case there was no loss but great gain in the gradual development of the framework. Browning in later days lost proportion. Tennyson, perhaps in part through Browning's influence, of which there are suggestions in several of the later poems, gained it.

But while fully admitting the importance of Browning's age in accounting for the excellence of his work between 1850 and

1869, I must point out that there were other forces at work. In the first place, it is necessary to take account of the influence of his wife, which was not confined to *Christmas Eve and Easter Day*, though there perhaps it is most directly felt. She died in 1861; but Browning never forgot; and in such a nature as his it would be only by slow degrees that time would lessen her influence. Her published work does not seem to have affected his to any appreciable extent. After his marriage he followed what was simply for him the natural line of development. The features of his style became more deeply marked with time, and the subjects in which he was interested were those which interested his youth, only widened and enriched with experience. But that Elizabeth Barrett as a woman influenced him profoundly cannot be doubted. Their marriage is the most conspicuous example in our literature of the union of kindred tastes. Every poet is dependent for success in great part upon the proper development of his emotional nature, and Browning undoubtedly found in his marriage the opportunity for such development. Plato thought that the ideal physician was he who had experienced all diseases. On the same principle it might be affirmed that the ideal poet is he who has experienced all emotions. Browning owed to Elizabeth Barrett the awakening in him of the most powerful, and for poetical purposes the most fruitful, of emotions. His biographer expressly tells us that when he met her he was "heart-whole".[1] This of course must not be taken to mean that at the age of thirty-two he was totally ignorant of the nature of the passion of love: if any evidence were needed, his own earlier poetry would prove the contrary. But it is one thing to feel sympathy with, and another to have fully experienced a great passion.

The importance of this experience to Browning will be acknowledged by all who have realised what a great part the poetry of love plays in his work. It is not to be estimated merely by its bulk, considerable as that is. We must further bear in mind that this is the one strain in which it may be asserted with confidence that Browning has surpassed all other poets who ever lived; and we must observe how he lifts the human passion into connexion with the great principle which in his conception rules the world. For variety, for elevation, and for truth his

---

[1] Mrs. Sutherland Orr's *Life*, p. 141.

love-poems are unrivalled. Always dramatic, they exhibit many phases of the passion: always true, they do not ignore the baser elements that mingle with it. The whole meaning of *Any Wife to any Husband* is just that the woman knows that the passion, perfectly pure in herself, has the stain of earth in him; and the very generality of the title gives it a sad significance. But Browning was no "man with the muck rake". Strong with a strength far beyond the realists, real to a depth their plummet could never sound, he nevertheless held it to be no part of the function of poetry to "paint the mortal shame of nature". The effect of his treatment of love is to elevate the passion on a Mount of Transfiguration, and, using little hyperbole himself, almost to excuse the hyperbole which other poets have lavished upon it. If anything could justify the enormous significance which Browning assigns to love in human life and in the scheme of the universe, it would be his own treatment of it. Calmer judgment may tell us that the perspective is false, but yet the effect is magnificent,—like the exaggerations of his favourite artist, Michael Angelo. It may not be "good to be here" always: it is unquestionably good to have breathed the air once. And only in Browning does this air exist for us to breathe.

It would be reasonable to conclude on *a priori* grounds alone that the influence of Mrs. Browning counted for a great deal in the creation of this wonderful body of poetry. But we have besides the fact that two of the most exquisite passages coming under this class were addressed to her. These are the *One Word More* of *Men and Women*, and the celebrated "Lyric Love" of *The Ring and the Book*. They form a small proportion, it may seem; but the reason will be plain to any one who reads the former piece with sympathy. Just because of the intensity of his love and of the reverence which mingled with it, there could be but one expression of it. The one poem of Rafael, the one angel of Dante, are impressive because they are unique. In this case above all there was force in that principle of reticence which Browning almost fiercely vindicated. He had no mind to unlock his heart with any key, and least of all this particular chamber of it. The step aside to the dramatic form was necessary; and probably, but for the suggestion of unreality conveyed by hyperbolic language in the ordinary love-poems, the necessity would have been more widely felt by poets.

It is necessary also to bear in mind the probable influence of the time upon Browning. During the third quarter of the century what may be described as the promise of the second quarter was realised, and that so brilliantly that probably no period in English history, except the generation following the French Revolution, and the age of Shakespeare, has equalled it in intense and successful intellectual activity. That activity was by no means purely literary; but even if we confine the view to literature the record is striking. The development of Tennyson has just been traced. Among other names in poetry were Matthew Arnold, Clough, Rossetti, Swinburne and William Morris, though the three last belong rather to the latter part of the period. In prose, Carlyle had done much of his most valuable work, but it was during those years that his influence was greatest. Ruskin was then at his best. The finest of Newman's prose lies within the period; and during it Macaulay completed—or rather left incomplete—his history. The best novels of Dickens were published earlier; but most of Thackeray's and all George Eliot's appeared during those years.[1] So did Darwin's great work, which is a valuable piece of literature, as well as an unequalled contribution to biology. It was impossible for Browning, with his intensely human sympathies, to remain unaffected by all this intellectual ferment. His youth had been by comparison a journey through a valley of dry bones. He had done what one man could to breathe into them the breath of life; but virtue goes out in doing so, and it was well for him that his maturer years fell upon a more responsive time.

Every worker feels the impulse of the work going on around him, the artist most of all, because the fact that he is an artist means that he is sensitive. The physical theory of matter which now finds favour supplies a striking analogue to what seem to be the facts in the region of mind. Atoms and molecules, we are told, in incessant motion, uniting, separating, attracted, repelled, transforming their energy into light and heat and sound, build up the complex and varied world we know. So thoughts, spiritual influences of every kind, emanations from mind to mind, set in motion activities previously unsuspected, and indeed, without such impulse, impossible. It is the meeting of the positive

---

[1] To be precise, *Daniel Deronda* was published just one year after the close of the quarter.

and the negative electricity that evokes the lightning-flash. It is the collision of spirit with spirit that draws "the spark from heaven". Where the strife of ideas rages fiercest, there is the proper field for the artist. In the political turmoil which shook half the thrones of Europe and laid the foundations of a democracy which only the tyranny of words hinders us from recognising as absolutely unparalleled in the history of the world; in the religious struggles wherein some saw the pangs of death and others the throes of a new birth; and in the triumphs of science opening fresh worlds for thought to conquer, there were problems enough to tax the faculties of the greatest genius. There were perhaps too many for all but the greatest: we shall see presently how the sense of complexity oppressed Arnold. But it exactly suited Browning. He was "ever a fighter," and the storm only roused his energies. Not by mere accident, and not wholly because he was then in his intellectual prime, does his work of those years stand pre-eminent.

Men and Women, as it stood in 1855, was a collection so various that it is difficult to choose out from it the dominant elements. It proclaims by its title the author's continued concentration upon human character; and the number of poems devoted to love indicates what element in character most fascinated him. But the remaining poems are of widely diverse character. Two or three, like the *Epistle of Karshish, Bishop Blougram's Apology*, and *Saul*, then first printed in its complete form, testify to the continuance and even the deepening of his interest in questions of a theological character, and may be thought to prophesy its further growth in *A Death in the Desert*, published nine years later. The *Epistle of Karshish* expresses admirably the temptation a thoughtful heathen might have felt to find Christianity true. The tone which runs through it of not daring to believe and hardly even daring to call attention to matters outside the ordinary laws of nature was probably suggested by the somewhat tyrannous attitude of modern science upon such questions. The poem, while dramatically true to the character of the Arab physician, contains a good deal that may also be safely set down as Browning's own feeling. The following lines hint at longings expressed by him so often, and under such various circumstances, that we must ascribe them to him :—

> The very God! think, Abib; dost thou think?
> So, the All-Great were the All-Loving too—

> So, through the thunder comes a human voice
> Saying, "O heart I made, a heart beats here!
> Face, my hands fashioned, see it in myself!
> Thou hast no power nor mayst conceive of mine,
> But love I gave thee, with myself to love,
> And thou must love me who have died for thee!"
> The madman saith He said so: it is strange (iv., p. 198).

In *Cleon* the poet approaches cognate subjects, again from the point of view of the heathen. The quotation from St. Paul with which it is headed, "as certain also of your own poets have said," gives the key. It is an epistle to a king from a poet and artist, not Christian, but with seeds of what might develop into sympathy with Christianity. Both have reached the evening of life, and both feel the horror of the doom, "to lie in cold obstruction". It is so horrible, says Cleon, that

> I dare at times imagine to my need
> Some future state revealed to us by Zeus,
> Unlimited in capability
> For joy, as this is in desire for joy (iv., p. 292).

But the hope is vain, for

> Zeus has not yet revealed it, and alas,
> He must have done so, were it possible! (*ibid.*)

The doctrine of St. Paul is at the close alluded to as that of one of whom the writer has heard, but only to pass it by:—

> Thou canst not think a mere barbarian Jew
> As Paulus proves to be, one circumcized,
> Hath access to a secret shut from us (*ibid*).

While Cleon and Karshish are vainly groping for a larger faith, Bishop Blougram is troubled with a superfluity of it—not in himself, but in what forms his world. The *Apology* is the defence of a man who professes to believe more than his intellect quite warrants. The original of the bishop was Cardinal Wiseman, and what Browning had in his mind was the Catholic revival in England. The whole argument is special pleading and some of it is sophistry; yet it seems probable that Browning had more sympathy with the character and the intellectual position than has generally been supposed. The bishop is worldly, but not wholly so. The fact that the argument is specially addressed to Gigadibs carries with it, for the bishop, both advantage and disadvantage. It makes the dialectical victory easier; but it intensifies the appearance of insincerity. Browning wishes the bishop to be understood as a man who, in his own words, lives a life of "faith diversified by doubt". He has no wholehearted belief, but faith rather than scepticism is his element. He wins the victory in part because he rather than his opponent has the poet's sympathy, at least his intellectual sympathy. If *Christmas Eve* is, in as great degree as it seems to be, a personal utterance of the poet, it shows that little as Browning liked Rome, he liked still less the German professor's lecture-room.[1]

Browning's special interest in Italy began with his first journey thither in 1838. After his marriage he lived there for many years, and *Men and Women* proves that "increase of appetite had grown with what it fed on".

> What I love best in all the world
> Is a castle, precipice-encurled.
> In a gash of the wind-grieved Apennine
>   (*Dramatic Lyrics: De Gustibus*, vi., p. 92).

But especially it shows what a hold Italian art had taken upon him. *Old Pictures at Florence*, *Fra Lippo Lippi* and *Andrea del Sarto* all deal with Italian painting and painters. The first, though fine in parts, is as a whole unattractive, but the two latter are masterpieces. Even though Browning never could himself handle brush or chisel to any purpose, the time he bestowed upon art was not thrown away if it helped him to perfect those two poems. It was at a later date that he learned to model, but they bear evidence that he had already given far more than the attention of the casual gazer to painting.

The two painters are besides among the most vivid and real of Browning's dramatic creations: his knowledge of art is in these pieces kept in due subordination to his main purpose of depicting men. They gain too by contrast. Fra Lippo lives quite contentedly a sensual life, and if somehow he paints higher things, he troubles himself little though they may not be the

---

[1] It is curious that in an article on *Men and Women*, said to be by Cardinal Wiseman himself, the writer says:—"Though much of their nature is extremely offensive to Catholics, yet beneath the surface there is an undercurrent of thought that is by no means inconsistent with our religion; and if Mr. Browning is a a man of will and action, and not a mere dreamer and talker, *we should never feel surprise at his conversion*" (quoted in Furnivall's *Bibliography of Robert Browning*, p. 54, n. 2).

highest. But the pathos of Andrea del Sarto's life lies in his consciousness of powers misused and a soul only half developed. He has chosen an earthly reward, and the consequence is that he lacks the spirit which should inform his otherwise perfect art. He can see and correct the technical faults of Rafael even, but is forced to confess at the same moment that "all the play, the insight, and the stretch" are beyond him. He has sold himself to beauty without soul, and even that which he appears to have is not his. His wife, Lucrezia, simply uses him to get the means for her own pleasures, and he is reduced to degrade his art and his own honour, to paint for gold and to shut his eyes to his own disgrace. And so he falls below men who as artists are far his inferiors.

> There burns a truer light of God in them,
> In their vexed beating stuffed and stopped-up brain,
> Heart, or whate'er else, than goes on to prompt
> This low-pulsed forthright craftsman's hand of mine
> 			(*Men and Women: Andrea del Sarto*, iv., p. 224).

Andrea del Sarto may be taken as a type of a nature essentially spiritual, but untrue to itself in the vital point. He knows that "a man's reach should exceed his grasp," yet stops short with what is within his grasp. Hence the conflict in his nature. Fra Lippo Lippi on the contrary is the sensual man with glimmering sympathies with a better life. He does not suppress those sympathies but gives them expression in his painting, where they seem even to puzzle himself. Meanwhile he lives with a single mind the life he enjoys. There is no reason for conflict. "The world is meant for each of us," and Fra Lippo Lippi has taken out of it all he was meant to take. Browning, like every dramatic genius, had a very large tolerance. It was to him as meaningless to judge men by any absolute standard as it would be to judge the lower animals because they are not men. He judges neither of the painters, they judge themselves; and the difference is that the lower man pronounces upon himself a verdict of acquittal, and the higher, one of condemnation.

Other forms of art besides painting received attention in *Men and Women*. *A Toccata of Galuppi's* and *Master Hugues of Saxe-Gotha* show that interest in music which culminated afterwards in *Abt Vogler*. But now as always it was poetry about which he most loved to write. Besides *How it strikes a Contemporary*, there were three poems in the collection devoted to that subject. *Memorabilia* may be described as a tribute to the greatness of the true poet. The mere meeting with Shelley is the one thing memorable in an ordinary life, as the moulted eagle's feather is the one thing memorable on a barren stretch of moorland. *Popularity* shows how the harvest may be reaped by some one other than him who sowed the seed. In this case the moral is pointed with the name of Keats. In "*Transcendentalism*" the poet shows how fully he was alive to an error he did not always himself avoid. Its doctrine is that the function of poetry is to drape "naked thoughts" "in sights and sounds".

Dramatis Personæ is a similarly varied collection, and most of the veins of thought worked in *Men and Women* are worked again here. The poetry of art is continued in *Abt Vogler, Deaf and Dumb, Eurydice to Orpheus,* and *A Face*. The second is an admirable example of Browning's keenly sympathetic way of reading a meaning into works of art.

> Only the prism's obstruction shows aright
> The secret of a sunbeam, breaks its light
> Into the jewelled bow from blankest white;
>   So may a glory from defect arise:
> Only by Deafness may the vexed Love wreak
> Its insuppressive sense on brow and cheek,
> Only by Dumbness adequately speak
>   As favoured mouth could never, through the eyes.[1]

Youth and Art, notwithstanding its name, must be classified otherwise. It is a poem, not exactly of love, but of what might have been through love. The opportunity is let slip, they "would not be rash". Success comes, but leaves life empty.

> Each life unfulfilled, you see;
>   It hangs still, patchy and scrappy:
> We have not sighed deep, laughed free,
>   Starved, feasted, despaired,—been happy.
>
> And nobody calls you a dunce,
>   And people suppose me clever:
> This could but have happened once,
>   And we missed it, lost it for ever.

[1] This little poem was first published in 1868, in the six-volume edition of Browning's works. It was the only new piece in that collection, and may be most conveniently treated as part of the *Dramatis Personæ*, where it is now placed.

The same lesson is enforced with more seriousness, and even bitterness, in *Dis aliter Visum*, where also ambition is the intervening cause of separation. These poems are the utterances of the women. The first has acquiesced at the time in the decision dictated by ambition, the second has not. Both condemn it on reflection, and Browning condemns it with them. The fruit in the latter case is four souls lost. "The devil laughed at you in his sleeve!" It is again the lesson that "a man's reach should exceed his grasp". A man must know when to dare something; if he abides content with what he is and has, he perishes.

> What's whole can increase no more,
> Is dwarfed and dies, since here's its sphere (*Dis aliter Visum*).

It is interesting to compare with these two poems the earlier piece, *The Statue and the Bust*, because it shows the immense importance Browning attached to decision of character. In the two instances just spoken of, failure comes from inability to decide upon a *right* act at the right time. In *The Statue and the Bust* two lives are frittered away because of inability to decide upon doing *wrong*. Browning would not defend the wrong, but he would and does say that the continued indecision betrays a fatal weakness of character, "the unlit lamp and the ungirt loin"; and he would doubtless have added that this life-long indecision was a greater crime than the purposed crime which served as the test.

Three others of the poems on love deserve special mention, *The Worst of It*, for a view which would probably have occurred to no one but Browning; *James Lee's Wife*, because it is less episodic than the other dramatic love-poems; and *Prospice*, because it is personal to the poet.

The Worst of It is almost if not quite the most wonderful poem on love even Browning ever wrote. The speaker is a man whose wife has betrayed him. He speaks with intense feeling, but with a love so strong that what moves him to agony is not the sense of the wrong done himself, but of the stain upon her. He even blames himself as the cause of it: he has bound her "by the vows that damn," and she has broken them as she ought. If he were judge she might treat as she pleased his own heart and a hundred like it, and be doomed to no remorse of conscience. But there are God and the devil to reckon with. "The worst of it" is that she seems to have forfeited "heaven for a snapt gold ring". But this he will not believe.

> She, ruined? How? No heaven for her?
>   Crowns to give, and none for the brow
> That looked like marble and smelt like myrrh?
>   Shall the robe be worn, and the palm-branch borne,
> And she go graceless, she graced now
>   Beyond all saints, as themselves aver.

This is incredible: her place of penance must be earth, and he will be called in the end to lend the devil the knife to stab her.

> He stabs for the minute of trivial wrong,
>   Nor the other hours are able to save,
> The happy, that lasted my whole life long:
>   For a promise broke, not for first words spoke,
> The true, the only, that turn my grave
>   To a blaze of joy and a crash of song.

What separates *James Lee's Wife* from the other love-poems of Browning is the width of its scope. It is not a single phase of feeling, but a series of phases; and it follows that it is not simply one poem but rather a series of connected poems. In this respect we may compare it with Tennyson's *Maud*, though the range of the latter is much wider. *James Lee's Wife* is the story of a love which lasts on the woman's side but dies on the part of the man. It opens with the first faint breath of suspicion that he may not be constant; it traces that suspicion to a certainty, first silent and unconfessed, then admitted and discussed; afterwards it moves through the gradual revival of the crushed mind to the tasks and duties of life, and ends with the separation.

This poem contains perhaps more of natural symbolism than any other of Browning's,—at least any other of similar compass. The first hint of change is associated with the changing year. Love supplanted by indifference is as summer displaced by winter and cold and darkness; but love entering life is like the brilliant-hued cricket and butterfly lighting up with their colours the scorched turf and the bare dry rock. But it is the wind that plays the chief part in this symbolism. The growth of the trouble is imaged in the rise of the tempest, its pathos is in "the wind with its wants and its infinite wail," and, following out the thought still further, Browning reprinted six stanzas, "Still ailing wind? wilt be appeased or no?" which had been originally published as far back as 1836. The style of this piece is Browning's own, and the introduction of the dying nun and of the dog in the closing stanzas is like no one but himself; but in the manner in which nature is associated with human life in the opening stanzas there are probably traces of the influence of the poets of the early part of the century.

> Still ailing, Wind? Wilt be appeased or no?
> Which needs the other's office, thou or I?
> Dost want to be disburthened of a woe,
> And can, in truth, my voice untie
> Its links, and let it go?
>
> Art thou a dumb wronged thing that would be righted,
> Entrusting thus thy cause to me? Forbear!
> No tongue can mend such pleadings; faith, requited
> With falsehood,—love, at last aware
> Of scorn,—hopes, early blighted,—
>
> We have them; but I know not any tone
> So fit as thine to falter forth a sorrow:
> Dost think men would go mad without a moan,
> If they knew any way to borrow
> A pathos like thy own?

Prospice is valuable not only because of its extreme beauty and lofty heroism, but because it is the lyrical utterance of the poet's own emotion. The principal subject is death and the spirit in which the speaker would meet it; but the passionate close may vindicate for it a place not only among the love-poems, but in that special class to which only *One Word More* and "Lyric Love," as wholes, belong:—

> For sudden the worst turns the best to the brave,
> The black minute's at end,
> And the elements' rage, the fiend-voices that rave,
> Shall dwindle, shall blend,
> Shall change, shall become first a peace out of pain,
> Then a light, then thy breast,
> O thou soul of my soul! I shall clasp thee again,
> And with God be at rest!

Perhaps however the most characteristic note of *Dramatis Personæ* is struck in the poems dealing with theology and religion. Four of the weightiest and most interesting pieces are of this description, viz., *Caliban upon Setebos, Rabbi Ben Ezra, A Death in the Desert,* and the *Epilogue.* In three of these poems Browning obviously bent his spirit to the subject more than he did in *Cleon* or in *Karshish.*

Caliban upon Setebos is an extraordinary poem with a strange attraction for the intellect. Does Browning read in it a lesson on the dangers of anthropomorphism? "Man never knows how anthropomorphic he is;" but it is easy to see how completely Caliban finds himself reflected in what is above him, and on consideration we may perhaps doubt whether his process is widely different from our own. Certainly sober theologians have arrived at conclusions as to the nature of the divine being not greatly superior to Caliban's, and this although they have not, like him, found themselves left entirely to the light of nature. *Caliban upon Setebos* is perhaps the only one of Browning's theological poems which presents nothing with which he himself would have agreed. There is much he would have accepted in *Cleon* and *Karshish*; very much, had he been placed in their time and in their circumstances. There is, as I have already said, a good deal even in Bishop Blougram. The bishop is a man of imagination and wide reach of thought, and he has even Browning's love for Euripides:—

> Just when we are safest, there's a sunset-touch,
> A fancy from a flower-bell, some one's death,
> A chorus-ending from Euripides,—
> And that's enough for fifty hopes and fears
> As old and new at once as nature's self,
> To rap and knock and enter in our soul,
> Take hands and dance there, a fantastic ring,
> Round the ancient idol, on his base again,—
> The grand Perhaps (iv., p. 245).

But in *Caliban upon Setebos* the point of view is too widely different from any one possible under any circumstances to the poet. And this fact gives the poem as a dramatic study a special interest. Many of Browning's critics have complained with reason that they found Browning himself in nearly all his characters. They will not find him in Caliban, though Caliban speaks in his style.

The key of the poem is given in its alternative title, "Natural Theology in the Island". It is the gropings of a nature such as Caliban's, penetrating though savage, for an explanation or first cause of things. After the fashion of early inquirers however he has only found a second cause, for as Fate overshadows Zeus, so the Quiet is dimly visible behind Setebos. The one principle which Caliban has to go upon in his musings is analogy from his own nature. He constructs a god impelled by such motives as would influence himself. He concludes that the impulse of Setebos to creation is mainly spite. The feeling of absolute power over his creatures is a satisfaction to a nature not at ease in itself, for "he dwelleth i' the cold o' the moon," and hates "that he cannot change his cold, nor cure its ache". It is a consolation that he can treat the creatures he has made as he pleases. They are

> What Himself would fain, in a manner, be—
> Weaker in most points, stronger in a few,
> Worthy, and yet mere playthings all the while,
> Things He admires and mocks too,—that is it.
> Because, so brave, so better though they be,
> It nothing skills if He begins to plague (vii., p. 152).

And as spite was the impulse to creation, so is caprice its law. Just as Caliban lets twenty crabs file past and stones the twenty-first, "loving not, hating not, just choosing so," in the same way does Setebos mete out punishment, or, if the whim seize him, reward, to his creatures. Moreover, the ways of Setebos are "past finding out". Not only so, but inquiry into them, or the presumption of understanding them, is the surest way to rouse his wrath. Cowering abject submission and humility, with not too much display of happiness, is the most promising attitude. But "never try the same way twice" to please him.

> Repeat what act has pleased, He may grow wroth,
> You must not know His ways, and play Him off,
> Sure of the issue. 'Doth the like himself:
> 'Spareth a squirrel that it nothing fears
> But steals the nut from underneath my thumb,
> And when I threat, bites stoutly in defence:
> 'Spareth an urchin that contrariwise,
> Curls up into a ball, pretending death
> For fright at my approach: the two ways please.
> But what would move my choler more than this,
> That either creature counted on its life
> To-morrow and next day and all days to come,
> Saying, forsooth, in the inmost of its heart,
> "Because he did so yesterday with me,
> And otherwise with such another brute,
> So must he do henceforth and always."—Ay?
> Would teach the reasoning couple what "must" means!
> 'Doth as he likes, or wherefore Lord? So He (vii., pp. 158-159).

These speculations have been carried on in the mire of a dark pit, where Caliban conceives himself safe from the observation of Setebos. Suddenly a raven flies overhead, going to reveal all to Setebos, and a storm bursts:—

> What, what? A curtain o'er the world at once!
> Crickets stop hissing; not a bird—or, yes,
> There scuds His raven that has told Him all!
> It was fool's play, this prattling! Ha! The wind
> Shoulders the pillared dust, death's house o' the move,
> And fast invading fires begin! White blaze—
> A tree's head snaps—and there, there, there, there, there,
> His thunder follows! Fool to gibe at Him!
> Lo! 'Lieth flat and loveth Setebos!
> 'Maketh his teeth meet through his upper lip,
> Will let those quails fly, will not eat this month
> One little mess of whelks, so he may 'scape (vii., p. 161).

There is something comically suggestive in all this of what many of us have heard gravely uttered from the pulpit; and if we wish a closer parallel than our own experience affords, we have only to search the sermons of a generation earlier.

A Death in the Desert may be set over against this piece as its natural antithesis. *Cleon* and *Karshish* from the dramatic necessities of the situation stand in a manner midway between the two. In *A Death in the Desert* there is no room for the humour which enlivens *Caliban upon Setebos*; but it is essential to remember that it also is dramatic, and that Browning himself does not necessarily accept all or any of the positions laid down in it. That its spiritual teaching is his cannot be doubted: "we needs must love the highest when we see it," and Browning has nowhere soared higher. We have here the same sort of sanction for partially identifying the poet with his creation that we have in the case of *The Pope*. The dramatic utterance in this case is made through the lips of St. John, and that which makes him its proper mouthpiece is the fact that he is the last surviving man who has seen Christ. The utterance is consistent with the character conceived; but when critics assert, as some have done, that it is free from anachronism, they seem to praise amiss. Much of it, on the contrary, was surely suggested by the polemics of the time. The argument on miracles is that of a writer of the generation of Strauss; but even if we admit this argument as conceivably an answer to the scepticism already rising at the close of St. John's long life, the voice of Browning is unmistakable in the doctrine that man's very limitations are the necessary conditions of his progress :—

> Such progress could no more attend his soul
> Were all it struggles after found at first
> And guesses changed to knowledge absolute,
> Than motion wait his body, were all else
> Than it the solid earth on every side,
> Where now through space he moves from rest to rest (vii., p. 144).

This thought runs all through Browning, but it was not within the reach of the age of St. John. The truth is that Browning has conceived a dramatic situation, and has most skilfully represented it. The old man dying in the lonely cave, last of all who had seen and known Christ, the faithful four around him, and the Bactrian sentry, "a wild childish man," crying his cry at intervals, "like the lone desert-bird that wears the ruff," form an impressive picture. He has conceived also a character, that of the beloved disciple, faithful through life to the highest because he has seen it; willing to "absent him from felicity awhile" if he may make others see it too; and recalled from the torpor heralding death by the words, magical to him, "I am the Resurrection and the Life". But it does not seem that he has even tried to limit the scope of this man's thought to that which was possible to his age. What special gain would there have been had he done so? In the cases of *Cleon* and *Karshish* there is a gain; for there the point is the struggle of a soul through darkness towards a clearer light. In *A Death in the Desert* the projection of the soul through centuries, its enrichment with the spiritual experience of many generations, in no way mars it as a creation, and immensely increases its significance to the poet's own time. This is clearly one of the poems which bear the marks of our time upon them, and which for that reason carry to it a lesson all the deeper.

One reason for Browning's choice of St. John for the utterance of some of his own most deeply felt thoughts has been stated. Another may be easily inferred. The apostle of love was a fit vehicle for the poet's dominant thought. Thus, it might be either St. John or Robert Browning who tells us that

> Life, with all it yields of joy and woe,
> And hope and fear,—believe the aged friend,—
> Is just our chance o' the prize of learning love (vii., p. 130) ;

or who speaks of "the love that tops the might, the Christ in God," or who insists that if God has merely might and man alone has love, then

> He is as surely higher in the scale
> Than any might with neither love nor will,
> As life, apparent in the poorest midge
> (When the faint dust-speck flits, ye guess its wing),
> Is marvellous beyond dead Atlas' self—
> Given to the nobler midge for resting place ! (vii., p. 148.)

This is surely the same voice as that which says, in *Christmas Eve*,

> The loving worm within its clod
> Were diviner than a loveless god
> Amid his worlds (v., p. 220).

Rabbi Ben Ezra, though closely allied to this poem, stands yet on a different plane. The theological element, though not the religious, has disappeared. There is no argument on matters of faith, no breath of the spirit of controversy. It is a dramatic piece, yet is removed in great measure from the influence of the play of events, and may be taken with confidence as representing Browning's own view. Twice, in this poem and in *The Pope*, he has imagined dramatic situations in which he could hardly give utterance to anything but his own philosophy of life. Both Rabbi Ben Ezra and the Pope are old men, conceived as the highest and best of their time and race, giving expression to their deepest thoughts with life behind them and eternity before. In such circumstances the poet was not only entitled but obliged to put into the mouth of his characters the best thoughts he could himself imagine. Dramatic circumstance becomes altogether subordinate. The Rabbi and the Pope look upon life almost as disinterestedly as disembodied spirits might. Its passions and entanglements are past, and they see them in the light of mature experience and ripe wisdom. Hamlet's rich reflectiveness is wedded to an irresolute character, and Othello's noble impulses are played upon and perverted by villainy; but Browning's two characters are idealised, their gold is unmingled with dross, their wisdom undimmed by passion. Thus they are different also from Browning's own St. John, whose arguments upon miracles it would be dangerous to treat as the poet's too. The fact that the Pope is a Christian and the Rabbi a Jew nurtured on the Old Testament might be thought by some an essential difference; but Browning's practical treatment of it may be taken as illustrating a remark once made by the Rev. Rowland Williams, that it is quite possible to have all that is really important in Christianity without the name or the forms. The Rabbi and the Pope are in thorough agreement as to the substance of their philosophy. The chief differences are that in the latter it is more full and comprehensive, while in the former it is presented with a lyrical fervour which makes it perhaps attractive to some who may miss the supreme beauty of *The Pope*.

It is difficult to quote from *Rabbi Ben Ezra*, for the temptation is to quote all; but a few passages will show how Browning's own view runs through it. His favourite thought, that difficulty and obstruction are not evil but are indispensable factors in the evolution of good, receives perhaps its finest expression in this poem. "A spark disturbs our clod," and to that intrusive spark we owe all. It is the discord which must mate with harmony to make music.

> Then, welcome each rebuff
> That turns earth's smoothness rough,
> Each sting that bids nor sit nor stand but go!
> Be our joys three-parts pain!
> Strive, and hold cheap the strain;
> Learn, nor account the pang; dare, never grudge the throe!

> For thence,—a paradox
> Which comforts while it mocks,—
> Shall life succeed in that it seems to fail:
> What I aspired to be,
> And was not, comforts me:
> A brute I might have been, but would not sink i' the scale.

Here too we find, what in such a context we might less expect, Browning's healthy belief in flesh as a thing which has as good a right to exist as spirit.

> Let us not always say,
> "Spite of this flesh to-day
> I strove, made head, gained ground upon the whole!"
> As the bird wings and sings,
> Let us cry, "All good things
> Are ours, nor soul helps flesh more, now, than flesh helps soul!"

But here too is the thought, shared by Browning in common with all imaginative natures, that a man's "work" is a thing not to be put in the scales and weighed, or set up and measured with a yard-stick, and that impulses and purposes must be reckoned in the sum as well as things accomplished.

> Thoughts hardly to be packed
> Into a narrow act,
> Fancies that broke through language and escaped;
> All I could never be,
> All, men ignored in me,
> This, I was worth to God, whose wheel the pitcher shaped.

It seems clear that on the whole *Dramatis Personæ* marks an advance even upon *Men and Women*. There is in it a greater proportion of poetry which must be ranked with the highest, and in each main department it presents examples which it would be difficult, if not to parallel, at least to surpass, elsewhere in Browning's works. *Abt Vogler* is probably the richest of the art poems; and if *James Lee's Wife* and *The Worst of It* are not the best of the love-poems, they are at any rate equal to the best. In what may be called the spiritual poems, as in the love-poems, the wealth to choose from makes choice difficult; but it may be said with confidence that the collection which contained *A Death in the Desert, Rabbi Ben Ezra* and *Prospice* had more of the highest quality than any previous collection. Perhaps the terrible personal experience of Browning in the death of his wife helped to enrich this section of his work. As her coming into his life deepened his tone, so likewise did her leaving it. It is in complete accord with his own philosophy to find in this "rebuff" an aid to his progress.

Browning was now near the highest point in his great course. In the closing months of 1868 and the beginning of 1869 appeared his longest, and, by almost universal consent, his greatest poem, *The Ring and the Book*. He had been working at, or brooding over, the story for more than six years. The manner in which he treats it is instructive, for it shows how completely he had learned the lesson that the drama was not for him. There are three principal characters in the story, the needy noble, Count Guido Franceschini, the hanger-on of the papal court; the girl Pompilia, the reputed daughter of two comfortable citizens, Pietro and Violante, who becomes Guido's wife; and the priest Caponsacchi, who helps her to escape from her husband. There are various minor characters, the reputed parents already mentioned, the count's brothers, priests, and his mother, living in a kind of squalid dignity in the family castle at Arezzo, their retainers who help in the murder, and the high ecclesiastics at Arezzo and in Rome. There is likewise plenty of action or of material for action,—the intrigue and parasitism of ecclesiastical society, the patching up of the marriage, with its trickery on both sides, the miserable life in the old castle, the flight, the pursuit, the capture, the murder, the trial. This would commend itself to any dramatist as the skeleton of a stirring drama, and no doubt Browning himself would have viewed it so in earlier days. The situation is not like that of his dramatic monologues, where as a rule one character speaks, and the presence of another is sometimes assumed and sometimes not. In the story of the Roman murder all are vitally interrelated. Yet Browning prefers to treat them one by one, and to enable himself to do so evolves the unique plan of *The Ring and the Book*.

That plan is in substance to tell over, or rather comment upon, the story from ten different points of view. Repetition is avoided by the assumption, after the introductory book, of a knowledge on the part of the audience of the outline of the story: what is given is the way in which it strikes the speaker. Hence action disappears out of the poem, and comment is at once narrowed and widened. It is narrowed because there is necessarily great concentration on three or four of the most prominent events, the marriage of the count and Pompilia, her flight and capture, and the murder. It is widened, because it gives the speaker full liberty to introduce anything and everything that seems to him essential. All restrictions necessary in the regular drama for the purpose of representation are swept away, and the picture becomes in each case a complete picture of an individual soul. This is the immense advantage which tempted Browning to adopt the seemingly clumsy plan, and in his hands it is its complete justification. He certainly could not, and it may be doubted whether any one else could, have produced equal results in any other way. At the same time, it is well to remember the accompanying disadvantage. The plan leaves no room, properly speaking, for the *development* of character. The poet may make the speaker review his or her life within any limits he pleases, but if and so far as the conception is dramatically true, every view and every word is influenced by the present situation. All the actors are steeped in that "hell's grim drench" of the murder; and when life moves after such an "awful parenthesis," it must move to a new measure.

The thing most to be regretted about *The Ring and the Book* is its excessive length and its consequent unevenness. About one-half of it is almost beyond praise, the other half is vastly inferior, and great part of it might be lost without detriment to the world. There is a reason indeed for the presence of all the books, but not a *sufficient* reason. We can understand why the two lawyers are introduced, but we should acquiesce in their introduction only if we found them, on the whole, equal to the other characters. Browning's plan was an elastic one. It necessitated a monologue from all the principal actors, but it left him free to bring in or to omit as he pleased *Half-Rome, Other Half-Rome, Tertium Quid, Dominus Hyacinthus de Archangelis,* and *Juris Doctor Johannes-Baptista Bottinius.* His great mistake was that he did not elect to omit them. These books are not destitute of fine passages, but there is not one of them that is worthy of a place alongside of the greater books of the poem, and the two lawyers are positively poor and wearisome. One great defect that runs through them is that they give low mean views in too large lumps, so to speak. In the regular drama, little bits of vulgarity and meanness, necessary from the characters introduced, are made effective by contrast, and are inoffensive because there is so little of them; but Roman gossip, stretched out through three whole books, fatigues and disgusts. Suppose Shakespeare had followed the same method; suppose that, in place of a few questions, answers, conjectures, criticisms here and there from 1st Citizen, 2nd Citizen and 3rd Citizen, representing the "rascal multitude," we had whole acts without break filled with their utterances? That would have wearied too. Browning seems to have failed to perceive a necessary result of his method. It concentrates the various dramatic elements and as a result alters their effect. When such a plan is adopted a different principle of selection and rejection ought to rule.

But the other parts of the poem magnificently atone for the shortcomings of these. The four figures of Guido, Pompilia, Caponsacchi and the Pope are certainly as great as any Browning ever drew. If Guido has not been held in equal estimation with the others, it is rather because he is disagreeable than because he is in any way less masterly as an artistic creation. In one sense it might even be held that he is greater than they, for probably in no other character has Browning so completely left himself behind. Guido also has the solitary distinction of appearing twice, and so gives unimpeachable evidence, not found elsewhere in *The Ring and the Book*, of the change which difference of circumstance makes in men. The first book devoted to him is entitled *Count Guido Franceschini*. In it he appears fresh from the torture, a miracle of craft, subtlety and intellectual dexterity, all rendered twice as telling by the inherited courtesy of an ancient house. "E'en the homely farm can teach us there is something in descent," and Browning was undoubtedly right in painting his Count Guido, scoundrel though he is, low-minded, intriguing, time-serving, criminal, as a man well able, when he pleases, to show that grace of manner, inborn in him from his long line of ancestry. His perfect courtesy brings his sufferings from the torture into just sufficient prominence to gain him all the advantage of his judges' pity. He is too well-bred to parade them, and too astute to hint blame of those in whose hands his life rests. He has done an act contrary to law, and what he is suffering is the necessary consequence. If he betrays that suffering by look or movement, it is the involuntary shrinking of the flesh. All his arguments are skilfully adapted to his audience. He speaks as a gentleman to gentlemen, as an almost life-long servant of the Church to Churchmen. He seeks to awaken all their prejudices in his favour. He makes the utmost of the trick that Violante has played upon him. He even makes the utmost of his own defects of character. He is speaking to men of the world, men upon whom Roman society has stamped its corrupting brand, and in whose eyes the absence of all pretence to lofty motive would be almost a virtue. In all this the true character of Guido is by no means ignored or concealed; on the contrary, the peculiar merit of the book is that the character shines through everywhere, yet leaves the defence the best possible in the circumstances. It is a wonderful triumph of intellect.

It takes the second book, *Guido*, to make the triumph perfect. The change of title is significant. In the former book we have the man Guido still in the setting of his social position and with his long descent behind him: he is count and he is a Franceschini. In the latter book we have his human nature stripped bare. The dramatic insight here is as true as that which in the earlier stage clothed Guido in the manners of his ancient house. "Scratch a Russian, and you find a Tartar." Try a man by the proper tests, and the inner nature will break through any veneer with which society may have overlaid it. Guido has received his death-sentence; and as soon as he is convinced that all hope is vain he lays aside his craft and stands out his undisguised self. It is a terrible character. His whole life has been a lie, and now that it can serve him no more he tears the lie to tatters. He will have no mock repentance. He is sorry for his punishment, but not for the crime which has brought it upon him. His contempt for all the hypocrisies of his former life is boundless; and it is stinging too, for he knows and shows that the lives of his hearers have been as mean, as unreal and as dishonest as his own. But the man is a coward after all. His last words, in the terror of the imminent doom, are a wild appeal to everything that he has wronged and disowned and poured abuse upon:—

> Abate,—Cardinal,—Christ,—Maria,—God,—
> Pompilia, will you let them murder me?

Giuseppe Caponsacchi, who gives his name to another book, differs from Guido as a man a little lower than the angels from a being no higher than the devils. He is a man not without faults, but with good impulses capable of being awakened into heroism. He is perhaps the most striking example in Browning of the power of a great and good motive to save a man from himself and his surroundings. Up to the moment of his call to help Pompilia he is living a life of easy self-indulgence in the Church, predestined to sink gradually lower as years pass, or, at best, to get "drunk with truth stagnant inside him". The call of Pompilia might have been his destruction: her character makes it his salvation. Her helplessness brings out his latent heroism. He devotes himself to her. To do so he has to over-leap convention and dare the judgment of the world. Her perfect innocence is her and his sufficient protection. The light frivolous man of pleasure emerges from the trial proud, strong and true, but marked for ever by its sufferings. "Work, be unhappy, but bear life, my son," is the Pope's sentence upon him.

Pompilia is certainly the finest female character ever drawn by Browning, and unsurpassed by any to be found in any poet. Her childlike innocence, her unmerited sufferings, and her patient fortitude make her one of the most pathetic figures in all literature. In the beginning she is merely a counter in the game played by the scheming Violante and the fortune-hunting Guido. Everything is against her, and, as regards character, she is to outward view a mere *tabula rasa* on which experience and the world may write anything. But unknown to any one there exists in her already a simple but clear conception of duty and a heroic resolution to act upon it. As Count Guido's wife her lot is one of unmixed suffering. On the unimpeachable evidence of Guido's self in book xi. she bears it patiently. Her simple philosophy helps her. There are many things which must be borne because they are so decreed:—

> God plants us where we grow.
> It is not that, because a bud is born
> At a wild briar's end, full i' the wild beast's way,
> We ought to pluck and put it out of reach
> On the oak-tree top,—say " There the bud belongs ! "
>
> (*Pompilia* vii., 301-305.)

For herself she is all meekness and submission to everything but sin. Her daring is born when she has another life to fight for. Then she summons Caponsacchi, and all her subsequent course is determined by the crowning fact that she has her child to think for and to protect. It is in the strength of this thought that she fronts and defies her husband at the little inn at Castelnuovo ; and it is the thought that she has saved the child that sustains her through all the subsequent suffering, and takes the sting from death. She is the one character who comes through the old Pope's scrutiny with unmixed praise :—

> Everywhere
> I see in the world the intellect of man,
> That sword, the energy his subtle spear,
> The knowledge which defends him like a shield—
> Everywhere ; but they make not up, I think,
> The marvel of a soul like thine, earth's flower
> She holds up to the softened gaze of God ! (*The Pope*, 1018-1019.)

The Pope is to many the highest point Browning ever attained. Viewed as a dramatic realisation of character, the book is inferior to *Caponsacchi* and to *Pompilia* and to *Guido ;* but as a poetical philosophy of life it is superior in depth, in grandeur and in comprehensiveness. It is dramatic too. The position of the old

Pope, called upon at the very close of life to pronounce sentence of death, is striking; and our rather weak-nerved age is indebted to him for his firmness. The closing passage is magnificent: he may die this very night, and he dares not die if he lets Guido live. The death of the criminal is due from the Pope to society. It is due to the criminal himself; for in this swift doom lies his one chance of repentance and salvation. On this question he never hesitates. Having examined the documents with all diligence and care he is convinced of the guilt of Guido, and he never shrinks from the responsibility of his position. He is human and may err, but the fact that he did his human best is defence sufficient. This wholesome saneness of mind and resolute acceptance of responsibility are among the most prominent features of the character. The long ruminations of the Pope are not, therefore, designed to clear away doubts which do not exist. There is in them perhaps some of the discursiveness of old age; but they are never irrelevant. God's vicar upon earth, called upon, by what may prove his last act in life, to pronounce doom upon five fellow-creatures, may well pause and reflect. Browning is not telling a story, and the pause disappoints no expectation of the reader. The Pope is the embodiment of wisdom and experience summing up the meaning of the story already told, and the worth of the characters which have already revealed themselves. Thus, among other peculiarities of the plan, we get from it not only the poet's concrete conception of each character, but also his own criticism of it,—for so doubtless the Pope's must be interpreted. But the Pope's great position leads him farther. To him, whose "loaded branch" lifts "all the world's cark and care," this spectacle of human passion, of greed, hatred, love, submission, heroism, revenge, opens out the whole question of the state of the world, its present, its past, and its future; and it is his reflections upon this question that make *The Pope* perhaps the greatest poem Browning ever wrote. They will receive consideration elsewhere: at present it must suffice to point out that here Browning came nearer than he ever did elsewhere to the fulfilment of the magnificent promise of *Paracelsus*.

CHAPTER VI.

MATTHEW ARNOLD.

It was in the year 1849 that the name of Matthew Arnold was added to the list of poets. He had previously written prize poems both at Rugby and at Oxford; but verse of this description rarely counts in the work of a great man's life, and we may therefore regard *The Strayed Reveller, and other Poems*, as his earliest contribution to literature. From the first his work was so delicately finished and so thoughtful that it established his right to be ranked among the great poets of his time: "established" that right, not by winning general recognition, but by virtue of those inherent qualities which we must believe will at last enforce such recognition. For recognised in any due degree Arnold is not yet. Indeed, now that death, which failed to do so in Arnold's case, has given the shock necessary to raise Browning above the danger of further neglect and depreciation, it is hardly too much to say that of all great Englishmen Arnold is the one who is farthest from the place he ought to hold in the hearts of his countrymen.

Experience proves that we must stand at the distance of several generations before we can finally and with absolute justice appraise the value of poetry. A moderate space of time is, it is true, generally sufficient to reveal the true dimensions of littleness once reputed great; but it is only from afar that we can take the angles by which to measure the mountain-peaks of thought. Some of the "kings of thought," like Carlyle and Browning, speak in the voice of the tempest and the earthquake. It is such men who are sure to be saluted at first with the loudest bray; but it is not they who are likely to be longest neglected or inadequately appreciated. They demand attention and at last receive it. The world is compelled to listen; and, unlike the Hebrew prophet of old, it discovers that the voice of God speaks in the storm and the convulsion. But what of the "still small voice"? It makes no clamorous assault upon the ear, it may go on indefinitely, whispering vainly to senses too dull by nature to hear, or so deafened by the rattle and roar of the world that they cannot hear. And yet surely there is truth as well as beauty in that old conception which finds the divine rather in gentleness than in violence.

It has proved to be so in the sphere of poetry. The polished and refined and reticent literary artists of the world, its Virgils and its Miltons, wear well; their smoothness has nothing of the nature of weakness. To this class Matthew Arnold belongs; and it is well worth while to make an effort to understand him more fully than he has yet been understood by England as a whole, because, rich as are the long rolls of English poetry in rugged strength and grandeur, they are comparatively poor in that classical purity and finish of which Arnold is our best example of recent times. He was partly the cause of his own eclipse. His excellent prose has to some extent overshadowed his still more excellent poetry. And more than that, he illustrates within his own works the way in which the loud voice drowns the lower and sweeter tones. The author of *Literature and Dogma* and of *God and the Bible* arrested the attention of men because he addressed himself openly and avowedly to current controversy; the voice of *Obermann once More* was heard by comparatively few. And yet the latter deals with essentially the same problems as the former, deals with them more profoundly and more wisely, and is free from the defect of a merely passing and temporary interest which is inherent in all controversy, and from which even the charm of Arnold's style will not permanently save his polemical writings.

And Arnold is valuable not only for what he is in himself, but for what he adds to the other two poets. He is probably the most faultless artist of the three. Browning sometimes provokes his readers to pronounce him not an artist at all, though again he redeems himself so magnificently that it becomes almost a pain to hint censure. Tennyson had very high artistic qualities, but in a tendency to excessive ornamentation, in the redundancy of *In Memoriam*, in the loose structure of the *Idylls of the King*, and in an occasional note that sounds like affectation in his metaphors and turns of expression, he showed that there were limits to those qualities. Thus, there is affectation in the metaphor, "closing eaves of wearied eyes" (*In Memoriam*, lxvii.), and in the intolerable translation of metropolis into "mother town" (*ibid.* xcviii.). One of the most frequently quoted passages in the *Idylls of the King* shows in its excessive antithesis a similar failure of taste :—

> His honour rooted in dishonour stood,
> And faith unfaithful kept him falsely true.

Arnold, narrower in his compass, within that compass makes fewer mistakes than either. Further, he is in some respects more than either of the others the voice of his own generation. That he is so may be due in part to his limitations; but be the reason what it may, the fact remains that if we wish to discover what men in the nineteenth century have thought on many important subjects, we shall do so more easily if not more surely in Arnold than in any of his contemporaries; and we shall find the way in which he gives expression to contemporary interests more lucid if not more profound.

Arnold was twenty-seven years of age when *The Strayed Reveller* was published. He was thus considerably older than Browning and Tennyson were when they first appeared as poets; for a difference of six years, though trifling in later life, is great between twenty and thirty. This is one reason why the chronological method is much less fruitful in the case of Arnold than it is when applied to Browning and Tennyson. At the date of his first publication he was far more mature than Tennyson, and he had far less to learn by way of experiment than Browning. Another reason for the same fact is that Arnold's whole period of poetic activity was short in comparison with the long careers of his two seniors. It began, as has been said, in 1849, and it practically ended in 1867; for the few poems published after that date cannot appreciably affect the judgment upon him.

The Strayed Reveller was withdrawn after only a few copies had been sold. So was the next work, *Empedocles on Etna, and other Poems*, published in 1852. Arnold's frequent changes of mind—or what must be interpreted as such—may be taken as indicating his extreme critical care, a care in his own case amounting almost to fastidiousness. It must be confessed that it is difficult to follow him; for poems are printed, omitted and reprinted in the most bewildering way. The puzzle is all the greater because in the end nearly everything reappears in the collected editions. Only eight published pieces, including the two prize poems, are omitted from the popular edition of 1890.[1]

---

[1] For the bibliographical facts I am indebted to Smart's *Bibliography of*

The Strayed Reveller, and other Poems proves by its contents how wonderfully complete already was Arnold's mental and moral equipment. He never changed as Tennyson did, he never even developed in the lesser degree that Browning developed. Even if we limit the view to equal spaces of time in their work, the conclusion is still similar. There is greater difference between the Tennyson of 1833 and the Tennyson of 1842 than there is through the whole literary career of Arnold. So too the Browning of *Bells and Pomegranates* changed more before he published *Dramatis Personæ* than Arnold ever did. The principal contents of this early volume, besides the piece which gave it its name, were *Mycerinus, The Sick King in Bokhara, To a Gipsy Child, The Forsaken Merman, In Utrumque Paratus, Resignation,* and the beautiful sonnets on *Shakespeare* and *To a Friend.* There is here the circle of Arnold's interests and of his thought nearly complete. It is true there is no specimen of what afterwards he did best of all, the elegiac, but there is plenty of the elegiac spirit. It is true also that he added much afterwards which we could ill spare; but these additions are less of the nature of fresh themes than of fresh illustrations of the themes already present in his first volume. Arnold however repeats, not with the monotony of mental sterility, but with the endless variety of commanding genius; and it is of the nature of the great thoughts in the region of which he moves that they will bear illustration indefinitely.

It is evident on the most cursory examination that Arnold has neither the magnificent optimism of Browning, nor the artistic aloofness which at first marked Tennyson. All the pieces mentioned are weighted with thought, but none of them has that firm trust in ultimate success which sustains Browning, and convinces him that the worst "apparent failure" can be no more than apparent. On the contrary, there is in them, one and all, the consciousness of a thwarting destiny. Even the sonnet on Shakespeare, alive as it is with the sense of the supreme triumph of the human intellect, has its glow darkened by reference to the "foil'd searching of mortality," and to the "weakness which impairs," and "griefs which bow". Far more deeply do the other pieces mentioned bear the traces of a spirit ill at ease, and with but little hope of finding in life the alleviation of his troubles. The poem entitled *Resignation* is peculiarly instructive. It differs from the others named as being, in greater

measure than they, a poem of nature. It is the best in this early collection to which that title can be applied, and one of the best Arnold ever wrote. We can easily gather from it Arnold's characteristic point of view. It is Wordsworthian, without the calm hopefulness of Wordsworth, for the younger poet was unable to "put by," as his master did, "the cloud of mortal destiny". For Arnold, to "put by" that cloud would have been equivalent to putting by his own nature. In a note to Fitzgerald's translation of Omar Khayyám there is quoted a pretty Persian story: "A thirsty traveller dips his hand into a spring of water to drink from. By-and-by comes another who draws up and drinks from an earthen bowl, and then departs, leaving his bowl behind him. The first traveller takes it up for another draught, but is surprised to find that the same water which had tasted sweet from his own hand, tastes bitter from the earthen bowl. But a voice—from heaven, I think—tells him that the clay from which the bowl is made was once *man;* and, into whatever shape renewed, can never lose the bitter flavour of mortality." So it is with Arnold. All nature has the taste of human destiny; and in that destiny there is something akin to bitterness.

This same poem, *Resignation,* prepares us also for Arnold's view of human life: and indeed in it man and nature are so intertwined that it is difficult to say on which the stress lies; only it is clear, here as always, that the latter is interesting to Arnold for the sake of the former. Resignation, the title of the piece, is the lesson the poet draws from his study both of nature and of the life of man:—

>Be passionate hopes not ill resign'd
>For quiet, and a fearless mind.

In all the other pieces the human element is more prominent and the lesson from nature is less directly taught. *The Forsaken Merman* is in one sense an exception, for it is not humanity that speaks in it at all; but it takes no great penetration to see that the wonderful pathos of the Merman is essentially human. It is more important to observe that here Arnold allowed his fancy a free play he rarely gave it; and he did so with the best results. The pictures of the sea-caverns are painted in beautiful verse:—

> Children dear, was it yesterday
> We heard the sweet bells over the bay?
> In the caverns where we lay,
> Through the surf and through the swell,
> The far-off sound of a silver bell?
> Sand-strewn caverns, cool and deep,
> Where the winds are all asleep;
> Where the spent lights quiver and gleam,
> Where the salt weed sways in the stream,
> Where the sea-beasts, ranged all round,
> Feed in the ooze of their pasture-ground;
> Where the sea-snakes coil and twine,
> Dry their mail and bask in the brine;
> Where great whales come sailing by,
> Sail and sail, with unshut eye,
> Round the world for ever and aye?
> When did music come this way?
> Children dear, was it yesterday?

To a Gipsy Child is at least as masterly in style as this. In it we find "the soil'd glory and the trailing wing," "the swinging waters," and the picture of him

> Who in mountain glens, at noon of day,
> Sits rapt, and hears the battle break below.

But it is impossible without fatal loss to separate any of its wonderful felicities of expression from their context. Arnold was a man who not only wrote beautiful lines but who, beyond most poets, had the skill to make them tenfold more beautiful by their setting. The piece is even more remarkable for its richness of thought than for its melody and verbal beauty. It is the "clouds of doom" on her brow that attract Arnold to the child. He reads into her his philosophy of life, and he prophesies that even if what the world calls success should come, she will before the end return to that mood which makes him think of her as "some angel in an alien planet born":—

> And though thou glean, what strenuous gleaners may,
> In the throng'd fields where winning comes by strife;
> And though the just sun gild, as mortals pray,
> Some reaches of thy storm-vext stream of life;
>
> Though that blank sunshine blind thee; though the cloud
> That sever'd the world's march and thine, be gone;
> Though ease dulls grace, and Wisdom be too proud
> To halve a lodging that was all her own—

> Once, ere the day decline, thou shalt discern,
> Oh once, ere night, in thy success, thy chain!
> Ere the long evening close, thou shalt return,
> And wear this majesty of grief again.

There is a certain similarity between *The Sick King in Bokhara* and *Mycerinus*. Both show the powerlessness of the highest position to remove the limits set to human will. "What I would, I cannot do," says the sick king, and all his rooms of treasure are powerless to console him. Mycerinus finds that even living well cannot alter the inexorable decree of fate. The poem is founded upon a passage in Herodotus which tells how Mycerinus, son of an unjust and evil-living father, "abhorred his father's courses, and judged his subjects more justly than any of their kings had done.—To him there came an oracle from the city of Buto, to the effect that he was to live but six years longer, and to die in the seventh year from that time." It is just after the receipt of this oracle that Arnold takes up Mycerinus. The king speaks "half in anger, half in scorn". The will of the great gods is plain: it is ill deeds and ill passions that reap their praise and are rewarded by length of years.

> My father loved injustice, and lived long;
> Crown'd with grey hairs he died, and full of sway.
> I loved the good he scorn'd, and hated wrong—
> The Gods declare my recompense to-day.
> I look'd for life more lasting, rule more high;
> And when six years are measured, lo, I die!

He asks whether it be that it seems to the austere powers above a light thing to spurn the pleasures of life; or whether it be that some superior force, "like the broad volume of the insurgent Nile," sweeps heaven and the gods along as well as earth and men; or whether it be that they simply live in epicurean indifference to human needs. If so, then all the "divinations of a will supreme" are lost labour,

> When the circumambient gloom
> But hides, if Gods, Gods careless of our doom.

He determines therefore to give the rest to pleasure, and in the "six drops of time" which remain to show the gods "revels more deep, joy keener than their own".

The end is in Arnold's own voice. Mycerinus laughed and made merry,

> And his mirth quail'd not at the mild reproof
> Sigh'd out by winter's sad tranquillity.

Yet Arnold conjectures that

> It may be on that joyless feast his eye
> Dwelt with mere outward seeming; he, within,
> Took measure of his soul, and knew its strength,
> And by that silent knowledge, day by day,
> Was calm'd, ennobled, comforted, sustain'd.

This prepares the way for the view implied in *In Utrumque Paratus;* for Arnold was invariably clear on the point that, whatever doubt might hang over man's ultimate destiny, it was always within his power and always his duty to live well the life he knew was his. If man has no second life, his injunction is, "Pitch this one high". So when the alternative is between a world made by God and a "wild unfather'd mass," the injunction is in the one case to remount "the colour'd dream of life" by lonely purity to its stainless source. In the other case it is that man, under that hypothesis the chief of all things, should moderate his triumph, remembering both that his knowledge is limited and that this primacy itself has in it nothing to satisfy his nature: "Who hath a monarch's hath no brother's part". There is no room for boundless triumph or lawless indulgence.[1]

Empedocles on Etna was withdrawn from circulation, as Arnold afterwards explained, because he held that a situation in which all was to be endured and nothing to be done was poetically faulty. With reference to this Mr. Hutton, who, though separated from Arnold by deep differences of view, is nevertheless one of the most sympathetic of his critics, has truly remarked that the insistence upon this principle would have condemned all that was most characteristic in Arnold's later work. It may be suggested however that the objection Arnold took to his own poem is one which applies to it principally as a long poem and as a drama. He objects to those situations "in which a *continuous* state of mental distress is *prolonged*, unrelieved by incident, hope, or resistance". In the lyric and the elegiac, which

---

[1] It is interesting to compare this with the Epilogue to Browning's *Dramatis Personæ*, where the Second Speaker, as Renan, conceives the same situation, man supreme over all things, and is similarly awed and sobered: "Oh dread succession to a dizzy post," etc. (vii., p. 253).

are Arnold's proper field, there is less reason why endurance should not be the dominant necessity. Moreover, when in 1867 Arnold republished *Empedocles on Etna*, he explained with pardonable satisfaction that he did so at the request of Browning. In the interval it had never appeared as a whole, though parts of it had been incorporated in various volumes of verse between its first publication and the issue of the *New Poems* in 1867.

Besides the title-piece, the volume thus withdrawn from circulation contained the greater part of the series afterwards entitled *Switzerland*, and of that now called *Faded Leaves*, and also *Excuse, Indifference* (afterwards *Urania* and *Euphrosyne*), *Tristram and Iseult, Memorial Verses, A Summer Night, Stanzas in Memory of the Author of "Obermann,"* and *Morality*.

Perhaps the most conspicuous new feature here is the attempt to deal with passion. The attempt is made lyrically in *Switzerland* and in *Faded Leaves*; while in *Tristram and Iseult* there is a dramatic thread interwoven with a treatment lyrical still. These poems are highly instructive, perhaps even more for what they do not than for what they do contain. They have been called cold. They are not cold, Arnold never is so; but they certainly do exhibit a spirit which seems incapable of resting in the affection for, or in the sense of the loss of, an individual. His " deep habitual smart " is due to a " something that infects the world," and thus turns the poetry of passion into a wail over destiny. The fifth poem of *Switzerland*, beginning " Yes ! in the sea of life enisled," laments the isolation of humanity. The poet's own loss is generalised in the feeling that in the sea of life " we mortal millions live *alone* ". So too the third poem, *A Farewell*, lays its stress upon that stern destiny whose doom is that

> We wear out life, alas !
> Distracted as a homeless wind,
> In beating where we must not pass,
> In seeking what we shall not find.

So too in *On the Rhine*, the fourth poem of *Faded Leaves*, the special passion is almost lost in the wider thoughts it awakens. Doubtless it is this that has led to the accusation of coldness; but the word is a mistaken one when applied to verse so charged with feeling :—

> Awhile let me with thought have done.
> And as this brimm'd unwrinkled Rhine,
> And that far purple mountain-line,
> Lie sweetly in the look divine
> Of the slow-sinking sun ;
>
> So let me lie, and, calm as they,
> Let beam upon my inward view
> Those eyes of deep, soft, lucent hue—
> Eyes too expressive to be blue,
> Too lovely to be grey.
>
> Ah, Quiet, all things feel thy balm !
> Those blue hills too, this river's flow,
> Were restless once, but long ago.
> Tamed is their turbulent youthful glow ;
> Their joy is in their calm.

Equally characteristic is *Tristram and Iseult*. The story upon which Arnold founds is one of passion as fiery and intense as any fiction presents. He selects the moment of its close. Tristram is lying

> Propt on pillows in his bed,
> Gazing seaward for the light
> Of some ship that fights the gale
> On this wild December night.

It is only in his fevered ravings that the dying knight retraces the events of a passion as delirious as the fever. Iseult of Ireland arrives just to see him die, and to die herself by his side ; and in death the beauty which, in life, passion had consumed and dimmed "like the desert-blast," returns to her :—

> Though the bed-clothes hide her face,
> Yet were it lifted to the light,
> The sweet expression of her brow
> Would charm the gazer, till his thought
> Erased the ravages of time,
> Fill'd up the hollow cheek, and brought
> A freshness back as of her prime—
> So healing is her quiet now,
> So perfectly the lines express
> A tranquil, settled happiness,
> Her younger rival's purest grace.

Professor MacCallum, in his *Tennyson's Idylls and Arthurian Story*, calls attention to "the meaning question at the close," the question, "What tale did Iseult to the children say?" The story she tells is the story of Merlin and Vivian ; and it is impossible to miss the lesson conveyed by the spectacle of the sage imprisoned, through his yielding to passion, in the "little plot of magic ground".

A grey light shadows all the later life of Iseult of Brittany. "Joy has not found her yet, nor ever will"—"she seems one dying in a mask of youth". She is freed from the turbid flow of passion and has found resignation but not happiness.

The extreme beauty of the descriptions in *Tristram and Iseult* calls for special mention. Arnold always had an exquisite power of describing nature ; but in the earlier poems he let this faculty for description play upon humanity more frequently than in later years. The picture of Iseult of Brittany's children asleep "in shelter'd nest" is one of the finest passages in the poem ; and that of Iseult of Ireland, though less varied, is hardly less admirable :—

> And she too, that princess fair,
> If her bloom be now less rare,
> Let her have her youth again—
> Let her be as she was then !
> Let her have her proud dark eyes
> And her petulant quick replies—
> Let her sweep her dazzling hand
> With its gesture of command,
> And shake back her raven hair,
> With the old imperious air !

Urania and *Euphrosyne*, to give these pieces the titles by which they are now known, might seem to serve as a means of transition to Arnold's more habitual themes. They deal with passion or the possibilities of passion, but rather from the point of view of a spectator than of a participant. *Urania* is an excuse for a character neither cold nor light though she seems both. What appears her fault has its root in the faults of men :—

> Eagerly once her gracious ken
> Was turn'd upon the sons of men ;
> But light the serious visage grew—
> She look'd, and smiled, and saw them through.

The companion piece, *Euphrosyne*, is a similar excuse for an opposite type of character, a character irresponsibly sunny The boon of such characters to the world is just this sunshine, and they are misjudged because they are asked to give something for which nature never meant them :—

> They shine upon the world! Their ears
> To one demand alone are coy;
> They will not give us love and tears,
> They bring us light and warmth and joy.

It is strange that Arnold is happier in this piece than in the former, for his natural sympathy was rather with the type of character depicted in *Urania*.

Memorial Verses, first printed in *Fraser's Magazine*, is in that vein of poetical criticism so distinctive of Arnold, and with the exception of two or three of the sonnets of the *Strayed Reveller, and other Poems*, was the earliest published, though not the earliest written, of its class. Arnold is rarely happier than in his criticisms in verse. Their peculiar charm is that they always penetrate to the heart of the writer criticised, and always bring into prominence his lesson to the world. Thus, in the *Memorial Verses*, it is the Titanic force of Byron, the vast intellectual sweep and penetrating sagacity of Goethe, and the soothing calm of Wordsworth, that he insists upon; and probably nowhere within equal compass is there such illuminating criticism of these writers. It is a remarkable illustration of Arnold's fine taste that he never in these critical verses forgets the difference between prose and poetry; we never feel that this would have been better said in plain prose. The *Stanzas in Memory of the Author of "Obermann"* are likewise largely critical. They are dated November, 1849, and were thus written before the *Memorial Verses*, the occasion of which was the death of Wordsworth. In portraying Senancour they reveal Arnold himself:—

> A fever in these pages burns
> Beneath the calm they feign;
> A wounded human spirit turns,
> Here, on its bed of pain.
>
> Yes, though the virgin mountain-air
> Fresh through these pages blows;
> Though to these leaves the glaciers spare
> The soul of their white snows;
>
> Though here a mountain-murmur swells
> Of many a dark-bough'd pine;
> Though, as you read, you hear the bells
> Of the high-pasturing kine—

> Yet, through the hum of torrent lone,
> And brooding mountain-bee,
> There sobs I know not what ground-tone
> Of human agony.

In these critical poems Arnold is quite different from Browning in his poems of art; because in the first place Browning always conceives his subject dramatically, and in the second place he tries, at least where he is dealing with poetry, to get at the principles of the art from the point of view of the poet he imagines. Arnold contents himself, both in *Memorial Verses* and in the stanzas on *Obermann*, with showing what, in point of fact, the writers spoken of do. It is enough for him to note the actual effect of Wordsworth's verse, he advances no theory as to how it is produced, still less does he attempt to speak in the voice of Wordsworth. In a later poem however, the *Epilogue to Lessing's Laocoön*, he did attempt, if not a complete theory of art, at any rate an explanation of the principal differences between the arts of music, painting and poetry; and within the limits he set to himself he was completely successful.

In the stanzas on *Obermann* the criticism of art merges so much in the criticism of life that we almost forget the presence of the former. In *A Summer Night* and in *Morality* the criticism of life is beyond doubt the keynote. The latter contrasts man with nature, his weary striving with her calm. So far it agrees with the earlier sonnet, *In Harmony with Nature*, drawn from the poet by a "restless fool" of a preacher who preaches what to him would be

> The last impossibility—
> To be like Nature strong, like Nature cool.

But in the sonnet Arnold's opposition to the preacher drives him to insist only on the contrast; in *Morality* he sees harmony as well as difference, and he implies that the strife of humanity is a higher thing than the calm and rest of nature,—a view habitual with Browning but rare in Arnold.

A Summer Night gives with greater completeness, and also with greater sadness, Arnold's gloomy view of life. The alternative is that the human being must be either a "madman" steering some false course across the ocean of life till he steers himself to ruin, or a "slave" bending languidly over "some unmeaning taskwork". This, in Arnold's opinion, is the case in his own generation, because the old motives which gave dignity and meaning to life have lost their force, and those which have taken their place are mean and low. His indictment against his own time is that it either neglects altogether the necessity of nourishing the spiritual nature, and bends its whole energies to a taskwork unmeaning except as subservient to spiritual needs ; or else it attempts to feed the spirit on the mere leavings of bygone ages, the husks which the swine *should* eat. Tennyson felt the same want, and he imagined that a remedy might be found in a war which should make men forget their petty interests and their absorption in their own personal comfort. He was not wholly wrong : any motive, if it will only lift above the immediate present and awaken the consciousness of union in cities and nations, will do the work in part. But Arnold saw farther and was less easily satisfied.

In 1853 Arnold published a volume of *Poems*, partly new and partly old. Of the new pieces the most noticeable were *Sohrab and Rustum*, *The Church of Brou*, *The Scholar Gipsy*, and *Requiescat*, the last of which, like Tennyson's " Break, break, break," compels mention by its extreme beauty. *The Church of Brou* is uneven, but it is memorable for its close, almost the finest piece of imagery in Arnold. He pictures the dead duke and duchess waking in their tomb on an autumn night :—

> Or let it be on autumn nights, when rain
> Doth rustlingly above your heads complain
> On the smooth leaden roof, and on the walls
> Shedding her pensive light at intervals
> The moon through the clere-story windows shines,
> And the wind washes through the mountain-pines.
> Then, gazing up 'mid the dim pillars high,
> The foliaged marble forest where ye lie,
> *Hush*, ye will say, *it is eternity !*
> *This is the glimmering verge of Heaven, and these*
> *The columns of the heavenly palaces !*
> And, in the sweeping of the wind, your ear
> The passage of the angels' wings will hear,
> And on the lichen-crusted leads above
> The rustle of the eternal rain of love.

The Scholar Gipsy is permanently associated with *Thyrsis*, first published in *Macmillan's Magazine* in 1866, and included among the *New Poems* of 1867. The early maturity of Arnold's work is illustrated by the fact that of these two poems, both among his best, most critics would probably give the preference to the one first written. One reason for this preference is that the pastoral form is better adapted to the subject of *The Scholar Gipsy* than it is to *Thyrsis*. That Milton chose the pastoral form has been frequently pleaded as an objection against *Lycidas*. It is certainly still more an objection against *Thyrsis*, two hundred years later, and dedicated to a closer friend than ever King was to Milton. But the form was in a manner determined for Arnold by his previous use of it in *The Scholar Gipsy*, for which it was admirably fitted. The two poems are so closely related in tone and treatment that Arnold rightly considered the advantage of making them companion pieces in outward shape as well, to be more than sufficient to balance the disadvantage arising from the artificial tone of the pastoral when used for the purpose of an elegy on a friend.

Sohrab and Rustum has the distinction of being the first considerable specimen, not dramatic, of Arnold's blank verse, and also the longest narrative he had yet published; for though *Tristram and Iseult*, which is about the same length, is classed as a narrative, it is in spirit much more a series of semi-dramatic lyrics. *Balder Dead* followed it in 1855. Perhaps the thing most to be regretted in Arnold's literary history is that he wrote no more poems such as these. Not that they are his best: there is more charm in his elegiac strain. Neither can it be asserted that they are eminently successful as narratives. There is no rapidity of movement in them. But in the first place the verse is singularly beautiful, and blank verse is that which can be longest read without weariness. More important however than this is the fact that this narrative form of verse promised Arnold a wider variety of themes than he seemed otherwise able to find. As elegiac poet and as lyrist he moved within a circle of emotions refined and elevated but not wide. His inborn melancholy gave to his work, even within that circle, a certain uniformity of tint. The narrative form would to some extent have taken him outside himself, and so have introduced greater variety. It is not to be supposed that he would have chosen subjects against the bent of his genius; neither is it to be desired. His choice of subject and his treatment of it in *Balder Dead* show how he remains himself in his narrative poems as well as in his lyrics; and it is well that he does so, for all that is most valuable in Arnold's verse comes from the reiterated disclosure of his own feelings and his own views. But he is not, to the same degree as in the lyrics, concentrated upon his own feelings. The legends of Balder and of Sohrab take him into an external world of men and gods, and force him to follow the course of events which have happened or are supposed to have happened. The stories, moreover, are too detailed and too coherent to be treated, like the legend of the scholar gipsy, as mere pegs upon which the poet may hang his own reflections.

It may be urged that in the earlier drama, *Empedocles on Etna*, and in the later one, *Merope*, Arnold had an equally good chance of escaping into a world external to himself. And this is true; but these very instances are sufficient to prove that the dramatic form was not suited to Arnold. There is much fine poetry in *Merope*, and still more in *Empedocles;* but their merits are not dramatic. On the other hand, *Sohrab and Rustum* and *Balder Dead* not only contain fine poetry, but they are good, though not excellent, as narratives. There seemed to be no reason why he should not have written an indefinite number of equally beautiful narratives; but *Balder Dead* was the last as *Sohrab and Rustum* was the first of the class; and they are the only considerable specimens, written under perfectly favourable conditions, of a blank verse not surpassed since the days of Milton for refinement and charm.[1] It is said that Arnold when asked by Browning why he did not write more poetry, replied that he could not afford it. If it was really so England has suffered and still suffers for her own want of taste and appreciation.

These poems are charged with the classical spirit and are full of phrases borrowed from or more frequently suggested by the classics. This influence is visible in the speeches, as in that of Rustum beginning "Go to! if Iran's chiefs are old, then I am older," and still more in the management of the similes, as for example the simile of the cranes in *Sohrab and Rustum* :—

> From their black tents, long files of horse, they stream'd ;
> As when some grey November morn the files,
> In marching order spread, of long-necked cranes
> Stream over Casbin and the southern slopes
> Of Elburz, from the Aralian estuaries,
> Or some frore Caspian reed-bed, southward bound
> For the warm Persian sea-board—so they stream'd.

---

[1] The verse of the dramas was not written under perfectly favourable conditions: the drama was too alien to Arnold's genius.

This passage illustrates also Arnold's love of harmonious geographical names. Careful students of his poetry will recall many similar examples ; and those who remember how he contrasted the ugliness of English with the euphony of Celtic names will readily believe that it is not by mere accident that those examples are to be found, and that the choice of names is far from being a haphazard one.

In both of these poems Arnold reveals himself in ways of thought as well as in turns of expression. He does so perhaps more in *Balder Dead* than in *Sohrab and Rustum*. Balder, it may almost be said, is Arnold himself; and Balder's weariness of the strife and carnage of Valhalla accurately reflects the poet's weariness of the turmoil and bustle of the world :—

> I am long since weary of your storm
> Of carnage, and find, Hermod, in your life
> Something too much of war and broils, which make
> Life one perpetual fight, a bath of blood.
> Mine eyes are dizzy with the arrowy hail ;
> Mine ears are stunn'd with blows, and sick for calm.
> Inactive therefore let me lie, in gloom,
> Unarm'd, inglorious ; I attend the course
> Of ages, and my late return to light,
> In times less alien to a spirit mild,
> In new-recover'd seats, the happier day.

This was always Arnold's method. He has constantly in his mind his own age and utters his own criticism upon it. Empedocles expresses the thoughts of Arnold; and *Tristram and Iseult* is a modern picture, with Arnold's moral drawn from it.

Balder Dead and *Separation* were the only new poems in the volume of 1855 ; but the *Stanzas from the Grande Chartreuse* appeared separately in *Fraser's Magazine* during the same year. Arnold seldom if ever wrote better than in these stanzas. In their range and tone of feeling they are similar to the *Obermann* poems, and the mention in them of *Obermann*, if that were needed, indicates the source of their inspiration. Three years later came *Merope, a Tragedy*, which will be noticed elsewhere, and in 1867 the *New Poems* almost closed Arnold's poetical career, though among his later verses *Westminster Abbey* and the three fine pieces on dead pets, *Geist's Grave, Poor Matthias* and *Kaiser Dead*, deserve special mention.

In that volume of 1867 Arnold returned to his early taste for the sonnet. There are none perhaps of the later sonnets quite equal to the best of the earlier ones, yet few either in Arnold or elsewhere surpass in happiness of conception *The Good Shepherd with the Kid*, and he has seldom expressed more clearly and finely than in the third of the series on Rachel his sense of the something amiss with the world. But what most distinguished the volume was the great proportion of exquisite elegiac poetry it contained. To this class belong *Thyrsis, Stanzas from Carnac, A Southern Night, Rugby Chapel, Heine's Grave, Stanzas from the Grande Chartreuse,* and *Obermann Once More*. The first, third and sixth of these pieces had been published separately, but they were then first gathered into the body of Arnold's poetry; and the others were new. When we consider the high quality of all these pieces, and add the other lovely elegies already mentioned, and the beautiful *Westminster Abbey*, one of the latest of Arnold's poems, it is not too much to claim for him the first position among English elegiac poets. Others have written single elegies exquisitely; Arnold alone among our great poets has written many, nearly all of which are in his highest strain. The secret of his success is not that he dwells upon death: rather, as has been pointed out in connexion with *Thyrsis*, he escapes from it as soon as possible. Neither is it his method to concentrate sorrow upon an individual. In the *Obermann* poems, in *Memorial Verses*, in *Heine's Grave*, in the elegies on his friends Clough and Stanley, and even when in *Rugby Chapel* his heart is filled with the memory of his father, he widens his view to human life in general. His great success is due to the fact that the mood of pensive reflection in which he is most at home is exactly right and natural in the elegy. But it is important to observe how wide is the range of this reflection; for on that depends largely the permanent interest and value of these poems. *Obermann Once More* contains the celebrated picture of East and West in the days of Roman sway, and traces the course of Christianity from the time of its vigorous early life to its decline and death, as Arnold conceived it,—death, that is, as a faith in a supernatural revelation. The earlier *Obermann* and the *Stanzas from the Grande Chartreuse* give the author's view of the world in his own day. So does *Thyrsis*, and so, sadly, yet with a ring of hope, drawn from the character of the dead man, does *Rugby Chapel*, the elegy on the poet's father. *A Southern Night* is the occasion for reflections, most musical if also most melancholy, on the author's countrymen, their ambition, their restlessness, their inability to "possess their soul"; and *Heine's Grave* contains the famous picture of overburdened England, "the weary Titan," staggering blindly on to her goal. This wealth of thought is never dragged in, but seems to spring spontaneously out of the subject. The exquisite style gives it that charm which in poetry nothing but style can give. Whoever glances over the list of the elegiac poems, and compares it with any other section of Arnold's poetry, will come to the conclusion that the true Arnold is there. Other things too he did beautifully; some of his sonnets and lyrics are hardly to be surpassed; but nowhere else is he so uniformly good.

One other poem in the volume of 1867 deserves special mention, not because it is superior to all the rest, but because it is the best expression of a mood of Arnold's mind rarely prominent in his verse, yet always present in it. His habitual view of the world was sad. He had no buoyant faith to help him to face the future. At times he seems almost driven to relinquish the struggle. But this is only in a momentary cry or two. He shows in *Pis-Aller* his scorn of those who cannot find outside of creeds any firm and sure principle of life. His own permanent mood was one of resolute endurance. If faith does not remain, duty does, and its call is clear. It would be difficult to find any utterance more resolute and inspiring than *The Last Word*:—

> Creep into thy narrow bed,
> Creep, and let no more be said!
> Vain thy onset! all stands fast.
> Thou thyself must break at last.
>
> Let the long contention cease!
> Geese are swans, and swans are geese.
> Let them have it how they will!
> Thou art tired; best be still.
>
> They out-talk'd thee, hiss'd thee, tore thee?
> Better men fared thus before thee;
> Fired their ringing shot and pass'd,
> Hotly charged—and sank at last.
>
> Charge once more, then, and be dumb!
> Let the victors, when they come,
> When the forts of folly fall,
> Find thy body by the wall!

There is in all this surprisingly little trace of development. But if there is not much evidence of any ment, there is ample proof that the younger poet important function of his own, distinct from that of either the two seniors.

Perhaps the first thought which strikes the student of Arnold is that in him more than in any English writer since Milton we find an incarnation of the classical spirit. In one respect even the exception of Milton need not be made; for there is nothing in Arnold so incongruous with the ideas of the Greeks as Milton's Puritan theology. There is much in him, no doubt, that was not and could not be in literature two thousand years earlier; but the sense of difference is reduced to a minimum by his way of viewing it. He is like the Greek of his own imagination, standing "in pity and mournful awe" before a fallen Runic stone. No dogma rises like a wall between him and the ancient classical spirit. The word which he took from the Greek and expounded to the Eton boys as expressing the ideal mental attitude might be applied to himself. He is eminently εὐτράπελος, flexible, sensitive to influences, ready to see the elements of truth which may mingle even with falsehood. Milton's theological panoply sometimes mars the stately magnificence of even his style; Arnold is rather the athlete, active and supple, encumbered by no dogma extraneous to his own thought. What he owed to Christianity blended easily with what he owed to Homer and Sophocles and Plato, because there was nothing in the one to which he was determined beforehand to make the others bend. In Milton it was otherwise. In him the theologian, who sees in the gods of Greek mythology the devils of true religion, stands in harsh contrast to the artist, conscious of the beauty of the old myths. The difference is largely one of time. Both Milton in the nineteenth century and Arnold in the seventeenth would have been different men. But the fact remains. Arnold, partly because he lived when he lived, partly because he was what he was, has given the best expression within recent times to the classical spirit, perhaps the most balanced expression it has ever received in English literature. In this respect he owed probably not a little to Goethe.

Arnold in his critical work was in the habit of fixing upon some one word as expressing more than any other the significance of the man or of the work or subject under discussion.

ever always careful not to bind himself hand and foot to any idea; the value of εὐτραπελία was just to prevent this. In such a matter it will be safe to follow, under the same limitation, one of the greatest of English critics.

If there is any one word which better than another will sum up what we mean by "the classical spirit," and especially by that spirit in contrast with the Gothic or Teutonic spirit, it is the word *restraint*. Classical poetry, in contrast not so much with modern as with Teutonic poetry, is distinguished for its orderliness, its proportion, its lucidity, its reticence. It nowhere gives the impression of a farrago of thoughts. In criticisms of poetry we frequently meet with metaphors drawn from mining for gold or precious stones: a fine thought or a happy expression is a nugget or a gem. The metaphor is never meant to be pressed, and it would be unjust to press it, but it is still suggestive of a truth beyond that which stands in the foreground. It implies that the surrounding mass is chaotic; and in the English or German poets this is not infrequently the case. But as applied to Greek poetry such metaphors would be inappropriate, or they would not carry with them the further suggestion. There the nugget is wrought and shaped, the gem is polished, and they have their place in a harmonious whole. In this respect Arnold was a Greek, Browning a Teuton, while Tennyson stood between the two, but much nearer Arnold than Browning. It is true that Browning denied the fact of the Greek perfection of form. It is even said[1] that one of his objects in translating the *Agamemnon* was to show how groundless was the opinion. If so, the best commentary on his attempt is perhaps the fact that I have heard an ardent Browningite, who is not a professed scholar, remark that he found the Greek easier than the English.

Another of Arnold's admirable habits as a critic was, on points of doubt relating to English literature, to resort to foreign opinion. He went to Scherer to learn what Europe thought of Milton. The same test may be applied to himself, and an answer may be drawn from the same man. "Mr. Matthew Arnold has, I should think," says Scherer, "as many ideas in his head as Carlyle, and as much poetry in his soul as Mr. Ruskin, and yet he does not think himself obliged to speak like a mystagogue." Even those who think the great French critic wrong must admit that his phraseology shows how a large part of our literature

[1] Mrs. Sutherland Orr's *Life*, p. 308.

affected a mind in most ways unusually sympathetic towards it. The French, it is generally admitted, have, more than any Northern nation, the classical sense of order, lucidity and proportion. It is the presence of these qualities in Arnold, it is their absence from Carlyle and Ruskin, that draws from him the word mystagogue. Now, it is more than anything else his self-restraint that stamps these qualities upon Arnold's work. He would not, like many of the greatest of his countrymen, follow any association which suggested itself. 'Εὐτραπελία is just the opposite of wilfulness. The association which satisfies the canons of art must be the most natural, the most appropriate, that which harmonises best with what has gone before and what is to come after. Hence a searching self-criticism, a severe repression, an austerity of taste stopping just short of fastidiousness. But for this Arnold would probably have written more: it is almost certain that he would have written less perfectly; and English poetry could spare most things better than a single one of its not too numerous specimens of perfect finish and perfect self-restraint. How inseparable these qualities were from Arnold's very nature is nowhere more conspicuously shown than in *Balder Dead*. The legend is Scandinavian, but the whole form and structure of the poem are classical. Valhalla is transformed into an Olympus conscious of modern needs and touched with modern feelings. The brawls and revels of the gods are as alien to Arnold as they were to Balder.

I have said that Tennyson in this respect stood between Browning and Arnold. As to the position of Browning there can hardly be a doubt, but some may dispute the judgment that Tennyson had less of the classical spirit than Arnold. In making this assertion I do not mean to imply that he was inferior, but that there were certain qualities, specially associated with the term "classical," in particular this power of restraint which is so important an element in it, that Arnold possessed in more liberal measure than he. Probably those who are not assured of this already will not be convinced by argument, and indeed the subject is by no means an easy one to argue about: it is rather a matter of feeling; but a few illustrations will help to explain my meaning.

Tennyson awakes to the sense of something amiss in the world around him, and gives utterance to his feelings in *Locksley Hall*. It is a good piece and quite sincere, yet it does not ring perfectly true in the artistic sense. There is a taint of violence and almost of rant about it. Arnold is never without this sense of something amiss; it is the prevailing thought of his poetry. But he has nowhere given the rein to his feelings as Tennyson did in *Locksley Hall*. He, like the world itself, *bears*. He contrasts the muteness of his own age in the face of seemingly irremediable evil with the passionate outcries of the preceding generation. The contrast was essentially true as regards himself. His art lay in the use of words and the stillness was not absolute; but there is always about his utterances this sense of restraint and the impression of power in reserve which restraint gives. Take again Tennyson's *Charge of the Light Brigade*. It won and has retained immense popularity; but it is loud rather than strong. There is absolutely nothing in Arnold which can be brought into comparison with this. He never makes this mistake. Even where he may be deemed to have exaggerated, we never have the sense that he has lost self-control.

> All pains the immortal spirit must endure,
> All weakness which impairs, all griefs which bow,
> Find their sole speech in that victorious brow.

This is almost as strong as language can be, perhaps too strong even as applied to Shakespeare. But the writer has himself well in hand, he says not a word more than he means to say, he is dignified, he never for a moment foams at the mouth. The Northern taste betrays itself in Tennyson's piece, the cultured South in Arnold's. A very fanciful critic might contend that descent had something to do with it. Tennyson had in his veins the blood of the sea-rovers, Arnold, in blood as well as in spirit, was related to France.[1]

The greatest man who ever bent his mind to criticism said that the end of tragedy was "to purge the affections by pity and terror". If we take away the element of terror we may describe this as the end of a great deal of literature besides tragedy. But everything depends on the way in which the pity is roused. The range is wide, from *King Lear* to, say, *East Lynne*. Probably if the two works were judged solely by the tears they have drawn, the latter would have to be pronounced the greater. The methods

---

[1] Perhaps in one solitary poem, *Pis-Aller*, Arnold forgets this restraint. There, religious bigotry draws from him just one impatient exclamation.

are different. In the one case we have King Lear with the dead
Cordelia in his arms :—

> She's gone for ever !
> I know when one is dead and when one lives ;
> She's dead as earth. Lend me a looking-glass ;
> If that her breath will mist or stain the stone,
> Why, then she lives.

It seems perfectly simple ; but only one man in all the world has ever done it just so. The recipe for the other is simple too. Take an erring but repentant wife and a little child on its death-bed. Put some innocent prattle in the lips of the latter. A childlike question or two about heaven adds to the pungency, and makes the effect certain. There are many grades between the prince of letters and the rank and file of its army ; but it is generally possible to discern whether a man is of the household of Shakespeare or not. Tennyson sometimes is, and is well worthy to wear the livery. He is so for example in the grand scene between Arthur and Guinevere, which is as majestic as it is touching. But unfortunately it is impossible to be assured of his constancy to the livery. The pathos of *Enoch Arden* is of the cheaper sort, and *The May Queen* is not beyond suspicion of a like taint. But Arnold never errs in this way, though he has frequently handled subjects which might have led him into similar error. There is tragic pathos in the close of *Sohrab and Rustum*, the agonised father sitting in the darkening sand by his dead son ; but there is no sentimentality. There is deep feeling in *Rugby Chapel* and *A Southern Night*, poems inspired by the loss of those nearest to the author in blood ; but there is no appeal to tears. There is pathos in *The Forsaken Merman*, the story of a husband and children deserted ; but it too keeps the higher tone :—

> Call her once before you go—
> Call once yet !
> In a voice that she will know :
> "Margaret ! Margaret !"
> Children's voices should be dear
> (Call once more) to a mother's ear !
> Children's voices, wild with pain—
> Surely she will come again !
> Call her once and come away ;
> This way, this way !
> "Mother dear, we cannot stay !
> The wild white horses foam and fret !"
> Margaret ! Margaret !

> Come, dear children, come away down ;
> Call no more !
> One last look at the white-wall'd town,
> And the little grey church on the windy shore ;
> Then come down !
> She will not come though you call all day ;
> Come away, come away !

Instances might be multiplied, but probably enough has been said to explain what is meant. Whether or not Arnold lost anything by this restraint I am not concerned to argue here: the point is that he possessed the quality, and that by reason of it he struck perhaps fewer false notes than any of his contemporaries. He has occasionally weak lines and unpleasing expressions, but they are of the nature rather of failures in execution than of defect in taste. For example, it is to be regretted that the beautiful *Westminster Abbey* is disfigured by the ugly word "cecity," introduced for the sake of the rhyme (and that a bad one); but no one supposes that Arnold's *taste* was at fault here : it is rather his command of language that on rare occasions fails. This restraint is the principal element in his style, and all the other elements are related to it; his lucidity, for he would not write until he could express his thought as clearly as, from its nature, it was possible to express it; his sureness of diction, for his habit was to pause to find not merely a good word, but the best. "Haste, half-work, and disarray" in literature he loathed. The lesson his example taught was or might have been invaluable. The fact that it is still so much needed is one reason why Arnold has never been appreciated as he deserves to be.

In the case of Arnold it is right and necessary to think first of all of style. The lesson of a severe and chastened but most expressive style was the one with which we could least dispense. But it was far from being the only one he had to give. On the contrary, in the substance of his thought his was pre-eminently the voice of his age. This assertion may seem paradoxical in view of the facts that he never was popular, and that in many passages he speaks of his own isolation and of his opposition to the opinions of the world. But at the same time it was the problems of his own generation, as they presented themselves to it, that interested him. If his treatment of them, or his solution, so far as he offered a solution, had been a common one, he must have been a common man. His greatness is indicated by the fact that his treatment was distinctive and personal. Arnold's thoughts and Arnold's way of viewing things are to be found nowhere but in Arnold. In Browning the one absorbing interest is character, especially in its moral aspects; and with regard to character the note of time is of subordinate importance. In Tennyson the same liberation seems to be brought about by the predominance of the artist's sense of beauty; for in that too the note of time, though not absent, sinks to an undertone. But in Arnold reflection is always wedded to artistic expression. There are poems, of the highest excellence too, of which it is difficult if not impossible to say what the thought means. Coleridge's *Christabel* and *Ancient Mariner* are examples; and perhaps Browning's *Childe Roland* may be another; at least the attempts at an allegorical explanation are not convincing. But this is never the case with Arnold. It is always possible to detect his thought. His characteristic mode of utterance is that which we find in the elegiac poems; and in them, and in the sonnets and lyrics only less clearly, we see that he is always occupied with the doubts and difficulties and ambitions special to his own time, and its seeming triumphs which often prove to be failures. His dominant thought is the war of contending powers in modern life. He gives utterance to the thought repeatedly, he sees the war raging everywhere. Rachel is to him typical:—

> Sprung from the blood of Israel's scatter'd race,
> At a mean inn in German Aarau born,
> To forms from antique Greece and Rome uptorn,
> Tricked out with a Parisian speech and face,
> Imparting life renew'd, old classic grace;
> Then, soothing with thy Christian strain forlorn,
> A-Kempis! her departing soul outworn,
> While by her bedside Hebrew rites have place—
> Ah, not the radiant spirit of Greece alone
> She had—one power, which made her breast its home!
> In her, like us, there clash'd, contending powers,
> Germany, France, Christ, Moses, Athens, Rome.
> The strife, the mixture in her soul, are ours;
> Her genius and her glory are her own.

No one else has expressed this sense of conflict, of the unexampled complexity of modern life, as finely as he.

The fact or view upon which Arnold works is always seen with the eye of an intellect exceedingly clear and penetrating;

but it is also seen as suffused with the "moist light" of a poetic and sensitive soul. In prose Arnold tried, as he was bound to do, to keep the light dry; in poetry he well knew that emotion was essential. Not only has his thought reference always to the present time, but it is also emphatically his own. The voice which he added to poetry was his natural voice undisguised. It is possible to get at the real Browning beneath the dramatic disguise, and at the real Tennyson beneath the semi-impersonality of the artist who is first of all an observer; but in Arnold the man himself is on the surface of his work, there is no disguise to penetrate. His self-revelation is indeed very different from that of Byron; it is quite free from the defiant and boastful and occasionally vulgar tone of the latter; and it is also free from personal detail about the *facts* of life. Arnold confines himself to the *thoughts* which life suggests. Yet in this way his self-revelation is complete. He did not succeed in portraying other characters, but he left his own clearly stamped upon his verse. He is specially valuable because his poems are *his* thoughts about *his* time.

Perhaps the time of Arnold's birth helped to make him the special exponent of the thought of the middle of the century. The early attraction of Tennyson to Byron showed that he at any rate had come under the sway of earlier forces as Arnold never did. It is true, Arnold all through life admired Byron; but he was never led away to imitate him. Browning from the first showed by his vast schemes, as revealed in *Pauline* and *Paracelsus*, and by his absorption in the study of character, that he must overleap the limits of the age. Arnold stood in years just far enough away from the forces which had their birth in the Revolution, and which he saw working themselves out, to be an observer interested in but not dominated by them. It was his fortune to belong to that English University which had the greatest share in shaping the thoughts of the generation then rising, and to be connected by blood and friendship with men who played a great part in so shaping them. And he brought with him just the disposition necessary to observe and to note the working of those forces and thoughts. Critic always, Arnold is never more a critic than in his verse. I do not refer merely to verses such as the *Epilogue to Lessing's Laocoön*, in which he gives utterance to literary criticism without losing the accent of exquisite poetry. There are more such pieces in Arnold than perhaps in any other poet; and he has more skilfully than any other combined the critical with the poetic spirit. But that spirit is far more widely spread through his poetry; it is indeed everywhere. Not without reason did he define poetry as "the criticism of life". This, with the added proviso that it was particularly life in his own century that he criticised, was specially Arnold's work. Not unnaturally too he held that the thing which Europe in his day most desired was criticism. There was great truth in the view; and if there was also some exaggeration it was the natural exaggeration of the man who unconsciously exalts that which he has to give.

CHAPTER VII.

TENNYSON AND BROWNING: THE CLOSING PERIOD.

We have traced Browning and Tennyson, in the one case to the publication of *The Ring and the Book*, in the other to the verge of the period of the dramas. The most interesting phase of Tennyson's further development is associated with the dramas and will be dealt with subsequently; his other poems may be treated with comparative brevity. At the same time, it is important to notice carefully their principal characteristics, because on the whole less justice has been done to the work of this period than to Tennyson's earlier poetry. Individual poems, like *Rizpah*, have been highly and deservedly praised; but the general excellence, and in particular the strength and thoughtfulness, of the miscellaneous poetry of the last twenty years of Tennyson's life has not been duly recognised. He was fortunate far beyond either of his great contemporaries in the general appreciation of his genius in early and middle life; and his fame secured him against anything approaching neglect in his old age. But it did not secure him against a false placing of his later in relation to his earlier work.

The trend of change which we have already detected in Tennyson continues down through his latest period. The object of his pursuit is still reality, not realism, and strength. In this development, which in the middle period brought gain almost unmixed, there is in later years a mingling of gain and loss. There is gain in the matter expressed by the verse, there is loss in the flow and melody and grace of style and versification. There is gain; for we find no longer that sinking to the verge of sentimentalism which is occasionally the fault of the earlier poetry. There is loss, as any one will feel who compares *Sir John Oldcastle* with the blank-verse of the *Idylls*. The style is broken and rough, almost harsh. But it should be noticed that in very great measure it is intentionally so. It was the choice of subject and the dramatic treatment that occasioned it. Frequently we find in these later poems that what at first seems harsh, in the end pleases the ear more than the smoothness of the earlier verse. Few, probably, for the first time read *Locksley Hall Sixty Years After* without being struck with what seems like a deterioration of style as compared with the earlier *Locksley Hall;* and yet can it be seriously doubted which is the better poem, in style as well as in matter? Tennyson has struck a harder vein of thought, and it gives at first a harder ring to the verse; but both verse and thought are true. Again, in *The Charge of the Heavy Brigade* we have only to notice with what consummate skill the verse echoes, as it were, the labouring uphill gallop of the heavy horse, to be convinced that Tennyson retained all his old skill. There are few of his earlier lyrics more beautiful and polished than *The Throstle* and *Crossing the Bar* in *Demeter*, perhaps there is none he ever wrote more deserving of praise for charm of verse and language than the exquisite song, " To sleep, to sleep," in *The Foresters*. He could therefore produce the old effects when he chose. If he did not choose as frequently as of old it was because he had now other interests. If we feel the sense of loss, as we must, we should set against it the compensating gain. The dramatic conceptions in which Tennyson now delighted expelled at times from his verse its old flow and smoothness ; they introduced instead a force it had not always possessed.

These dramatic conceptions are by no means confined to the dramas. Next to the plays themselves, the most striking characteristic of the later work is the presence of a number of pieces which though not plays are full of the dramatic spirit. It was not a new departure on the part of Tennyson. He called *Maud* " a monodrama " ; and he had already written *The Grandmother* and *The Northern Farmer*, the latter a piece which in its own class he never equalled. But never before had pieces of this kind such prominence. *The Northern Cobbler, Rizpah, The First Quarrel, Sir John Oldcastle, Columbus, Locksley Hall Sixty Years After, Owd Roä* and *Despair* are examples which by no means exhaust the class. There is a dramatic spirit also in some of the most remarkable of the ballads, such as *The Revenge* and *The Defence of Lucknow*. In short, with few exceptions the poems generally selected from the productions of those years as most admirable, are marked by this dramatic spirit, and help to show that it was not from caprice but by an inevitable process of development that Tennyson turned to the writing of plays.

Tennyson had from his earliest period been accustomed to put verse in the mouths of imaginary characters; but his treatment was idyllic, not dramatic. Take for example *Œnone* :—

> O mother Ida, harken ere I die.
> Far-off the torrent called me from the cleft:
> Far up the solitary morning smote
> The streaks of virgin snow. With down-dropt eyes
> I sat alone: white-breasted like a star
> Fronting the dawn he moved; a leopard skin
> Droop'd from his shoulder, but his sunny hair
> Cluster'd about his temples like a God's:
> And his cheek brighten'd as the foam-bow brightens
> When the wind blows the foam, and all my heart
> Went forth to embrace him coming ere he came.

This is fine, but not dramatic. The writer has time for much besides portraiture; indeed, neither in this passage nor elsewhere in the poem can he be said to trouble himself with portraiture at all. Compare with this *Sir John Oldcastle* :—

> Eh! how I anger'd Arundel asking me
> To worship Holy Cross! I spread mine arms,
> God's work, I said, a cross of flesh and blood
> And holier. That was heresy. (My good friend
> By this time should be with me.) "Images?"
> "Bury them as God's truer images
> Are daily buried." "Heresy.—Penance?" "Fast,
> Hairshirt and scourge—nay, let a man repent,
> Do penance in his heart, God hears him." "Heresy—
> Not shriven, not saved?" "What profits an ill Priest
> Between me and my God? I would not spurn
> Good counsel of good friends, but shrive myself
> No, not to an Apostle."

The mode of conception here is quite different. The poet's object is no longer first of all to make beautiful verse. It is to think the man's thoughts in the man's own way; the beauty must shine through the character. Hence, as I have said, the harsher and more broken versification. Not that the dramatic conception always involved this sacrifice. There are lines in *Columbus* and in *Becket* which show that Tennyson could still wield blank verse with all the melody of the *Idylls*, and with the dignity of their finest passages. The following passage is from *Columbus* :—

> Chains for the Admiral of the Ocean! chains
> For him who gave a new heaven, a new earth,
> As holy John had prophesied of me,
> Gave glory and more empire to the kings
> Of Spain than all their battles! chains for him
> Who pushed his prows into the setting sun,
> And made West East, and sail'd the Dragon's mouth
> And came upon the Mountains of the World,
> And saw the rivers roll from Paradise!

In many of the other pieces the dramatic nature of the conception is still more conspicuous, and the success of the poet is greater. The frequent use of dialect, which seems to be another outcome of Tennyson's development, indicates the dramatic spirit. The eighteenth century scorned dialect for serious poetry. Burns showed its power; and in the present century many writers in various dialects have followed in his steps. Sometimes the use of a provincial form of speech is little better than a caprice, and many poems have been written in such forms merely to gain the factitious kind of interest which attaches to anything out of the common. In Burns's hands, it need hardly be said, the use of dialect was absolutely sincere. So was it in Tennyson's, for a different reason. Burns wrote dialect first and chiefly because he knew nothing else equally well; Tennyson wrote it because the subjects demanded its use. His *Northern Farmer* and *Northern Cobbler* could not be translated into literary English. They are studies of human nature, not in gloves and spotless linen, but smocked and hornyhanded, and their language has to be made to suit. The strength and raciness of Tennyson's lines proves the success of his study. His cobbler who put a quart of gin in his window in preference to a pint, because he "liked a bigger fellow to fight wi' an' fowt it out," is a living man ; and there is an even stronger pulse of life in the Northern Farmer, who supports the squire and listens regularly (at least while his wife lives) to the parson on Sundays :—

> An' I hallus coom'd to 's choorch afoor moy Sally wur deäd,
> An' 'eärd 'um a bummin' awaäy loike a buzzard-clock ower my 'eäd,
> An' I niver knaw'd whot a meän'd but I thowt a 'ad summat to saäy,
> An' I thowt a said whot a owt to 'a said an' I coom'd awaäy.

Not the least surprising feature of Tennyson's later poetry is its revelation of this fund of humour, a quality of which earlier he seemed so destitute. There is no quality which more proclaims the man. It has been prominent in nearly all the poets who have been conspicuous for their interest in things mundane. It was fitting and almost necessary that Tennyson should develop humour; for without it there can be no safety in handling human character. The absence of it indicates a certain want of sympathy, and want of sympathy is fatal to the dramatic artist. Now, it is remarkable that the majority of the figures Tennyson drew from humble rural life are humorous conceptions. The farmer who thought the Creator was making a mistake in taking him, " wi' aäf the cows to cauve an' Thurnaby hoälms to plow," may not have been a humorous man himself, but the artist who painted him certainly was. He proves himself so too with his spinster and her views of children :—

> Mashin' their toys to pieäces an' maäkin' ma deäf wi' their shouts,
> An' hallus a joompin' about ma as if they was set upo' springs,
> An' a haxin' ma hawkard questions, an' saäyin ondecent things
>
> (*The Spinster's Sweet-Arts*, vi., p. 275).

There is humour too in the church-warden, with his shrewd advice to the curate :—

> If iver tha meäns to git 'igher,
> Tha mun tackle the sins o' the Wo'ld, an' not the faults o' the Squire,

and his fears that the Baptists who washed their sins in his pond had poisoned his cow in doing so. In all this Tennyson is genuinely humorous, because he is genuinely sympathetic and fully enters into the life he is painting.

Along with this growth towards the drama, which was by far the most important change in Tennyson's later years, we observe, not indeed a similar growth, but at least a continuance in full vigour of all the more human interests of his earlier poetry. His patriotism was from the first a distinctive feature of his poetry. *The Revenge, The Charge of the Heavy Brigade*, and *The Defence of Lucknow* prove that the passion was as vigorous as ever. Some lines in other poems show that it was a little less hopeful. He was not sure of the outcome of modern democracy:
"Babble, babble, our old England may go down in babble at last ". But along with the similarity in spirit between these poems and the earlier patriotic poems there runs an instructive difference.

In his first period the poet's favourite mode of conception is abstract. He sees Freedom seated on the heights, and enjoins love of country for reasons drawn from the general course of her history. After the turn of the century he prefers to associate his patriotism with a great life, as in the *Ode on Wellington*, or with a political situation, as in *The Third of February, 1852*, or with some stirring event, as in *The Charge of the Light Brigade*. In the last period he keeps true to this more concrete mode of conception; indeed the poems of this period are even more concrete than those of the one before it. They are not better than the *Ode on Wellington*, nor as good; but they show more devotion to fact. The poem on the Heavy Brigade is far more historical than its predecessor on the Light Brigade. One of the great merits of the former is its minute and accurate embodiment of facts; while the latter, though not inaccurate, is vague.

In the same way, Tennyson's continued interest in questions of religion and in all the deeper social problems is manifested in these poems. Probably *Locksley Hall Sixty Years After* is in this respect the most comprehensive poem he ever wrote. It is an old man's review of nearly all that he has found to interest him in life. He touches upon patriotism and on the state of politics. He reviews the hopes of his youth in the light of his mature experience, and finds many of them hollow. He examines the boast of progress, and finds little to justify it. Though the form is dramatic it is impossible to doubt that the heart of Tennyson is in most of these poems; and even in cases like *Despair*, where the voice is not at all his voice, it is easy to read between the lines his condemnation of both extremes.

"The wonderful flower-show," as Browning called it, of Tennyson's earlier verse, is thus in his closing years varied with the gnarly oaks of a greater thought. In Browning himself the character of the change was so far similar; but the point of departure was not the same, and in consequence the effect was different. In much of his later work Browning almost ceases to be artist, and becomes the philosopher writing verse. Its variety after *The Ring and the Book* is at first somewhat bewildering. The subjects are Greek, English, Italian, French, ancient and modern, serious and light. The manner and method are varied also; and it is in this variety that we detect the characteristic difference from the work of the preceding period. We have seen that the years between *Pauline* and *A Soul's Tragedy* may be fairly regarded as years in which the poet through a series of experiments, in narrative and in the regular drama, convinced himself what was the special form of poetry best adapted to his genius. From the latter date down to the completion of *The Ring and the Book* he faithfully adhered to that form. In the closing period, through his growing interest in problems directly philosophical rather than dramatic, he in great part openly and still more in spirit renounced his allegiance to it. What I call the open renunciation is illustrated in *La Saisiaz*, where the poet argues by logical methods the question of immortality; but there is equally a renunciation in the spirit illustrated by the *Parleyings*, where the method is no longer dramatic but openly critical. Both Browning and the world were losers by the change. He never found any other form of poetry in which he could so well express himself as in the dramatic monologue, and consequently he remains as a poet best represented by the works of his intermediate period.

Browning did not revert to the regular drama: his translations from Æschylus and Euripides, because they are translations, can hardly be considered a reversion on his part. On the contrary, he became less dramatic in his work than he had ever before been. At the same time, he did not altogether abandon the method which had succeeded so admirably in *Men and Women* and in *Dramatis Personæ*. In some of his works really and in more outwardly he adhered to it. In the *Dramatic Idyls* we look for something to compare with the *Dramatic Romances*. Many of the poems in *Jocoseria* and in the volume containing *Pacchiarotto* are of the same description. *Numpholeptos*, a wonderful poem whose full import is apt to be missed until it has been read many times over, though it contains less than usual of the circumstance of actual life, is true to Browning's earlier method. The meaning is hinted in the title. The speaker is "taken by a nymph," and the poem is the utterance of his passion, almost hopeless because subjected to an almost impossible condition. He is to "obtain experience of each tinge" of the broken lights of life, and to return to "the quintessential whiteness," "jewelled as with drops o' the urn the rainbow paints from". He returns instead spotted with the stains of experience and the world, until at length he is driven into a revolt only to end in submission and a renewed despairing quest.

Cristina and Monaldeschi is, as a specimen of a kind of work like that we find in the earlier poems, even better. The character of Cristina is dramatically conceived, and she is presented, in Browning's favourite way, at a fateful moment. Here love has changed to hate and is on the verge of a terrible revenge. *A Forgiveness* is an equally profound and impressive study, and in it too love passes through the stage of hate and leads to an act of vengeance. *Ixion*, with its beautiful conception of an eternal hope wrung out of an eternal torment, is likewise dramatic. So are *Martin Relph* and *Ned Bratts*; and though in these the poet's aim is lower than it is in the other pieces mentioned, he hits the mark as full as he ever did.

These pieces, taken from *Pacchiarotto*, *Dramatic Idyls* and *Jocoseria*, belong not to the beginning but to the middle portion of the period. They are selected as, though not nearest in time, yet on the whole nearest in spirit to the poetry of the time ending with *The Ring and the Book*. There are however other poems of this period kindred in spirit and method to Browning's earlier work. The translations from the Greek, as translations, stand by themselves. The fact that Browning did translate in his old age is singular and interesting, but it is not directly connected with the development now under discussion. In *Balaustion's Adventure* however there is a considerable portion of original work, and in *Aristophanes' Apology* the bulk of the original verse much exceeds that of the translation. The beautiful romance of Balaustion, which runs through both, may be classed along with his work of the second period; and in Balaustion herself he has depicted a character which must take a high rank among his conceptions of women. His Aristophanes is even more powerful if less charming. He discusses once more those questions of poetic art which had such an endless interest for Browning; and the poet, notwithstanding his love for Euripides, presents the case of comedy, through the lips of Aristophanes, in such a way as to impress the reader with the conviction that there is, not pure truth in it, but a strong infusion of truth. The form of the poem is not monologue, but dialogue, as it is in *Paracelsus* and is likewise in *The Inn Album*, published in the same year as the *Apology*. The fact that the dialogue is narrated by Balaustion makes practically little difference. But in neither the *Apology* nor *The Inn Album* is the dialogue of that broken and rapid character which Browning found it hard to manage.

These poems have much of the kind of merit shown to perfection in *The Ring and the Book;* and perhaps of the longer poems of this period none is so fully admirable as *The Inn Album*. It deserves the pre-eminence for the fine conception and masterly execution of all the characters. In Browning's gallery of female portraits the heroine is probably surpassed by Pompilia only; and the villain is in his own execrable way only less perfect.

Thus there are still in those later years several poems which breathe the spirit of Browning at his best. But the greater part of the work of this time is different. Even in those collections, like *Dramatic Idyls*, *Jocoseria*, and the volume containing *Pacchiarotto*, where we naturally expect to find the example of the earlier collections followed, there are many pieces which betray the change that was passing over the poet. *At the Mermaid*, *House* and *Shop* are openly critical. In the first Browning indeed speaks on behalf of Shakespeare; but it is impossible to say that there is any realisation of the character of Shakespeare, or even any attempt to realise it. He is not a *dramatis persona*, he merely, in his capacity of dramatist, pronounces an opinion as to the personal relation between himself and his work, or between himself and his audience. He declares that he stands apart from his plays.

> Which of you did I enable
> Once to slip inside my breast,
> There to catalogue and label
> What I like least, what love best,
> Hope and fear, believe and doubt of,
> Seek and shun, respect—deride?
> Who has right to make a rout of
> Rarities he found inside?

If Browning had wished to depict Shakespeare, it is not such a question as this he would have chosen. What the poem does is rather to proclaim our ignorance than to increase our knowledge. We learn that Shakespeare is not in his works; we do not learn where he is. The poem next to it, *House*, where the dramatic form is discarded, throws almost as much light upon the character. "With this same key, Shakespeare unlocked his heart," quotes Browning; and he retorts, "Did Shakespeare? If so, the less Shakespeare he." So too the *Epilogue* to the same volume differs from *At the Mermaid* only in the person who is supposed to speak. It is the utterance of Browning himself.

But it is critical in character, not a dramatic presentment of him; and so far as it is self-revealing, it is so indirectly.

But perhaps the difference between this period and the last is best seen in poems which approach the old form. One such is *Iván Ivánovitch*. The story is powerfully told and it leads up to a most impressive moral judgment. The whole poem was made for the sake of that judgment and of the act in which it was expressed, not for the sake of the miserable woman who died by it, nor for the ghastly tale itself. But the principal character practically appears only in that act; the rest is narrative subsidiary to it and the comments of others on what he has done. The same relative prominence of circumstances is seen in *Pheidippides*. The relations of Athens and Sparta and the great old struggle divide the interest with the man; and the facts are brought forward, not dramatically, but by narrative. So it is too with *Pietro of Abano*. Old Pietro is less an individual than a type. This, Browning wishes to teach, is the way in which the world treats men who dare to be too far in advance of their time. The personality of Pietro is subordinate. In true dramatic work, and in Browning's own best work, the character *is* the lesson, the personality is of primary importance. In the earlier poems each character paints himself, in words it is true rather than deeds, but still to the life. This is the case with all the great actors in *The Ring and the Book*, with the Bishop of St. Praxed's, with Bishop Blougram, with Sludge, with Andrea del Sarto and Fra Lippo Lippi, and with Cleon,— a varied multitude, but each admirable in his way.

We can trace the same kind of change even in *Clive*. It is an admirable piece, and perhaps no one but Browning ever imagined such a situation as that in Clive's mind after the firing of his own pistol. In comparing *Clive* with the best work of *Men and Women* or of *Dramatis Personæ* the question is not one of superiority or inferiority, but of difference. The method is different. There is, as in *Iván Ivánovitch*, more of narrative leading up to just the one point of interest, and a more intense concentration upon that point. It was always Browning's habit to concentrate upon a single situation; but as a rule he diffused the interest through the whole poem. The speaker is generally painting himself in every line, and one line is more or less equal in value to another. There is a turning-point in the lives of Pompilia and Caponsacchi; but the character of neither is concentrated all in that, it is gradually revealed in each case through the whole book devoted to it. But in the case of *Clive* the narrative leading up to the culminating point is relatively commonplace. It does something to reveal the man, but this something is insignificant in comparison with the blaze of light which shines from the duel. As the meaning of the threatening blackness is revealed by some sudden lightning-flash, so the fact that Clive's soul is not like other souls of men endowed with physical courage is revealed in the situation which his defencelessness opens before his mind, and in the course which to him seems the only possible one :—

> Suppose the man,
> Checking his advance, his weapon still extended, not a span
> Distant from my temple—curse him!—quietly had bade me "There!
> Keep your life calumniator!—worthless life I freely spare :
> Mine you freely would have taken—murdered me and my good fame
> Both at once—and all the better! Go, and thank your own bad aim
> Which permits me to forgive you!" What if, with such words as these,
> He had cast away his weapon? How should I have borne me, please?
> Nay, I'll spare your pains and tell you. This, and only this, remained—
> Pick his weapon up and use it on myself. I so had gained
> Sleep the earlier, leaving England probably to pay on still
> Rent and taxes for half India, tenant at the Frenchman's will.

This is in Browning's earlier style; but it is the moment to which all the rest leads up; and in the path he follows to it we see the symptom of change.

It is still more evident in the later collections of short poems, *Ferishtah's Fancies*, *Parleyings with certain People of Importance*, and *Asolando*. For the most part, they hardly even pretend to be dramatic. *Ferishtah's Fancies* is in effect a series of lessons which are really Browning's own, though they are inculcated through the dervish Ferishtah. *A Bean Stripe* treats of the mingling of good and evil in human life. They are so related that no life is either wholly black or wholly white. *A Pillar at Sebzevar* deals with his favourite problem of the relation of love and knowledge in life, with that tendency to exalt the former at the expense of the latter, which is visible in his poetry from the first, exaggerated to a dogmatic decision. *Two Camels* is a parable meant to inculcate the rights of the body as against the exaggerations of asceticism. One camel, unduly abstemious, on the eve of a journey sups on mouldy bran instead of the liberal meal provided, and in consequence breaks down midway; the other eats the meal and so obtains strength to struggle through to the end.

> Do thy day's work, dare
> Refuse no help thereto, since help refused
> Is hindrance sought and found,

is the teaching. *Mihrab Shah* puts Browning's familiar view of pain on a new footing, representing it as the great instrument to awaken sympathy. Mihrab Shah is evidently Browning himself; and instead of a dramatic conception we have what is in essence a philosophical problem threshed out.

The method of the *Parleyings* is highly significant. Here Browning stands apart and comments on and criticises the men whose names furnish the titles to the poems. Thus *George Bubb Dodington* is a piece of pure criticism of life. It is criticism suggested indeed by the particular life of Bubb Dodington, but it is not a dramatic presentment of the man. Still less is *Bernard de Mandeville*. The poetic disguise is very thin and the artistic value slight. It is purely a piece of reasoning, and the subject is the optimism of Browning himself *versus* the pessimism of Carlyle. Perhaps the most instructive poem of all, as regards the change which had come over Browning, is the epilogue of *Fust and his Friends*. It is in dramatic form, but in spite of that the stress falls not on the *character* of Fust but on his *work*, and the piece embodies views of that work.

If we look to some of the longer poems we see equally clear evidence of the change. *Red Cotton Nightcap Country*, which came near the beginning of the period (1873), has some kinship with the earlier work; but there is also a noticeable difference. It is a study of the development of certain souls with the poet's comments interspersed. Browning, it is true, always commented on occasion, as for example in *The Statue and the Bust*, where he states in his own person the moral that for the purpose of a test a crime will serve as well "as a virtue golden through and through". But in earlier years he did this sparingly. Now, to use his own contemptuous words, he takes his stand, "motley on back and pointing pole in hand," beside his characters. He adopts voluntarily the very method which in *Sordello* he describes as forced upon him by an unappreciative audience. At every critical point he is ready to tell us what we ought to think, what is the inner meaning of the events narrated and their psychological value. The summing-up of the characters at the end is in keeping with the whole. The actual events on which the poem is founded led to a trial; and Browning takes the seat of the judge, pronounces his judgment and gives the reasons for it:—

> Clara, I hold the happier specimen—
> It may be, through that artist-preference
> For work complete, inferiorly purposed,
> To incompletion, though it aim aright.
> Morally, no! Aspire, break bounds! I say,
> Endeavour to be good, and better still,
> And best! Success is nought, endeavour's all.
> But intellect adjusts the means to ends,
> Tries the low thing, and leaves it done, at least;
> No prejudice to high thing, intellect
> Would do, and will do, only give the means.
> Miranda, in my picture-gallery,
> Presents a Blake; be Clara—Meissonier!
> Merely considered so by artist, mind!
> For, break through Art and rise to poetry,
> Being Art to tremble nearer, touch enough
> The verge of vastness to inform our soul
> What orb makes transit through the dark above,
> And there's the triumph!—there the incomplete,
> More than completion, matches the immense,—
> Then, Michelagnolo against the world! (xii., pp. 167-168).

Contrast this with *The Inn Album*, published two years later. There we have a thread of narrative, but only a thread, connecting the dramatic situations, and comment there is none. The curtain falls before the effect of the last tragic scene is disclosed: it is left to the imagination of the reader. And each character has spoken for and interpreted itself.

Here are two methods, the one fully dramatic, the other partially so. In the one Browning is stage-manager: he brings the characters on, but leaves them to make their own impression. In the other he is still that, but he is at the same time the man in the pit: he adds to the character *his* interpretation of it. We are passing from the creative to the critical point of view. In spite of exceptional works like *The Inn Album*, it is the latter that is specially characteristic of the closing period; and *Red Cotton Nightcap Country* stands at the parting of the ways;

while other works of the period, like *La Saisiaz, Ferishtah's Fancies* and the *Parleyings*, have quite left the old track.

Prince Hohenstiel-Schwangau stands likewise at the parting of the ways; but notwithstanding the dramatic form the bias towards the new path is stronger. It is well known that the poem was suggested by the character and history of Napoleon III., and the speaker is supposed to be the Emperor himself, in exile again, an exile combining the companionships and the outward circumstances of his early life as an adventurer, with the memories proper to the time subsequent to his overthrow by Germany. But who can accept the Prince as a true counterpart of the Emperor of the French? Browning takes a point of view, symbolised by the act of the Prince in drawing a line between two blots. He is the man who cannot make what is absolutely new, who will not "mar what is already well enough," but whose function is to "turn to best account the thing that's half-made". Is this either Louis Napoleon as known to his Maker, or Louis Napoleon as he would have pleaded in defence of himself after his overthrow? It ought to be one or other, the former if the dramatic conception were of the highest class, the latter at least if it were of the second rank. It is very doubtful if it is either.

But further, the scene beheld from this point of view is very largely what would have been visible to the eyes of Browning. The poem is rich in thought, but all through the first quarter or so, and here and there through the rest, we are conscious that it is the thought of Browning himself. In other words, the poem is not in reality a dramatic representation at all. For instance, is the admirably satirical passage on the bard belittling man and magnifying the ocean, appropriate to Napoleon or to Browning?—

> How did the foolish ever pass for wise
> By calling life a burden, man a fly
> Or worm or what's most insignificant?
> "O littleness of man!" deplores the bard;
> And then, for fear the Powers should punish him,
> "O grandeur of the visible universe
> Our human littleness contrasts withal!
> O sun, O moon, ye mountains and thou sea,
> Thou emblem of immensity, thou this,
> That, and the other,—what impertinence
> In man to eat and drink and walk about

>   And have his little notions of his own,
>   The while some wave sheds foam upon the shore!"
>   First of all, 'tis a lie some three times thick:
>   The bard,—this sort of speech being poetry,—
>   The bard puts mankind well outside himself
>   And then begins instructing them : " This way
>   I and my friend the sea conceive of you!
>   What would you give to think such thoughts as ours
>   Of you and the sea together?" Down they go
>   On the humbled knees of them : at once they draw
>   Distinction, recognise no mate of theirs
>   In one, despite his mock humility,
>   So plain a match for what he plays with. Next,
>   The turn of the great ocean-playfellow,
>   When the bard, leaving Bond Street very far
>   From ear-shot, cares not to ventriloquize,
>   But tells the sea its home-truths : " You, my match?
>   You, all this terror and immensity
>   And what not? Shall I tell you what you are?
>   Just fit to hitch into a stanza, so
>   Wake up and set in motion who's asleep
>   O' the other side of you in England, else
>   Unaware, as folk pace their Bond Street now,
>   Somebody here despises them so much!
>   Between us,—they are the ultimate! to them
>   And their perception go these lordly thoughts :
>   Since what were ocean—mane and tail, to boot—
>   Mused I not here, how make thoughts thinkable?
>   Start forth my stanza and astound the world!
>   Back, billows, to your insignificance!
>   Deep, you are done with!" (xi., pp. 145-147).

It is not too much to say that in the whole of this long passage there is not a thought or a word appropriate to the character of Napoleon. Neither is it Napoleon, but Browning, who a little farther on speaks in the language of evolution. Napoleon is in fact forgotten by the poet. There is, it is true, something similar to this in the earlier poems. As I have said elsewhere, there is hardly a character created by Browning in which it is not possible to detect the accent of Browning. But in the earlier poems what we find is rather a different person who agrees with Browning on certain fundamental points and in his manner of expressing them. Paracelsus does so, and Caponsacchi, and even Pompilia. But we never lose in them the impression of a personality vitally different from his. In the case of Prince Hohenstiel-Schwangau it is otherwise. We observe in the first place that what may be called the Browning portion of him has grown very much; it is more than an accent, it is almost the whole speech. But further, it is even more important to notice that the interest awakened is only in a subordinate degree interest in a character. In Caponsacchi it is not the opinions in themselves that captivate; it is the spectacle of a fine nature in the balance between good and evil, and determined in a moment by a great opportunity which might also have been a great temptation; it is the fiery ardour bursting through the "sudden smoke from hell". In Pompilia it is beautiful pure simplicity made great through tribulation. Even in Paracelsus, though he is less dramatic than these, the issue of the pursuit of truth is vitally related to the character of the man who pursues it. A narrower nature might not have felt the failure. George Eliot's Casaubon would not have felt it,— supposing he could have conceived the aim. Because Paracelsus was greater than his aim as well as less, he was led beyond it. It is otherwise with Prince Hohenstiel-Schwangau. Not the man but the views are interesting, not the dramatic situation, but the "criticism of life". Compare Arnold's *Empedocles*. There too, in still larger measure than in Browning's poem, the thoughts are the writer's thoughts, and the interest in Empedocles *as a man* is of the slenderest kind. The fact that the comparison is possible goes to show that Browning was either losing, or for some reason did not choose to exercise, his dramatic faculty.

This impression is strengthened by *Fifine at the Fair*, in some ways among the most characteristic of Browning's poems. It is at once psychological and ethical, and he loved to be both, and was habitually both in the works of the second period. It has been generally, and with good reason, regarded as one of the most puzzling of his works. The difficulty is partly inevitable. Much of Browning's profoundest thought is to be found in *Fifine*, and profound thought is by its nature difficult. . But the difficulty is greatly increased by representing this as the thought of a Don Juan, and mingling truth with sophistry in almost inextricable entanglement.

The poem is a story of a husband and wife who, strolling through a fair, see a gipsy, Fifine, beautiful but destitute of character. The husband's admiration rouses the anger of the wife. He defends himself, admitting the moral inferiority of Fifine to Elvire, yet insisting that every creature has its supreme worth. He therefore who knows and reverences what is higher may nevertheless turn to the lower with admiration for that in it wherein it is supreme. The fact that what he does turn to is a woman, not a man, is explained on the ground that "man turns upon himself. Women rush into you, there remain absorbed." But further, the husband insists that what is commonly called inconstancy is really inseparable from spiritual growth. Everything changes; all forms of art and thought, and even morality, must adapt themselves to the time. Changelessness means stagnation. It is true he ends with the declaration,

> Inconstancy means raw, 't is faith alone means ripe
> I' the soul which runs its round (xi., p. 337);

but he proves his insincerity immediately by carrying inconstancy into act. In revenge the wife deserts him.

The poem then is an argmentative justification of inconstancy leading to the commission of an immoral act, which may be regarded as the poet's warning that the arguments are not to be accepted without careful scrutiny. Why then should Browning be blamed, seeing that he puts the arguments in the mouth of an imaginary person, and makes them lead to an indefensible result? It is said that Thackeray, when censured for the marriage of Esmond and Lady Castlewood as an offence against taste, replied, "I did not do it,—they did it". Is the artist's defence not good for Browning also? For answer we must turn to the other side and see how much of Browning's self enters into the piece.

It speedily becomes evident that a great deal of Browning does enter into it. The fundamental conception, the passing of contraries into one another, is his, and runs through all his work.

> I want, put down in black and white,
> What compensating joy, unknown and infinite,
> Turns lawlessness to law, makes destitution—wealth,
> Vice—virtue, and disease of soul and body—health? (xi., p. 228).

This problem, which the Don Juan of the piece sets out to solve, is Browning's own. It is illustrated in numerous passages elsewhere in his works, and it reappears several times in this very poem in forms indisputably his too. The author of *Rabbi Ben Ezra* and of *Rephan* is evident in this :—

> Are we not here to learn the good of peace through strife,
> Of love through hate, and reach knowledge by ignorance?
>
> (xi., p. 312.)

The same thought is only more fully developed in the fine image of the swimmer :—

> I liken to this play o' the body—fruitless strife
> To slip the sea and hold the heaven,—my spirit's life
> 'Twixt false, whence it would break, and true, where it would bide.
> I move in, yet resist, am upborne every side
> By what I beat against, an element too gross
> To live in, did not soul duly obtain her dose
> Of life-breath, and inhale from truth's pure plenitude
> Above her, snatch and gain enough to just illude
> With hope that some brave bound may baffle evermore
> The obstructing medium, make who swam henceforward soar :
> —Gain scarcely snatched when, foiled by the very effort, sowse,
> Underneath ducks the soul, her truthward yearnings dowse
> Deeper in falsehood! ay, but fitted less and less
> To bear in nose and mouth old briny bitterness
> Proved alien more and more : since each experience proves
> Air—the essential good, not sea, wherein who moves
> Must thence, in the act, escape, apart from will or wish.
> Move a mere hand to take water-weed, jelly-fish,
> Upward you tend! and yet our business with the sea
> Is not with air, but just o' the water, watery :
> We must endure the false, no particle of which
> Do we acquaint us with, but up we mount a pitch
> Above it, find our head reach truth, while hands explore
> The false below (xi., pp. 274-275).

This is Browning's philosophy. Again, we recognise a characteristic and recurrent thought in the idea that there is nothing, however insignificant in appearance, but has "its supreme worth".

> Where is the single grain of sand, 'mid millions heaped
> Confusedly on the beach, but, did we know, has leaped
> Or will leap, would we wait, i' the century, some once,
> To the very throne of things ?—earth's brightest for the nonce,
> When sunshine shall impinge on just that grain's facette
> Which fronts him fullest, first, returns his ray with jet
> Of promptest praise, thanks God best in creation's name!
>
> (xi., pp. 239-240.)

So too it is impossible to doubt that the theory of art in *Fifine at the Fair* is Browning's own,—as it has been in essence the theory of others besides him. The artist, by some "chemic secret" evolves beauty. What he sees, though a reality, is a product of his own imagination, as distinct from that to which it is attributed as flame is from fuel. And Browning himself is once more apparent in the contrast between man and woman; man, typified in the bubble-fish which, though nine parts water, shows when stranded and drained that there is a tenth part, skin, alien in nature from the water. It has taken all, but refused to be absorbed in that to which it is indebted. Woman is the rill which hurries down to lose itself in the sea. Or again, as he most strikingly expresses it:—

> To obtain the strong true product of a man,
> Set him to hate a little! Leave cherishing his root,
> And rather prune his branch, nip off the pettiest shoot
> Superfluous on his bough! I promise, you shall learn
> By what grace came the goat, of all beasts else, to earn
> Such favour with the god o' the grape: 't was only he
> Who, browsing on its tops, first stung fertility
> Into the stock's heart, stayed much growth of tendril-twine,
> Some faintish flower, perhaps, but gained the indignant wine,
> Wrath of the red press! (xi., p. 289.)

Thus any trespass on it makes the personality of the man all the more intense, presses from it "the indignant wine": woman on the contrary "takes nothing and gives all".

I have illustrated this point at some length in order to show that the argument of *Fifine at the Fair* is, not in a mere turn of phrase or casual expression of opinion, but vitally and almost everywhere Browning's own. The Don Juan of the piece is a mere shadow. The interpretations of his character put forward by critics are mainly their own creation; in the poem itself he hardly impresses us as a character at all. He is rather a mouthpiece of arguments. Further, in so far as Browning's Don Juan is really a man, he is misleading. His indeed is the guilt, and his the sophistry which turns truth into falsehood by unwarranted applications; but the backbone of the argument and the general view of the world are not his. The principal character is Don Juan with the soul of Browning; and the mixture is artistically indefensible. There is an instructive triplet of drawings by Thackeray labelled respectively Ludovicus, Rex, and Ludovicus Rex. The first represents a puny, starved, shrivelled, miserable little naked mortal; the second, "the trappings and the suits" of royalty without the man inside; and the third is a picture of the starveling transformed into a Jove by the help of high heels, imposing wig and flowing mantle. Browning in *Fifine at the Fair* has gone to work just the other way about. The naked soul, his own, seen in the fundamental arguments, is magnificent; but it is clothed upon with a garment of flesh altogether belittling.

In *La Saisiaz* we see the characteristics of the closing period fully developed. It is frankly non-dramatic, and professes to be nothing but what it is, a discussion of the question of immortality, subtle, resourceful and suggestive; but the poem throughout is almost as much a discussion of a philosophical question in the philosophical manner as is Kant's *Critique of Pure Reason*. In that respect it is better than what may be called the intermediate poems. We know what we have to expect; we are free from the confusions arising from an incongruous blending of methods. As Browning had gone so far we may welcome the last step; but we must regret that he had gone so far.

We have found the change which had been gradually passing over Browning to mean, negatively, that he was becoming less dramatic. Positively, it means that the dramatic was being replaced by a philosophic element. There is reason to believe that if he had cast off the dramatic form at an earlier time it would have been in favour of the apocalyptic vision such as we find in *Christmas Eve and Easter Day*. The interest would have shifted from character as such to truth seen under a highly emotional exaltation. But in his later works Browning stands out clearly as the poet turned philosopher. He is largely so in *Prince Hohenstiel-Schwangau* and *Red Cotton Nightcap Country*, to a still larger extent in *Fifine at the Fair*, almost wholly in *Ferishtah's Fancies* and the *Parleyings*, and altogether in *La Saisiaz*. That the philosophic element was present in him from the first is plain; but for long it was only an element. He insisted frequently that it was the artist's business to teach truth by symbols. But in his later years he lost the balance of his youth and his maturity. He forgot that the artist's attack upon " the forts of folly " must be a covert one, by mining and zig-zag trenches, and marched straight against the walls with drums beating and colours flying, protecting his advance by a fire of syllogisms. Such an attack must be met by a similar defence, and both attack and defence lie outside the sphere of art. It is no longer a question of detecting a hidden connexion between poetry and philosophy; the connexion is avowed and passes almost into identity.

There is nevertheless, as has been partly seen already, much that is exceedingly fine in the works of this last period. The poet retains to the end all his old reach of thought, and writes at times with all the old fire. Few of his poems can be placed above *The Inn Album*, and, notwithstanding the fundamental incongruity, few better repay study than *Fifine at the Fair*. But when we ask the question what was gained and lost in the course of his development through this period, the answer must be that the losses far outweigh the gains. From the point of view of the student, the later poems have the great advantage that they frequently give the means of settling questions as to Browning's personal opinions which the dramatic form of the earlier poems must have left doubtful. But the want of proportion between the thought and its artistic dress—in respect of which he was at all periods too often faulty—and the absence of the charm of character, are losses which there is nothing to counterbalance.

CHAPTER VIII.

THE DRAMAS.

I HAVE reserved from the general chronological investigation of the poems the subject of the dramas. It is a wide one, it opens important questions with regard to the development of literature, and though the dramatic period of Tennyson is far removed in time from that of Browning, it seems on the whole best to view them together.

It has been said that the nineteenth century has produced no great dramatist. Nearly all the more memorable poets, Byron, Shelley, Browning, Tennyson, Arnold, Swinburne, have attempted dramatic composition; and in their dramas they have embodied great poetry. Yet it remains a matter of dispute whether the whole century has enriched the English language with a single play great in the sense in which scores of the Elizabethan plays are great. There is doubtless exaggeration in the unqualified censure sometimes passed upon the nineteenth century drama; yet the censure is not without foundation. For some obscure reason a fate seems to hang over the modern play-wright: either his plays will not act or they are not great poetry. Good they may be, great they very seldom are. More than one of the poets have bowed to this fate, and by their choice of the Greek model have, as it were, proclaimed that they did not intend their plays to be acted. Yet a dramatic piece which is not to be acted is in a sense a play that is no play. Others, and among them Browning and Tennyson, have written plays with the purpose that they should be acted; but they have rarely risen in them to the level of their best work. How does it come that in the Elizabethan age nearly everybody who could write at all could write dramas, while in the present century the highest powers accompanied by the best will do not ensure success?

With regard to two of the three poets under consideration it might with reason be contended that the inability springs not from the age but from the individual. Their endowments, it might be argued, were not dramatic, and had they lived in an age of dramatists they would have stood out as exceptions, as Spenser did among the Elizabethans.

Clearly, in the case of Arnold the personal explanation is sufficient. His own action may be interpreted as a tacit and perhaps unconscious admission of the absence of the dramatic faculty. We may detect such an admission, not merely in his choice of the Greek model, but in the fact that neither of his dramatic experiments permanently pleased him. Not only was *Empedocles* withdrawn before fifty copies were sold, but *Merope*, first published in 1858, was absent from the collected editions of Arnold's poems till 1885. His hesitation in admitting these dramas to a place among his works is instructive; and if we view the two pieces purely as dramas we must pronounce it to be justified. There is some fine poetry in *Merope*, and a great deal in *Empedocles*, but in neither of them is the merit of a dramatic nature. They are not even dramas for the study, they are poems which have been somewhat arbitrarily thrown into the dramatic form. No character stands out vividly, the long-past age in which the action is laid does not live again. Neither *Merope* nor *Empedocles on Etna* restores the Greek drama as Swinburne's *Atalanta in Calydon* does. The attitude and the arguments of Merope are modern rather than Greek, a fine expression of an essentially Christian rather than pagan shrinking from vengeance and bloodshed. Womanhood, and the fears of a mother, will partly explain it, but not entirely. It is not so that the women of Æschylus and Sophocles speak and think.

Even more obviously modern in spirit is *Empedocles*. The problems which fill the mind of Empedocles are in a sense as old as civilisation, but the form they take in Arnold's drama is modern. The sphere of thought is that within which Arnold always moved, that of the *Obermann* poems, of *Thyrsis*, and of all that is most personal in his work. This is just another manner of saying that in *Empedocles on Etna* there is no realisation of character at all. Empedocles *is* Arnold, his thoughts are Arnold's thoughts, his words Arnold's words. His view of the position of man in the world could only have been taken after the rise of Christianity, and further, after the commonly received Christianity had been battered by the shocks of modern scepticism. Moreover, *Empedocles* is best just where the poet is himself with least disguise. Everywhere the charm of Arnold, to those who feel his charm at all, lies in the revelation of a refined, penetrating, sensitive intelligence, loaded with a melancholy due to the pressure of a world not made for the gratification of human desires. The same melancholy, due to the same pressure, is throughout evident in Empedocles. His closing confession might with a few changes have been written of the poet himself:—

> Slave of sense
> I have in no wise been;—but slave of thought? . . .
> And who can say : I have been always free,
> Lived ever in the light of my own soul?—
> I cannot; I have lived in wrath and gloom,
> Fierce, disputatious, ever at war with man,
> Far from my own soul, far from warmth and light.
> But I have not grown easy in these bonds—
> But I have not denied what bonds these were.
> Yea, I take myself to witness
> That I have loved no darkness,
> Sophisticated no truth,
> Nursed no delusion,
> Allow'd no fear.

"Far from my own soul, far from warmth and light": this is Arnold's constant lyrical refrain. And he too never grew easy in the bonds. In one point however there is a great difference between the poet and Empedocles,—in the suicide, which Arnold took from the legend, though he turned it to suit his own purpose. He held it a duty to fight his way through "the mists of despondency and gloom"; and he did it.

The self-revelation of a gifted mind must be always fascinating, but what we principally seek in the drama is insight into *another* mind. In this *Empedocles on Etna* fails, and so in a less degree does *Merope*. This is a point of far greater importance than the fact that these two dramas are really modern in tone. A drama profoundly anachronistic may nevertheless be great as a drama, but not one which does not present clearly defined and living *dramatis personæ*. But moreover, *Empedocles on Etna* fails, as a drama, in balance. Empedocles is not only the dominant character, he may be said to be almost the sole character; for Pausanias and Callicles exist only for his sake, and the poet neither feels himself nor inspires in his readers any independent interest in them.

We are forced to the same conclusion if we look at the question from another point of view. If success in characterisation is the first requirement of the drama, action is the second. We may doubtless have poems of high merit, dramatic in nature, yet destitute of action. But such poems are not *dramas*. The very meaning of the literary form of the drama is to permit the union of these two elements, action and the development of character. The Greek drama, it is true, was so constructed as to permit action to sink into a very secondary place; and perhaps Arnold's *Merope*, though it has not much action, is not conspicuously deficient in this respect. His *Empedocles* certainly is. It is practically, as he soon felt, one long pause on the verge of suicide. Action, it would seem, was as foreign to Arnold as the delineation of character. If we turn to poems of a form which, though not dramatic, normally presents this quality of action, we find confirmation of the impression produced by *Empedocles*. *Sohrab and Rustum* and *Balder Dead* were not written for the sake of the movement in the story. On the contrary, their charm would be destroyed, or would be totally different in kind if there were in them any sense of hurry. Rest rather than motion, reflection rather than action, constitute their beauty. They are as far as possible removed from the vigorous speed and hurry of the narratives of Scott and Byron.

It seems safe then to conclude that a man who has created no great character, and who has nowhere displayed the power of reproducing rapid action, was not meant by nature to be a dramatist. In another time and amidst other surroundings other powers might have been evoked; but they certainly did not spring up spontaneously.

The case of Tennyson is less clear; but the majority of his readers look upon him as deficient in dramatic talent, and quite recently an elaborate criticism of him (Mr. Stopford Brooke's) has been written without even a cursory mention of his principal dramas. In a large volume in which separate chapters, and sometimes more than one, are devoted to the principal poems, such as *The Princess, In Memoriam*, the *Idylls of the King* and *Maud*, the plays of *Queen Mary, Harold* and *Becket* are not only not criticised, they are, I believe, not even named. From this fact and from occasional dicta in his book it seems safe to draw the conclusion that Mr. Brooke did not consider them worth naming. This is striking, but the view is only an exaggeration of the common opinion as to the relative value of Tennyson's dramas in comparison with his other work.

The poet's own history is from the point of view of the drama remarkable. His early poems were as destitute as they could well be of the dramatic spirit. His literary career had been already prolonged beyond that of most men, and his life had almost covered the allotted span, before he published his first play. Previous to *Queen Mary* he had never approached nearer to the dramatic form than in the "monodrama" of *Maud*, a piece essentially lyrical in structure as well as in spirit. After *Queen Mary* however he returned again and again to the drama, and this in spite of either condemnation on the part of the critics, or what was at best, as applied to Tennyson, faint praise. The most natural and obvious division of his later works is that which ranges them under the heads of dramas and non-dramatic poems; and of these the former are more bulky and in some respects more striking, though with one exception certainly less valuable than the latter. They are more striking, if only because of the surprise of finding an old man, long trained in art, and by no means inclined to undervalue training, suddenly leaving the path his own footsteps had beaten hard and smooth, and attempting a new and difficult way. Did the impulse to do so spring from the tardy development of some power hitherto latent? or, if not, to what other cause is it to be ascribed?

It is astonishing to find a development of such a kind at an age so advanced; yet a fair examination of the dramas, side by side with the contemporaneous poems, seems to reveal it. We have already seen how large a proportion of the poems is partially dramatic. One remarkable fact such an examination certainly does reveal,—that Tennyson, even after the age of seventy, still possessed, in a degree almost as marked as ever, the capacity of growth. There is, in the series of his principal dramas, a steady rise which even those who most disparage them will probably acknowledge. Whatever merit we ascribe to *Queen Mary*, we must ascribe more to *Harold*, and more still to *Becket*. The last is the culminating point, in the dramatic form, of Tennyson's genius. His other dramatic pieces, *The Falcon*, *The Cup* and *The Promise of May*, which all appeared upon the stage before *Becket*, and *The Foresters*, which is of later date, are all lighter in build and inferior in worth to it. *The Falcon* has little either of incident or character, and the turning point in it, the sacrifice of a hawk, is according to modern ideas too trivial. *The Cup*, notwithstanding some fine situations and fine poetry, is on the whole frigid, and the characters, though distinct and consistent, lack greatness. There are disagreeable elements in the story of *The Promise of May*. The story of a seduction may legitimately be put upon the stage; but there must be strong reasons indeed to justify the representing at length, as a principal character, a man capable of supposing that by marrying one sister he can atone for the ruin and supposed death of the other. *The Foresters* and the volume containing *The Death of Œnone* are the only works of Tennyson which unequivocally show the signs of the failure of mental power through age. There may be some failure in *Demeter* too, but it is less marked. The trivial puns which deface *The Foresters* would almost certainly have been expunged if the author had retained his full vigour. If they are imitations of the Elizabethans, the choice was ill-judged. Their presence and the general weakness of the story bear witness to the decline of Tennyson's faculties; and it is all the more astonishing to find his lyrical power in at least one case as exquisite as ever.

In estimating the value of the dramas two different standards may, or rather must, be taken. We may appraise them absolutely, or we may appraise them in relation to their author's other work. In the first case the question to answer is simply, Is the play a good play? In the second case we ask, Is it as good as the *Idylls* or as *In Memoriam*? Judged by either standard *Queen Mary* must be pronounced wanting. That it falls beneath Tennyson's standard of work hardly need be said. That it is a poor play is equally true. It betrays defective technical knowledge. The stage is overcrowded. There are no fewer than forty-five named characters, besides the crowd of lords, attendants, citizens, peasants and so on. Nowhere except in *Henry VI.*, which he only patched, has Shakespeare a list of *dramatis personæ* at all like this; as a rule he has not more than half. Tennyson discovered his mistake, and in the later plays kept his list within manageable limits. *Harold* has twenty-three named characters, and *Becket* twenty-five. More important than this is the fact that, with the exception perhaps of the sketch of Elizabeth, there is not a single well-drawn character in *Queen Mary*. The situations too are uninteresting, and the action drags. What is more surprising is that the piece is inferior as a poem. When it was first announced that Tennyson was writing a play, there were probably few who expected that the great lyrist would prove to be also a great playwright; but many would have freely prophesied that even an unsuccessful play by him would contain a great deal of fine poetry. They would have been wrong. *Queen Mary* does contain some verse not unworthy of the previous work of its author, but it does not contain much. The dramatic form seems to mar the grace of his verse, and he has not in this instance succeeded in giving it that rapidity and energy which might atone for the want of grace.

Harold gives evidence that the poet was successfully grappling with the technical difficulties in his way. There is vigour in the principal characters, and dramatic interest throughout. The subordinate characters too leave a more distinct impression than those of the earlier drama. Still, the dramatic art is somewhat crude, and the scenes appear, as they do also in *Queen Mary*, to be tacked on to one another. The author also shows himself wanting in resource and inventiveness. Harold's vision at the end, so obviously suggested by the vision of Richard III., would never have been introduced except by an inexperienced dramatist at a loss for a device,—or by a very experienced one indifferent to the comparison. Shakespeare himself, we may be sure, would not have hesitated to use it; but he could afford to do many things that lesser men dare not do. The scene of the battle of Hastings is unsatisfactory; but the defect here is perhaps due rather to the form of art than to the artist. The stage-battle has always verged upon the ludicrous, the mechanical resources are so inadequate for the purpose. In this respect the epic is immeasurably superior. Tennyson tried to graft its advantages on the drama by making a spectator, Stigand, report what he saw to another, Edith, who is supposed to be too deeply interested to look for herself. The idea was not a happy one, but perhaps the effect is as good as the conditions allow. A more serious defect is the unworthy treatment of the character of William. A contrast was doubtless needed to Harold, but there is something wrong with the dramatic art which fails to impress us with the greatness of a man who has left so deep a mark on history. Ungenerous and selfish he may be, but he ought to strike the reader as great, and Tennyson's William the Conqueror does not. But after all deduction is made for defects, there is still in *Harold* a marked and even surprising advance upon *Queen Mary* in the principal merits proper to the drama.

In *Becket* the point reached is still higher, and probably the interval between it and *Harold* is even greater than that between the latter and *Queen Mary*. The character of Becket himself is worthy of all praise. Its principal features are strongly marked, yet it is free from the vice of exaggeration or caricature. Becket is hot, impulsive, apt to take his own will for the will of heaven, and unconscious of his foible; but at the same time he is strong, generous, great and honest. There is nothing of the intriguing priest in Tennyson's conception of him. He is, to begin with, a man full of human passions. This is the source of the great weakness upon which John of Salisbury lays his finger:—

> May there not be something
> Of this world's leaven in thee too, when crying
> On Holy Church to thunder out her rights
> And thine own wrongs so pitilessly? Ah, Thomas,
> The lightnings that we think are only Heaven's
> Flash sometimes out of earth against the heavens
>
> (act v., sc. ii.).

But it is the source likewise of his charm, and gives him that colour of flesh so infinitely more attractive than the pale purity of sainthood. Manliness is stamped deep upon his character. He is soldier and statesman before he is churchman, and he carries into his churchmanship the courage of the soldier and the intellectual breadth of the statesman. If he renounces the world he well knows what he is renouncing. In the fine prologue to the play Henry jests at Becket's appreciation of the good things of life.

> A sauce-deviser for thy days of fish,
> A dish-designer, and most amorous
> Of good old red sound liberal Gascon wine (*Prologue*),

is the king's description of him; and Becket admits both this and what naturally follows:—

> Men are God's trees and women are God's flowers;
> And when the Gascon wine mounts to my head,
> The trees are all the statelier, and the flowers
> Are all the fairer (*Ibid.*).

But appreciation is a different thing from abuse, and the suggestion of abuse he repels.

The crucial question with regard to Becket's character is whether its keynote is or is not mere ambition. Whatever may have been the case with the historical Becket, as regards Tennyson's Becket, with whom we are concerned, the answer must be negative. Ambitious Becket doubtless is, and it may be added that he ought to be. That ambition which impels a man conscious of great powers to seek a field for his activity is a duty rather than a vice. But it was not Tennyson's view that Becket simply used Henry as a ladder by which to reach the pinnacle of his ambition, and that the subsequent conflict between Church and Crown was equivalent to kicking down the ladder. One object of the prologue evidently was to clear away this misconception. What the careless eye is prone to miss is the fact that new relations carry with them new duties. Becket the servant of Theobald, Becket the Chancellor of England, and Becket the Archbishop of Canterbury were three different persons. The principle upon which an honest and true man acts is no doubt always the same, but the outward shape his acts take under the guidance of that principle may vary greatly. Hence in many cases the charges of dishonesty and inconsistency which the shallow mind brings against a larger nature whose sole fault is that it is too big for the critic to comprehend.

Becket knows how he is liable to be misinterpreted. He is not even without "compunctious visitings" himself, for he knows the alloy of earth in his own character, an alloy not of a kind to defile it, but rather such as to make him fit for the work he is called upon to do. Becket is no spotless saint, fit only for an imaginary heaven all gold crowns and trumpets and unending psalms and hallelujahs. Something of iron, a metal liable to corrode, but eminently serviceable, had to mix in a composition which was to stand the rough work of a very rough age. The poet accordingly depicts Becket as a man not wholly free from the stains of the world (perhaps those only are, if any are, who do none of its work), yet essentially pure. Self has its place in his scheme of life, but above self he enthrones duty. Becket's self-criticism, partly expressed and partly suggested, is thoroughly sound. Of Theobald he says :—

> He did prefer me to the chancellorship,
> Believing I should ever aid the Church—
> But have I done it? He commends me now
> From out his grave to this archbishoprick (*Prologue*).

And just as his acts as chancellor might, as he hints, have disappointed Theobald, so he is fully aware must his acts as archbishop disappoint Henry. He owes the two great steps in promotion to expectations which in the one case he at any rate does not, and which in the other case he clearly foresees that he cannot, fulfil. There are two possible explanations. The easier and more obvious is that his conduct is governed by mere selfish ambition, unmixed with any nobler ingredient. Theobald in the first instance is disappointed because it "pays" Becket, as chancellor, to curry favour with Henry. Henry in his turn is disappointed because the mask has served its end—or the net has caught the fish. Becket becomes the mere "pestilent priest" because, when he has got all that Henry can give, the secular power of the Crown is an obstacle in the way of his ambition. Tennyson's explanation however, and Becket's own in Tennyson's play, is subtler. If in his chancellorship he had more than once gone against the Church, he had done so to please not merely the king, but the King of kings :—

> For it seemed to me but just
> The Church should pay her scutage like the lords (act i., sc. i.).

As officer of State his first duty was to the State; and that duty obliged him, not to oppress the Church, not to make unjust exactions, but to see that just exactions were not evaded. But as servant of that very Church he was bound first of all to uphold her rights, not bound to make wrong right, but bound to see that no right was infringed, and disposed, as every strong man in such a position must be, rather to err in magnifying than in minimising those rights.

The weakest point in Becket's moral position is that, clearly realising the course he must take and also the expectations of Henry, he accepts the gift of office from the king's hand without warning him; for a casual expression, such as occurs in the *Prologue*, when Becket tells Henry he would be no easy father confessor, can hardly be considered a warning. Becket is himself sensitive on this point, and would fain believe, but cannot, that Henry has had little to do with his elevation. The play gives no answer to the question how far Becket was blameworthy in this, or whether he was blameworthy at all. It was no part of the dramatist's business to come forward with his answer; and it may be left to each man's private judgment to determine whether the man conspicuously fit for an office is bound to tell the weaker donor of it that his administration will not follow just the course the donor expects.

That Henry totally misjudges Becket's character is clear. It ought to have been evident that a man so strong as Becket must needs steer an independent course. Henry, self-centred, sees in him only a man who has been hitherto the efficient instrument of his will; and he never doubts that, bound by affection and gratitude, he will continue to be so. He fails to make the due allowance for the sense of duty, and forgets that in new relations duty may point in a new direction. In other words, he takes as wholly personal to himself the service which in Becket's case is largely due to the higher consideration of justice. He ignores the fact that as Archbishop of Canterbury Becket becomes the representative and champion of that spiritual power which in the middle ages claimed a position, even in politics, co-ordinate with the temporal, and in the last resort superior in kind. Tennyson accordingly, with true dramatic intuition, makes his hero resolute from the first moment as to his line of action. He has qualms, as we have seen, about the means by which he gets the office, but none as to his conduct in it. The gratitude and the affection to which Henry trusts are quite real, and Becket's vision of the effect of the course he is resolved to take is quite unclouded; but he never hesitates. "O Herbert," he cries,

> O Herbert, here
> I gash myself asunder from the king,
> Though leaving each, a wound; mine own, a grief
> To show the scar for ever—his, a hate
> Not ever to be heal'd (act i. sc. i.).

This is inevitable. Having taken the office Becket cannot but do in the main as he does. The strong man necessarily acts according to the law of his strength.

This is a great character, happily conceived and powerfully executed. It may be thought, and perhaps it is true, that there is less subtlety in it than in the highest creations of dramatic genius; but it is at least a character which challenges comparison with those creations. It is far nearer the level of Shakespeare's Wolsey than it is to that of the churchmen, Cranmer, Gardiner and Cardinal Pole in *Queen Mary*. There is nothing, not even in the tragic close of *Becket*, to compare for pathos with the fall of Wolsey, no speeches as touching or as full of poetic beauty as those of the great cardinal in his eclipse, but there is the accent of greatness in Becket too.

Becket is one of those dramas in which one figure overtops the rest, but it is not a single-character play. Tennyson has avoided the mistake into which Browning fell. The rest of the *dramatis personæ* of Becket are indeed made of thinner stuff, and they are altogether less fascinating than the hero of the piece; but several of them are nevertheless of high merit. The portrait of Henry is very well drawn. In several respects he closely resembles Becket. Like him he is fiery, like him too he is masterful. "Even in a palace life may be lived well." The saying of Marcus Aurelius implies that living well under such circumstances is exceptionally difficult. If it is hard for a rich man to enter into the kingdom of heaven it would seem to be tenfold hard for a king. Henry's position lifts him above the wholesome necessity of restraint. The lessons of his earlier life are forgotten. His fierceness degenerates into ungoverned self-will, darkens really fine gifts of disposition and intellect, and superadds to his natural inferiority to Becket an acquired inferiority. This turns a friendship founded upon resemblance into a connexion which has in many respects the effect of contrast, and leads to the grand mistake as to the character of Becket whereon the whole play turns.

The female characters are of less merit. Rosamund is a somewhat commonplace conception, with few features to distinguish her from the ordinary heroine of the second-rate novel. Eleanor of Aquitaine however is neither commonplace in conception nor in execution. She has the grace of the poetess added to the grace of womanhood, of high birth and of a buoyant southern race. The charm of the beautiful lyric snatch she sings in the Prologue partly clings to her throughout. In Tennyson's plays there is a tendency to drag in lyrics, as if the author was more confident of himself as lyrist than as dramatist; but Eleanor's song comes quite naturally and is quite in keeping with her character. Her moral nature contrasts with her artistic nature. She has been bred in a society where the rules of right and wrong which bind the vulgar crowd are hardly recognised; and those feelings, half religion, half superstition, which in that age for many natures took the place and did the work of the rules of right and wrong, have little or no place in her soul. Hence

Eleanor's hardness. She is equally pitiless, remorseless and unscrupulous. Yet the feeling is left that under more favourable conditions she might have developed very differently. "Louis of France loved me, and I dreamed that I loved Louis of France: and I loved Henry of England, and Henry of England dreamed that he loved me." Her growth, in what is to the normal woman the most vital of all ways, has been stunted. Here, as in so many other points, the Prologue gives the key to what follows. A strong passionate nature endowed with a fine sense of beauty, but a nature never softened by healthy human relations,—such is the groundwork of the character of Eleanor. "Even in a palace life *may* be lived well," but Eleanor succumbs to those adverse conditions.

If the play be examined from the point of view of its action an almost equally favourable judgment must be pronounced. The subject is great. No larger motive could have been found within the middle ages than the warring claims of Church and State; and those claims are represented by two of the most gifted and high-placed men of their time. There is a steady march of events from beginning to end, the various threads are kept well in hand, and the artistic obligation to bring everything into relation with the central character is not forgotten. Few dramatic pieces leave on first reading so clear an impression of the story, still fewer bear so well to be read repeatedly. It is however very long. For representation it needs curtailment, and it was considerably curtailed by Mr. Irving before his very successful enactment of it.

Becket is then a successful play. Is it too much to say that if there is one exception to the rule mentioned at the beginning of the chapter, we find it here? Taken all round, *Becket* has probably the best claim among the plays of the century—English plays of course—to rank as a great drama. Other dramatic pieces, like Byron's *Cain* and Shelley's *Cenci*, display great power and high poetic gifts, but for one reason or another they are not acting plays. Neither do they contain any character equal to Becket. The poet of seventy-six, persevering in the face of dubious approval, mixed with disapproval not at all dubious, proved his mastery, for once at least, over the new art. To rank him on that ground as a great dramatist might be unwise. Becket is his one unqualified success; but this one success is itself astonishing, and the steady advance in the old poet's knowledge of the conditions necessary to success is hardly less so.

We must revert now to the question with which we started upon this investigation. Was it a late development of new powers, or was it some external impulse which turned Tennyson in his old age to the drama? Probably the true answer is affirmative to both questions. On the one hand, it is difficult to believe that Tennyson would have achieved the success he did achieve if the new departure had been made thirty or forty years earlier. In the early poems there is scarcely to be seen one stray characteristic of the poet of dramatic gifts; and the absence of those characteristics is almost conclusive evidence that the gifts did not exist except in the most rudimentary form. We are driven to conclude therefore that in Tennyson's case the dramatic faculty was abnormally late in reaching maturity. On the other hand it is probable that but for the reaction of circumstances upon him the faculty would never have displayed itself. We have seen that in Tennyson's early work there are signs as of a man vaguely groping for a great subject and a great interest. Life and experience year by year enriched him with new interests or widened and deepened those he already felt. The history of literature, or at least of English literature, probably presents no example of more consistent and sustained progress in one direction. As years go on his grasp of the concrete grows more and more firm. Now, the point to be noticed in this connexion is that there is no form of literature which, without losing ideality, takes so strong hold of the concrete as a skilfully handled drama. The drama therefore was the natural goal towards which Tennyson, both by the law of his own development and by the action of circumstances upon him, moved. It was not caprice or wilfulness, or any mistake as to his own gifts, that drove him to it, but a kind of necessity. His great contemporary has finely expressed the restless struggle of instinct for its appropriate surroundings:—

> As the inland-hatched sea-creature hunts
> The sea's breast out,—as, litter'd 'mid the waves,
> The desert-brute makes for the desert's joy,—

so man, thwarted though he may be, turns to his "true resource". Such, except that we must exclude the idea of unfitness in the early surroundings, was the case of Tennyson. He was born in that Beulah-land of "golden languors" and "tranced summer calm". He was no stranger there. He took kindly to its orchards and vineyards and to the sun that shone day and night. Nevertheless, "the bells did so ring and the trumpets continually sound so melodiously," that he could not sleep. "Some life of men unblest he knew," and "his piping took a troubled sound". He was forced to seek the sea's breast out and to make for the desert's joy.

So viewed, there is something pathetic as well as deeply interesting in the great poet's later development. Many still uncompromisingly pronounce the dramas a series of mistakes and failures. Those who, like the writer, rise from each perusal of *Becket* with a deepened sense of its power, will ask for at least a modification of this judgment. But all must admit that Tennyson's dramatic career was at best a success chequered with failure. The courage of the man of sixty-six (Tennyson's age at the publication of *Queen Mary*) in venturing such an experiment, the fidelity to his art which, if I have rightly interpreted him, inspired the attempt, and the tenacity with which he maintained his resolution to succeed, are beyond all praise.

"On earth there is nothing great but man: in man there is nothing great but mind," was the motto which Sir William Hamilton caused to be inscribed on the walls of his class-room. We may take it as an evidence of the truth of this maxim that so large a proportion of the highest literary genius has been devoted to the delineation of this one great thing, the human mind. The three great tragedians of the Attic stage, Shakespeare, Cervantes, Moliere, Goethe, the four supreme intellects, in literature, of four great modern nations, are examples at once of the inexhaustible interest of its study, and of the reverence which its successful study compels. And this reverence in turn makes it almost a pain to pronounce a word of adverse criticism upon any one who has shown such mastery. The loftiest genius displayed mainly in other ways meets with its due measure of censure. Dante's treatment of his enemies is unsparingly condemned, and no one hesitates to point out the limitations of Milton's Puritan theology. But it is a different matter with "Euripides the human" and Sophocles in his "mellow glory"; and for Shakespeare, the critical eye sees him in Elysium calmly brushing aside censure, saying with a smile that "he knew it, and it did not matter".

If there is any recent writer to whom this reverence must attach it is Browning. Not since Shakespeare has English literature, or perhaps any literature, produced such a master of the secrets of the soul. Some enthusiasts would not even make the exception of Shakespeare. Time alone, which is the final judge in such matters, can pronounce authoritatively whether they are right or wrong; but at any rate they have so much to say for themselves that even those who differ most from them may treat their opinion with respect. Here then, it might seem, we have an instance sufficient in itself to disprove the alleged rule that the nineteenth century is inimical in spirit to the drama. On the contrary, it may prove that this is just the instance which most demonstrates the rule. In the case of the other two poets, the fact that their genius was in the main non-dramatic may be otherwise explained. Arnold, it is clear, was not endowed by nature with the dramatic faculty. Tennyson long kept aloof from the stage; and it is by no means evident that the partial character of his success, when he did write for it, is to be ascribed to any disability laid upon him by the circumstances of his time. If however Browning, whose work is throughout "dramatic in principle," who held that the "development of a soul" is alone worthy of study, and who pursued that study with such success that thoughtful and balanced minds have challenged comparison for him, in this respect, with its supreme master for all time,—if such a man nevertheless falls short of success in the drama, we must clearly look abroad for an explanation. All the more is explanation necessary when it is added that Browning was by no means deficient in the sense of action. It is true his interest seldom centred in events for their own sake; but he could tell a story vigorously when he pleased.

For the present purpose it is necessary to exclude all pieces which, however dramatic in spirit, are not regular dramas. *Pippa Passes* therefore will be left out of view. So will *In a Balcony*, for, although it is dramatic in form as well as in spirit, it is rather like one act in a drama than a complete play. The pieces which remain to be considered are, in the order of publication, *Strafford, King Victor and King Charles, The Return of the Druses, A Blot in the 'Scutcheon, Colombe's Birthday, Luria,* and *A Soul's Tragedy*. Are these or any of them successful dramas? and if not, why is it that they fall short of success? It may be well to repeat that success must be understood as relative to the author's standard. A mighty exhibition of strength in Lilliput would have been ludicrous weakness in Brobdignag. There is also the further ambiguity of the word as applied to the drama. We may mean by "successful," successful on the stage, or successful as appealing to the student. We ought strictly to mean both.

The question of the stage success of Browning's plays is slightly complicated by his unfortunate misunderstanding with Macready. On account of that, *A Blot in the 'Scutcheon* at least had something less than a fair chance. On the other hand, he had the advantage of some exceptionally good acting, in particular the acting of Macready himself and that of Helen Faucit. Mrs. Sutherland Orr's *Life of Browning* shows that his friends were inclined to think that the inequality of the acting told against the plays. No doubt it did; but what cast, in England at least—we are told that they manage things better in France—is ever anything but unequal? And the fact that explanation is necessary shows clearly that the measure of success achieved was very limited. The plays did not keep the stage when they first appeared, and they have not regained it since.[1]

Are the dramas then more successful in the other sense, as subjects for private study? To call them failures except in the sense explained, the *relative* sense, would be unjustifiable. So great a man could not, at any rate repeatedly, write what was positively bad. But if relative value be tested by a general consensus of opinion among admirers of Browning, the dramas must sink, at best, to a secondary place. It is in dramatic monologue that we find the real Browning.

An examination of the substance and structure of the plays reveals one or two facts which go far to explain the comparative failure. In the first place, they are deficient in action; secondly, most of them prove to be studies of single characters; and thirdly, the hands may be the hands of Valence or of Luria, but the voice is the voice of Browning. It must be explained hereafter under what limitations this is to be understood.

[1] I am not referring to occasional revivals. There is an understood though indefinable distinction between a play which has established itself on the stage and one which has failed to do so. Browning's dramas all belong to the latter class.

As to the first point: As a rule the action of Browning's plays stagnates, because his interest is not in it. They are rather psychological studies. *In a Balcony* is typical. Very little is enacted on the stage. There is some interaction of the characters upon one another leading up to a critical situation, and there the curtain drops. In *Colombe's Birthday* there is but one large question, and the whole play is filled with discussions regarding the answer to it. In *Luria* too the interest centres in the psychological problem of the effect upon the Moor's mind of the discovery that he has all along been suspected and watched. It is significant that in both these plays Browning finds it easy to observe the unity of time, which Shakespeare was obliged to cast aside. Shakespeare did so because his scheme of action was too large to be compressed within a day. Browning sometimes kept himself within the limit, not because he had any more respect than Shakespeare for the unity, but because he was indifferent to action, and worked best when he was concentrated on a moment.

That the plays are single-character plays is still clearer, and is also more important. The play of *Strafford* is little more than the character of Strafford encompassed by shadows. Nobody, unless it be here and there an enthusiast, would turn to it for a living Hampden, or a living Pym, or a living Vane. Charles too is pitiably, unnaturally weak, and yields at once where there should be at least a struggle. None of these characters disturbs the historical conception, whatever it may be, with which we approach the play. It has been remarked with truth that Shakespeare and Scott have in large measure written English history for the multitude; and careful students have sometimes shown themselves aggrieved by the mistakes and misrepresentations of the poet and the novelist. The false view has taken so firm hold that it is difficult to uproot it and plant the truth instead. Whether the historian of the future, or of the present, differs from Browning or not, he need be under no apprehension on this score, except perhaps with reference to Strafford himself.

The same fault, for dramatically it is a fault, is conspicuous in several of the other plays, and is more or less visible in nearly all of them. It was not the result merely of inexperience. On the contrary, *Strafford* is the only play of Browning's which has a fairly long list of *dramatis personæ*. The others range from four to ten or eleven. *A Soul's Tragedy* is what its title denotes, a soul's tragedy. The poet is concerned only with the fate of Chiappino, who vanishes disgraced; as regards the rest of the *dramatis personæ* the end is darkness. In this case however the judgment must be qualified by the admission of high merit in the slight sketch of Ogniben. *Luria* is even more decidedly a study of the character which gives the title to the piece. His lights and shades are brought out, not by the men around him, but by an abstract something, Florence, in the background; and it is in precisely the same way that the character of Pym in *Strafford* is moulded by his conception of England. *The Return of the Druses* and *King Victor and King Charles* stand in an intermediate position. They are more complex than the plays previously mentioned, yet they present just the same feature. The former hinges on the character of Djabal, and though Loys, Khalil and Anael have some life and reality, it is hardly sufficient to give the play its proper balance. The latter is essentially a study of the character of Charles, though not in the same degree as *Strafford* is a study of the character of Wentworth. Though they are subordinate there is some degree of substance in Victor, D'Ormea and Polyxena. Still, is it the kind of substance which Shakespeare gave to his subordinate characters? The play of *Hamlet* has passed into a proverb as the one in which the principal character is *par excellence* the principal. Yet in which of Browning's plays do the minor characters live as Polonius, Laertes, Horatio, Ophelia and the clowns live? Compare Ophelia with Polyxena! Compare Polyxena with any female character in Shakespeare who fills a similar place. Browning's drama is like a tree flourishing and healthy in its stem, but feeble and sickly in the minor branches. Shakespeare's is a tree full of vigour and life down to the smallest twig.

Colombe's Birthday is a finer and subtler piece than any of these. The characters are interesting. Valence is grand with his fire and eloquence and unselfishness. Berthold is a fine study of the man of the world, clear-sighted, selfish, yet capable of generosity and with something of a heart, though he is too deeply involved in affairs to follow its dictates. In his reading of others he makes mistakes through trusting too much to the selfish view. His confidant, Melchior, the student-observer of life, less entangled in affairs than Berthold, and less inclined to measure all with the measure that fits most, is right in the case of Valence and Colombe where Berthold is wrong. Colombe herself is rather the centre round which the others play than a figure of great interest for her own sake. Of the courtiers, Guibert is worthy of study. In him, the struggles of a disposition naturally good with the tendencies begotten of demoralising surroundings and mean companionships are exceedingly well depicted. Contact with Valence rouses in him the better nature which would else have slept, and in the end he rises to the height of following the ruined fortunes of his mistress. There is a touch of melodrama in the conclusion; but it is justified and made natural by the air of romance thrown over the whole.

So too *A Blot in the 'Scutcheon* rises above the ordinary level of Browning's dramas. The conception is fine and the moral insight shown is deep. But the merits are not in the main of a dramatic nature. The characters fall just short of excellence. In Thorold the scholar and the genealogist are overdone, and so is the bashful boy in Mertoun. Mildred's character is almost summed up in the moral situation in which she is placed; there is no opportunity to know her otherwise. The inferiority of the pure drama as handled by Browning is well seen by comparing her with Pompilia. The monologue allows Browning to paint the latter as he pleases, and in consequence we get an impression of the whole being. In the play he is fettered by the conditions of the stage, and we get little more than a single aspect. There is, dramatically, more merit in the lighter character of Gwendolen, whose criticism of Mertoun's request for Mildred's hand is sound and piquant, and who proves herself afterwards to have heart and principle as well as wit.

The great fault of *A Blot in the 'Scutcheon* is that in it the moral situation overtops the characters, whereas the true dramatic method is to express the moral only in and through the characters. Endless moral discourses have been founded on such characters as Macbeth, Hamlet and Shylock; but no one, except perhaps a German commentator, ever dreamed of viewing them as mere illustrations of the discourses. In *A Blot in the 'Scutcheon* however they may almost be regarded in that light. A minor defect is that the piece seems to be inconsistent with itself. For the general conduct of it we must suppose a considerable difference in age between Thorold and the lovers, Mertoun and Mildred.

Thorold is the all-accomplished scholar whose reputation overawes Mertoun. Yet towards the end we discover that Thorold and Mildred have been accustomed to wade together for water-lilies and have been rescued from peril by old Gerard.

Another fault in Browning's dramas is the fault of style. There is no necessity to express an opinion here as to the merits of Browning's style when he speaks in his own person. In a sense it may be said that a dramatist need not have a style of his own at all; but if he escapes this obligation he incurs a more onerous one, he must have not one style but twenty. This is where Browning fails. He *has* a style of his own, a style for good or evil conspicuous for its strongly marked traits; and this he carries with him through all his dramas and in the delineation of all his characters. The ideal dramatist changes his style to suit each figure he brings upon the stage. One man is abrupt and sententious, another smooth and flowing; one is florid, another simple and severe. In Browning there is audible all through an accent which is unmistakably Browning's. Who can miss it in these lines from *Colombe's Birthday*?

> He holds you—you, both form
> And mind, in his, where self-love makes such room
> For love of you, he would not serve you now
> The vulgar way,—repulse your enemies,
> Win you new realms, or best, to save the old
> Die blissfully—that's past so long ago!
> He wishes you no need, thought, care of him—
> Your good, by any means, himself unseen,
> Away, forgotten! (iv., p. 166.)

So in the speech of Pym near the end of *Strafford* :—

> I never loved but one man—David not
> More Jonathan! Even thus, I love him now:
> And look for my chief portion in that world
> Where great hearts led astray are turned again
> (Soon may it be, and, certes, will be soon:
> My mission over, I shall not live long),—
> Ay, here I know I talk—I dare and must,
> Of England, and her great reward, as all
> I look for there; but in my inmost heart,
> Believe, I think of stealing quite away
> To walk once more with Wentworth—my youth's friend
> Purged from all error, gloriously renewed,
> And Eliot shall not blame us (ii., p. 304).

Illustrations might easily be multiplied, but it is scarcely necessary, as the fact is generally admitted. It may be well to add however that the same feature is even more conspicuous in the poems " dramatic in principle " which are not in form dramas. It is only necessary to recall any of the *Dramatic Romances* or *Dramatic Lyrics*. Browning's turns of expression, Browning's abruptness, all his peculiarities are reproduced under twenty different names. The varieties of character are well marked, but the thought of all is cast in the same mould. *The Ring and the Book* abounds with instances. All through *Pompilia* in particular they arrest attention, just because Pompilia, a woman, young, gentle, unlearned, more than most demands a style different from Browning's. Violante, if possible, even more imperatively demands variation of style, but we do not find it in her words as reported by Pompilia. It would be hard to discover lines more characteristic of Browning's own style than these :—

> If I put before him wholesome food
> Instead of broken victual,—he finds change
> I' the viands, never cares to reason why,
> But falls to blaming me, would fling the plate
> From window, scandalize the neighbourhood,
> Even while he smacks his lips,—men's way, my child!
>
> (*The Ring and the Book*, b. vii., lines 539-544.)

It is equally marked in the following passage from *The Inn Album* :—

> I transcribed
> The page on page of sermon-scrawlings—stopped
> Intellect's eye and ear to sense and sound—
> Vainly: the sound and sense would penetrate
> To brain and plague there in despite of me
> Maddened to know more moral good were done
> Had we two simply sallied forth and preached
> I' the "*Green*" they call their grimy,—I with twang
> Of long-disused guitar—with cut and slash
> Of much-misvalued horsewhip he,—to bid
> The peaceable come dance, the peace-breaker
> Pay in his person! Whereas —Heaven and Hell,
> Excite with that, restrain with this! So dealt
> His drugs my husband; as he dosed himself,
> He drenched his cattle: and, for all my part
> Was just to dub the mortar, never fear
> But drugs, hand pestled at, have poisoned nose!
>
> (xii., pp. 254-255.)

In matters of this kind questions of style are also questions of substance. Browning's men and women are marred as men and women because they always speak his language. There is nothing in the thought of the passages quoted inappropriate to the person who speaks it, yet something of the sense of fitness is lost because of the manner. It is far worse when the thought itself is such as could never have occurred to the speaker; and even into this error Browning occasionally, though happily not often, falls. Violante again furnishes an example:—

> 'Tis arranged we never separate,
> Nor miss, in our grey time of life, the tints
> Of you that colour eve to match with morn
> (*The Ring and the Book:* Pompilia, 559-561).

We have in Browning then a man of one fixed and somewhat inflexible style. Moreover, his dramas as a rule present only a single carefully developed character; and in his absorption in character or in ethical problems he is prone to forget the need of action. For these reasons his success in handling the regular drama was limited. But he was not mistaken in adopting the dramatic principle. He not only succeeded, but, notwithstanding the faults noticed, succeeded splendidly in the creation of character. For him however each individual had to stand apart. The interaction of man upon man and the play of circumstance he could understand, but could not dramatically represent. He could penetrate the individual to the soul; but it was a condition of his art that he must be left for the time undistracted to identify himself with that soul, and must view the whole universe from its standpoint. But this is only a statement of the fact in other words, it does not reveal the cause.

Of all forms of literature, the drama is pre-eminently the literature of action. It almost pre-supposes for its full development and perfect health an age of action resolute, single-minded and not unduly troubled by doubts. It is well known that this was the case with the golden age of the English drama. Even more strikingly, if possible, was it the case with the drama of Athens. It is remarkable that Æschylus in the prime of manhood fought at Marathon, Salamis and Plataea, that Euripides is said to have been born on the very day of Salamis, and that the life of Sophocles almost exactly spans the great period of

Athenian activity. As Marlowe and Shakespeare were the children of a new birth of their country, so the Athenians seem to have drawn their inspiration from that great political impulse which Herodotus singles out as the cause of the almost bewildering progress of the city in the fifth century B.C. The connexion —or coincidence—between a flourishing drama and a period of great and somewhat youthful national activity, is perhaps not so conspicuous in any other country as in England and Athens; but neither have the fruits of the drama in any other country been so rich.

On the other hand, the drama can scarcely arise among a primitive people. It is a complex form of art, and it demands, besides energy and decision, a considerable advance in reflection. Narrative is simpler; and accordingly we find that the early poetry of all races is narrative in form, the simple narrative we call a ballad. If the poetic instinct of a race is powerful, its ballad poetry is sure to be varied, and to be enriched with vivid flashes of dramatic intuition; but in the early days of even the most poetic races we do not find either the skill in artistic construction, or the capacity of interweaving several threads of thought which the drama requires. Therefore the drama is never a very early growth. Neither, on the other hand, can it well be the latest. It requires a balance between thought and action which, as a rule, only an intermediate period can afford. No doubt the succession of literary forms may be modified by many circumstances; by the influence, for example, of foreign literatures, as the literature of all modern Europe has been influenced since the Renaissance by that of ancient Greece; or by the political history of a particular nation. A great triumph may hasten its development, or a great disaster may break its spirit and kill its literature altogether. But variations of this kind do not affect the principle.

The application of this principle may perhaps help us to understand the failure of this century in its dramatic attempts; for with few exceptions there has undoubtedly been failure. It is assuredly not reflection that is wanting. Neither, if we consider it alone, can it be said to be action. Our century is active enough, perhaps more active than most. It is rather the perfect balance between the two that we miss. In literature the reflective faculty has partly paralysed the faculty for action. The spirit of philosophy either overcomes art, as it does in Browning's later works ; or art, when examined, proves to be philosophy in another shape, as it does in Arnold and in much of Tennyson. And it is not in England only that this is the case : the same holds true emphatically of Goethe. Neither is the difference felt only in dramatic poetry. It is the secret of the heavy tone of the modern in contrast with the inimitable spontaneity of the Elizabethan lyric. The contrast can be most conveniently illustrated here. There is a song in John Wilbye's *Second Set of English Madrigals* which runs thus :—

> Love not me for comely grace,
> For my pleasing eye or face,
> Nor for any outward part;
> No, nor for a constant heart!
> For these may fail or turn to ill:
> So thou and I shall sever.
> Keep therefore a true woman's eye,
> And love me still, but know not why!
> So hast thou the same reason still
> To doat upon me ever.[1]

Mrs. Browning in her *Sonnets from the Portuguese* strikes upon the same theme, perhaps quite unconsciously. The difference of treatment is most remarkable :—

> If thou must love me let it be for nought
> Except for love's sake only. Do not say
> " I loved her for her smile—her look—her way
> Of speaking gently,—for a trick of thought
> That falls in well with mine, and certes brought
> A sense of pleasant ease on such a day " ;—
> For these things in themselves, Belovèd, may
> Be changed, or change for thee,—and love, so wrought,
> May be unwrought so. Neither love me for
> Thine own dear pity's wiping my cheeks dry,—
> A creature might forget to weep who bore
> Thy comfort long, and lose thy love thereby!
> But love me for love's sake, that evermore
> Thou mayst love on, through love's eternity.

The spirit of the sixteenth and of the nineteenth centuries is in these two pieces. It is a kindred change that has made the drama in this later time so difficult. The load of introspection is too heavy for it to bear.

But further, we must consider not only the degree but the

[1] Printed in Bullen's *Lyrics from Elizabethan Song-Books.*

kind of reflection. The division of the age against itself has been already touched upon. The phrase, "an age of transition," rather meaningless, because every age is necessarily such, has, after all, as applied to the present century, a shade of truth and of special significance. Our neighbourhood to one of the great historical convulsions of the world makes the process of transition specially difficult and specially important to us. Reflection under such conditions cannot easily be wedded to action. Singleness of purpose has gone from life, and it goes from the drama too.

Can we on these grounds explain Browning's failure? Do they at the same time account for his success? What is the difference, as regards the faculties called into play, between the drama and the dramatic monologue? What type of mind, capable of succeeding in the latter, might fail in the former?

We must distinguish here the two great methods of the human intellect, the intuitive and the critical. The intuitive is the method of art, the critical that of philosophy; the former partakes of the nature of instinct, the latter is a deliberate exercise of reason. In the highest work, both of philosophy and of poetry, they blend; but intuition ought to prevail in poetry, and criticism in philosophy. Now, it is evident that a form of art in which criticism plays a large part may succeed in dramatic monologue; but with what prospect of success can it be applied to the drama proper? For a great price, paid in mental energy, a man may be able, by a process of reasoning, to make himself one with another, and to clothe himself in the vesture of that other's thoughts and emotions. But what human faculties would avail, by any conscious process, to identify a poet at once with a whole stage? What faculties would enable him to draw off and on character with the ease of a glove, to make every utterance in keeping with the speaker, and on the one hand to observe from beginning to end a due subordination of parts, on the other to remember that the leading parts must not be suffered to obliterate those of minor consequence? This was not Shakespeare's method, and we may be sure that, vast as were his powers of reason as well as of intuition, they would not have sufficed for such a task. But it *was* Browning's method; and just because it was so he failed in the drama. This is not a matter merely of inference from his works. Mrs. Sutherland Orr records Browning's conviction that his wife's genius was higher than his own. It was based on the ground just explained. She was the inspired seer, he the capable and industrious workman. We need not accept his conclusion; genius, like faith, is best judged by works. But he knew his own method, and his judgment upon that is entitled to attention.

It is not of course meant that Browning was all reason and no intuition : if that had been the case he would have been no poet, though he might have been entitled to a high place as a philosopher. He was a poet in whom the philosophic element was relatively strong, and who did much of his work by a method largely philosophical. He is the philosopher among poets, as Plato is the poet among philosophers. Even if Browning's early poems might be supposed to leave this in doubt, his later works conclusively establish it; and no careful reader will question that the later works are but the full development of tendencies which were present in germ, or rather in bud, from the first.

Browning then realised character by a process which was in great part conscious. He could not realise a dozen at once. He could not transfer himself in a moment from soul to soul. Hence the fact that most of his dramas resolve themselves, as we have seen, into studies of single characters. To give his powers their freest play, he had to devote them uninterruptedly to one individual. Dialogue he could not manage. Hence too, perhaps, the persistence of his own style throughout, and the frequent recurrence of certain favourite ideas which we recognise as his. In the critical process the identification of the creator with his creation is less complete than it is in the intuitional. Notwithstanding his defiant, " No foot over threshold of mine," we trace Browning in his men and women as we certainly do not trace Shakespeare in his. In chemical change, we are told, there is always one fact which remains constant through all mutation. Weigh the compound, and we find that its weight tallies with the joint weights of the elements which have disappeared to produce it. So with Browning: he disappears in his characters, but the identity beneath is betrayed by his style and by a certain fundamental conception of the universe which is always present in his work. A few men in the course of human history have possessed the bewildering power of concealing themselves without leaving even this trace of identity. But in this respect the age had set its mark upon Browning. The critical and conscious method was too strong for the intuitional and unconscious, and absolute identification with another character was impossible.

I have said that the drama demands a balance between thought and action, and that in the nineteenth century the perfect balance between them is destroyed. We can see from another point of view how this fact influenced Browning. As a rule, the events of his dramas are few, he prefers to make his characters talk rather than act. He likes to dwell upon what goes on within the soul, and has always time to pause and reason out this process. Outward circumstances are important only as they bring about an inward change; nay, in the fascination of the inward change they are in danger of being forgotten. The scientific view of evolution is that outward circumstances act upon the living being, and that the living being reacts upon the outward circumstances. The ideal dramatist is impartially just to both, though no doubt the inward is to him first. Browning on the contrary cares for little but the reaction, and as far as possible he strips his characters of their clothing of circumstance. Hence much of the difficulty of *Sordello*. Hence the rhetorical ring of *Colombe's Birthday*, for action is extruded by speech. Hence the tendency, illustrated in *Karshish, The Confessional, Cleon, Andrea del Sarto*, and so many of Browning's richest and most characteristic poems, to take the character musing, moralising, philosophising, reflecting on the past, speculating on the future, doing anything but acting. The reason is not that Browning could not put action into verse, but that other things almost always seemed much more important. So for some purposes they are; but in the drama action cannot without detriment be put in the background, and Browning in his dramas as elsewhere shows a desire to thrust it there. How full of incident are Shakespeare's historical plays as compared with *Strafford* or *King Victor and King Charles*. The reader of *King John* or of *Henry V.* or of *Richard III.* carries away a tolerably clear idea of the principal events of the period in which the scene is laid; the reader of Browning gets only the barest outline, and that rather by allusion than by enactment on the stage. *Colombe's Birthday* is even a better illustration of Browning's method. In the drama as the Elizabethans handled it there is a series of events sloping up, as it were, to the keystone, and another series of events sloping down to the catastrophe. In Browning's play it is as if everything were concentrated in the catastrophe. The structure of events, outside that, is of the slightest description. A woman, two principal male characters, certain steps, almost jumped over, by which they are brought together,—there is little else. A critical decision has to be taken and everything pauses at that. The arguments for and against, the revelation of character which they cause, the hesitation of Colombe and the decision which reveals her,—these constitute the interest. We have in a word the poet's whole power concentrated on an inward struggle. The action in which it is expressed is to him altogether subordinate. The arguments of the characters are important, what they do is secondary. Such is the case too in *A Blot in the 'Scutcheon*. The illuminative utterances of Mildred and Mertoun are words which refer to past action. Their characters are formed and their destiny fixed by that, the play does not show them in the making.

Contrast with this Shakespeare's method. There too we have argument, as in the soliloquies of Macbeth and Hamlet. But Macbeth in action is a different man from Macbeth communing with his own soul. Through his deeds he is born anew, not in fresh innocence, but with the brand of Cain upon his brow. He is another man after the murder. The catastrophe does not spring from something which lies behind the play, but from what is enacted in its course. So too in *Hamlet*, though it is one of the least rapid of Shakespeare's plays, we have only half of Hamlet in his soliloquies and discourses with his friends. For the other half we have to look to what he does or fails to do. But all Valence is present in his speeches. The character is formed beforehand, not developed as the play proceeds. This is one of the results of what may be called Browning's catastrophic method.

In Browning's case then we have at once something to account for and the means of doing it. We have, to begin with, genius of the highest order. We find that genius, "from first youth tested up to extreme old age," clinging persistently to a dramatic mode of expression and displaying in it powers almost unparalleled. And yet it is true that the possessor of this genius is not a great dramatist. Born too late for such success as the Elizabethans easily won, he is obliged to evolve for himself a form of poetry "dramatic in principle," yet not adapted to the stage. The best expression of his genius is found in studies of single characters, where reflection naturally predominates, where action becomes as subordinate as the writer may desire, and where there is no distraction due to the conflicting claims and diverse peculiarities of other characters.

CHAPTER IX.

THE POETRY OF NATURE.

IN all the poetry of the last three generations the treatment of nature has played so conspicuous a part that it demands special consideration. The reason why this is the case will perhaps be best given in the next chapter; meanwhile, we have to do with the universally admitted fact. At an earlier date even great poets were apt to be perfunctory in their treatment of nature, and they often merely adopted without examination the tradition handed down to them by their predecessors. They did not write "with their eye on the object". It seems to be proved that there is a great deal of mere convention in the birds of Shakespeare; though as he has made for England a history of his own, which is not altogether that known to the disciples of Freeman, so he has contrived in part to create an ornithology. In spite of the inaccuracies alleged by careful observers, his few favourite birds are stamped upon literature with the habits he chose to give them.

The three great Victorian poets were all in different ways poets of nature. Browning indeed is not usually regarded as such, and it is true that his first interest is always in humanity; but nevertheless nature plays a large part as subsidiary to man. Arnold, the pupil of Wordsworth, could not fail to be a student of nature. He views it in a different light from Browning. While Browning goes to nature in order to find backgrounds to his characters, and to illustrate them, Arnold seeks an anodyne to his own sufferings. He is throughout more self-centred than the elder poet. Tennyson may be said to be the most disinterested of the three,—meaning by the phrase that his studies of nature have less frequently than Arnold's direct reference to his own mood, and have also less frequently than Browning's direct reference to the mood of other men. That is, he more than either of his contemporaries takes the purely artistic view, and enjoys the beauty of nature for its own sake, without regard to its healing power, or to the light it may shed on a psychological problem. Of course Tennyson does use nature for such purposes, and in the poetic treatment of nature the reference to humanity is never far in the background. The appeal to the sense of beauty is human as well as the appeal to the sense of hunger, and more distinctively so. Still, there are important differences in degree. Tennyson is the poet in whom the reference to humanity is least direct and obtrusive; Browning looks at nature in the light of humanity at large; and Arnold views it through the glass of self.

Tennyson is then, in his treatment of nature, first and chiefly the artist. Simple beauty seems at times sufficient for him. He sees it, describes it, and leaves it to produce what effect it may. But secondly, and especially in his later development, he is also the moralist, and as such more nearly approaches the point of view of his contemporaries. These may be described as the two principal strains in the Tennysonian poetry of nature, existing side by side all through his work, but the first dominant in his earlier, and the second more conspicuous in his later poetry.

The artistic sense finds expression in the poet's rejection of the idea of utility:—

> Oh, to what uses shall we put
> The wild-wood flower that simply blows?
> And is there any moral shut
> Within the blossom of the rose?

There may be a use even in the wild-wood flower, and a moral in the rose; Tennyson would hardly deny that; but to the purely artistic mood the moral is so indirect and the use so far away that they may be neglected. They are certainly not before the artist's own mind. Now, the mood of careful, loving and exact observation is more habitual with Tennyson than with either of his contemporaries. The lime is "a summer home of murmurous wings," and it "feathers low". It has ruby-coloured buds, and they break into young leaves of emerald green,—"a million emeralds break on the ruby-budded lime". These are facts, real aspects of the beauty of nature, and that is why they are in Tennyson's verse. Again, the sea is "crisped," or it is "wrinkled". The latter is indeed an epithet taken from the human face, but it is purely descriptive. Tennyson might immediately after have written, with Byron, "Time writes no wrinkle on thine azure brow". The idea of age is not in his mind at all, nor any human characteristic, only an aspect of external nature, which he describes by the most pictorial word he can find.

This impulse to describe the beautiful simply as such frequently makes Tennyson pause and dwell upon the scene before him with loving minuteness. Probably no poet has painted in words so many scenes that could be transferred at once to colour. He gives every detail with something of Pre-Raphaelite exactness. Thus in *The Gardener's Daughter* he wishes, for no particular reason except that it is beautiful, to describe the space between the garden and the minster clock, and he does it thus:—

> Between it and the garden lies
> A league of grass, wash'd by a slow broad stream,
> That, stirr'd with languid pulses of the oar,
> Waves all its lazy lilies, and creeps on,
> Barge-laden, to three arches of a bridge
> Crown'd with the minster-towers.

But though here leisurely in spirit, the poet is wonderfully terse: every word adds to the pictorial effect. There is the same condensation and the same readiness to dwell on detail in the passage in the *Idylls* describing the spot where Arthur and Lancelot found the ruby necklace:—

> A stump of oak half-dead,
> From roots like some black coil of carven snakes,
> Clutch'd at the crag, and started thro' mid air
> Bearing an eagle's nest (*Idylls: The Last Tournament*, p. 340).

And even more terse and more minutely accurate in observation is the picture of a small stream painted by Percivale in *The Holy Grail*:—

> A brook
> With one sharp rapid, where the crisping white
> Play'd ever back upon the sloping wave,
> And took both ear and eye (p. 298).

But perhaps this side of Tennyson is best illustrated from *The Daisy*, because that which suggested it might have led him into other paths. It is a poem purely retrospective. The daisy, plucked on the Splugen and dried, is found long afterwards in "the gray metropolis of the North," and calls up the memory of past travels in Italy. It is remarkable that the memories are almost exclusively of scenes of natural beauty or the beauty of art, the campanili and the amaryllis in the bays, and the "sombre, old, colonnaded aisles". They are a little vague from distance, but they are hardly tinged at all by the hues of personal feeling, which under similar circumstances would have coloured the work of most poets. Thus in the beautiful and delicately painted scene of the distant Alps viewed from the roof of Milan Cathedral the poet's own feeling scarcely enters. He is merely silent and observant:—

> I climb'd the roofs at break of day;
> Sun-smitten Alps before me lay.
> I stood among the silent statues,
> And statued pinnacles, mute as they.
>
> How faintly-flush'd, how phantom-fair,
> Was Monte Rosa, hanging there,
> A thousand shadowy-pencill'd valleys
> And snowy dells in a golden air.

The purely physical character of the retrospection is remarkable here. The poet does not recall moods, he recalls scenes. Not he but Monte Rosa is the centre of the picture, and he gets himself into position not for the sake of giving utterance to his reflections, but for the sake of describing the mountain. His method is as widely separated as possible from that of Wordsworth, whose Yarrow poems, for example, are not properly descriptive at all, but reflective. In these the order of importance is reversed. Not the scene with its lights and shades and colours, but the man with his feelings about it, is first in importance. Tennyson, especially in the early poems, has little of that reflectiveness which is the most conspicuous feature of Wordsworth's treatment of nature. Neither did he ever develop in its fulness the Wordsworthian view. He does not theorise about the relation of man to nature. No such conception as that which Wordsworth works out in *Ruth*, and refers to in many other poems, is to be found in his poetry:—

> The wind, the tempest roaring high,
> The tumult of a tropic sky,
> Might well be dangerous food
> For him, a Youth to whom was given
> So much of earth—so much of Heaven,
> And such impetuous blood.

THE POETRY OF NATURE.

This sense of influences passing into man from nature does indeed occasionally tinge Tennyson's work, as it tinges that of nearly all the successors of Wordsworth, but hardly so as to form an integral part of it. Tennyson seems on the whole ✓ to take the commoner view of an analogy between nature and man, not direct communion between them, or identity of the laws underlying both. Thus there is an obvious relation between the picture of the moated grange and the mood of Mariana; but it is not represented that the one passes into and is the cause of the other. No doubt Tennyson would have acknowledged the possible importance of "an impulse from a vernal wood"; and no doubt he too had felt the shock which "carried far into his heart the voice of mountain torrents". The sense of such things is at the root of all sympathetic poetry of nature. But in Tennyson we do not find that steady insistence upon such points which makes Wordsworth's poetry what it is. The daisy, crushed and dry, suggesting memories of cities and cathedrals and mountains, is instructive. Wordsworth sees the same flower, and the result is two stanzas of reflection on the concord between the flower and humanity. There is gain and loss in both methods. On the one hand, Tennyson cannot rival Wordsworth in the deep sympathy and rich suggestiveness of his treatment of nature; on the other hand, he is superior as a pictorial artist. Wordsworth's method lays too great stress upon a single object: it is impossible to make a picture out of the celandine alone. Tennyson passes from object to object, giving each just that degree of prominence which its relation to the whole requires.

The most striking illustrations of the pictorial quality in Tennyson's poetry are to be found in *The Palace of Art*. The scenes delineated by the poet are there supposed to be transcribed from pictures; they could be immediately re-transferred to canvas :—

> One seem'd all dark and red—a tract of sand,
>   And some one pacing there alone,
> Who paced for ever in a glimmering land,
>   Lit with a low large moon.
>
> One show'd an iron coast and angry waves.
>   You seem'd to hear them climb and fall
> And roar rock-thwarted under bellowing caves,
>   Beneath the windy wall.

> And one, a full-fed river winding slow
>   By herds upon an endless plain,
> The ragged rims of thunder brooding low,
>   With shadow-streaks of rain.
>
> . . . .
>
> And one, an English home—gray twilight pour'd
>   On dewy pastures, dewy trees,
> Softer than sleep—all things in order stored,
>   A haunt of ancient Peace.

Here are four scenes of distinct and well-marked types. The three last are as definite as words can make them; the first is purposely veiled in a haze of vagueness, in harmony with the "low large moon" which lights it. But the vagueness is not at all in the poet's conception: he sees this picture as clearly as he sees the others; but a fine taste convinces him that the moonlight glimmer over all is better for bringing out the feeling he wants than the sharp precision of clear day.

Sometimes, it may be thought, this pictorial vividness of conception leads the poet away from the immediate subject in hand, and induces him to bring in details not quite to the point; but they are generally so true and beautiful that it is impossible to regret their presence. This seems to be the case in a passage in *The Last Tournament* :—

> And Arthur deign'd not use of word or sword,
> But let the drunkard, as he stretch'd from horse
> To strike him, overbalancing his bulk,
> Down from the causeway heavily to the swamp
> Fall, as the crest of some slow-arching wave,
> Heard in dead night along that table-shore,
> Drops flat, and after the great waters break
> Whitening for half a league, and thin themselves,
> Far over sands marbled with moon and cloud,
> From less and less to nothing; thus he fell
> Head-heavy (pp. 358-359).

This is in the spirit of the classical similes of wolf or lion roaring round the fold or against the hunters. But it is evident that the details of the breaking of the wave in no way illustrate the fall of the knight. The resemblance ends with the first dash; but the image of the table-shore and the breaking wave is so clear before the poet's mind that he is led on to complete the picture. We have hitherto had chiefly in view the precision, clearness, sharp outline and minute detail of Tennyson's descriptions of nature. But he was a master of the effects of haze and obscurity almost if not quite as great as he was in the other style. His distant Alps, and the "glimmering land" with its "low large moon," are hints of his power. He knew well the heightened effect which comes from partial concealment, and from time to time wraps his verse in the mystical atmosphere of a landscape by Turner. There is something Turneresque in his architecture too. He is careful to leave Camelot half-shrouded in mystery :—

> All the dim rich city, roof by roof,
> Tower after tower, spire beyond spire,
> By grove, and garden-lawn, and rushing brook,
> Climbs to the mighty hall that Merlin built
>   (*Idylls: The Holy Grail*, p. 287).

He knows too the effect of repetition. Camelot is again

> Our Camelot,
> Built by old kings, age after age, so old
> The King himself had fears that it would fall,
> So strange, and rich, and dim (*ibid.* p. 292).

And if we move from the realm of romance to that of reality we find Milan Cathedral depicted with the same gorgeous suggestiveness :—

> O Milan, O the chanting quires,
> The giant windows' blazon'd fires,
> The height, the space, the gloom, the glory!
> A mount of marble, a hundred spires! (*The Daisy.*)

The vagueness of these passages, in contrast with the clear outline of the former pictures, is due to the fact that the poet's purpose was different; and his method is in each case right.

It is noticeable that Tennyson produces effects of this kind chiefly, not when he is, as in the passages earlier adduced, describing nature mainly for her own sake, but rather when he wishes to create a scene in harmony with some human mood which fills his mind. The impulse which led him to act upon this principle was doubtless, whether conscious or not, artistically sound. The border-land where the law that rules mind touches the law that rules nature must necessarily be in twilight. There are perhaps no better illustrations than those which may be found in that exquisite poem, *The Lotos-Eaters* :—

> All round the coast the languid air did swoon,
> Breathing like one that hath a weary dream.
> Full-faced above the valley stood the moon;
> And like a downward smoke, the slender stream
> Along the cliff to fall and pause and fall did seem.
> A land of streams ! some, like a downward smoke,
> Slow-dropping veils of thinnest lawn, did go ;
> And some thro' wavering lights and shadows broke,
> Rolling a slumbrous sheet of foam below.
> They saw the gleaming river seaward flow
> From the inner land : far off, three mountain-tops,
> Three silent pinnacles of aged snow,
> Stood sunset-flush'd : and, dew'd with showery drops,
> Up-clomb the shadowy pine above the woven copse.

Nowhere probably has the effect of a hazy, listless, opiate-laden atmosphere been better given. It is the natural analogue to the moral character of " the mild-eyed melancholy Lotos-eaters ". The reference to humanity is everywhere conspicuous in it, and we are conscious that the poet has depicted the scene in order to illustrate the characters of the men. In doing so he has not departed from the truth of nature : the picture is not less correct, but only more deeply charged with meaning from its suggestion of something beyond. Just because of this superior suggestiveness it would be more difficult to paint the scene. It comes indeed within the limits of " the painter's sphere " as defined in Arnold's *Epilogue to Lessing's Laocoön* ; but they are very few who can fill landscape so full of human emotion.

This is from an early poem. It is however in his more mature years that we find Tennyson most freely interweaving human feeling with his descriptions of nature ; and in his later days it is comparatively seldom that he paints nature at all without a clear reference to man. The development of his manner may be best shown from *The Passing of Arthur*. The greater part of it was first published as a fragment in 1842 under the title of *Morte d'Arthur*, and it appeared as one of the *Idylls* in 1869. It is remarkable that the scenic setting of the original part of the poem is quite different from that of the later addition. The two parts cannot indeed be called inconsistent, for the change is explained by the rise of " a bitter wind, clear from the North ". The introductory part, which is the later in date of composition, describes the day of battle and the time preceding it; the sequel narrates the events of the night after the battle, when the King, wounded to death, gives Sir Bedivere the brand Excalibur and charges him to fling it into the lake. This is the landscape :—

> The winter moon,
> Brightening the skirts of a long cloud, ran forth
> And sparkled keen with frost against the hilt:
> For all the haft twinkled with diamond sparks,
> Myriads of topaz-lights, and jacinth-work
> Of subtlest jewellery (*Idylls: The Passing of Arthur*, p. 408).

Notwithstanding the sea-wind, " shrill, chill, with flakes of foam," it is rather cheering. There is doubtless a reason for it. Without the moon sparkling keen with frost " the wonder of the hilt " could hardly have dazzled Sir Bedivere. Still, we have to notice that for this there is sacrificed the harmony between the scene and the human feeling of the actors in it,—Arthur at the point of death, and Sir Bedivere, "first made and latest left of all the knights," alone remaining to attend upon him. In the introductory part on the contrary every feature of nature is carefully adapted to the feelings inspired by the "last, dim, weird battle of the west". Lyonnesse itself is a fitting scene for the passing away of an old order of things. Every feature in the description is carefully chosen for its power of suggestion :—

> A land of old upheaven from the abyss
> By fire, to sink into the abyss again ;
> Where fragments of forgotten peoples dwelt,
> And the long mountains ended in a coast
> Of ever-shifting sand, and far away
> The phantom circle of a moaning sea
>   (*Idylls: The Passing of Arthur*, p. 402).

Shifting sand and phantom sea, the land raised from the abyss and doomed to sink into it again, the inhabitants themselves mere "fragments of an earlier world,"—it is impossible to mistake the purpose which inspired the choice of these details. Equally clear is it in the more ephemeral phases of nature which surround the " dim, weird battle " :—

> A death-white mist slept over sand and sea:
> Whereof the chill, to him who breathed it, drew
> Down with his blood, till all his heart was cold
> With formless fear (*ibid.* p. 403).

And again, after the battle,

> The wan wave
> Brake in among dead faces, to and fro
> Swaying the helpless hands, and up and down
> Tumbling the hollow helmets of the fallen,
> And shiver'd brands that once had fought with Rome,
> And rolling far along the gloomy shores
> The voice of days of old and days to be (*Idylls*, p. 404).

Of these three quotations the two former are marked by the vagueness already noticed; the third is perfectly definite; for sometimes, though not generally, it is possible to suggest human feeling in a picture as clear and precise as any painted with a single eye to nature. This is admirably done in the lines in *Guinevere* which describe the feeling of Modred after he has been plucked from the wall by Lancelot:—

> Ever after, the small violence done
> Rankled in him and ruffled all his heart,
> As the sharp wind that ruffles all day long
> A little bitter pool about a stone
> On the bare coast (*Ibid.*, p. 373).

Similarly clear and true is the fine picture of Sir Bedivere in *The Passing of Arthur*:—

> But the other swiftly strode from ridge to ridge,
> Clothed with his breath, and looking, as he walk'd,
> Larger than human on the frozen hills.
> He heard the deep behind him, and a cry
> Before. His own thought drove him like a goad.
> Dry clash'd his harness in the icy caves
> And barren chasms, and all to left and right
> The bare black cliff clang'd round him, as he based
> His feet on juts of slippery crag that rang
> Sharp-smitten with the dint of armed heels—
> And on a sudden, lo! the level lake,
> And the long glories of the winter moon (*Ibid.*, p. 413).

These quotations have been taken mostly from the *Idylls*; but similar illustrations could be found in many parts of Tennyson's works. As might be expected, *In Memoriam* furnishes chiefly descriptions vividly coloured with human emotion; but the emotion is not unduly obtruded, nor is it purely the author's emotion. The sea, which earlier had been to the disinterested artist's eye the "crisped" or the "wrinkled" sea, when loaded with the freight of feeling, becomes the "vast and wandering grave" of the sailor whose "heavy-shotted hammock-shroud" drops in it. Its sounds also acquire a new meaning; they are "the moanings of the homeless sea". But in *In Memoriam* too we find the descriptions, while still full of emotion, as accurate as those of science. For example:—

> Short swallow-flights of song, that dip
> Their wings in tears, and skim away (*In Memoriam* xlviii.).

Whoever has watched swallows flitting about the surface of a river will recognise this as a faithful picture. There is equal truth in the highly imaginative description of a cloud in a stormy sky,

> That rises upward always higher,
> And onward drags a labouring breast,
> And topples round the dreary west,
> A looming bastion fringed with fire (*ibid.* xv.).

These two strains in Tennyson's poetry, namely, that of the accurate observer and that of the observer who looks through a coloured atmosphere of human feeling, and who sees a unity behind the difference between man and nature, may, in the language of philosophy, be described respectively as the objective and the subjective views; but it must be understood that the "subject" here embraces all humanity, not merely the individual, and that the "object" is nature outside of humanity. It is not pretended, of course, that these two are ever cut completely asunder from one another. A subjective view of nature, without any objective element, is impossible; and equally impossible, though perhaps to some minds less evidently so, is a purely objective view. We must discriminate according to the relative importance of the two. In some cases the two threads, the objective and the subjective, are interwoven in such a way that the passage may be brought under either head or both. It is so for instance with the "swallow-flights of song" just referred to. Here the subjective element is conspicuous. It is solely to illustrate an emotional state that the swallow is brought in. But on the other hand the objective fact remains objective. The swallow-flight is not itself imbued with the emotion it is used to illustrate. Contrast this with the "death-white mist" of Arthur's last battle. There the natural fact *is* imbued with the emotion: it not only illustrates the emotion but is felt to be the same in kind with it. Or contrast the passage already quoted about Modred with that about Sir

Bedivere. Both are equally accurate pictures of natural scenes; but in the one case the sharp wind, the little bitter pool and the bare coast are the natural analogue of the small, loveless, rankling and bitter heart; while in the other case the human form "clothed with his breath," the dry clang of the armour and the other details certainly help to bring out the feeling of the scene, but they are not so peculiarly and almost exclusively adapted to it.

It is evident that Tennyson in his more mature work partly bridged the distance which originally separated him from Wordsworth. But he never did so completely; and throughout there is in his verse less of the "pathetic fallacy" than there is in the verse of the majority of recent poets.

Browning, unlike Tennyson, very rarely describes purely for the sake of the description. His own declaration, already more than once quoted and alluded to, that little else interested him besides the incidents in the development of a soul, cannot be too carefully borne in mind. At the same time, his interpretation of what constitute the incidents in that development was extraordinarily wide. The most cursory reading makes it plain that his concentration on the soul had not the effect of excluding anything from his view. His curiosity was universal. He saw the far-off trains of cause and consequence which linked or might link the soul to what was seemingly most foreign to it; and we must therefore be prepared to find him go far abroad for his incidents.

There are, broadly speaking, two types of mind, which we may call provisionally the concentrative and the expansive. The one, in an extreme form, is exemplified in the monks of Mount Athos, who thought to find wisdom, or holiness, or whatever they chose to call it, by an intense contemplation each of his own navel. The other ventures forth into the world, perhaps only to seek his father's asses, but perhaps also to find a kingdom. The one concentrates itself upon an object, and that alone, with the result that at the end of the threescore years and ten he knows just as much about it as at the beginning. The other treats the object in its relations to surrounding forces. Instead of fruitlessly poring over a lump of iron ore, he tries the ore by fire, and reveals new qualities in it. Browning's mind belongs to the expansive class. To the familiar Latin adage which teaches us that nothing human is alien from man, he would have added that nothing natural is alien either. Because therefore Browning is essentially the poet of the human soul, we must not expect that nature will be indifferent to him; but we shall find that he uses it principally to illustrate the soul. He seldom studied nature in the disinterested spirit, as I have called it, of Tennyson.

Just as little however did Browning adopt the Wordsworthian view. That view involves the elevation of the natural almost to a level with the spiritual. The well-known line which expresses Wordsworth's faith that every flower "enjoys the air it breathes," illustrates his inclination to obliterate as far as possible the marks of division. There is no such inclination in Browning: he recognises the distinctions, and is ready on occasion to insist upon them. He rather looks upon the natural world as the theatre of man's exertions, as that which affords him the conditions of life, as a thing therefore which must be studied and comprehended, but also as a thing to be used as a means, not to be elevated into an end.

Vast knowledge is one of the marks of Browning; knowledge historical, scientific, philosophical, knowledge in short of every kind. He had read enormously, and he proved the catholicity of his taste by his sympathetic treatment of the diverse stores of his mind. One of the first questions that occur with regard to his treatment of nature is whether his taste here is as catholic as it is elsewhere. Has he kept his eyes as wide open to nature as to books? When we ask the question we speedily find that he differs from contemporary poets, not in possessing less knowledge of nature or less accurate powers of observation, but in his manner of using his knowledge and his powers of observation. The sea, though he laughed at the affectations of poets regarding it, the mountain and the forest he had evidently watched closely. But in the first place he frequently manifests a characteristic tendency to translate feeling into knowledge, to penetrate beneath appearances to causes. The well-known description of the making of the ring is typical. The interest centres not in the completed object, but rather in the action of one natural force upon another. Hence Browning, more perhaps than any other poet, embodies the results of science in his verse. And in the second place (and this is essential), the impulse to knowledge has its root in the desire to make nature subservient to man. All Browning's treatment of nature is, after a fashion of his own, determined by the view he takes of humanity.

First and principally, Browning's irrepressible optimism is the key to much that we find him. There is a livelier lilt in his strain than there is in almost any other poet. "How good is man's life, the mere living!" he makes David exclaim in *Saul;* and the pleasure simply in life as life, in the unrestrained play of all its powers, has seldom if ever been expressed better than it is expressed there:—

> Oh, our manhood's prime vigour! No spirit feels waste,
> Not a muscle is stopped in its playing nor sinew unbraced.
> Oh, the wild joys of living! the leaping from rock up to rock,
> The strong rending of boughs from the fir-tree, the cool silver shock
> Of the plunge in a pool's living water, the hunt of the bear,
> And the sultriness showing the lion is couched in his lair.
> And the meal, the rich dates yellowed over with gold-dust divine,
> And the locust-flesh steeped in the pitcher, the full draught of wine,
> And the sleep in the dried river-channel where bulrushes tell
> That the water was wont to go warbling so softly and well.
> How good is man's life, the mere living! how fit to employ
> All the heart and the soul and the senses for ever in joy! (vi., p. 104.)

This is refreshing and tonic in an age when the question whether life is worth living has so often been asked. The question was not an open one to Browning: the evidence, to him, that it was worth living was so overwhelming everywhere that he did not need to ask it, any more than he had to trouble himself about the rising and setting of the sun.

> This world's no blot for us,
> Nor blank; it means intensely, and means good.

The words are put in the mouth of Fra Lippo Lippi, but the sentiment is Browning's own as well.

In this faith Browning looked at the world. He devoured it, as he devoured libraries. It is a faith which fills him with interest in all things, but does not itself furnish him with an artistic principle. *That* he finds when he gets nature centred in some soul. It is in relation to the soul that nature has meaning, and with reference to it that the meaning is good. If Browning fails to find the soul, or if he fails to make it the centre of interest, he pours out the stores of his observation in rich but disorderly profusion. *The Englishman in Italy* is, not indeed one of the best, but one of the most instructive of his poems,—instructive, I mean, as regards his own method. It is classed among the *Dramatic Romances;* but the dramatic element in it is unusually slight. Observation of nature (still however with a keen eye to the needs and the delights of life) pushes it into the background. The result is not a picture, nor a series of pictures, but a medley. The poem is saved from being a catalogue, because it is lighted up everywhere with imagination and sympathy. There are indeed pictorial elements in it, as for instance :—

> Quick and sharp rang the rings down the net-poles,
>   While, busy beneath,
> Your priest and his brother tugged at them,
>   The rain in their teeth (v., pp. 55-56).

But there is not the self-restraint necessary for a clearly-outlined picture. We have seen from the study of the manner of Tennyson that a poetic picture may be painted almost in a stroke, or it may be rich with many details; but in the latter case the details must be chosen with a view to a general effect. This is the case, for example, in the picture of the country of the Lotos-eaters. It is the case also in the lines quoted about Sir Bedivere. In the latter instance the human figure furnishes a centre, and makes the choice of details comparatively easy; but in the former, where there is no such obvious central point, the effect of unity is just as surely attained. The artist has in his mind a definite conception of an impression he wishes to produce, and that supplies him with the principle of choice. But in *The Englishman in Italy* Browning seems to have been guided by no such conception. The poem is difficult to quote, because it is hard to decide where to begin. Perhaps the lines immediately following those already given will do as well as any. The two men tugging at the net-poles with the rain driving in their teeth would, in Tennyson, have been the point round which all the other details would have been grouped. Not so in Browning. The poem goes on thus :—

> And out upon all the flat house-roofs
>   Where split figs lay drying,
> The girls took the frails under cover ;
>   Nor use seemed in trying
> To get out the boats and go fishing,
>   For, under the cliff,
> Fierce the black water frothed o'er the blind-rock.
>   No seeing our skiff

> Arrive about noon from Amalfi,
> —Our fisher arrive,
> And pitch down his basket before us,
> All trembling alive
> With pink and grey jellies, your sea-fruit ;
> You touch the strange lumps,
> And mouths gape there, eyes open, all manner
> Of horns and of humps,
> Which only the fisher looks grave at,
> While round him like imps
> Cling screaming the children as naked
> And brown as his shrimps ;
> Himself too as bare to the middle
> —You see round his neck
> The string and its brass coin suspended,
> That saves him from wreck (v., p. 56).

Tennyson is said to have criticised Browning on the ground that he took too long to say what he had to say. If so, the criticism was, according to the ordinary meaning of words, singularly inept ; for seldom has thought been expressed with greater condensation than by Browning. But probably Tennyson had in his mind the *pictorial* effects ; and in that case he was right. By skilful selection a picture could frequently be produced in half the space Browning takes ; but not a word could be spared without cutting out something from the meaning. The passage just quoted bears witness to extraordinary keenness of observation ; but this very keenness, while it is a merit, is also the source of a great defect. It tempts Browning to say everything. He is not verbose, and what he says is not unworthy to be said ; but he does not select. It is safe to say that such a piece as this is not to be found in the whole of Tennyson, or of Arnold, or of any poet who is artist first and chiefly. It might not be easy quite to parallel it elsewhere from Browning himself, though the passage could be multiplied by four from the same piece. But the same *kind* of thing, if not in the same degree, is frequent in him. There is a good deal more than a suggestion of it in the passage already quoted from *Saul*. The description in *Red Cotton Nightcap Country* of the " meek, hitherto un-Murrayed bathing place " belongs to the same class. The manner in which the poet there introduces himself and his tastes and habits is full of meaning. In a simple picture of nature there would be no place for him ; but there is place when the object is to give prominence to the effect of nature upon man, not visually alone, but in his life.

The secret of Browning's manner of treatment in all these cases, and in many others which might be adduced, is the same. His principal object is not to paint nature, but rather to illustrate the pleasures human life derives from nature. For this purpose multiplicity of points of contact, rather than orderliness or artistic arrangement, is important. And it will be acknowledged that it is "no scanty tide" of the results of observation that he pours out.

It must not be understood that Browning was incapable of being pictorial. Occasionally he is so without more intimate reference to humanity than is present in all poetry. The fine opening of the second part of *Paracelsus*, already quoted, is an instance; another is the description quoted from *Sordello* of the wood lying black beneath the fiery sunset; and better than either is the splendidly imaginative picture of the storm from the scene of Ottima and Sebald. Sometimes a few words suffice to bring a scene before the eye, as in the reference to the castle in the Apennines. But still Browning's overmastering interest asserts itself. The pictorial style is most commonly used to illustrate some human state or succession of states,—a different thing from illustrating the pleasures or the troubles of life in general. In *Saul* there is another striking passage where we see the pictorial quality which is not to be found in the former quotation. The object is to find an analogue to the awakening of Saul from his torpor:—

> Have ye seen when Spring's arrowy summons goes right to the aim,
> And some mountain, the last to withstand her, that held (he alone,
> While the vale laughed in freedom and flowers) on a broad bust of stone
> A year's snow bound about for a breastplate,—leaves grasp of the sheet?
> Fold on fold all at once it crowds thunderously down to his feet,
> And there fronts you, stark, black, but alive yet, your mountain of old,
> With his rents, the successive bequeathings of ages untold—
> Yea, each harm got in fighting your battles, each furrow and scar
> Of his head thrust 'twixt you and the tempest—all hail, there they are!
> —Now again to be softened with verdure, again hold the nest
> Of the dove, tempt the goat and its young to the green on his crest
> For their food in the ardours of summer (vi., pp. 106-107).

This is not one picture; there is a movement in the poetry which painting could never give. But it is three related pictures.

There is an obvious reason why the pictorial quality, absent from the earlier quotations, is present here. The poet had to bring before the mind three states of the man Saul,—what he had just been, what he was now, and what he might again become; and he could not do so except by something in which there was unity as there was in the man. That lawless multiplication of instances, which, if not altogether admirable even in general illustrations of life, is yet not without its advantages, would in this case be inadmissible, because it would defeat the end in view. So too in the description of the inn where Pompilia rested we see how the human action of which it was the scene enforces unity. Only what is relevant to that can be admitted, and the keenest flash of imagination in the description is directly suggested by it :—

> I found the wayside inn
> By Castelnuovo's few mean hut-like homes
> Huddled together on the hill-foot bleak,
> Bare, broken only by that tree or two
> Against the sudden bloody splendour poured
> Cursewise in day's departure by the sun
> O'er the low house-roof of that squalid inn
> Where they three, for the first time and the last,
> Husband and wife and priest, met face to face
> (*The Ring and the Book*, i., 507-515).

To return to Browning's delight in life, and in nature as furnishing the means for it, and its setting. It is not of course suggested that Browning was a mere pleasure-lover. On the contrary, no one knew better than he that pain and sorrow and resistance were valuable, and indeed indispensable, to any high life, or rather to any *higher* life. They are conditions of progress. But he loyally accepted all sides of experience because he too looked upon the world, and saw that it was *all* very good. Having found a place and use for evil, he did not stumble, as many have done, at that which the unsophisticated mind views as its irreconcilable opposite.

But the pleasure he contemplated in life was far more than a purely personal one. It was rather "joy in widest commonalty spread"; for it was "the mere living" that was so good. If, as might and did happen, the joy was missed, this was not normal but abnormal. If circumstances curtailed the opportunities for it, the balance might be partly redressed by intensity of enjoyment when opportunity did come. Browning had the keenest sympathy with those whose fortune stinted them of the full measure of delight life might yield; and just because of that sympathy he knew how, in a well-balanced nature, compensation might be found for this stinted measure. He has described it in the opening of *Pippa Passes*. The poor mill-girl, with her one holiday in the year, and her heart hungry for the beauty which she has only then leisure to enjoy, is yet happier than any of those whom she esteems "Asolo's happiest ones". The aids to happy life, like the aids to noble life, are all within. The passage to which I have referred is well known; yet it is necessary to quote it. There is none that better expresses Browning's sense of the joys nature can impart to life; and very few within the compass of his works that so well satisfy the common idea of what poetry is.

> Day!
> Faster and more fast,
> O'er night's brim, day boils at last:
> Boils, pure gold, o'er the cloud-cup's brim
> Where spurting and suppressed it lay,
> For not a froth-flake touched the rim
> Of yonder gap in the solid gray
> Of the eastern cloud, an hour away;
> But first one wavelet, then another, curled,
> Till the whole sunrise, not to be suppressed,
> Rose, reddened, and its seething breast
> Flickered in bounds, grew gold, then overflowed the world.
> Oh, Day, if I squander a wavelet of thee,
> A mite of my twelve hours' treasure,
> The least of thy gazes or glances,
> (Be they grants thou art bound to or gifts above measure)
> One of thy choices or one of thy chances,
> (Be they tasks God imposed thee or freaks at thy pleasure)
> —My Day, if I squander such labour or leisure,
> Then shame fall on Asolo, mischief on me! (iii., pp. 5-6.)

We see then that Browning's optimism supplies the key to his treatment of nature. "The world is made for each of us," and the product we extract from it is good. Hence the triumphant ring of his utterances about nature. At the same time, "all's right with the world," not because everything is smooth and easy from the start, but just as much because of the occasions for strife and victory which the world presents. And this is true both in the moral and in the natural sphere. In each we have to welcome obstruction as well as smooth-flowing success. In the passages already quoted it cannot escape notice that, in the poet's conception of a world that "means intensely, and means good," difficulties to be overcome are at least as prominent as pleasures to be enjoyed. Browning disbelieved in pessimism :—

> The sourly-Sage, for whom life's best was death,
> Lived out his seventy years, looked hale, laughed loud,
> Liked—above all—his dinner,—lied, in short (xvi., p. 80).

But he did not disbelieve in adversity, physical, mental, or even moral. The physical pleasures which appeal to him are generally those of intense action, those which spring from something overcome.

> The hunt of the bear,
> And the sultriness showing the lion is couched in his lair,

have their place among "the wild joys of living". No one who knows Browning can doubt that in the mental sphere he not only faces but covets difficulties. "Our interest's on the dangerous edge of things," he makes Bishop Blougram say; and he himself loves to take his stand on this dangerous edge. Earth is higher than Rephan. In this obstructed planet the work may "drop groundward," yet the worker reach a heaven unattainable in a sphere

> Where weak and strong,
> The wise and the foolish, right and wrong,
> Are merged alike in a neutral Best (*Asolando : Rephan*).

We may say then generally of Browning's treatment of nature that he consistently and purposely subordinates it to humanity. It has to him a derivative and reflected interest. So it has indeed to every one; but he is conscious of the fact and makes it prominent in his verse. He seldom rests in pure contemplation of nature in itself. He regards it as the environment of man, an environment which gives him some part of the means of life without appreciable effort, but far more as the result of struggle. It is a field in which "winning comes by strife". Hence although study and contemplation are indispensable, they are not ends in themselves. To Browning as to Paracelsus Knowledge may be translated into Power. His attention is purposely given to nature because he sees its influence upon life.

Arnold in his treatment of nature is unlike both his contemporaries. He agrees with Browning in looking at nature mainly with direct reference to humanity; but as Arnold is not at all dramatic, while Browning is so in a high degree, the human element is in the younger poet differently presented. He agrees with Tennyson in being frequently pictorial; but when he is so his pictures are as a rule painted for the sake of the sentiment they suggest, not simply for their beauty. Moreover, there is a severity in Arnold's style and an absence of colour and movement suggestive of sculpture rather than painting. He differs from both the others in the space nature fills in his poetry. Of the great poets of the Victorian era, Arnold is emphatically the poet of nature. Less than Tennyson, and far less than Browning, is he the poet of man; but more even than Tennyson, and far more than Browning, he has enshrined nature in his verse.[1] To understand this aspect of his work it is first of all necessary to find his point of view.

Arnold is in his verse almost always self-centred. He rarely describes from the pure and unmixed desire to represent beauty. This, as we have seen, Tennyson in his earlier years frequently did. This Keats too did. Neither does Arnold, like Browning, fill his pages with the stir and bustle of life and of thought not his own. These may be regarded as gates by which the poet can escape outside himself. Arnold hardly ever does so escape. His characters speak his speech and think his thoughts; and the simple feeling that "this is beautiful" is in him rarely dissociated from the further feeling that "it affects my life, harmonises with it or contrasts with it, in such-and-such a way". Thus he finds himself in nature. It is either a type of his own mood, or he sees in it what by contrast soothes and calms, more rarely what stirs and invigorates him. Though he is a disciple of Wordsworth, his view of nature is very far from being a transcript of Wordsworth's. He learnt from Wordsworth that nature had much to give for the satisfaction of human needs; but his own needs were so different from his master's that what he found was necessarily far other than what the elder poet found. Wordsworth was prevailingly cheerful; Arnold bore through life a refined melancholy which has given to his verse perhaps its most characteristic note. Wordsworth was serene; so was Arnold. But while the one attained his

---

[1] In saying so I have regard to the proportion the treatment of nature bears to the whole of Arnold's verse. He wrote much less than either of the other two, and, as I have elsewhere said, his range was narrower.

serenity, if not without a struggle, at least after a short one which left no permanent trace, the other owed it to that stoic attitude of mind which proudly ignores the strife as unworthy. Landor's line, "I strove with none, for none was worth my strife," might have been written of him. Along with the fact that Arnold was a Wordsworthian, we must, before we can understand him, remember that he was likewise a disciple of Goethe. In Goethe Arnold found those elements of life which Wordsworth ignored but he could not ignore.

It follows from this that Arnold's view of nature stands in the strongest possible contrast to Browning's. In the eyes of Browning, as we have seen, nature was the stage on which human life was enacted; and that life was vigorous and triumphant, and all the stronger for the resistance it encountered. Browning never rested in nature, but was drawn on perpetually by "the need of a world of men". Arnold viewed that world of men with very different eyes. He saw in life little of the conquering energy which Browning saw; and therefore he turned to nature, not to find room for a fuller life, but to escape from that in which he found so little satisfaction. In *Resignation* he depicts the poet contemplating the world. It was an early piece, but Arnold held to the end of his days the view there expressed. It is the very antithesis of Browning's sense of the joy of life:—

> Lean'd on his gate he gazes—tears
> Are in his eyes, and in his ears
> The murmur of a thousand years.
> Before him he sees life unroll,
> A placid and continuous whole—
> That general life, which does not cease,
> Whose secret is not joy, but peace;
> That life, whose dumb wish is not miss'd
> If birth proceeds, if things subsist ;
> The life of plants, and stones, and rain,
> The life he craves, if not in vain
> Fate gave, what chance shall not control,
> His sad lucidity of soul.

"Whose secret is not joy, but peace." This is the key-note to Arnold's view of nature. It takes all his philosophy to say, as he does in *Youth and Calm*, " Calm's not life's crown, though calm is well ". His longing is always for peace. It is peace which is the sufficient reward of her whom he celebrates in that exquisite lyric, *Requiescat :—*

> For peace her soul was yearning,
> And now peace laps her round.

In *Bacchanalia*, again, the new age is pictured entering riotous and triumphant; but though the observer has to admit that the flush is lovely on the cheeks, he adds,

> Ah, so the quiet was,
> So was the hush!

Approaching nature in this spirit, Arnold seeks from it, not, like Browning, a sphere for his activity, since activity brings with it so much that is evil, but an anodyne. His favourite attitude therefore is, like Wordsworth's, an attitude of contemplation; and the favourite objects of his contemplation are those in which there is something subdued,—mist rather than cloudless brightness, moonlight rather than sunlight, sounds of gentle melancholy rather than the roar of the tempest or cataract, the slow imperceptible operations of growth and decay rather than sudden throes and convulsions. Arnold's love of moonlight is very noticeable; and it can hardly be a mere fancy which connects with it his habitual mood of mind. It is a moonlit sea on which the poet looks in *A Southern Night;* the scene of *A Summer Night* is moonlit also; and it is the same light he chooses for gazing upon Dover Beach. Moonlight in literature has had several functions. It is widely associated with romance, because its glamour leaves the fancy less confined than the full daylight. But in Arnold's poems its function is not to deepen the sense of mystery; it is rather to tone down the colours to an eye weary of the world. And in harmony with his love of moonlight we do in fact find both that he is sparing in his use of colour and that the tints he delights in are subdued. His heroine's hair is ash-coloured. Her eye is neither blue nor grey, but something between which eludes description. He delights in the cold pale purity of snow-crowned peak and glacier. When something brighter must necessarily be introduced his words are apt to be vague and general. It is "glorious" or "glittering". It would seem that his eye felt the beauty of the warmer tones, but dwelt with more minute observation on the paler and more subdued colours. In this Arnold contrasts with Browning, who likes colour, and likes it strong and vivid. There is no such piece in Arnold as *On the Cliff* in *James Lee's Wife*, which is all colour from beginning to end.

The same spirit is evident in Arnold's treatment of sounds. He hears the wind *washing* through the mountain pines. The Alpine torrent itself is heard at a distance which reduces its roar to a hum, as in "*Obermann*"; or position produces the same effect, and it becomes in *Switzerland* a "rock-strangled hum". The word and the sound are favourites with Arnold, and for the sake of its subdued soothing voice the mountain-bee appears repeatedly in his verse. In a similar spirit, the sound of the sea upon the beach is a "tremulous cadence slow," and it brings "the eternal note of sadness in"; or it is the "murmur" of the "Midland deep". Arnold's own mood is evident in all this, with its calmness

> Tinged with infinite desire
> Of all that *might* have been.

"The exulting thunder" of another race he regards, not with sympathy or admiration, but with dislike.

The sense of loneliness, so characteristic of Arnold, almost necessarily goes along with such tastes as these. The din of a bustling life suffers no sounds but the loudest to be distinguished; it is the fate, as Arnold himself tells us, of every voice, not of thunder, to be silenced. Surrounded by a crowd of objects competing for attention, we "glance, and nod, and bustle by"; and the glance falls, not upon what is most beautiful, but upon what is most glaring. His opposition to evil tendencies of this kind strengthened Arnold's love for the more subdued aspects of nature. The feeling of triumph over nature and of delight in life for its own sake is not only in the main a social feeling, but is most powerfully felt where men are gathered in the densest crowds. Arnold could not feel the sense of triumph, because he could not throw himself into the deepest current of life. He must "possess his soul," and to him possessing his soul meant quiet, freedom from distraction, the unhurried contemplation of things that were in danger of being lost to view in the crowd. To him the separation of one soul from another was a deeper fact than any union possible between them. "What heart knows another?" he asks, and immediately adds, "Ah, who knows his own?" "Thou hast been, shalt be, art, alone," is the sentence he pronounces upon himself, and he corrects himself merely to say that his solitude is modified only by companionship with other things as lonely:—

> Or, if not quite alone, yet they
> Which touch thee are unmating things—
> Ocean and clouds and night and day;
> Lorn autumns and triumphant springs
>
> (*Switzerland: Isolation*).

This loneliness of humanity is reflected in nature; and as among men the highest are the most lonely, so it is in nature:—

> The solemn peaks but to the stars are known,
> But to the stars, and the cold lunar beams;
> Alone the sun arises, and alone
> Spring the great streams (In *Utrumque Paratus*).

And this isolation which marks the great features of nature prevails also in the lower animal world. In his later years Arnold gave a great share of his poetic talent to the celebration of dead pets,—*Kaiser Dead, Geist's Grave, Poor Matthias*. These poems are full of Arnold's delicate grace. They are full also of a pathos half playful yet wholly serious. It is the sense of an insuperable barrier between the bird and man that gives this pathos to *Poor Matthias*. The bird sits upon his perch, sickening with mortal illness, while his unconscious human companions mock him with offers of cake and sugar and seed, and with praises of his beauty:—

> Gravely thou the while, poor dear!
> Sat'st upon thy perch to hear,
> Fixing with a mute regard
> Us, thy human keepers hard,
> Troubling, with our chatter vain,
> Ebb of life, and mortal pain—
> Us, unable to divine
> Our companion's dying sign,
> Or o'erpass the severing sea
> Set betwixt ourselves and thee,
> Till the sand thy feathers smirch
> Fallen dying off thy perch!

There follows the characteristic application to humanity. This severance between the bird and those who control its little life is pathetic. But is there not the same severance between man and man?—

> What you feel, escapes our ken—
> Know we more our fellow men?
> Human suffering at our side,
> Ah, like yours is undescried!

> Human longings, human fears,
> Miss our eyes and miss our ears.
> Little helping, wounding much,
> Dull of heart, and hard of touch,
> Brother man's despairing sign
> Who may trust us to divine ?
> Who assure us, sundering powers
> Stand not 'twixt his soul and ours ?

But to Arnold the sea is the great type of the power which thus isolates one being from another and sentences each to stand alone. Other poets as well as Arnold have felt this sense of loneliness, and others too have looked upon the sea as typifying the gulfs between soul and soul; but to none has the sense been more constantly present, and no one has ever expressed it more exquisitely. To him it is "the unplumb'd, salt, estranging sea"; and life itself is a sea with this power of separation :—

> Yes ! in the sea of life enisled,
> With echoing straits between us thrown,
> Dotting the shoreless watery wild,
> We mortal millions live *alone* (*Switzerland: To Marguerite*).

In these passages and in many more Arnold sees his own mood reflected in special phases of the world around him. In at least one poem already referred to, *Resignation*, he sees in the whole of nature evidence of agreement with his whole tone of feeling. Arnold was driven by the necessities of his thought to an attitude of resignation. Experience, in his opinion, gave no countenance to large hopes of pleasure and delight in life. The wise man's task was therefore to set aside expectations which could only result in disappointment; and in *Resignation* he attributes the same attitude of endurance to the whole powers of nature :—

> Yet, Fausta, the mute turf we tread,
> The solemn hills around us spread,
> This stream which falls incessantly,
> The strange-scrawl'd rocks, the lonely sky,
> If I might lend their life a voice,
> Seem to bear rather than rejoice.
> And even could the intemperate prayer
> Man iterates, while these forbear,
> For movement, for an ampler sphere,
> Pierce Fate's impenetrable ear ;

THE POETRY OF NATURE.

> Not milder is the general lot
> Because our spirits have forgot,
> In action's dizzying eddy whirl'd,
> The something that infects the world.

Still more frequently however Arnold goes to nature for the sake of contrast. Her calm is set against the turmoil of life, the slow motion and orderliness of her processes against the hurry and disorder characteristic, as Arnold thought, especially of the present century. Her permanence is opposed to the ephemerality of man, her wide generosity to his narrow selfishness. Both the latter points of contrast are finely expressed in *A Wish*, where the poet utters his desire, when death comes, to be

> Moved to the window near, and see
> Once more, before my dying eyes,
>
> Bathed in the sacred dews of morn
> The wide aerial landscape spread—
> The world which was ere I was born,
> The world which lasts when I am dead;
>
> Which never was the friend of *one*,
> Nor promised love it could not give,
> But lit for all its generous sun,
> And lived itself, and made us live.

The sense of permanence is present in *Resignation:*—

> The world in which we live and move
> Outlasts aversion, outlasts love,
> Outlasts each effort, interest, hope,
> Remorse, grief, joy.

The calmness of nature finds a heightened expression in the impressive contrast of *A Summer Night*. On the one hand is the picture of the man not low-spirited enough to live contentedly the life of the "brazen prison," yet incapable of steering his way on an ocean torn by the "trade-winds which cross it from eternity":—

> Awhile he holds some false way, undebarr'd
> By thwarting signs, and braves
> The freshening wind and blackening waves.
> And then the tempest strikes him; and between
> The lightning-bursts is seen
> Only a driving wreck,
> And the pale master on his spar-strewn deck

> With anguish'd face and flying hair
> Grasping the rudder hard,
> Still bent to make some port he knows not where,
> Still standing for some false, impossible shore.
> And sterner comes the roar
> Of sea and wind, and through the deepening gloom
> Fainter and fainter wreck and helmsman loom,
> And he too disappears and comes no more.

Over against this picture of toil and trouble ending in defeat, of the blind longing which is, after all, only for "some false, impossible shore," there is set the contrasting picture of the

> Heavens whose pure dark regions have no sign
> Of languor, though so calm, and, though so great,
> Are yet untroubled and unpassionate;
> Who, though so noble, share in the world's toil,
> And, though so task'd, keep free from dust and sd.

It is in this contrast that Arnold finds the principal lesson nature can give to humanity; and in this lies his fundamental difference from Wordsworth. Where Arnold finds contrast, Wordsworth sees only harmony; and in Arnold the sense of the contrast is apt to shine through lines where the Wordsworthian spirit is most conspicuous. There are few passages more deeply imbued with the sentiment of nature than that which I have quoted elsewhere from "*Obermann*"; yet it is too little to say that the contrast is present in that passage. It is to bring out the contrast that the lines are written.

I have spoken of Tennyson's pictorial power, and have contrasted Arnold as rather the sculptor of poetry. The contrast is grounded partly upon a certain severe purity and stately calm in Arnold's style and manner of conception, and partly on that absence of colour to which reference has also been made. It would be a mistake to understand it as implying incapacity to bring a scene before the mind. It is however true that Arnold is only on comparatively rare occasions a purely descriptive poet. The reference to man is generally so near the foreground that nature can hardly be said to be pictured alone. And it is not the concrete individual whom Arnold has in view, but rather the abstract "life in general". There are of course exceptions; as, for example, the majestic and beautiful lines on the Oxus at the close of *Sohrab and Rustum*. Mr. Hutton is doubtless right in regarding these lines as written to satisfy the poet's sense of beauty, not for the vague analogy the course of the river presents to human life. In this instance the scene is described with all the detail it admits of. More frequently a picture is condensed into a single word, as in "starlings *swirling* from the hedge," "the *swinging* waters," or in the celebrated and almost equally terse line on Oxford, "that sweet city with her dreaming spires". This last example, suffused as it is with human sentiment, returns to Arnold's habitual manner. The same feature is present throughout the beautiful descriptions of *Thyrsis* and *The Scholar Gipsy*, where not only Arnold's intimate familiarity with the physical features of the scenes, but his intense sympathy with their sentiment, has contributed to enrich his verse even beyond its wont. The famous lines in *The Scholar Gipsy* deserve all the praise they have received :—

> Thee at the ferry Oxford riders blithe,
>   Returning home on summer-nights, have met
> Crossing the stripling Thames at Bab-lock-hithe,
>   Trailing in the cool stream thy fingers wet,
>   As the punt's rope chops round ;
> And leaning backward in a pensive dream,
> And fostering in thy lap a heap of flowers
>   Pluck'd in shy fields and distant Wychwood bowers,
> And thine eyes resting on the moonlit stream.

Very fine too in its perfect simplicity is the contrast drawn in the winter picture between the snowy ridge of Cumner and "the line of festal light in Christ-Church hall". These examples, while rich in human emotion, are, it will be noticed, less imbued with the personal feelings of Arnold than some of those previously quoted. The same may be said of the passage elsewhere given from *The Church of Brou*, great part of the charm of which comes from the interweaving of the sentiment of the buried pair with the scene where they lie.

A remarkable feature in Arnold is that he nowhere, except ✓ perhaps in the sonnet, *In Harmony with Nature*, complains against nature. The exception may be explained by the circumstances in which, as the poet tells us, the sonnet was written. It assuredly is not consistent with Arnold's prevailing mood. The rise of the philosophy of evolution has been accompanied by the rise, on the part of some, of a feeling that nature is cruel. As Tennyson tells us, she sacrifices the individual to the type ; and the type itself disappears the moment it ceases to be in harmony with its surroundings. The law by which this takes place is inexorable in its rigidity, and few have been able to accept it uncomplainingly. Economists, politicians and social reformers, as well as poets, have risen in revolt against the system under which they live. A loud-voiced, but perfectly futile, insurrection against facts has been a feature in much of the reasoning, especially of the socialistic and economic reasoning, of recent times. The Malthusian law of population, in particular, has been denounced in terms generally reserved for personal injuries. The conclusion seems too hard that some are, by the conditions on which they hold their lease of life, foredoomed to destruction. Sometimes the indignation thus aroused is turned against the law, sometimes against those who promulgate it. Arnold denounces neither. He is prepared to find the law of nature hard, and he is too reasonable to blame those who discover what it is. It may be argued that such questions lie outside his domain as a poet; but this is not the case. He is constantly moving in spheres of thought in which such views, if he held them, could not but find expression. But he justifies nature, as we have just seen, on the ground that it promises nothing it cannot give, and lights for *all* its "generous" sun. The law may be hard, as it is certainly unbending, but it is perfectly equitable. Error arises through men claiming rights they do not possess. Diving into his conscience Arnold finds that he has no rights, only duties. Man therefore, so placed, cannot complain that he is deprived of that which never was his. He has come into a system older than himself, and he must bend to it rather than expect it to bend to him:—

> We mortals are no kings
> For each of whom to sway
> A new-made world up-springs,
> Meant merely for our play;
> No, we are strangers here; the world is from of old.

The so-called cruelty of nature is therefore, to Arnold, no cruelty, because nature owes no duties to man. He has his place, and equal measure is impartially meted out to him and to the inferior creatures; but coming in a stranger he has no right to claim as his own "the children's bread". Nature has in this sense no children, none to whom she owes duties or for whom she is bound to provide happiness.

CHAPTER X.

THE INFLUENCE OF SCIENCE.

THAT the good done by science is mingled with evil, and that there is reason in the protests of Ruskin against the confusion of "material" with "human" progress is not to be denied. Nor could the poets fail to be at one with Ruskin in the spirit of this protest. The poet by his very nature is bound to look upon merely material results as at best insufficient. It is true there have been exceptions. Macaulay, the literary apostle of material progress, had more of the poetic character than recent criticism has been disposed to credit him with; but the character was inconsistent with the opinions he professed. The votary of the philosophy of Fruit and Progress has no business with poetry. Fruit is something that can be eaten, and the Progress he speaks of is something that can be measured with a foot-rule. In the celebrated contrast between the Baconian philosophy and the "barren" ancient philosophy, there is no hint of a suspicion that "fruit" and "progress" can mean anything else. But nearly sixty years have passed since the publication of the essay on Bacon, and we have now to reckon with the fact that the "barren" philosophy of Plato and Aristotle has far more influence on thinking men than the "philosophy of fruit," and bids fair to outlive it.

Science however really means knowledge; and to the true man of science the machines which have so much occupied attention are but as the by-products of some chemical process, valuable perhaps, but not the thing aimed at. If, instead of fixing our eyes on the machinery, we regard science in its true light, it is clear that there must be innumerable points of contact between it and poetry. Intellect has an emotional side, and the emotions, especially those that are of any value for poetry, are often highly intellectual. All who believe in the essential oneness of the mind of man ought to hold that the growth of any single faculty will normally stimulate the growth of all the others. We should expect that the poetic view of nature and of man, though different from the scientific, would not only be influenced by it, but influenced for good.

But in this instance, so deep has been the sense of the difference that some have gone so far as to hold that the complete triumph of science involves the decay and death of poetry. Poetry, it is felt, rests upon the mystery which bounds the human intellect on every side. When we can arrange our thoughts in syllogisms we have bidden farewell to poetry; so long as our reach exceeds our grasp there is still room for the play of imagination. In the days before exact science was, imagination peopled nature with spiritual powers, with nymphs and dryads and fairies. These recede before science, and in the full blaze of knowledge there is room for nothing but a prosaic statement of facts.

Views of this kind have been held not merely by many ordinary men but by some far from ordinary. Even Carlyle, a poet at heart, though he lacked the gift of versification, shared the opinion that the day of poetry was past. Others, without accepting the conclusion, betray the influence of the argument by looking upon poetry as an elegant amusement, one of the refinements of civilisation, and not as also a part of the "sterner stuff" of life. But the doctrine involves a threefold error,—a false view of the relation between the pure intellect and intellect "touched with emotion," an exaggerated confidence in positive knowledge, and a narrow and inadequate conception of poetry.

With regard to the first point, it is only a false abstraction which thus opposes "pure" intellect to intellect touched with emotion. There is no such thing as intellect that is *not* so touched. The difference between art and science is not a difference in the *kind* of intellect exercised—we have only one,— but rather a difference in the sphere of its activity. Art is bound by its nature to be sensuous; but what is sensuous may be in the highest degree intellectual; and in the last resort there is nothing intellectual that does not rest on a basis of sense. Again, there can be no doubt that the emotional element is more prominent in art than in science, and that in the case of many of the hard facts with which the latter deals it is inappreciable. We feel no thrill in contemplating the equation, $2+2=4$. Nevertheless, there was a time when even this equation was a new discovery, and we may be sure that the discoverer did feel a thrill; and if we do not it is because we have grown beyond it. Just in the same way we grow out of forms of art. The thin tinkle of the savage harp is not music to the cultured ear, nor is the empty jingle of words poetry; but they are the beginnings of both, as this equation is the starting-point of mathematics.

But further, science does not consist exclusively or principally of hard facts. The problems which at any given time fill the mind of the man of science are as speculative as those of philosophy and as imaginative as the conceptions of the poet. The nature of electricity, or of the ether filling space, or of the atoms and molecules which constitute matter,—these are questions demanding the exercise of faculties closely akin to the poetic, and their solution is undoubtedly accompanied by emotions similar in kind to those which move the poet. So too with regard to what many consider the greatest scientific conception of recent times. Darwin, who in his later life had, by devotion to pure science, grown insensible to the beauty of poetry, in his great generalisation took a view of nature intimately related to the poetic. He did not first gather his full array of facts and then form his theory; but with broken fragments of proof in his possession, like the rising piers of an unfinished bridge across the stream of nature, he made his daring leap, and afterwards filled in the arches. The great discovery was an act of imagination, and it shows a direct contact between the scientific spirit and the poetic.

In reality, the truth about nature is not unpoetic, though partial conceptions of it may be so; and the complete triumph of science would be far more likely to result in a vast development of poetry than in its extinction. Even had the confidence in positive knowledge been well founded, the results anticipated would not have flowed from it. But the confidence was not well founded. Though the ideal of science is perfect knowledge, it is an ideal which never has been and never can be attained. Not only is the secret of the universe inviolate, the secret of its minutest part is never fully known. Science is

> But an exchange of ignorance for that
> Which is another kind of ignorance.

If poetry can subsist on mystery, there is little prospect that it will soon be scanted of food.

Moreover, the notion we have been examining implies a narrow view of poetry. In the first place it is forgotten that poetry is neither only nor chiefly concerned with nature: its great province is life. The nymphs and fairies themselves would never have been created but for that interest in life which, from Homer down to Browning, has been the pivot whereon poetic thought has turned. There still remains in the mystery of life ample room for poetic intuition as well as for the precision and the patient investigation of science. And in the second place—what I chiefly wish to insist upon here—the facts with regard to the poetry of nature are in irreconcilable conflict with this theory. It is most remarkable that just where, according to the view under discussion, poetry ought to exhibit the most conspicuous decay, it has made the most marked advance, if it has not achieved its greatest triumphs.

At no period in literary history has the poetry of nature held so great a place as in the last hundred years. No very great poet before Wordsworth ever built a reputation mainly upon his treatment of inanimate nature. No poet of any sort, great or small, ever set about, before the rise of exact science, to make nature the principal subject of his study. Virgil's Georgics are no exception to the rule, for there the study of nature was not disinterested, but was made with an ulterior end in view. The Roman farmer is closer to Virgil's mind than his crops and his ploughs; and nature is investigated, not for the sake of pure knowledge or of poetic emotion, but for "fruit". But at the very dawn of experimental science, or at least about the time when its results began to permeate the general mind, we observe the beginnings of a closer study by the poets of natural phenomena. Early in the sixteenth century this is already visible in one or two of the more quietly reflective poets. Drummond of Hawthornden not only gives greater proportionate attention to external nature than it had received before, but shows an appreciation of aspects which had previously been viewed with repulsion and dislike. The conventional May morning had satisfied the poets for generations. They were not themselves disposed to seek for variety, and their audience were not sufficiently interested to demand it. A century later we find the poetry of nature developed almost in proportion to the development of science. James Thomson would probably have been impossible at an earlier date; we certainly do not find his equivalent. Later still, this branch of art may be said to culminate in Wordsworth. No one after him bestows quite so large a proportion of his attention on the lower and inanimate creation; yet in most of the great poets subsequent to him it holds a prominent place, and in none of them is it inconsiderable. Coleridge, Byron, Scott, Shelley and Keats were all lovers of natural beauty, and have all devoted a great deal of their verse to descriptions of it. The last chapter has shown how the same spirit lives on in the Victorians, and how even Browning, absorbed as he is in the development of the soul, is nevertheless a poet of nature as well.

Nor is it in poetry alone that the coincidence between the development of science and the development of art is noticeable. It is equally conspicuous in landscape painting. If Wordsworth is the poetic high-priest of nature, Turner among painters holds the same position towards her. While it is perhaps more than doubtful whether in the plastic arts generally recent times have equalled either the golden age of Greek art or the great days of the Renaissance, it is certain that in landscape we have surpassed the artists of the Renaissance, and, notwithstanding our imperfect knowledge of Greek painting, few would doubt that we have also surpassed the Greeks. There have been in recent times not only greater individual men, but a higher average and a wider distribution of talent among those who have devoted themselves to this branch of art. The same minute attention which was long ago bestowed upon the human form, has now been given to inanimate nature. The great artists of the Renaissance studied anatomy, because they knew that they could not reproduce even the surface play of life unless they understood the causes at work beneath. In the same spirit some of the more far-seeing of the modern landscape-painters have studied natural science and learnt to use the microscope, confident that the knowledge so acquired, though it could never be directly applied to their art, would not be useless. It is characteristic of investigation in this exhaustless field that the "interrogation" of nature not only may but constantly does lead to answers not at first contemplated by the questioner.

Has this double coincidence between the development of science on the one hand, and on the other the development of the poetry of nature and of the skill to paint landscape, been purely accidental? It is not easy to believe so; yet if we question it we must be prepared not merely to modify but to reverse what has been the general view as to the effect of science upon poetry. It would seem that science, far from narrowing the scope of poetry, has widened it by the addition of a great province in earlier days very imperfectly explored and occupied. And on reflection it is not difficult to suggest reasons why this should be the case. After all, the nymphs and fairies were, when regarded merely as poetic explanations of natural phenomena, no better than a kind of machinery. They had, of course, especially the creations of Greek mythology, other aspects, but these are not here to the point. As a machinery for the explanation of nature, their poetical capabilities were very limited. There was too much of the element of caprice in the conception of them, and law is invariably greater and more fruitful than caprice. The art which is content to copy, or more properly to study and idealise nature, is always superior to that which by a lawless imagination frames monsters. The Venus of Milo and the Apollo Belvedere are greater than the best of the fauns and satyrs of ancient sculpture. So too a Hamlet from the hand of Shakespeare or a Pompilia from that of Browning is superior not merely in execution but almost by the nature of the case to a Lamia by Keats.

So it has proved with regard to the physical world. It took men hundreds of years to learn that the best way to subdue nature was to begin by obeying her. Till within the last three or four centuries they went on, with here and there a rare exception, such as Roger Bacon, substituting their own vain imaginings for the facts of nature. As Francis Bacon insisted, the true method was to "interrogate" nature, to listen to the answer, and to believe that and that alone. On the vast growth which has resulted from the adoption of this method it is unnecessary to insist; but evidently such a growth could not take place without exercising wide-spread influence beyond its own strict limits. It has reacted upon philosophy, as it would be easy to show that philosophy has in turn reacted upon science; it has changed the method of history; it has profoundly influenced theology; and it has breathed a soul into the poetry of nature instead of taking life and spirit from it.

For the poet too has had to substitute "the reign of law" for his old empire of caprice, and like his brother the man of science, he has found his profit in doing so. Nature, closely studied, has once more proved richer than the human mind ringing the changes upon a few superficial facts or appearances. In the study of nature, the abandonment of the idea that the key must be or could be found within man's inner consciousness seemed at first to take the investigator out into a cold, distant, alien world; but, like the trader in an unknown sea, he returned enriched by his venture. There are, says Browning,

> Two points in the adventure of the diver,
> One—when, a beggar, he prepares to plunge,
> One—when, a prince, he rises with his pearl.

The man of science and the poet have each secured a pearl. Accurate observation, the spirit "that watches and receives," has been only less fruitful in poetry than in science.

That the change in the attitude of the poets towards nature has been strongly influenced, if not caused, by the change in science, is thus rendered probable by the fact that it is a change of the same kind. There are doubtless poetical conventions still, and numerous proofs of the poets' ignorance. Even such a close observer as Tennyson falls into the notorious blunder of making the may blossom on the black-thorn. But the stock of accurate observation has increased enormously. Versified science, like Erasmus Darwin's *Botanic Garden*, need not be taken into account, though even that is instructive as indicating a sense of the relation between poetry and science; what it is really important to notice is the spirit of close observation, cognate to that of science, which pervades nearly all recent poetry,—how, for example, in *Maud*, Tennyson's imagination plays round the shell found on the Breton coast, and from the shell conceives its vanished tenant pushing a golden foot or fairy horn "thro' his dim water-world". Just as geographical discovery fired the imagination of the Elizabethans, and as the promise of the French Revolution roused the enthusiasm of those who were young when it occurred, so have the triumphs of science coloured the thought and brightened the hopes both of the revolutionary poets and, still more, of the Victorians. *Locksley Hall* bears witness to this influence. *Paracelsus* would probably never have been written but for it.

It would be difficult to exaggerate the power of hopefulness in furthering the progress of the human spirit and determining the direction of that progress. Without reasonable hope of results strenuous exertion will not long continue to be made. Now, it was science that first inspired the hope of such results in the region of nature, and made the hope assurance by actually producing the results. Comparatively recent though the date is, we have already almost forgotten that the inspiration was ever necessary. Socrates dissuaded his pupils from physical investigations on the ground that they were too difficult, and gave no hope of success. The prudent man, he held, would rather busy himself in the easier sphere of moral and philosophical inquiries. The facts before Socrates gave some support to his opinion. In the present day, we have so completely reversed the view that we even forget it was ever maintained. It was not only maintained, but for centuries it governed the practice of men. There need be little wonder that, while this opinion reigned, the poetry of nature did not thrive, that it was meagre in amount, and that it tended to become conventional. The poet too must be induced to believe in the existence of the pearl before he will dive; and it was science that implanted in him this faith.

Science then seems in point of fact to have influenced poetry for good; and there is strong reason for believing that every increase of knowledge must ultimately do so. But it is by no means certain that its immediate effect will be beneficial. There was a time when it appeared likely that science would be harmful to art. In an earlier part of this book it has been necessary to call attention to the symptoms of hesitancy in the poetry of the third decade of the century. The poets seemed as if they would justify the opinion that they were triflers. The explanation already given, that this hesitancy arose from the failure of the motive supplied by the Revolution, is true so far as it goes. But a negative explanation is seldom the whole truth. The failure and decay of one impulse means as a rule the growth of another. Early in the present century the ground left vacant by fading social and political ideals began to be occupied by the ideals of science. But the poetic aspect of the latter was not at once evident as that of the former had been; and though, as an element among others, science had hitherto been helpful, as an all-pervading force it threatened destruction.

The tendency to regard science as purely an affair of "facts," and to set its facts in sharp contrast to "ideas," considered as mere figments of the mind, was probably stronger in the second quarter of the present century than it has been since or than it ever was before. It is true, the popular consciousness of the contrast reached its full growth at a somewhat later time; but already, before the middle of the century, it was beginning to lose hold on the men whose opinion ultimately rules, and it afterwards found no such champions outside the ranks of pure science as it had in those earlier days. Reference has already been made to Macaulay's brilliant essay. John Stuart Mill went further, he made a philosophy for it. Mill was, notwithstanding his limitations, a great man, and he did a great work. But no philosophy more unpoetical than his was ever formulated, and, so far as it represented the spirit of the time, it proved that spirit to be inimical to the free play of imagination.

There were never wanting some who protested against this conception of the universe. All through his life Carlyle stood in determined opposition to it. But for many years Carlyle's was the voice of one crying in the wilderness; and the fate of *Sartor Resartus*, both before and after publication, goes far to show how entirely foreign to public opinion was anything savouring of idealism. The opposite doctrine was not only accepted readily, it hardly stood in need of proof. We cannot wonder therefore that the accents of poetry faltered. A versified Mill was impossible; and yet there were few who could without misgiving venture to express another conception of the universe. It was easier to evade the difficulty than to solve it, and to the smaller minds the temptation was irresistible to play only upon the surface of things.

Even when the poets begin to throw off the shackles they still show the marks of them. The hero of *Locksley Hall* sees "the heavens fill with commerce". The wars of the future, in his imagination, take their character from the mechanical contrivances used in them. He is impressed, not by the ideas at the root of science, but by her material triumphs. He is indeed aware of the intermixture of evil with them: for though "knowledge comes" (and knowledge here means control over matter), yet "wisdom lingers," and the individual withers. But he is still far from the view of his old age, when he sees those material triumphs "staled by frequence, shrunk by usage into commonest commonplace"; and moreover sees the world, thus familiar with such triumphs, not appreciably better or happier than of old. The great task for poetry at the opening of the Victorian era was to live down this materialism, to absorb the truth in science and yet not to treat it as the whole truth. This it had done, partly by its internal development, partly by the rise of new forces outside it, before the turn of the century, and by that time the temporary danger that the influence of science would be prejudicial had passed away.

There are two ways in which the effect of science upon modern poetry might be estimated. It might be done by a survey of the cases in which the poets embody in their work particular and definite results of science. They do so frequently, and there would be little difficulty in showing, especially from Browning, how details of the most unexpected kind, from physiology, from chemistry, from the physical theory of light, and from many other branches of science, have passed into verse. This may be a matter of merely subordinate importance, or on the other hand it may be the promise of a fresh and unexpected development of poetry. There probably was a time when the poets' references to nature seemed hardly more noteworthy. But in any case the adequate treatment of the subject after this fashion would demand a knowledge of science to which the writer cannot lay claim. It will certainly be easier, and perhaps also in the present state of poetry more profitable, to view the influence "writ large" in the greater impulses and tendencies communicated by science to poetry. We have already seen how one such impulse almost created the poetry of nature; it remains to see how the poets' wider conceptions of life and of their whole function were affected.

In *Paracelsus* Browning proclaimed, as it were by sound of trumpet, that the spirit of science had entered into poetry. The poem may be regarded as at once a celebration of the greatness of the scientific ideal, and a warning of its possible one-sidedness. It is impressive just because the man Paracelsus is great. He is the man of science idealised, and following out his aim as such to the exclusion of everything else. He fails, not on account of remissness or incapacity in pursuit of the ideal, but because the ideal itself is wrong. Physiology teaches us that a man may die of starvation with food all round him, if the food be of one kind only and have not in it every element his nature needs; and similarly Paracelsus, the man of profoundest knowledge, starves for want of spiritual nourishment. It is the irresistible cravings of nature that rouse him to the closing struggles to repair his own fatal mistake. *Paracelsus* is perhaps the most striking sermon ever preached on the solidarity of human nature. Browning himself afterwards lost this luminous breadth of view, and fell into the opposite one-sidedness of not giving knowledge its fair place as a factor in life. But no apology has on this ground to be made for *Paracelsus*: it is, though perhaps not wholly free from traces of bias, a fair demonstration that the pursuit of the scientific ideal *alone* is a mistake.

If Browning himself fell from this height, none of his contemporaries ever fully attained it. For that very reason they are as examples in some ways more instructive than he. Tennyson oscillated between two views, and it was not till the latter part of his career that he clearly showed he had made the scientific spirit his own. In this respect once more Arnold is the man who most obviously and simply exhibits the influence of the forces of the time. He does so notwithstanding the fact that his references to science are few, and that he more rarely than either of his contemporaries embodies its results in his verse. What science gave him was rather its method, its trust in reason, and its demand for clearness and certainty, than any more specific ideas. But these are of immense importance. Without the previous scientific work, and, it may be added, without the work of Goethe, who had already wedded the spirit of science to poetry, Arnold's poetry could not have been what it is. Whoever has read it carefully must have been struck with the pervading sense of an obligation to examine all old beliefs. Nothing is accepted on authority. The foundations of the old beliefs seem to have crumbled away at the advance of science. Arnold does not conceive it possible " to curse or to deny the truth " science teaches. He accepts it, and only seeks to apply it more closely to life, and to estimate the results. The great problems of modern life, as they appeared to him, were largely the creation of science.

That Arnold did not adopt more from science may, paradoxical as it seems to say so, be ascribed to the influence of science itself. The demand for clearness and assurance with respect to human life was one which even science could not altogether meet. Not that Arnold was the man to run atilt against the law of gravitation because its whole meaning is a mystery, or to insist that everything should be proved according to the principles of

Euclid. But it must be remembered that a great part of the influence of science during the present century has been due less to its achievements in the past than to the hope it has inspired for the future. It is in this respect that Arnold finds it wanting. On examination he discovers no sufficient ground for the expectations which were cherished, and turns the sceptical attitude of mind against the source of the scepticism. He keeps before his eye the conditions which knowledge of nature must fulfil if it is to satisfy the aspirations and needs of humanity, finds that it does not and cannot satisfy them, and turns from it in distrust and almost in indifference. This is the spirit of *Empedocles on Etna*. The lesson there drawn from experience is rather that of the limitation of human powers than of their greatness. The idea of a world made for man is swept away as an illusion, for man is but an item in the whole. "Experience, like a sea, soaks all-effacing in," and we learn from it that we must obey the law of the universe, not hope to control it. This is likewise the lesson of science, but Arnold throws the stress upon what we cannot, not upon what we can do; upon what nature, viewed in the light of science, cannot give us, not upon what she can give. Universal curiosity only opens before us a vaster gulf of ignorance. "Our hair grows grey, our eyes are dimm'd, our heat is tamed" in the effort to know what in the end we only discover that we can never know.

This however is only part of Arnold's teaching. He repeats in his own way the lesson of *Paracelsus*. The demands of human nature can never be met by the most complete success of science; the heart must be soothed as well as the head satisfied. Conduct, Arnold tells us elsewhere, is at least three-fourths of life, and it is doubtful how far the most thorough knowledge of nature can contribute to that. The comfort which he drew from nature was not due, at least directly, to science; it had its source in feeling rather than in knowledge. When we seek to understand we are driven to the verge of despair:—

> The world, which seems
> To lie before us like a land of dreams,
> So various, so beautiful, so new,
> Hath really neither joy, nor love, nor light,
> Nor certitude, nor peace, nor help for pain;
> And we are here as on a darkling plain
> Swept with confused alarms of struggle and flight,
> Where ignorant armies clash by night (*Dover Beach*).

But joy and love and light are just the food human nature demands, the food on which it has heretofore been nourished, and without which " man's life is cheap as beast's ".

It is at this point that Arnold does not indeed part company with science, but pronounces it insufficient. What it has taught remains true, but either there is something omitted, or life is not worth living. It is not merely that the quantity of satisfaction to be derived from a knowledge of nature is less than had been imagined, but its kind is not the kind required, or rather is not the *only* kind required. Hence the failure is not temporary but permanent. As Midas starved in the midst of wealth, so will the soul that only understands. Widely as Arnold dissented from the theologians, he agreed with them on the vital point that man demands more than the satisfaction merely of the thirst for knowledge; and so far as it seemed to deny or to ignore this demand he regarded science, or rather the thinner voices speaking in her name, with as much dissatisfaction as he felt for theology, and with far more impatience.

> We admire with awe
> The exulting thunder of your race;
> You give the universe your law,
> You triumph over time and space!
> Your pride of life, your tireless powers,
> We laud them, but they are not ours
>   (*Stanzas from the Grande Chartreuse*),

are the words in which he addresses the " sons of the world "; and the contrast between his language to them and the sympathy, notwithstanding intellectual disagreement, he shows for the monks, indicates to which side his heart inclined. The "triumph over time and space" dispels any doubt that might be felt as to the class whom the poet regards as " sons of the world ". He calls his own time an "iron age" because of its hardness of intellect; and that hardness of intellect is most conspicuously present in those "sons of the world".

If the heart therefore could have given the answer, there can be no doubt what Arnold's answer would have been. It is to his lasting honour that he refused to take this easy way. Science and the other forces of modern life bring him face to face with the possibility that life may in very truth be not worth living. He does not shirk the possibility. He does not shelter himself, as even Browning does, under the argument that "being weary" proves that man has "where to rest". No poet of the century is intellectually more sincere. He walks by the light of "the high white star of truth," and only insists that we must pay equal regard to all its rays. He quarrels only with those who, looking through glasses which intercept some, insist that the remaining rays are the sole light. Theology, in his view, falls into this error by denying the facts. Science, he thinks, falls into it likewise by prematurely closing the discussion and insisting that what may prove to be only part of the truth is the whole truth. Theology had combated this one-sidedness by denying the right of unlimited inquiry; Arnold did so by insisting that the inquiry had been unduly limited, and that therefore the result was only partially true.

How far he himself by this method advanced towards a positive conclusion will appear in more detail hereafter. In the meantime it will suffice to state the general result. His prose as well as his poetry proves that Arnold accepted the spiritual rather than the material interpretation of the universe. If he is obliged to reject creeds, he rests still in a "moral plan" firm and sure without their support. His polemical writings are an attack on most of the articles of faith his countrymen accepted; but they rest on an interpretation of experience the same in kind as that involved in the creeds. It is curious that, while Arnold's disagreement with the party of faith has been more than sufficiently insisted upon, his agreement with them on the questions at the root of all has been comparatively unheeded. Yet the fact that an intellect so clear and sane, so imbued with the love of truth, and so indisposed to accept it on authority, did nevertheless adopt their view of those questions, is surely an impressive testimony to the inherent strength of their case.

> Leave then the Cross as ye have left carved gods,
> But guard the fire within (*Progress*),

is his cry. The Cross here represents the "creed outworn," "the fire within" is the truth it bore witness to, deeper still than that partial truth which, if this be neglected, leaves the soul to perish of cold.

Thus Arnold rejects the claim of science to be sufficient for life; but while he does so he is deeply influenced by science. He accepts its method, and also, within the limits proper to the

sphere of inquiry, its results. The confidence in investigation
rather than authority, and the trust in reason rather than
tradition, are characteristic of his whole attitude of mind. If
in the solution of the problem thus arising he seems to part
company with some of the followers of science, it is only to
vindicate their principles against themselves.

But while the influence of science upon Arnold is great, he
maintains a habitual reticence with regard to it. He simply
adopts its fundamental principles. He does not, to any considerable extent, embody its particular results in his verse, nor
does he often refer to the source whence he draws his principles.
He maintains this reticence even with regard to the supreme
scientific idea of the century—supreme at least in its bearing
upon poetry,—the idea of evolution, probably because, although
its power is visible in his verse, he did not understand its importance. The greater part of his poetical work had been done before
the theory of evolution was moulded into its most impressive
shape. His references to it are indirect. He would almost
certainly have condemned as unmeasured the intellectual turmoil
it caused, for he was as little disposed to be carried away by new,
as to yield unquestioning allegiance to old ideas. This practical
application of the principle, $\mu\eta\delta\grave{\epsilon}\nu\ \check{\alpha}\gamma\alpha\nu$, is the poet's weakness
as well as his strength. It makes him the best critic of the new
time, but it takes from him the possibility of being its prophet.
Arnold did indeed absorb and embody in his verse the larger
results of evolutionary thought,—the conception of life as a
whole, the conception that thoughts befitting one age and
helpful to it must and do drop away from another like a worn-out garment, the conception of morality as a growth out of
"nature". Even this position, ordinary as it seems to most of
us now, was not attained without effort. Carlyle for half a
lifetime struggled to gain acceptance for it; and the battle is
not wholly won even yet. Arnold's critical spirit, here akin to
scepticism, prevented his fuller acceptance of such ideas, and
above all choked the spring of hope which might have burst
from them and given his verse a buoyancy it does not possess.
But to wish that it had this would be to wish away its peculiar
charm, and the very suggestion serves to show how futile must
be the regret that a great man is not other than he is.

This idea of evolution however is the one by which the
influence of science upon the other two poets is best measured.

By means of it, far more than anything else, science has coloured modern thought outside its own bounds. The reason is plain. It positively revolutionised men's conceptions of life, and their chief interest must necessarily be in life. The idea itself is by no means the exclusive property of science; on the contrary, the earliest, widest and most satisfactory expression of it was given in philosophy; and we find it even in poetry before the date of its adoption in science. Still, it is certain that but for the working of it out by Darwin, the idea of evolution would not have had the tithe of the influence it now possesses; and the weapon belongs to him who can best wield it. Though therefore it is in part misleading to treat as the outcome of science what is really due to the whole current of modern thought, it is perhaps less misleading than any alternative arrangement.

We, who have grown up in the light of this idea, already find it difficult to realise a world in which it was unknown. Some indeed still dread and reject it, but they cannot help seeing by its light. Its influence has been almost universal. Under the reign of the old thought the sense of law, even among the intelligent, was imperfect. The domain of chance girdled it round. And not only so, but, with regard to living beings, the law was looked upon as discontinuous from age to age. The truth was seen in glimpses, just as there were anticipations of the theory of evolution itself; but previous to the present century the natural result of the theory of special creation showed itself. Species were regarded as in the main fixed and stationary; and the view was by no means limited in its consequences to natural history. In the case of humanity, the hopes of those who were inclined to believe vaguely in progress were more than balanced by the pessimism of those who saw the highest attainment of the race in a golden age of the past. There were ideals, it is true, like the Christian ideal; but as they were then understood they were essentially ideals for the individual. A soul was a soul. "The pomp on Buonarroti's brow" counted for no more than the happiness of the humblest spirit that ever entered Paradise. Perhaps it ought not to count for more. But it has to be added that there was no sense of a movement of the race towards that pomp. On the contrary, the garden of Eden was the cradle of man, his later dwelling-place was an earth bringing forth thorns and thistles for his sake. Regress, not advance, degeneracy, not improvement, was what the eye saw in the past of the race. Progress, so far as there was social progress at all, was looked upon as the result of social machinery. It hardly dawned upon men's minds that a general spiritual advance might co-operate with, and indeed help to make, the machinery.

Once apply the doctrine of evolution, and the view must be entirely changed. We must conceive of society as a continuous growth, not as loosely linked from age to age; its unity as vital and necessary, not as capricious and semi-accidental. We must conceive also of the individual as drawing increased wealth of meaning from all the generations previous to him. The last generation is "heir of all the ages" in a sense not previously dreamed of. It is impossible to set bounds to the influence of this great idea. It has banished for ever conceptions which, like the theory of Rousseau, were, only a century ago, not only possible but dominant. It has been the great solvent of the extreme individualism which till the other day governed English thought in politics as well as in religion. It has suggested new conceptions as to the nature and limits of responsibility. It is applied in all spheres, with the partial exception of the sphere of religion. When we reflect that it goes nearer than any other idea to the root of the problems of life, and that the great subject-matter of poetry is life, we must admit at any rate its potential importance in poetry.

Both Browning and Tennyson were evolutionists, but both rejected those conclusions drawn in the name of scientific evolutionism, which seemed to go beyond the strict domain of science, and also, as they thought, beyond the limits of proof. In their acceptance of evolution we find, in part, the secret of the buoyant optimism of Browning, and the more chastened optimism of Tennyson. For this philosophy of development is an emphatically hopeful one. It can find for a large amount of suffering and evil a place and a meaning more satisfactory to reason than the bare assertion that "all is for the best in the best of all possible worlds," or than the Manicheism which ascribes it all to a principle of evil somehow permitted to exist by another principle all-powerful and all-good, which yet does not choose to abolish the evil. It is true there is another side to the shield. If there is evolution, there is also " Reversion ever dragging Evolution in the mud ". But when full allowance has been made for it, the fact still remains that all the evidence of the past points to a movement on the whole upwards, however diversified by partial and temporary regression.

Tennyson's references to science are much more numerous than Arnold's, though probably its real influence upon him was less. Every reader must have noticed how his imagination dwells upon the discoveries of modern astronomy. He was profoundly impressed by the conception of multitudes of "peopled spheres" as well as earth. He was interested in the discoveries of physiology, and in *In Memoriam* borrows a striking fact from embryology. But we find in his acceptance of the evolutionary view his principal point of contact with science. Of Tennyson's direct references to evolution, some of the most emphatic, and probably the best known, are in *Locksley Hall*, considerably prior to the formulation of the theory by Darwin. Even disappointed passion does not long dash the confidence of the hero that the course of the world is forward; and if he refers to the belief in a golden age away back in the simpler past of the race, it is only to reject that belief with disdain. The idea of evolution is present too in *Maud*:—

> A monstrous eft was of old the Lord and Master of Earth,
> For him did his high sun flame, and his river billowing ran,
> And he felt himself in his force to be Nature's crowning race.
> As nine months go to the shaping an infant ripe for his birth,
> So many a million of ages have gone to the making of man:
> He now is first, but is he the last? is he not too base?

The same idea may be likewise traced in a number of pieces where it is not distinctly expressed. The spirit of it inspires and moulds the *Idylls of the King*, which neither depict a far-past age, nor present an ideal to be striven for by the solitary aspirant after purity and moral elevation. The ideal is social in its nature, to be reached only by man through the help of man, and in the course of ages, each generation working upon the vantage-ground gained for it by its predecessors.

Contrast with this such a conception as that of Milton's *Paradise Lost*. All Milton's greatness could not lift him above the individualistic views of his time. He recognises the hereditary character of evil; but he is by no means so clear as to the hereditary character of good. Even the visiting of the sins of the fathers upon the children is rather a theological mystery, an imputation of guilt by arbitrary will upon the person not guilty, than a profound fact in the constitution of the universe, to be searched into and if possible explained. The dealings between God and man are personal dealings, and each individual must work out his own salvation.

There was and still is a most important truth in this; but it was the characteristic defect of the Protestant Reformation that it exaggerated the truth to the complete eclipse of the opposite truth. This opposite truth modern thought has revindicated, and we see it passing into the poetry of the nineteenth century. Tennyson's political poems are charged with a sense, new to history or enormously increased in strength, of a political development from age to age. He cannot sufficiently condemn the "catastrophic" view of progress, the violent overturns characteristic of France after the Revolution. He cannot sufficiently praise the quiet, slow, sure growth of English freedom. The process he praises is that which agrees best with the general law of progress in nature, the process he condemns is analogous to that which early science thought to be the general law, but which later science has either wholly rejected, or degraded to a position altogether secondary. Trust the imperceptible [but sure growth of ages and distrust the spirit of revolution which seeks to shrivel up earth and heaven like a scroll in order to make them anew, is the moral of Tennyson's political pieces. Look with hope to minute, almost infinitesimal variations, which by accumulation may become great, and expect nothing from the monstrous birth of nature, is the lesson of evolutionary science.

In Memoriam likewise contains this evolutionary faith. One of its best-known passages is that in which the poet speaks of the succession of the types of nature; and the poem ends with the promise of a gradual development from age to age. The moon is invoked to rise,

> And touch with shade the bridal doors,
>   With tender gloom the roof, the wall;
>   And breaking let the splendour fall
> To spangle all the happy shores
>
> By which they rest, and ocean sounds,
>   And, star and system rolling past,
>   A soul shall draw from out the vast
> And strike his being into bounds,
>
> And, moved thro' life of lower phase,
>   Result in man, be born and think,
>   And act and love, a closer link
> Betwixt us and the crowning race

> Of those that, eye to eye, shall look
>   On knowledge; under whose command
>   Is Earth and Earth's, and in their hand
> Is Nature like an open book;
>
> No longer half-akin to brute,
>   For all we thought and loved and did,
>   And hoped, and suffer'd, is but seed
> Of what in them is flower and fruit.

All these references are to poems published before the appearance of *The Origin of Species*. Tennyson's grasp of the principle became much firmer after that date. There are two thoughts which seem to have struck him with special force. One is the sense that any great change must be very slowly brought about. Men calculate time by centuries, nature measures it by millions of years. But though the process is slow no limit can be set to its power. Man may be developed into something far higher than he is:—

> Man as yet is being made, and ere the crowning Age of ages,
> Shall not æon after æon pass and touch him into shape?
>   (*The Making of Man*).

Or again he may pass away altogether:—

> Many an æon moulded earth before her highest, man, was born,
> Many an æon too may pass when earth is manless and forlorn
>   (*Locksley Hall Sixty Years After*).

The same sense of immeasurable time in the past, and of the indissoluble relation of human life to the whole scheme of things, is expressed once more in *De Profundis*:—

> Out of the deep, my child, out of the deep,
> Where all that was to be, in all that was,
> Whirl'd for a million æons thro' the vast
> Waste dawn of multitudinous-eddying light—
> Out of the deep, my child, out of the deep,
> Thro' all this changing world of changeless law,
> And every phase of ever-heightening life,
> And nine long months of antenatal gloom,
> With this last moon, this crescent—her dark orb
> Touched with earth's light—thou comest, darling boy.

The other thought of these later poems is the possibility of reversion, a possibility which gave to Tennyson's later accent a less confident ring. In the earlier poems, evolution seems to him to promise a sure movement upwards, and this, concurring with the hopefulness of youth, issues in an exultant optimism. But age, and the wider view experience opened of the complex problems presented by the world, modified this optimism. The result is a change to a tone still hopeful, but no longer, as of old, triumphant. We have just seen how the sense intrudes that the progress, even if sure, is exceedingly slow; and in *Locksley Hall Sixty Years After* we see the shadow of Reversion projected over Evolution. The conception of the difficulties in the way is far more just than any the poet ever showed in his earlier years.

> All the full-brain, half-brain races, led by Justice, Love, and Truth;
> All the millions one at length, with all the visions of my youth?
>
> All diseases quench'd by Science, no man halt, or deaf or blind;
> Stronger ever born of weaker, lustier body, larger mind?
>
> Earth at last a warless world, a single race, a single tongue—
> I have seen her far away—for is not Earth as yet so young?—
>
> Every tiger madness muzzled, every serpent passion kill'd,
> Every grim ravine a garden, every blazing desert till'd,
>
> Robed in universal harvest up to either pole she smiles,
> Universal ocean softly washing all her warless Isles.
>
> Warless? when her tens are thousands, and her thousands millions, then—
> All her harvest all too narrow—who can fancy warless men?
>
> Warless? war will die out late then. Will it ever? late or soon?
> Can it, till this outworn earth be dead as yon dead world the moon?

It is clear that Tennyson before he wrote this had lost a good deal of his old hopefulness. A wider study of the poems proves that the change is not to be explained away by pleading that *Locksley Hall Sixty Years After* is dramatic; but it also proves that it is far from being a change to pessimism. The change is for him gain. Optimism must justify itself at the bar of experience, and Tennyson's earlier optimism scarcely made the attempt. A subdued hopefulness after facing such hard facts as these is a more encouraging thing than unclouded confidence not founded on due consideration of them.

But it was Browning who grasped the principle of evolution in by far the firmest fashion, and it was on him that the science and philosophy of the century left the deepest marks. Take from him, in fact, this principle, and the greatest motive and purpose of his poetry is gone. His conception of the universe is ruled by it.

Browning was not only the poet who made most use of evolution, he was also the one who first expressed its meaning adequately. Tennyson, as we have seen, had dim previsions of it before the adoption of it in science; but Browning had already grasped its whole significance, and all we can trace in his later poetry is merely some enrichment of detail due to the influence of Darwin's theory, and some criticisms directed against conclusions drawn from but not warranted by the theory. It was therefore not so much the influence of science as the influence of all contemporary thought that led him to the idea of evolution. But for the fact that we are assured he did not in his youth know German philosophy, that would naturally have been thought to be the source from which he borrowed. As it is, we must consider this one more instance of a great idea, when "the times are ripe" for it, occurring to several minds independently.

The extraordinary precision and clearness with which Browning had, when little more than a boy, conceived the meaning of evolution, is evident from the powerfully thought and beautifully worded close of *Paracelsus*. Seldom, even to this day, has the idea received a more satisfactory expression; and the passage, while permitting the philosophical idea to shine through, yet remains truly poetical. The speaker, Paracelsus, begins by showing how God is immanent in everything, and how all leads up to man:—

> Thus he dwells in all,
> From life's minute beginnings, up at last
> To man—the consummation of this scheme
> Of being, the completion of this sphere
> Of life: whose attributes had here and there
> Been scattered o'er the visible world before,
> Asking to be combined, dim fragments meant
> To be united in some wondrous whole,
> Imperfect qualities throughout creation,
> Suggesting some one creature yet to make,
> Some point where all those scattered rays should meet
> Convergent in the faculties of man.
> Power—neither put forth blindly, nor controlled
> Calmly by perfect knowledge; to be used
> At risk, inspired or checked by hope and fear:

THE INFLUENCE OF SCIENCE.

> Knowledge—not intuition, but the slow
> Uncertain fruit of an enhancing toil,
> Strengthened by love: love—not serenely pure,
> But strong from weakness, like a chance-sown plant
> Which, cast on stubborn soil, puts forth changed buds
> And softer stains, unknown in happier climes;
> Love which endures and doubts and is oppressed
> And cherished, suffering much and much sustained,
> And blind, oft-failing, yet believing love,
> A half-enlightened, often-chequered trust:—
> Hints and previsions of which faculties
> Are strewn confusedly everywhere about
> The inferior natures, and all lead up higher,
> All shape out dimly the superior race,
> The heir of hopes too fair to turn out false,
> And man appears at last. So far the seal
> Is put on life; one stage of being complete,
> One scheme wound up: and from the grand result
> A supplementary reflux of light
> Illustrates all the inferior grades, explains
> Each back step in the circle (ii. pp. 168-169).

But this is only the beginning. As creation has climbed by countless steps to man, so must man by struggles ages long rise from what he is to what he is to be. "Man's general infancy" is but beginning when all mankind are levelled up to the height here and there attained by some powerful mind, and even when man has passed from this infancy to maturity, there is still another stage of evolution to begin:—

> All tended to mankind,
> And, man produced, all has its end thus far:
> But in completed man begins anew
> A tendency to God. Prognostics told
> Man's near approach; so in man's self arise
> August anticipations, symbols, types
> Of a dim splendour ever on before
> In that eternal circle life pursues.
> For men begin to pass their nature's bound,
> And find new hopes and cares which fast supplant
> Their proper joys and griefs; they grow too great
> For narrow creeds of right and wrong, which fade
> Before the unmeasured thirst for good: while peace
> Rises within them ever more and more (*Ibid.* pp. 171-172).

In the view of the young poet then evolution covers the whole scheme of things, and prevails through all existence from lowest to highest. And in this belief Browning was firm to the end. In *Prince Hohenstiel-Schwangau* we find it again, with a colour due to his study of the scientific theory which had been formulated in the interval :—

> I like the thought He should have lodged me once
> I' the hole, the cave, the hut, the tenement,
> The mansion and the palace ; made me learn
> The feel o' the first, before I found myself
> Loftier i' the last, not more emancipate ;
> From first to last of lodging, I was I,
> And not at all the place that harboured me.
> Do I refuse to follow farther yet
> I' the backwardness, repine if tree and flower,
> Mountain or streamlet were my dwelling-place
> Before I gained enlargement, grew mollusc ?
> As well account that way for many a thrill
> Of kinship, I confess to, with the powers
> Called Nature : animate, inanimate,
> In parts or in the whole, there's something there
> Man-like that somehow meets the man in me (xi. p. 165).

But further, to Browning's mind evolution finds its own explanation in God. A creator was vital to his conception of the universe. Herein of course the poet differs from many of the scientific exponents of evolution ; but within the limits proper to biology the question scarcely arises. Evolution may be the true explanation of the diversity of the forms of life, as it is beyond comparison the best yet advanced ; but as to the *origin* of life it is silent ; and life as protoplasm is as much a mystery as life manifested in man. This is the real meaning of that passage in *Francis Furini* which has sometimes been read as if it were a thoroughgoing attack on evolution. It is not so, except in the sense in which it is an attack on all knowledge. "All around ignorance wraps" man. The very width of this attack deprives it of all special point as against evolution. The only assault the poet makes on evolution in particular is directed against inferences to things beyond the chain of proof :—

> 'Tis the tip-top of things to which you strain
> Your vision, until atoms, protoplasm,
> And what and whence and how may be the spasm
> Which sets all going, stop you (xvi. p. 186).

Were it otherwise, were *Francis Furini* really an assault upon the *principle* of evolution, then it would be necessary either to explain it away as dramatic, not Browning's own thought, or as a temporary aberration. For evolution is no chance idea or occasional illustration with him. He is distinguished from both his contemporaries by the immense importance he attaches to it and the great part he makes it play in his poetry. Their conceptions of life are affected by it, but not always with their own full consciousness. His are in the first place affected more deeply, and in the second place he has far clearer knowledge of the bearing of the principle.

A moral purpose is never far in the background of Browning's work. Like Milton, though in a different way, and though also he repudiates the design, he is impelled to "justify the ways of God to man". He does so principally by two arguments, which are really inconsistent with one another. One is that curious doctrine of necessary ignorance already referred to. Knowledge is ultimately impotent, and only on the ground of this impotence is faith possible. If so, alas for faith! This is the weakest point in Browning's poetical philosophy. He resorts to it only when he is in what seems to be an insuperable difficulty; and he proves his unconscious insincerity by using the plea of ignorance as a platform from which he may strain towards knowledge. This singular position may be regarded as a negative influence of science upon his mind. He was determined to save the spiritual interpretation of the universe at all costs, and he did not always see his way to do it at less than this ruinous price. For it ought to have been evident to a smaller mind that the negation of knowledge is the most sceptical of all theories.

But Browning has another explanation besides this merely negative, and in the last resort self-contradictory one. It is evolution. By means of evolution he can explain many of those stubborn facts in experience, otherwise apparently irreconcilable with the conception of a beneficent government of the universe. Evolution explains evil in all forms. It explains evil in the form of physical pain; for are not sympathy and love evolved through pain?—

> Put pain from out the world, what room were left
> For thanks to God, for love to Man? Why thanks,—
> Except for some escape, whate'er the style,
> From pain that might be, name it as thou mayst?
> Why love,—when all mankind, save me, suppose,
> Thy father, and thy son, and . . . . well, thy dog,
> To eke the decent number out—we few
> Who happen—like a handful of chance stars

> From the unnumbered host—to shine o'erhead,
> And lend thee light,—our twinkle all thy store,—
> We only take thy love! Mankind, forsooth?
> Who sympathizes with their general joy
> Foolish as undeserved? But pain—see God's
> Wisdom at work!—man's heart is made to judge
> Pain deserved nowhere by the common flesh
> Our birthright,—bad and good deserve alike
> No pain, to human apprehension! Lust,
> Greed, cruelty, injustice, crave (we hold)
> Due punishment from somebody, no doubt:
> But ulcer in the midriff! That brings flesh
> Triumphant from the bar whereto arraigned
> Soul quakes with reason (*Mihrab Shah*, xvi. p. 37).

The same principle explains moral evil. The Puritanical explanation, that evil is allowed to exist in order to test man's obedience, is too crude for the nineteenth century : we have outgrown it and must seek for another. Browning finds it in the view that resistance, of which moral evil is one form, is indispensable to all progress. This doctrine permeates Browning's thought from youth to age. Already in Sordello evil is "the scheme by which, thro' ignorance, good labours to exist". It is the whole motive of the poem *Rephan*, the changeless star, where

> The wise and the foolish, right and wrong,
> Are merged alike in a neutral Best;

where, just for that reason, life is stagnation; and whence advance means removal to earth. For earth is higher, not in spite but because of its limits and doubts, its hopes and fears. Illustrations might be multiplied indefinitely, for there is no thought in Browning more frequently recurrent. Throughout he is firm in accepting evil as a result no less natural than good. Nay, it is necessary. All the highest virtues are linked to evil as their negative condition. It is through strife that the moral being rises to peace: if the peace is reached without strife, it is not moral in kind. The "rebuffs" and "stings" of earth are to be welcomed as impulses to higher progress. Even temptation is a blessing to those who are able to face it:—

> Pray,
> " Lead us into no such temptations, Lord!"
> Yea, but, O Thou whose servants are the bold,

> Lead such temptations by the head and hair,
> Reluctant dragons, up to who dares fight,
> That so he may do battle and have praise!
> *(The Ring and the Book: The Pope, 1187-1192.)*

Here is the most courageous and thoroughgoing application possible of the idea of evolution. Just as the forms of life are evolved through the stress of conflict with material circumstances, so the moral being grows to the fulness of his stature through conflict with evil. It must not be supposed that Browning's theory hangs upon a distinction between physical and moral evil. His language in the passage quoted above is perfectly clear, and it is too often repeated to leave room for the supposition of inadvertence. He tells us even that we are "by hate taught love"; and though it is Bishop Blougram he causes to speak of "the blessed evil," we feel that he would himself use the same adjective. He finds therefore in a scientific principle the groundwork of his whole scheme of morals, that without which the world he lives in is to him inexplicable.

CHAPTER XI.

THE SOCIAL AND POLITICAL ASPECTS OF THE POETS.

In turning from science to social and political life we approach nearer to the essence of poetry. What the pure intellect can give, so long as its end is knowing rather than living, is only certain regulative ideas. These may indeed be of almost incalculable importance, but they become poetical only in relation to life in the concrete. The poet therefore is apt to view with comparative unconcern the waxing and waning of theories. "Our little systems have their day," he thinks; and though during that day they may influence him more perhaps than he knows, he waits with calmness for another morning after it has set. To some extent the same is true even of changes directly affecting life. The particular social forms in which its needs have found expression are not essential to the poet, and the silent changes they undergo may therefore pass unnoticed by him. But he can hardly remain unmoved by those great revolutions which seem to alter every feature of life. They may lift him into a heaven such as no purely intellectual triumph could open, or plunge him into a gulf to which intellectual failure could not sink him. It is a commonplace of criticism that the former was the fate of the poets during the closing years of last century and the beginning of the present one. I have already said that in a modified degree the latter was the state in which the poets at the end of the first quarter of the century found themselves. The bitterness of their disappointment was proportioned to the eagerness and extravagance of the previous hopes, and it led to a lassitude which only by slow degrees passed away.

Browning, it is true, never sank under the influence of this lethargy. The question why he escaped it must remain for consideration in a later part of this chapter. Tennyson, it is also true, was never wholly subject to it. Still, as we have already seen in part, its brand is stamped deep upon his early work. I have in an earlier chapter referred to the sense of loss left upon him and others by the death of Byron. With Byron seemed to die a great generation with its hopes and aspirations; and there was no young leader of thought who at the moment saw what was to take their place.

But Tennyson almost, as Browning wholly, deserved the praise reserved by the old Romans for those who in troublous times had not despaired of the Republic. The horizon of his hopes was narrowed indeed, and the fact, as we have seen, showed itself both in his choice of subjects and in his manner of treating them. But we have seen also that even in those early days he had formed his own political ideals and given them noble expression. There is no more characteristic note in his poetry than that which rings in his political pieces.

The fact has been already pointed out that Tennyson held opinions in this respect widely different from those of the revolutionary poets. It remains to show wherein precisely the difference consisted at the beginning, and how it was affected by the course of events and by the poet's gradual development.

If we take Byron as representative of the poetry of the revolutionary period, we may say broadly that in all his poetry Byron speaks for man; Tennyson in his political pieces writes as an Englishman for Englishmen. The barriers levelled by the Revolution had been built up again; and the sense of division overpowered once more the sense of unity. Tennyson's three early political pieces, already noticed, are a glorification of English ideals of freedom and English political methods. The sense of full satisfaction with the practical results of these methods, and the poet's mode of presenting them, were both modified with advancing years; but the same spirit animated him throughout. It found forcible expression again in the beginning of the middle period, and the events of the revolutionary year, 1848, deepened the sense of opposition to France with which it was accompanied.

> God bless the narrow seas,
> I wish they were a whole Atlantic broad,

is the exclamation of "the Tory member's elder son" in *The Princess*.

The comparative narrowness of view here implied is far from being purely matter for regret. Bacon condemned as one of the errors to which the human mind is prone the tendency to grasp prematurely at universality. The Revolutionists had certainly fallen victims to this tendency. In their revolt against false divisions they asserted a unity impossible in the time and circumstances, and by doing so provoked a reaction hardly less exaggerated than their own revolt. If Wordsworth answers at all to Browning's Lost Leader, it is because he fell under the influence of this reaction, as Tennyson did after him. But Tennyson was right in believing the differences between nation and nation to be, not perhaps as vital as the points of agreement, but here and now the more immediate and practical business. He was at least not wholly wrong in postponing the unity to a distant future. The point in which he is really open to criticism is that he is grudging and half-hearted wherever he goes much beyond his own time and country. There was a strain of conservatism deep in his nature. His habit was to rest in the view of the day, modified as a rule, if the view was at all a gloomy one, by a vague and undefined trust in the future. This is the keynote of his utterances on religion; it is the keynote too of his political pieces. The extraordinary interest of his poetical development lies in the opportunity it affords of observing how circumstances without, acting upon native powers within, gradually undermined this disposition to accept what is.

The observation of this habit of mind is important because, though it does not fix Tennyson's place in literature, it helps to determine the sphere within which that place must be found. He does not belong intellectually to the class of which Shakespeare is the head, a class distinguished by a width of range and a flexibility not to be found in Tennyson. In Tennyson we always have the sense of an intellectual "beyond"; in Shakespeare we have not. He may not have settled, or even tried to settle, the subject with which he is dealing, for he is singularly free from dogmatism. But he invariably leaves the impression that he has seen all round it. Tennyson on the contrary belongs to the class of which we may take Milton for the type,—the class of minds intense and strong, but comparatively narrow; and he nowhere shows this more clearly than in his political references, which have both, on the one hand, a Miltonic

CH. XI.] SOCIAL AND POLITICAL ASPECTS. 261

intensity of strength, and, on the other, a Miltonic narrowness.[1]

Tennyson betrays his limits in the answer he gives to the exclamation already quoted from *The Princess* :—

> "Have patience," I replied, "ourselves are full
> Of social wrong : and maybe wildest dreams
> Are but the needful preludes of the truth :
> For me, the genial day, the happy crowd,
> The sport half-science, fill me with a faith,
> This fine old world of ours is but a child
> Yet in the go-cart. Patience ! Give it time
> To learn its limbs : there is a hand that guides (iv. 142).

"The sport half-science" is a reference to the telescopes, toy railways, fire-balloons and mimic telegraphs with which, as we learn at the beginning, the holiday crowd were amused. As if to give these lines the emphasis they certainly need, Tennyson adopts them as his own answer to "the Tory member's elder son". But the acknowledgment of social wrong is perfunctory beside the heart and vigour he puts into the description of the scene across channel, where

> Whiff ! there comes a sudden heat,
> The gravest citizen seems to lose his head,
> The king is scared, the soldier will not fight,
> The little boys begin to shoot and stab,
> A kingdom topples over with a shriek
> Like an old woman, and down rolls the world
> In mock heroics stranger than our own ;
> Revolts, republics, revolutions, most
> No graver than a schoolboys' barring out ;
> Too comic for the solemn things they are,
> Too solemn for the comic touches in them (iv. 141).

Contrast with this Tennyson's references to the history and political institutions of his own country. It is the stability of English freedom, the fact that it is no mushroom growth, but a thing handed down through centuries and steadily increasing, that has impressed him. No lines he ever wrote are better known than those in "You ask me why, tho' ill at ease," where he describes this freedom as slowly broadening down "from precedent to precedent". In "Of old sat Freedom on

---

[1] It may be well to insist that the narrowness is only comparative—it is Miltonic.

the heights," this personified liberty is pictured gazing down from her isle-altar :—

> Her open eyes desire the truth.
> The wisdom of a thousand years
> Is in them.

The third piece opens with the exhortation,

> Love thou thy land, with love far-brought
> From out the storied Past, and used
> Within the Present, but transfused
> Thro' future time by power of thought.

In each case it is permanence that is insisted upon. The lesson of French political instability had sunk deep ; and probably but for that lesson these pieces would not have been written, or the stress would have fallen somewhere else.[1]

The lines in which Tennyson mocks the "sudden heat" of France evidently take their colour from the disturbed state of the Continent at the time when they were written. Those entitled *The Third of February, 1852,* are similarly influenced. But no temporary state of continental politics can afford a full explanation of the feeling displayed. It is the reverse to which a passionate admiration and love of England is obverse. Tennyson cherished a haughty pride in his country; and, if such a feeling can be made consistent with perfectly even-handed justice to other countries, it has at least not been made so yet.

[1] I do not wish to deny that Tennyson is one-sided in his admiration for the slow, steady, practical politics of England, and his detestation of the revolutionary methods of France. But when, as by Mr. Stopford Brooke in his recent volume on Tennyson, the poet's right to take such a view is almost denied, it is surely time to protest. And a protest has already been made in an able article in the *Spectator,* July 7, 1894. The writer of it objects with reason to the inclusion of Wordsworth and Coleridge among those who took the opposite side to Tennyson. With reference to Tennyson's position on social questions he says :—" In his very last book Mr. Brooke complains that Tennyson puts the laying of the 'Ghost of the Brute' in man, and the millennium for which they are looking, in the dim and distant future. ' We are far from the noon of man, there is time for the race to grow.' ' Time !' exclaims Mr. Brooke impatiently, ' when half the world and more are in torture,' reminding us of that enthusiastic social reformer who exclaimed with equal impatience and a half-comic despair :—' I am in such a desperate hurry ; and the worst of it is, God is in no hurry at all '." It is good to remember that "God is in no hurry at all ". It is good also to remember the reason :— " God," says Hegel, " lives in eternity, and therefore he has plenty of time "·

Patriotism has always carried with it a sense of opposition, deep in proportion to its intensity. Tennyson felt that England had a special function in the world, and did not hesitate to speak his conviction, whatever sensibilities he might wound in doing so:—

> As long as we remain we must speak free,
> Tho' all the storm of Europe on us break;
> No little German state are we,
> But the one voice in Europe: we *must* speak
> (*The Third of February*).

Britain, he repeats, cannot palter with public crime:—

> Better the waste Atlantic rolled
> On her and us and ours for evermore (*Ibid.*).

He is proud of this position and of its responsibilities, proud to think of himself as one of that people

> Whom the roar of Hougoumont
> Left mightiest of all peoples under heaven
> (*Idylls of the King: To the Queen*, p. 420).

He is bitterly hostile to anything that may seem to threaten this pre-eminence. Hence his much-censured love of war; which is not properly a love of war, but rather the expression of a belief that there are worse things than war. Peace, he thought, might sap the spirit and manhood of a nation; and it is far from certain that history gives him the lie. He had to oppose a party whose motto was peace at any price. He had to insist that even peace may be bought too dear if it salves tyranny.

> Though we love kind Peace so well,
> We dare not ev'n by silence sanction lies
> (*The Third of February*).

Hence the welcome of war in *Maud*, and hence the heartiness with which, from youth to extreme old age, the poet always sang of warlike themes. Hence also he ranks with Campbell as one of the two best singers of the glories of the English arms; for, absurd as it would be to put Campbell on a level with him in other respects, even Tennyson's war-poems are no more than equal to *Ye Mariners of England*.

It is to be noticed however that Tennyson's patriotism is by no means wholly summed up in the sense of opposition. Neither is it wholly based on an acceptance of things as they were in the England of his own day. Great rights carry with them correspondingly great duties. It is clear from the passages already quoted that Tennyson recognised this in the public as well as in the private sphere. The lofty position he claims for England is hers because she alone has the power to perform the duty it entails. To Tennyson, just as to Wordsworth, England is above all precious as the last voice of freedom, not as the mistress of brute force. But freedom is impossible without force, and is not likely to survive long the dying away of the "tone of empire". This is the reason for Tennyson's hatred of the spirit, so prevalent among the politicians of that time, which shrank with horror from the bare thought of undertaking any new burdens, and would fain have thrown off even those assumed by former generations. Tennyson feared as well as hated this spirit. If England, says he, knows her greatness "and dreads it, we are fall'n". He hopes rather that the dread of responsibility may spring from not knowing the greatness. He does his best to spread the knowledge. It must be said to his honour that in the days when the Manchester school reigned he consistently refused to bow the knee to the gods it would have set up. "We are not cotton-spinners all," he cries; and over and over again he reiterates that the single pursuit of money is death, and the peace which seeks that alone worse than war, which at any rate keeps manhood alive.

But there is one poem, the *Ode on the Death of the Duke of Wellington*, which as an expression of Tennyson's political faith overtops all others. It is not purely political: the human character which gives it a heart lifts it high above the limitations of which Goethe spoke when he said to Eckermann that a political poem is at best only the organ of a single nation. But all that is in it harmonises with the writer's political views and feelings. The poet is in perfect sympathy with his hero, his pulse quickens as he writes about him, and the result is a poem almost as massive and strong as the man about whom it was written. The very speed with which it was executed proves how the subject had taken hold of the writer's mind; for, after full allowance has been made for the changes subsequently introduced, it is still remarkable that a poem of such length and finish should have been published on the day when the Duke was buried.

The character of Wellington as it is worked out under Tennyson's hand is a kind of incarnation of the spirit of England as he conceives it ought to be. Without wishing to diminish in the least the just pride of Ireland in her son, it must be said that the great soldier's character seems to have been drawn rather from the land of his blood than from the land of his birth. For this reason he was just the man with whom Tennyson was capable of feeling unbounded sympathy, and whom he could fully understand. Wellington therefore gave the poet the incalculable advantage which in art always attaches to the concrete. His pride in England passes into pride in him who had led England to victory, his trust in English character and English political wisdom becomes trust in the greatest Englishman of his time. It is strange that the Ode was in general ill received on its first appearance, and perhaps even more strange that the condemnation, or the faint praise, has been more than once repeated in recent years. But the hostile critics are at variance with respect to the grounds upon which they object to the Ode. One condemns it as a whole on grounds of art, another is offended by the political tone of the seventh section.

The seventh section bears its character on its face. "A people's voice! we are a people yet," it begins, echoing *The Princess*, where the reason given for the blessing pronounced upon the narrow sea is that it "keeps our Britain, whole within herself, a nation yet". This section stands or falls therefore with the poet's other political utterances, though the most hardened of objectors must surely have found it difficult to steel his heart against the spirit which leads the poet to

> Thank Him who isled us here, and roughly set
> His Briton in blown seas and storming showers.

The themes of his praise are the same that we meet with in the other poems. England is "the eye, the soul of Europe," and what saves her helps

> To save mankind
> Till public wrong be crumbled into dust.

It is sanity, political sobriety and "loyal passion" for "temperate kings" that are her attributes. To preserve these, in the name of him whose voice is for ever silent in the council-hall, the poet calls upon surviving statesmen to obey his behest and "guard the sacred coasts".

Turn from this to the picture of the man whose death is the occasion for it. It is just the same worked out in greater detail and with even greater effect, because in him the poet sees clothed with flesh the spirit he had only imagined as the abstract of national qualities. He is praised for his "long-enduring blood," he is "moderate, resolute," "a man of well-attempered frame," "rich in saving common-sense". He is destitute of show even as his country is; for English freedom is "sober-suited". He is "one that sought but Duty's iron crown". His warfare itself is distinguished principally for its patient resolution. Its most characteristic feature is the stubborn standing at bay at Lisbon, and the slow gain in strength afterwards till the final victory. The "day of onsets of despair" was similar, for Wellington's function was till the close simply to beat back those onsets steadily as they were made. And if on occasion, as in the clash "against the myriads of Assaye," he could show that unconquerable resolution is no way inconsistent with headlong daring, that too has its analogue in English history. The rule is steady obedience to law, but the end for which law exists is not forgotten. Tennyson notes the exceptions in *The Third of February*, and approves:—

> From our first Charles by force we wrung our claims.
> Prick'd by the Papal spur, we reared,
> We flung the burthen of the second James.

Wellington's very speech is the speech of his countrymen idealised. Too busy to talk much, he lets "the turbid stream of rumour flow". When he does utter his thoughts, it is in

> Language rife
> With rugged maxims hewn from life.

This great picture too must therefore be judged along with the more directly political utterances. If there is no defence for them, neither is there for the idealisation of that character in which England and the spirit of English institutions seem to be gathered up into a unity.

In his old age Tennyson seldom gave direct expression to his political views. He wrote with even greater freedom and frequency than before of the past exploits of his countrymen; and for a few of them, like Gordon and Lord Stratford de Redcliffe, he wrote epitaphs after their death. On occasion, but rarely, he was still ready to use his pen with the view of influencing public action. The lines entitled *The Fleet*, drawn from him by a discussion raised in 1886 on the condition of the navy, show the old spirit and the old practical interest in his country. But the very form of these verses seems to proclaim them as the words of a man who has done with such things. He does not pronounce dogmatically, he puts the question by way of hypothesis :—

> You, you, *if* you shall fail to understand
> What England is, and what her all-in-all.

Certainly Tennyson when younger would not have used the "if"; certainly too in 1886 he knew its weakening tendency. The presence of the word means that he leaves it now for younger men to determine the facts, he only points out consequences.

This remark leads to the consideration of the principal features of Tennyson's later work in this department as contrasted with his earlier work. It may be summed up by saying that the attention earlier given to political forms is now devoted to social conditions. In other words, the poet's development has gone in the direction of greater "inwardness". This is just another instance of the kind of change of which we have already seen a still more striking case in his movement to the drama. The earlier praises of freedom and political stability are admirable, but they furnish no evidence of a knowledge of the deeper facts of life. The lines already quoted from *The Princess*, with the acknowledgment of "social wrong," rather raise the presumption of ignorance, so vague and inadequate are they. That presumption is strengthened by a consideration of *The Princess* as a whole. The feebleness and shallowness of the poem, if we regard it as dealing with one of the principal social questions of the time, has been already touched upon. The subject of *In Memoriam* almost shuts out questions of the kind. That of the *Idylls of the King* does indeed encourage them to a certain extent; but the romance transports them into a distant world. In *Maud* the heart of the writer seems to be sometimes more deeply moved by the social circumstances of his own generation. But there is a slight taint of superficiality about the social references in

Maud, and more than a slight taint about those of *Locksley Hall*.

This reproach cannot be brought against the various collections from the *Ballads and other Poems* of 1880 onwards. It cannot be brought against any body of poetry which seriously seeks to deal with the concrete facts of life. Prior to his dramatic period Tennyson very seldom made the attempt, and almost as soon as he did we detect a significant change. The stress shifts from the political forms to the facts of which they are merely a more or less imperfect expression. The poet discovers that although on one side of the channel freedom is the steady growth of ages, while on the other "a kingdom topples over with a shriek," yet the human nature which produces both results is much the same. The discovery widens and humanises Tennyson's poetry, and lifts it completely above the reproach, never wholly just even if we confine the view to this aspect, of being the organ only of one nation.

It was not by generalising that Tennyson won this higher station; little ever is won by merely generalising, and hardly anything in the sphere of art. On the contrary, his philosophy of life deepens as he descends more and more to the individual, and his results are a striking corroboration of the philosophic doctrine that the knowledge which is most particular is at the same time most universal. In his earlier poetry he is prone too much to set the class Englishman against the class Frenchman, and he exaggerates the differences because he finds them to take the tangible shape of a constitution. In his later poetry he takes individuals, the Northern Farmer (though he is exceptionally early), the Northern Cobbler, Rizpah, the husband and wife of *The First Quarrel*, and many more. In these cases there is incomparably more of local colouring and of local peculiarities of character and life than there is in the earlier poems; but there is also more of that human nature which will not be bounded either by narrow seas or by seas "a whole Atlantic wide". In his idyllic strain Tennyson seems to touch the rough facts of life with a dainty caution. The farming life of *Dora* and the sea-faring life of *Enoch Arden* are softened and transmuted. They are like the Arcadia of poetic convention beside the actual shepherd-life as known to Wordsworth and as lived by James Hogg. No one would say this by way of reproach against Tennyson. The pastoral and the idyll are legitimate and valuable

CH. XI.]   SOCIAL AND POLITICAL ASPECTS.   269

forms of poetic art. The point here is that there are certain aspects of truth they do not embrace and certain qualities they do not develop. Human nature as seen in the actual English rustic proves to be a deeper thing than human nature as imagined in the English Arcadian.

This study of human nature drives Tennyson to fill in what ✓ in his earlier poetry is at most only a slight sketch. The "social wants" and "social lies" of *Locksley Hall* take substance and solidity in *Locksley Hall Sixty Years After*. The vague admission of *The Princess* that "ourselves are full of social wrong" becomes a body of concrete instances of wrong, constantly relieved by the flash of spirit rising superior to wrong. Under these influences politics sink into a secondary place :—

> Raving politics, never at rest—as this poor earth's pale history runs,—
> What is it all but a trouble of ants in the gleam of a million million
>   of suns?
> Lies upon this side, lies upon that side, truthless violence mourned
>   by the Wise,
> Thousands of voices drowning his own in a popular torrent of lies
>   upon lies;
> Stately purposes, valour in battle, glorious annals of army and fleet,
> Death for the right cause, death for the wrong cause, trumpets of
>   victory, groans of defeat (*Demeter: Vastness*).

This confusion seems to leave little ground for hope; and the hope is not increased by an examination of the facts beneath the confusion.

> Is it well that while we range with Science, glorying in the Time,
> City children soak and blacken soul and sense in city slime?
> There among the glooming alleys Progress halts on palsied feet,
> Crime and hunger cast our maidens by the thousand on the street.
> There the Master scrimps his haggard sempstress of her daily bread,
> There a single sordid attic holds the living and the dead.
> There the smouldering fire of fever creeps across the rotted floor,
> And the crowded couch of incest in the warrens of the poor
>   (*Locksley Hall Sixty Years After*).

Yet Tennyson was never a pessimist. The same poem in which he paints this gloomy picture closes in the confidence that "love will conquer at the last," and with the injunction,

> Follow Light, and do the Right—for man can half control his doom—
> Till you find the deathless Angel seated in the vacant tomb.

The difference in this respect between the poet's view in age and his view in youth is, that while both are in essence optimistic, the optimism of the former is founded upon an adequate view of the facts, while that of the latter is not. But in neither case is it fully worked out. There is a gap between the facts and the hope founded upon them.

Arnold's different nature shows itself from the first. The interest in society was always, with him, while it was not always with Tennyson, deep and strong. Partly at least for this reason the note of his poetry is social rather than political. He has none of Tennyson's early contentment with things as they are. In what is perhaps his most decided political utterance in verse, the famous passage in *Heine's Grave* about the "weary Titan," we see that it is not the success of his country he dwells upon, but her failure, her incapacity for her task, her inability to preserve as factors in her life "glory, and genius, and joy". This is as far removed as possible from the spirit of Tennyson, whose fear is just that England may, like Arnold, dread the too vast orb of her fate.

It is almost as widely different from the political utterances of the poets of the revolutionary period, with their tone of bitterness, occasionally verging upon hatred, against their country. Arnold sees and deplores her weaknesses, and admits the substantial justice of Heine's criticism, but he sees no other social or political system to which he can turn with any more hope and confidence. The Revolutionists were naive in their hope and confidence. Rousseau's faith in a natural, happy state of men, to be reached not by building up but by knocking down, was wide-spread. Sweep away obstructions and abuses, the more or less wilful wrong done by man to man, and the age of gold will return. Such, or nearly such, seems to have been at bottom the creed of those who were directly influenced by the Revolution. It was held in its fulness and freshness only by those who were young men just approaching maturity when the Revolution broke out; and even on their minds it soon lost its hold.

Coleridge's ode, *France*, discloses the exultation felt by the most gifted of the younger men, and in the same breath the bitter disappointment which followed. The later Revolutionists are less hopeful. It is the "Titanic strife" raging in the soul of Byron that draws attention to him. In his eyes, everything is wrong, "the world is out of joint". Yet if we look a little below the surface we see that there is dimly present to his mind the idea that the evil is not insusceptible of cure. Fundamentally he agrees with Rousseau. He might be happy if only he could have a desert for his dwelling-place.

Arnold came after the stormful passions of that period had had time to settle into calm,—a calm not without hope but with narrowly bounded hopes. It is in this respect, perhaps above all, that he is the child of his age. No doubt there were in his youth, and there are still, hopes of wild extravagance as well as —it would be a mistake to say no less than—a hundred years ago. We have had specifics that were to work miracles in free trade, in co-operation, in a hundred things good in themselves but ludicrously insufficient to revolutionise the world. But, viewed as specifics, these have been the property of the British Philistine,—Arnold's own name for those of his countrymen who are prone to go astray because of narrow views and limited mental horizon. Such soaring hopes have not been, as similar hopes were a century ago, accepted by the best intellect of the time. Least of all have they been so accepted if we may take that intellect to be embodied in poetry, which Arnold held, probably with justice, to be the loftiest product of the human mind.

That Arnold at least refused to put faith in any of the panaceas of his time is too obvious to need proof. In his view of the present state and future prospects of society he is essentially critical. Further, his criticism may be described as a wide, enlightened and thorough criticism from the point of view of the time itself. In thoroughness and adequacy as a poetical expression of contemporary thought it far surpasses anything that Tennyson attained until almost the close of his life; in apocalyptic quality it is inferior to the verse of Browning, who for that very reason is more the voice of the future than of the present.

To Arnold the French Revolution was, if the phrase be not too hackneyed for use, epoch-making. It swept away the older world, and left the new generation the gigantic task of building up another. Arnold reviews the past and deliberately records his judgment that

> Of the spirits who have reigned
> In this our troubled day,

he knows but three who have seen their course clearly. One of those three is Wordsworth, whose vision, though clear, is limited, for he turns his eyes away "from half of human fate". Another is Goethe. The third is Étienne Pivert de Senancour, author of *Obermann*. The attraction of this man for Arnold is extremely significant. Two of Arnold's noblest poems are associated with the name of *Obermann*, and a third, equally noble and beautiful, the *Stanzas from the Grande Chartreuse*, though it does not bear the name in its title, draws its inspiration from the same source. The secret of the attraction is not hard to find. In a note on Senancour appended to the *Stanzas in Memory of the Author of "Obermann,"* Arnold has himself explained what he found in him. "The stir of all the main forces, by which modern life is and has been impelled, lives in the letters of *Obermann*; the dissolving agencies of the eighteenth century, the fiery storm of the French Revolution, the first faint promise and dawn of that new world which our own time is but now more fully bringing to light,—all these are to be felt, almost to be touched, there." When we add that *Obermann* is "a collection of letters from Switzerland treating almost entirely of nature and of the human soul," and that Senancour "has a gravity and severity which distinguish him from all other writers of the sentimental school," the spiritual kinship between this sentimentalist and his admirer is completely explained. Not only are the principal interests of Senancour identical with those of Arnold, but his attitude towards the world is closely similar. It is "that air of languor, cold and death" which brooded over the Frenchman's soul that draws the English poet to him. It is because the former has scanned well "the hopeless tangle of our age" that the Englishman is content to sit at his feet and learn from him. The concentration on nature *and* the human soul is significant in connexion with the work of one who rarely concentrated upon nature except with reference to the human soul. So deep is the communion that it may be questioned whether anywhere within equal space there is to be found so much of the real Arnold as in the three poems just referred to.

There is no mistaking Arnold's attitude as revealed in these poems and in many others; for his opinions are reiterated again and again in some of the most musical and thoughtful verse of the century. The poet is

> Wandering between two worlds, one dead,
> The other powerless to be born.

This, more than all else, is the secret of his melancholy. For him, the old order has changed: there is not yet a new to take its place. There are plenty of negations, and plenty also of materialism; but Arnold sees too deeply to be satisfied with the former; and whether from depth of vision or not, he at any rate cannot rest content with the latter. Yet he has no positive which commends itself to him to put in the room of the negations; and the very key to his intellectual position is the fact that he is in revolt against the accepted spiritual interpretation of the universe. All past effort seems to have been vain. The vast revolutionary upheaval has brought to pass none of its high promises: it is represented only by "blocks of the past, like icebergs high," floating "on a rolling sea". The sense of fruitless effort and the apathy which follows upon it are expressed in some beautiful verses in the *Stanzas from the Grande Chartreuse*, in which the poet asks of what avail has been the haughty scorn of Byron, the musical wail of Shelley, the "sad, stern page" of Obermann. They have added nothing to the sum of human joys, they have made life no lighter; and the result is that the very expression of pain is felt to be useless. Men are no more content than of old, but they give no voice to their discontent. Why should they, when even the "Titanic strife" of Byron has been so useless?—

> Achilles ponders in his tent,
> The kings of modern thought are dumb;
> Silent they are, though not content,
> And wait to see the future come.
> They have the grief men had of yore,
> But they contend and cry no more.
>
> Our fathers water'd with their tears
> This sea of time whereon we sail,
> Their voices were in all men's ears
> Who passed within their puissant hail.
> Still the same ocean round us raves,
> But we stand mute, and watch the waves.

The past is a record of strivings without result, of hopes whose blossom never set in fruit. That age just gone by which promised the new birth of all things, what has it been but

> Europe's dying hour
> Of fitful dream and feverish power?

Its struggles have proved to be not the throes of birth, but "the turmoil of expiring life". Hence the age succeeding that day of delusive promise is one of "sick fatigue" and "languid doubt". Modern life is a "strange disease,"

> With its sick hurry, its divided aims,
> Its heads o'ertax'd, its palsied hearts.

And that unrest, that "fever of the soul," which is the general characteristic of our latter days, is the special inheritance of the poet's own country. In that pathetic poem, *A Southern Night*, he moralises upon the graves of his brother and that brother's wife, the one at Gibraltar, the other farther still from home:—

> For there, where morning's sacred fount
> Its golden rain on earth confers,
> The snowy Himalayan mount
> O'ershadows hers.

It is a "strange irony of fate" that keeps for two jaded English such graves as these. We of a bustling race, who traverse restlessly every land under heaven, and "never once possess our souls before we die," should rest in cities.

> Not by those hoary Indian hills,
> Not by this gracious Midland sea,
> Whose floor to-night sweet moonshine fills,
> Should our graves be.

The exquisite beauty of this stanza, its charm of sound and the singular felicity of the adjectives to the Indian hills and the Midland sea, all heightened by its skilful contrast with the stanzas immediately preceding it, give a glimpse of Arnold's art in one of its highest phases, as well as a revelation of what he thinks the defect of English life.

If we extend the view more widely over Arnold's poetry the result is still the same. His fundamental conception of society is that the old impulse on which men had lived from the rise of Christianity, which had been rejuvenated at the Reformation and strengthened by that other impulse from the Renaissance, had been exhausted before the Revolution. The Revolution shattered the tottering fabric without building anything in its place. But this absence of moral shelter from the elements makes modern life a chaos. Health seems scarcely possible except to those who are able more or less completely to withdraw from it. Hence Arnold's sympathy with Wordsworth and with the Scholar Gipsy, as well as with Senancour. He is attracted to the Scholar Gipsy, because he early left the world,

> With powers
> Fresh, undiverted to the world without.

And he has his reward :—

> No, no, thou hast not felt the lapse of hours !
> For what wears out the life of mortal men ?
> 'Tis that from change to change their being rolls ;
> 'Tis that repeated shocks, again, again,
> Exhaust the energy of strongest souls
> And numb the elastic powers.
> Till having used our nerves with bliss and teen,
> And tired upon a thousand schemes our wit,
> To the just-pausing Genius we remit
> Our worn-out life, and are—what we have been.

But this freedom from strife is exceptional. The fate of the scholar in Arnold's own day would rather be that of Thyrsis, who, unable to wait the passing of the storm, wanders out into the storms of the world, and dies.

The post of intellectual leader of such a day is a sad one. It would be a mistake to suppose that Arnold has been speaking only of the ordinary world, and that in the fierce light which beats upon the poet's throne we shall see life clearly. In *The Strayed Reveller* he tells us that it is with labour and in pain that the wise bards behold their visions and sing their songs ; and in *The Scholar Gipsy* he depicts the intellectual king of his own age. We, " light half-believers of our casual creeds," are waiting " for the spark from heaven " :—

> Yes, we await it !—but it still delays,
> And then we suffer ! and amongst us one,
> Who most has suffer'd, takes dejectedly
> His seat upon the intellectual throne ;
> And all his store of sad experience he
> Lays bare of wretched days ;
> Tells us his misery's birth and growth and signs,
> And how the dying spark of hope was fed,
> And how the breast was soothed, and how the head,
> And all his hourly varied anodynes.

This is all the wisest can give, not cure, but alleviation.

Supremacy of suffering, not power to heal, is the title to the throne.[1]

Beneath the level of this throne there is indeed confidence and self-satisfaction in plenty, but it is a confidence not founded on knowledge. The destructive forces of the Revolution have evoked or set free a vast amount of individual energy which on certain lines and within certain limits seems triumphant. Whoever can absorb himself in "business," or rest content with merely material results, or can even silence the question what is the character of the results, may live envied and outwardly successful. But there is a double failure in such a life. The secret of its failure on the side of the individual has been partly seen already. We have no leisure to "possess our soul". Hardly for one little hour "have we been ourselves". In the struggle for life we forget the deeper purposes of life. Bright and fast therefore

> The stream of life may roll,
> And no man may the other's hurt behold ;
> Yet each will have one anguish—his own soul
> Which perishes of cold (*Progress*).

But this is only part of the cost of the modern life of restless bustle and triumphant "business". It maims the soul before killing it with cold :—

> But we, brought forth and rear'd in hours
> Of change, alarm, surprise—
> What shelter to grow ripe is ours?
> What leisure to grow wise?
> (*Stanzas in Memory of the Author of "Obermann"*.)

It is clear then that in Arnold's view the revolutionary energy is by no means altogether wholesome for the individual. As little can it be wholesome for society. When, in his favourite phrase, he insists upon the vital importance of "possessing our soul," Arnold does not mean to preach the value of solitude. Retirement from the world may indeed accidentally and temporarily prove the only way of being our true selves; but it is at the best an evil necessity. Arnold regards it in the spirit of Plato's famous metaphor. To retire behind a wall from the hurricane of dust and rain may be the wise man's only resource; but the ideal is rather to live his life under such conditions

---

[1] It will presently appear how Arnold modifies this judgment.

as the world affords. The monastery is only a "living tomb". The abandonment of life in the world is the blankest confession of failure. It is no better than the wisdom of the ostrich, the cry of peace, peace, when there is no peace, the meaningless assertion that the dead old world is not dead but alive. Not so can the new birth come. Monasticism, to Arnold, is fatally insufficient, because it is selfish,

> And who can be *alone* elate,
> While the world lies forlorn?

Again, he praises his father because he would not be saved *alone*. The fact that it is the poet's father who is praised thus, and that it is Senancour, the man with whom his spirit was in most intimate communion, to whom these lines are ascribed, gives an added meaning to this assertion of the insufficiency of a solitary salvation.

Further, not only is the struggle a duty, but success in it is, though difficult, still possible ; indeed, if success were not possible the struggle could hardly be a duty at all. There are three men in recent times whom Arnold believes to have succeeded. Goethe did so by the path of intellect; and his own father, by virtue of his moral greatness :—

> We were weary, and we
> Fearful, and we in our march
> Fain to drop down and to die.
> Still thou turnedst, and still
> Beckonedst the trembler, and still
> Gavest the weary thy hand.
> If, in the paths of the world,
> Stones might have wounded thy feet,
> Toil or dejection have tried
> Thy spirit, of that we saw
> Nothing—to us thou wast still
> Cheerful, and helpful, and firm!
> Therefore to thee it was given
> Many to save with thyself;
> And, at the end of thy day,
> O faithful shepherd! to come,
> Bringing thy sheep in thy hand (*Rugby Chapel*).

The third was Arthur Penrhyn Stanley; and though this "child of light," sharing a mortal lot, " knew care and knew unrest," and finally sank beneath "the crowning impotence of death," yet he was "victorious" while he lived, and his coming was a pledge of good to atone for ill. It is true "the flux of mortal things" sways backwards and forwards, but all the while it is "moving inly to one far-set goal" :—

> And thou, O Abbey grey!
> Predestined to the ray
> By this dear guest over thy precinct shed—
> Fear not but that thy light once more shall burn,
> Once more thine immemorial gleam return,
> Though sunk be now this bright, this gracious head!

The first condition of progress is the admission of the death of the old world. "Le roi est mort" must precede "Vive le roi". Arnold makes the admission freely; he is not so ready to proclaim the new king. It is evident, however, that the principle upon which the new world is to be based must be a social one. Arnold's criticism of the individual strivings of his time rests just upon this, that they are destitute of such a basis. There is no thought in his verse more frequently reiterated or more beautifully expressed than that of the loneliness of humanity. The soul "perishes of cold" because it is isolated. Ripeness and wisdom come not out of solitude but out of society; and the condemnation of the individual for his lack of ripeness and wisdom is on its other side a condemnation of society because it does not furnish them. The bonds have not the strength necessary to draw men close enough. It is only by a real union with their fellows that men can escape, even in part, that doom of isolation which is the severest of all punishments; and even so they can escape it only in part. The "severing sea" divides us from ourselves as well as from our brother men. Still, a true social ideal in part breaks down the barriers: the pity is that in the din and turmoil of modern life men have been losing the vision of the ideal. In the simpler life of the past they could see the truth at once and follow it. "What bard," asks Arnold,

> What bard,
> At the height of his vision, can deem
> Of God, of the world, of the soul,
> With a plainness as near,
> As flashing as Moses felt
> When he lay in the night by his flock
> On the starlit Arabian waste?
> Can rise and obey
> The beck of the Spirit like him? (*The Future*.)

"The beck of the spirit" summoned Moses to lead a people,—at first, it is true, only into the wilderness, but thence towards a promised land, though he himself was doomed never to enter there.

Arnold too has his Mount Nebo, which gives a glimpse, if a distant one, of a land of promise. He would not be half as interesting as he is, if he did not, partially at least, rise above his own melancholy and the "icy despair" of *Obermann*. But it is characteristic of the man that he is never borne away on swelling waves of expectation. Standing between the dead old world and the world "powerless to be born," he sees far off "the vision of the future". What he offers is the most benignant medicine possible to a "physician of the iron age," for it is the promise that after all the birth will come. To supplement the passages already quoted from *Rugby Chapel* and *Westminster Abbey*, I turn for illustration to the closing stanzas of *Obermann once More*. The gloomy vision ends significantly with the injunction to tell "hope to a world new made". After it has vanished the poet, vaguely stirred, turns aside along the banks of Naye :—

> Past Sonchaud's piny flanks I gaze
> And the blanch'd summit bare
> Of Malatrait, to where in haze
> The Valais opens fair,
>
> And the domed Velan, with his snows,
> Behind the upcrowding hills,
> Doth all the heavenly opening close
> Which the Rhone's murmur fills ;—
>
> And glorious there, without a sound,
> Across the glimmering lake,
> High in the Valais-depth profound,
> I saw the morning break.

Unquestionably there is a reference to something beyond the physical dawn in these lines. If any doubt were possible it is set at rest by the prose note to the poem, already quoted. There we are told that there is even in Senancour himself "the first faint promise and dawn of that new world which our own time is but now more fully bringing to light". Much more is the dawn visible in Arnold. *Thyrsis* too closes with promise for the future :—

> Too rare, too rare, grow now my visits here !
> 'Mid city noise, not, as with thee of yore,
> Thyrsis ! in reach of sheep-bells is my home.
> —Then through the great town's harsh, heart-wearying roar,
> Let in thy voice a whisper often come,
> To chase fatigue and fear :
> *Why faintest thou ? I wander'd till I died.
> Roam on ! the light we sought is shining still.
> Dost thou ask proof ? Our tree yet crowns the hill,
> Our Scholar travels yet the loved hill-side.*

Even *A Summer Night*, one of the gloomiest of Arnold's poems, ends with the exclamation,

> How fair a lot to fill
> Is left to each man still !

He repudiates the attempt of the philosophers to "rend in a thousand shreds this life of ours," because

> Deep and broad, where none may see,
> Spring the foundations of that shadowy throne
> Where man's one nature, queen-like, sits alone,
> Centred in a majestic unity
>
> (*Sonnet written in Butler's Sermons*).

And it is the very greatness of human nature that makes him marvel why men will not listen to the "voice oracular" when they hear it. They pass on, "scornful, and strange, and sorrowful, and full of bitter knowledge " :—

> Yet the will is free ;
> Strong is the soul, and wise, and beautiful ;
> The seeds of godlike power are in us still ;
> Gods are we, bards, saints, heroes if we will
>
> (*Sonnet written in Emerson's Essays*).

It may be well to pause here and consider what result we have attained. We have seen a spirit fallen, like Shelley's, "upon the thorns of life," reduced to the verge of despair, and even in a momentary cry or two seeming to renounce

> The heavy and the weary weight
> Of all this unintelligible world.

But the cry is only momentary. The poet never consents to be less than an actor in the struggle, result how it may. Even if his own doom be defeat, he will still charge "the forts of folly," confident that at last the victors will come and find his body by the wall. We have seen, moreover, that the source of his trouble is the failure of the social and spiritual principles on which mankind had lived hitherto. It still further appears that to him high gifts and faculties mean only, or rather mean *first*, added intensity of pain. It is given to no one to work out his *own* salvation. Neither in this particular case is it given to the whole generation, though the success of the few choice spirits proves that failure springs from the insufficiency of individuals, not from something in the scheme of the universe. Still, the salvation must be a social one, and the poet in a spirit of prophecy has glimpses of a good to come in which he and his age can participate only by sympathy. The nature of this good is nowhere clearly defined. But vague as they are, these intimations of a progressive future may well prove to be among the most noteworthy utterances of their author. The thoughts a man fully grasps and can express in logical formulæ are often a trifle commonplace. It has been truly said with respect to Plato that when he is struggling with an idea of which he is only half master he takes refuge in myth. Subsequent ages have found in those myths the most pregnant hints the philosophy of Plato contains. And so time may show it to be in the case of Arnold. His ultimate hopefulness is a great thing, just because it was preceded and is accompanied by such a profound sense of the difficulties of the time. It is more noteworthy than Tennyson's trust that "*somehow* good will be the final goal of ill," because, though Arnold knows the *how* no more than Tennyson, he has weighed the ill more scrupulously than the latter did.

An examination of Browning yields what may seem at first sight a curious result. He, whose interest in man was certainly deeper than the interest of either of his contemporaries, has practically nothing to say about politics, and not much even on wider social questions,—not much, I mean, directly bearing upon them; for indirectly nearly his whole work may be interpreted as dealing with such subjects. One of Browning's few sonnets is an answer to the question, "Why I am a Liberal"; *The Lost Leader* indirectly answers the same question still better, and bases the liberalism on reasons which appeal not to one country only but to humanity. We have already seen how fervid are the few patriotic lines of *Home Thoughts from the Sea*. The enthusiasm for Nelson expressed in *Nationality in Drinks* need not in itself be referred to patriotic feelings, for Nelson's was a character to win the admiration of Browning whatever had been his country. But if we take it in conjunction with the former piece, we see clearly that the sentiment of country is present in it too. There are also here and there through Browning's works direct references, generally scornful, to contemporary political questions, and far more numerous references to contemporary forms of social and intellectual problems. His scorn is not of the problems which really demand solution, but of the childish forms in which they present themselves to many men. He has no patience with "thrilling views of the surplice question". He is deeply convinced that the universe is spiritual, but he despises spiritualism. He is "a liberal," but the things which must perforce occupy the mind of the practical politician sometimes seem to him as "thrilling" as the "surplice question," not because they are unimportant, but because they are painfully obvious. *The Englishman in Italy* closes with a contemptuous allusion to the burning political question of the time. He has just been describing the celebration of "the Feast of the Rosary's Virgin ":—

>   —" Such trifles ! " you say ?
>   Fortù, in my England at home,
>   Men meet gravely to-day
>   And debate, if abolishing Corn-laws
>   Be righteous and wise
>   —If 't were proper, Scirocco should vanish
>   In black from the skies !

If an exhaustive list were made of the passages in Browning's works bearing directly upon politics, it would not be long, and it would seem to show an interest poor and feeble compared with that of Tennyson. The passage quoted above gives the clue to the explanation. Political questions seemed to Browning to shape themselves in local and temporary ways, and he preferred to look at things in their universal and permanent aspects.

It is said that, while he was a passionate Unionist, "the question of our political relations with Ireland weighed less with him, as it has done with so many others, than those considerations of law and order, of honesty and humanity, which have been trampled under foot in the name of Home Rule ".[1] If this was Browning's feeling we have in it a further indication of the fact that he was more concerned with social facts than with politics. He stands in one respect therefore nearer to Arnold than to Tennyson. While Tennyson's first interest is England, Arnold's is Europe, and Browning's the whole world. Arnold's mind dwells by preference on the social state determined for the civilised world by the French Revolution. To Browning too it was important, but only as a step in the onward march of humanity. He never regarded it as a destruction of the old world, and therefore never doubted the destiny of the new. *The Lost Leader*, however much or however little of Wordsworth we may suppose to be in it, shows Browning's view of those who deserted the cause, not of this revolution alone, but of any revolution carried out in the interest of humanity at large: Milton, Burns and Shelley, the first actively engaged in one revolution, the others openly and avowedly in sympathy with another, are his examples of those who stand in the van among the freemen. To stand there is a sacred duty, to desert the post the deepest disgrace, but the end in either case is never doubtful:—

> We shall march prospering,—not thro' his presence;
> Songs may inspirit us,—not from his lyre;
> Deeds will be done,—while he boasts his quiescence,
> Still bidding crouch whom the rest bade aspire:
> Blot out his name, then, record one lost soul more,
> One task more declined, one more footpath untrod,
> One more devils'-triumph and sorrow for angels,
> One wrong more to man, one more insult to God!

In the first place then, to discover the social views underlying Browning's work we must look wide. We shall find them embodied not in the political forms of this country rather than that, nor even in those of any country at all. It is the men who give the forms meaning, not the forms that make the men. The Florence which looks so fair and attractive to the eyes of Luria proves when tested to be full of deceit and treachery and meanness. The simple trust and reverence with which the Moor had looked to the great city were superior to anything within it; his own ruder race had bred something nobler than the most polished state in the world could show;

[1] Mrs. Sutherland Orr's *Life*, p. 374.

and the social forms cannot be good which do not produce good men. Neither shall we find Browning's opinions on society linked to any particular time. It is true that what is near must loom larger in the eyes of even the prophetic bard than what is distant, and so beget a tendency to treat subjects which, if farther removed in time, might not have seemed large enough for poetic treatment. *Sludge the Medium* and *Tray* are instances in point. But on the other hand, there is probably more force in the consideration that distance, if it diminishes apparent size, reveals relations and proportions, and so makes artistic treatment much more easy. Browning at any rate seems to have chosen his subjects pretty impartially from every age as well as from every country, and his inner convictions are to be found scattered through them all.

It almost follows from this that the social element in Browning merges in the human; or in other words that his interest centres not in the man *qua* member of a particular society at a particular time, but in the man *qua* member of *human* society, a character of which it is impossible to strip him. To Browning there is neither Greek nor barbarian, Jew nor Gentile, bond nor free. He shares with Shakespeare and Goethe a cosmopolitan character which probably belongs to no other poet in equal measure. In this respect he stands in contrast to Tennyson, and he differs widely from Arnold too. The latter, as we have seen, is always absorbed in the present state and future prospects of the civilisation around him. Further, he is not dramatic. The emotion uppermost in his mind is almost always his own, and hence his true means of poetic utterance are the lyric and the elegiac. Browning, on the other hand, it need hardly be repeated, is almost always dramatic, even in his lyrics. This does not mean that social facts are unimportant to him, but that he sees them in and through the individual soul.

The question then, what are Browning's social views? merges in the wider question, what are his views of man? and that has been partly answered already. It will however conduce to clearness to give special prominence to the aspects suggested by the narrower form in which the question arises here.

In the first place, it is beyond doubt that Browning considers all specially human qualities as the outgrowth of society. The idea of a life, independent and self-sufficing, in a tub, was ridiculous to him; and in face of the Aristotelian doctrine that the solitary being must be either a wild beast or a god, he would have had no difficulty in choosing his alternative. History bears him out in his choice, for all the greatest men have been on his side. Cynicism has been the resort, as a rule, of the intellectually commonplace, and in exceptional cases of the intellectually insufficient. Swift was a cynic, not because he was great, but because he was not great *enough* for the problems which confronted him. Religious solitude has been similarly the resort of the morally commonplace. The Pauls and Hildebrands and Loyolas and Luthers of the world, widely as they differed, have all done a work social in its character. The hermits of the Thebaid doubtless produced an effect, but it was in a double way like that produced by the coral insects. In the first place, it was such that the work of the individual was lost in the mass; and in the second place, it was but an island after all. The continents are the creation of the Pauls and Luthers, the social workers.

For a full and adequate recognition, in recent times, of the social principle, we must turn to Browning. We find it in Tennyson, but not fully; he is too much absorbed in temporary and local forms. The same is true of Arnold, who as we have seen betrays now and then the longing to escape the harder task and save his soul alone. We have seen how Browning lays the greatest stress on the principle of love, which is in its very nature social. This is the law of human life, and the law of the universe as well. We have seen also the fate which overtakes Paracelsus, because he seeks his end in solitude, or mingles in society only in a way that is anti-social; for in the 'first part of his career he simply uses men for an end which, meanwhile at least, is purely his own, and of which the possible outcome is too distant to produce any practical effect. His first aspiration is for power—power to use nature and to use man for ends which may not be selfish in a narrow or bad sense, but of which the social bearing is at least secondary. It ends in ruin, and he learns that it is "love, hope, fear, faith" that "make humanity,"—all social principles, all taking the individual outside himself and making him recognise other beings with reciprocal rights, and possibly superior beings. The lesson of the poem is that every wholesome aim must be social.

The same thought runs through all Browning's poetry. It is conspicuous in the dramas. What impresses us as wholesome and sound in them is always what conforms to the requirements of the " love, hope, fear, faith," that " make humanity ". They leave room for the widest differences in detail, but not for difference in the essential principle. Strafford and Pym, on opposite sides, are both men to be admired, because they are each true to a social principle, the one seeing the state embodied in the king, the other seeing it in the just aspirations, as he considers them, of the popular party. Charles is contemptible because he is true to nothing but self. In *King Victor and King Charles* the two kings differ in the same way. In *The Return of the Druses* even the trickery of Djabal is not wholly unpardonable, because it is never wholly divorced from the desire to serve his race. Throughout Browning's plays, in short, all great failure springs from unfaithfulness to a social ideal, and all great success from fidelity to it.[1] In *A Blot in the 'Scutcheon* Thorold goes astray because concentration on the 'scutcheon makes him forget larger and greater facts; and Valence in *Colombe's Birthday* succeeds because he bases the rights of the ruler upon his duties; and he succeeds most of all in the end, when he applies his principles to himself, stands aside, and pronounces what is right and wrong as if he and his feelings had no existence.

It would be a mistake to suppose that Browning thinks the individual either does or ought to sacrifice himself to society. If in one sense he does so, in another he finds his profit in the sacrifice. Valence is ready to surrender his hopes of Colombe, not in obedience to something external, but at the dictates of a spirit of manhood and a law of duty which are more his own than even the love of Colombe disjoined from them. Sordello in forgetting himself becomes more truly himself than he could ever otherwise have been.

Browning has left no doubt possible as to his opinion of renunciation for its own sake, or for the sake of a future life unnaturally divorced from the present life. His treatment of monasticism is very instructive, and may be interpreted as

---

[1] I do not of course refer to the *outward* success of life. Browning was the last man to teach the copy-book morality of "honesty is the best policy". In *Colombe's Birthday*, Berthold, a self-seeker, though no ordinary one, wins the Duchy; but he admits that he is poorer than Colombe who loses it:—

> You can so well afford to yield it me,
> And I were left, without it, sadly lorn.

revealing in a negative way his conviction of the need of the world, *i.e.*, of society, and of society in the fullest sense. I have already referred to the *Soliloquy of the Spanish Cloister*, where the two monks may be taken as types of the opposite effects a rebellion against nature might be expected to produce. Brother Lawrence is the man of lowered energies and narrowed interests, meek, mild and absorbed in his flowers, which somehow do not thrive,—because the other Brother keeps them "close-nipped on the sly". The slanders which this nameless Brother whispers against the poor lover of flowers are false, for Lawrence has not the energy to sin that way; he has taken too well the colour of his surroundings, and all is neutral and subdued about him. His enemy is a man of greater natural activity, whose energy, dammed back by monastic rules from its natural channels, finds its outlet in an intense hatred of the effeminate Brother whose harmless commonplaces he is doomed to hear day by day. This second monk is a good illustration of the saying, "Naturam expellas furca, tamen usque recurret". The Church bent its strength to thrust out nature, and the whole monastic system was a protest against it; yet here, in the shadow of the cloisters, is nature rank and luxuriant. The monk's force of character expends itself in hatred and malice and in petty persecution, which is not persecution on the large scale only for lack of opportunity. Though he is not by nature theologically minded, yet want of occupation drives him back upon the points of orthodoxy. He illustrates the Trinity in his very drinks, and he dwells with exultation on the "great text in Galatians" with its "twenty-nine distinct damnations".

Browning's full-blooded sympathy with life stood him in good stead in drawing this picture. He could never have become himself the sensualist, like his Spanish monk; but his whole being cried out against the suppression of any part of human nature for the behoof of another; and if anything could have forced him to sensualism, it would have been the attempt at suppression. The poet is far from thinking that all the right is on the side of the holy Brother Lawrence, and all the wrong on the side of the more worldly monk. There is virtue in the very vigour of his hate. The flesh has its rights as well as the spirit. Browning's own protest, in *Sibrandus Schafnaburgensis*, against the pedantry that misses all the joys of life, was Rabelais and a bottle of Chablis. Long afterwards, in *Ferishtah's Fancies*, he returned to the theme, and in the *Two Camels* taught not only the right but the duty of taking advantage of every slightest help, through sense as well as through soul, on the road of life.

Fra Lippo Lippi inculcates a moral similar to that of the *Soliloquy of the Spanish Cloister*. Society is essential to the man depicted, and even while yielding to questionable indulgences he is still feeding his soul. It is true, he

> Did renounce the world, its pride and greed,
> Palace, farm, villa, shop and banking house,
> Trash, such as these poor devils of Medici
> Have given their hearts to—all at eight years old.

He renounced, in short, everything he had not and could not hope to get, for "the mouthful of bread" the renunciation secured to him. And he found in the end that all his education of any value was that which had come to him from the relations of the street, where at any rate he was still in the world and brightening his intellect by the sharp, and not altogether unwholesome, contact with facts. "All the Latin I construe is 'amo' I love." But in the streets he had learnt

> The look of things, and none the less
> For admonition of the hunger-pinch.

To "renounce the world" is for average human nature unhealthy. Average human nature rarely does it in more than name. If it gets nothing else out of the renunciation, it gets at least the "day-long blessed idleness". But that, though a seductive bribe, brings with it consequences reason can hardly approve. It brings the lowered energy of the one Spanish monk, and the concentration on petty spite of the other. It even degrades the higher feelings, until the love of beauty itself becomes, as in the Bishop of St. Praxed's, the miserly gloating over a stolen lump of *lapis lazuli*, mingled in this instance again with feelings as far as possible removed from Christian charity towards other men. The life of the family, the life of the state, the life of the world, make the complete man,—even "worldliness" is better than "other-worldliness".

It would seem then that in Browning's opinion healthy human life demanded healthy and natural relations with other men. It does not matter how such relations are lost or forfeited, the penalty must be paid. Monastic life affords perhaps the most striking, but by no means the only illustrations. Paracelsus and

Sordello, each in his own way, illustrate the fact too. And though the poems mentioned have hitherto been chiefly poems of the earlier period, Browning never altered his opinion. In *The Ring and the Book*, all the moral elevation on the one hand, and all the moral ruin on the other, flow from fidelity to, or from implicit rejection of, the principle on which the social relations rest. Guido is, logically, a solitary, for there is no reason in his conduct why men should admit obligation to him. If he is not left wholly alone it is just because the most antisocial action cannot all at once strip the wrong-doer of the privileges earned for him by the better life of other men. Caponsacchi is perhaps the most striking instance in Browning of the effect of the opposite course of conduct. He alone among the Churchmen brought in contact with Pompilia rises to the height of duty; and he has his reward in the transformation of a self-centred dilettante into, not indeed the "rose," Pompilia, but

> The other rose, the gold,
> We grave to imitate God's miracle (*The Pope*, 1097-8).

And again, in *The Inn Album*, a social wrong works to the ruin of the man sinning, but to the moral glory of the woman sinned against.

Prince Hohenstiel-Schwangau is for the present purpose peculiarly interesting, because it represents not merely a man in society, but a ruler of society; and though it is dramatic, great part of it accords too well with the general scheme of Browning's thought to be dismissed as not representing his own opinion. The speaker shows that high position brings no release from duty, but only makes it more stringent. Moreover, it makes duty wider in its scope; and it makes the agent not less, but rather more, the child of circumstance. "What he will he cannot do." The possibilities of his position are determined for him by others than himself. It is only the irresponsible man, the man who is not obliged to *act*, who can talk of good in the abstract. When the wheels of the actual world have to be put in motion, allowance must be made for friction. The "voice and nothing more" may shout,

> Light in Rome, Law in Rome, and Liberty
> O' the soul in Rome—the free Church, the free State!
> (*Prince Hohenstiel-Schwangau*, xi., 159.)

or,
> Unfettered commerce! Power to speak and hear,
> And print and read! The universal vote!
> Its rights for labour! (xi., 159.)

But, clothed with responsibility and power,

> Such eyes I saw that craved the light alone,
> Such mouths that wanted bread and nothing else,
> Such hands that supplicated handiwork,
> Men with the wives, and women with the babes,
> Yet all these pleading just to live, not die! (*Ibid.*, 161.)

The character of the duty is not in the least changed by the elevation of the agent. Whether the immediate task be "how to manage Europe," or "how keep open shop," in every case the whole meaning of life is determined by its social bearings. Neither would the case be different were the Prince a regenerator, not a mere "saviour" of society. Gifted with greater powers, he would only be "loftier," not more "emancipate".

Browning is then, on the one hand, comparatively indifferent to political forms. There is one vital thing, liberty, which these forms must preserve or give; but after that all is secondary; and liberty is vital because from it comes "all I am and all I hope to be". But on the other hand, this indifference by no means indicates a low view of the importance of society. On the contrary, it is clearly implied that society makes the individual; and all the great crises, all the turns for good or ill in the lives of men, Browning traces to the soundness or unsoundness of their relations with others. Though he worked by monologue, those relations, implied if not expressed, colour the monologue.

The present century has been, beyond most, a period of political change and experiment. If there is any truth in the theory that the principal forces at work during any time must show themselves in its poetry, we should expect to find abundant evidence of the political turmoil in the Victorian poets. And we do. Arnold all through life insisted upon the difficulties and complexities, the strife and unrest, of an age when society has to be made anew. This is the prevailing note of his poetry, or if there is any rival to it, we find it in the expression of the more spiritual aspects of the same difficulties. The immense importance of the political element in the poetry of Tennyson is equally obvious. In his youth he is triumphant, rejoiced that his country has come safely through the fiery trial, and he sings her glories whole-heartedly. A little later he is defiant, because dangers have begun to threaten. In old age he is touched with doubt. Where is this wild democracy driving to? The ignorance of those who are now to rule, and the wanton outrages of a populace becoming conscious of political freedom before they have learnt to control themselves, almost terrify him. But whatever the form it assumes the subject is always a great one in his eyes. In Browning we do not find it in this shape, but we do find that to him the whole meaning of life lies in its social relations. No one, in his opinion, can live his life alone. In his sympathies he is with the Greek philosophers, who ascribed nearly everything to society, rather than with the popular thought in his own day, which sought to limit the functions of society almost to police duties.

CHAPTER XII.

FAITH AND DOUBT.

WITHIN the last hundred years two forces have seemed at times to threaten with imminent destruction every spiritual interpretation of the universe; or perhaps it would be more accurate to speak of them as one force showing itself in two different aspects. Through the agency of the red republicans the materialising philosophy of the eighteenth century secured a practical triumph, and the bells that celebrated the enthronement of the Goddess of Reason sounded to many like the death-knell of the elder goddess, Faith. And unquestionably the alliance of the Church with a doomed political system, and that tenacious championship of abuses which is the special danger of a conservatism so intense as that fostered by the system of catholicism, did in truth lay it open to a wound from which, in some parts of Europe, it has not yet recovered. The progress of physical science, in the second place, has led to results in some respects similar. As, point by point, the intimate connexion between matter and spirit was demonstrated, the conclusion seemed inevitable that the supposed division was a mere illusion; and only a few thought that it might be as legitimate to say that all is spirit as it would be to assert that all is matter.

When such forces were at work it was almost impossible that any powerful mind should remain quiescent. It was also probable *a priori* that the real handling of the questions involved would fall to those who were some little distance in time removed from the starting point of them. The soldier in the heat of the fight knows less about what is taking place than the spectator from a distance. The actor in a violent struggle merely feels; it is only he who reflects at leisure who knows. Thus, Shelley's crude atheism, contradicted, if we interpret it strictly, by almost every line of his poetry, was in reality only an expression of sympathy with those who in the interests of reason rose up against authority. "I used it [the word atheism]," he said, ".to express my abhorrence of superstition. I took up the word as a knight takes up a gauntlet in defiance of injustice."[1] Similarly, Byron's attitude of intellectual and moral revolt was, in its excess, the result of reaction; for mere revolt is impossible as a permanent state. On the other hand, the conservatism of Wordsworth was equally the result of the reaction, upon a spirit of another kind, of the excesses of the Revolution. Goethe, it is true, though he lived through this period, contrived to regard it with a luminous and comprehensive wisdom not yet surpassed. That he did so was partly due to his own qualities, and partly to the condition of his country. Germany was intellectually riper than England, and Goethe was undoubtedly greater than any contemporary Englishman.

When after the great convulsion the world began to settle down and count its gains and losses, when doubts began to spring up whether mere material progress could possibly lead to any "islands of the blest," there were two principal ways in which an interest in more spiritual things showed itself and made headway. From the beginning of his career Thomas Carlyle laboured to spread a knowledge of the heterodox, but still idealising and spiritual, thought of Germany. He traced the progress of a soul fallen on evil times, but resolute to work out its own salvation, not by ostrich-like ignoring the danger, but by facing the problem and solving it; and just when the century was at its turning-point he was thundering in *Latter-Day Pamphlets* against "dismal sciences" and "mud philosophies" and all that tended to materialism. There are still, and there may always be, wide differences of opinion as to the value of Carlyle's solution of the fundamental problems of life; but at any rate his was one of the two methods by which, it would seem, the solution must be attempted. Either the individual soul stands erect, not foolishly casting away the help to be got from others, nor ignoring "the long result of time," but still in the last resort responsible for its own solution and owning no appeal except to reason. The other method was attempted, just a little later, by the band of scholars who headed

---

[1] Trelawny's *Records*, quoted in Dowden's *Life of Shelley*, p. 117.

what is known as "the Oxford Movement". Newman, the most penetrating intellect among them, went over to Rome, but the majority found a satisfactory *via media* within the pale of Anglicanism, and only emphasised the principle of authority as against the Protestant conception of individual right and individual responsibility.

There was, then, a choice of three paths open to the thoughtful Englishman of the middle period of the present century. There was, in the first place, the path of the native philosophy, dominated by the Utilitarians and the economists. They were materialistic in their tendency, and generally negative in their attitude towards questions of a spiritual character. There was, secondly, the path of faith, leading to an acceptance of views on such questions, not as proved, but on authority, as incapable of proof. The third attempted the solution of the problem by reason, like the Utilitarians, but found under the guidance of reason not a materialistic but a spiritual solution. It is not the business of a poet to range himself either with or in opposition to any school of philosophers or theologians; but no poet, if he thinks, can help being influenced by the views current around him as to the ultimate meaning of life; and certainly neither Browning nor Tennyson nor Arnold escaped their influence.

It will be easy to trace this influence in the case of all from the beginning of their work; but it was not till near the middle of the century that questions of this sort seemed to reach maturity. It is remarkable that in 1850 both Tennyson and Browning gave more formal and decisive expression to their convictions than they had hitherto done, the former in *In Memoriam*, the latter in *Christmas Eve and Easter Day*. Tennyson's subject, made for him by the death of his friend, naturally suggested such treatment; but Browning was free to choose, and his choice was probably, at least in part, determined by the events of the time. As for Arnold, he from the beginning showed that he considered such questions, or the same questions in their social aspects, the most interesting of all; and though he is last in time it will be convenient, for a reason already assigned—that he reflects more clearly than either of the others the spirit of the age—to treat him first.

Arnold may be described as the poet of doubt whose reason nevertheless points to another kind of faith. This position is in harmony with that which, as we have already seen, he takes with regard to all great human interests. One of the most remarkable features of his work is the perfect consistency of one part with another: a second is the close articulation of his thought. His opinions on religion are plainly of a piece with his social and political views, and all flow from the one fundamental conception of an old world which has been worn out and which has therefore fallen to pieces, leaving to the present century the task of beginning to build up a new one in its stead.

The very position in which fortune placed Matthew Arnold seemed partly to mark out what he was to be. The son of Dr. Arnold of Rugby, the friend of Arthur Penrhyn Stanley, could hardly miss sympathy with the party of faith. But theirs was a faith based upon a broad foundation of reason, and reached by a method not fundamentally different from that which led the sceptical philosophy to its results. Matthew Arnold followed their method with a greater courage and a more inexorable logic. On the other hand, his famous, but by no means happy, prose definition of the power behind the visible order of nature as "a stream of tendency, not ourselves, which makes for righteousness," proves how far he had gone with the opposite school of scepticism. But it also proves that he refused to take, or rather found himself on grounds of reason precluded from taking, the last and greatest step. This alone would be cause sufficient for ranking Arnold in this respect with the other two poets, both of whom agree with him in rejecting the materialistic explanation. All their points of difference are subordinate to this point of agreement.

In a passage already quoted Arnold speaks of the "rigorous teachers" who seized his youth. The reader of Arnold owes much to that habit of self-revelation which, while never obtruding trifles, rarely fails to give a clue to the most important facts of his spiritual experience. The guidance is peculiarly valuable here. The teachers in question were principally German. Goethe has had no more faithful follower and panegyrist in English verse than Arnold. It was he alone who, in Arnold's judgment, taught how to front the troubles of the age, not to put them by, and how to act in face of them, not passively to endure. It was from Goethe that he drew his uncompromising love of truth. Like Goethe, he saw no guide but reason; and he determined to accept its teaching, whatever it might prove to be. The resolution involved to Arnold much sacrifice and much pain. He has been widely regarded, chiefly on the score of his polemical works, as the jubilant sceptic, the triumphant iconoclast, the light-hearted and pitiless assailant of a venerable creed. Others, better informed, have yet imagined that they detect a note of calm superiority in his references to what he regarded as a fallen faith. Neither view is right. Arnold from the beginning rejected the popular creed, but he did so with sorrow and pain. The heaviest cloud that darkened his world had its source just in the fact that it was an impossibility for him, an anachronism as he believed, a thing which now must divide the human spirit against itself. He could not accept the street preacher's specific for trouble of this kind,—" believe, believe, don't question, don't reason, only believe ". He was far too clear-minded, too great and too honourable to seek an ignominious refuge from the task his genius laid upon him of searching for the truth and as far as he could teaching it. When, even for a moment, he seems inclined to seek shelter from his troubles, he hears the voice of his rigorous teachers asking what *he* does in a living tomb. His scepticism was the melancholy acceptance of a stern, unwelcome intellectual necessity. He has himself expressed its character in words of surpassing beauty:—

> The Sea of Faith
> Was once, too, at the full, and round earth's shore
> Lay like the folds of a bright girdle furl'd. .
> But now I only hear
> Its melancholy, long, withdrawing roar,
> Retreating, to the breath
> Of the night wind, down the vast edges drear
> And naked shingles of the world (*Dover Beach*).

It ought to be added that there is nevertheless a reason for the popular conception, so opposed as it is to the reality. Arnold was a master—few more skilful—of the keen weapons of irony and satire. He was also apt to be dominated by scorn of the Philistines and all related to them. And so he has sometimes allowed himself to speak with contempt of beliefs which had ceased to be possible to himself, but which remained precious to many of his countrymen,—beliefs the decay of which he has himself lamented in eloquent and touching verse. In this he was inconsistent with himself, and untrue to his better nature.

Believing what he believed about the past and present of the world, his criticism, even of the less intelligent forms of the popular creed, ought to have been always temperate and respectful. It was, though hostile, always temperate; but it was not always respectful. In this matter his prose is much more frequently to blame than his verse; but even in the latter, notwithstanding the self-restraint which high poetry imposes upon its author, there is an occasional note of impatience, an occasional gleam of scorn of the fools who cannot see eye to eye with the poet.

We must seek the key to Arnold's religious position in his general view of the world. The essence of it, as we have already seen, lies in the belief that the principles on which life had hitherto proceeded have failed, and that from the failure has sprung the typical disease of modern life, its aimless unrest. But Arnold does not leave the matter thus vague, he has a more specific answer to the question whence this disease springs. It is expressed most clearly, perhaps, in *Obermann once More*. In that poem Arnold draws a magnificent contrast between East and West in the days of Roman sway,—between the outward grandeur of Rome and the rottenness within, the legions thundering in conquest over the world and the "brooding East" bowing before the blast. But then as now it is not he who wields the sword, but the master of the soul, who really rules; and that mastership belongs to the East. The brooding results in the birth of a new religion; and the West in turn passes under the dominion of the East. The latter issues her edict and is obeyed:—

> "Poor world," she cried, "so deep accurst,
> That runn'st from pole to pole
> To seek a draught to slake thy thirst—
> Go, seek it in thy soul."

Few pictures have been painted more impressive than that of the effect of this mandate,—the eagles veiled, the sword snapped, sceptre and crown abdicated, art and philosophy, "lust of the eye and pride of life," all abandoned as vain and empty. And the West finds salvation in what to the materialist looks like ruin:—

> Tears wash'd the trouble from her face!
> She changed into a child!

> 'Mid weeds and wrecks she stood—a place
> Of ruin—but she smiled![1]

Such then is Arnold's conception of the influence of early Christianity. It lasted long, but it decayed at last, because, in his view, it rested upon error. The "gracious Child" and "thorn-crown'd Man" lived while faith in him remained; but faith passed away, and

> Now he is dead! Far hence he lies
> In the lorn Syrian town;
> And on his grave, with shining eyes,
> The Syrian stars look down.

We must perforce abandon our "all too human creeds," and find, if we can, the divine way by efforts of our own.

Arnold never retracted these negations. If his poetry left the question in any doubt, his prose would settle it. But in one of his latest poems, *Geist's Grave*, he speaks of death as the

> Stern law of every mortal lot,
> Which man, proud man, finds hard to bear,
> And builds himself I know not what
> Of second life I know not where.

[1] There is a passage in Browning's *Christmas Eve*, § 11, singularly like this of Arnold's in conception, and even in an occasional phrase, though quite different in execution. The passage is worth quoting for the sake of the comparison with Arnold's better known lines:—

> Oh, love of those first Christian days!
> —Fanned so soon into a blaze,
> From the spark preserved by the trampled sect,
> That the antique sovereign Intellect
> Which then sat ruling in the world,
> Like a change in dreams, was hurled
> From the throne he reigned upon:
> You looked up and he was gone.
> Gone, his glory of the pen!
> —Love, with Greece and Rome in ken,
> Bade her scribes abhor the trick
> Of poetry and rhetoric,
> And exult with hearts set free,
> In blessed imbecility
> Scrawled, perchance, on some torn sheet
> Leaving Sallust incomplete (v. 235).

Arnold's poem was much later in date than Browning's; but I quote the passage, not to suggest plagiarism, for I do not believe there has been anything of the kind, but to draw attention to the curious parallelism of thought between two writers who do not often exhibit it.

He rejected the supernatural wholly from his belief and his life. Some will think that in doing so he rejected religion, and that consequently the discussion of him in his religious aspects is, except negatively, rather futile. Such however was not his own view. He believed in a scheme of things surely setting towards righteousness. His life was guided and his verse inspired by that belief, and to ignore it would be to ignore its vital principle.

The fact that there is so little that is positive in Arnold's religion accounts in part for its characteristic tone. The "melancholy, long, withdrawing roar" sounds through it always, and there is no after flood-tide to fill the bare expanse of shingle. We have seen already that the hope to which he looks in the end is in the first place distant and in the second vague. His own age can do no more than make a beginning.

> Ein guter Mensch in seinem dunkeln Drange
> Ist sich des rechten Weges wohl bewusst
> (*Faust, Prolog im Himmel*),

says Goethe. This, if the emphasis be laid strongly on the dark strivings, is an exact description of Arnold's good man. The way is dark, all the more because the times grow increasingly complex, and it is only "somehow" that the best can know the way. "From gloom we come, and vanish into gloom"; but it is never to be forgotten that the darkness is flecked with a spiritual light.

The man who would rear a structure to last through ages must dig down to bed-rock for his foundation. The man who in modern days would construct a stable faith must begin by a deep-reaching scepticism. In the thoroughness of his scepticism, in his perfect faith in reason and absolute intellectual sincerity, Arnold had the promise of a faith more sure than either Browning or Tennyson reached. As we shall presently see, they stopped short and would not face the last difficulties of all. Arnold did face them, but he attained only the beginnings and the faint promise of a faith. This was doubtless because he was not sufficiently master of the truths he saw. His wail about the complexity of his age is full of meaning. He felt that he had not grasped the whole of experience; and therefore though there is a positive side to his thought it is not fully worked out.

Of the other two poets Browning may be taken as the more closely akin to Arnold. They differ widely in their conclusions, but there is a fundamental similarity in their method, for both begin by a reasoned investigation, the results of which show through their verse. But Browning was less purely critical in his verse, and far less negative in his results, than Arnold. On the other hand, he was more critical than Tennyson, and less disposed to accept beliefs as he found them. In the case of Browning, however, we must discriminate between the earlier and the later work. Professor Jones has once for all pointed out how the poet, failing to find a solution of his difficulties, towards the end fell back upon a denial of knowledge and accepted faith blindly, without reason and even against reason. Herein he is in contrast with Arnold, who, under the guidance of his " rigorous teachers," accepts reason as his law, and never swerves from his allegiance, though his " lyric cry " from time to time betrays his suffering.

During the earlier part of Browning's career it may be said that the religious element is chiefly implicit in his work, in the middle period it is explicit, but is still reached by the critical method, and exists side by side with other elements. The characteristic of the closing period is that faith threatens to oust everything else, and that it is no longer reached by a method truly critical; or rather the criticism is only a step in the process of proving that criticism is ultimately impossible.

That a deeply religious spirit is from the first implicit in Browning's poetry is plain. By calling it implicit I mean that he does not deliberately set himself to treat religious questions, nor does he write poems professedly upon them. Notwithstanding this, it is present in nearly every poem from *Pauline* onwards. *Pauline* is a revelation of the inner life of the speaker, and the extreme importance of the religious element in this inner life appears repeatedly :—

> I have always had one lode-star; now,
> As I look back, I see that I have halted
> Or hastened as I looked towards that star—
> A need, a trust, a yearning after God :
> A feeling I have analysed but late,
> But it existed, and was reconciled
> With a neglect of all I deemed his laws,
> Which yet, when seen in others, I abhorred.

> I felt as one beloved, and so shut in
> From fear: and thence I date my trust in signs
> And omens, for I saw God everywhere;
> And I can only lay it to the fruit
> Of a sad after-time that I could doubt
> Even his being—e'en the while I felt
> His presence, never acted from myself,
> Still trusted in a hand to lead me through
> All danger; and this feeling ever fought
> Against my weakest reason and resolve (i. 15).

Again :—

> My God, my God, let me for once look on thee
> As though nought else existed, we alone!
> And as creation crumbles, my soul's spark
> Expands till I can say,—Even from myself
> I need thee and I feel thee and I love thee.
> I do not plead my rapture in thy works
> For love of thee, nor that I feel as one
> Who cannot die: but there is that in me
> Which turns to thee, which loves or which should love (i. 37).

And the poem ends with the expression of belief "in God and truth and love".

The belief could easily be traced through *Paracelsus* and *Pippa Passes* and all the principal poems of the early period. To say that it is implicit therefore must by no means be understood to imply that it is weak or indistinct. Clearly Browning had never to grope, or, if the hint dropped in the first passage quoted from Pauline be autobiographical, had not to grope long, for the essential principle of a faith. But the only apparent exception in the first period to the implicitness of religion in the sense I have explained is *Saul*; and it is no more than apparent, for the part which affords the best ground for regarding this poem as exceptional did not appear in 1845 when it was first published among the *Dramatic Romances and Lyrics*. Only the first nine sections were then printed, sections 10-19 being added in 1855 when the poem reappeared among *Men and Women*. The difference between the two parts in matter and tone is very instructive. In the earlier sections David is engaged in trying to win back Saul from his gloomy "possession" by playing the various tunes of the wholesome shepherd life—the tune which gathers the sheep, that which attracts the quails, "the help-tune of our reapers," even the song "when the dead man is praised on his journey," then "the glad chant of the marriage," and last of all the splendid song of "our manhood's prime vigour". In all this there is nothing of that prophetic quality which is the special mark of the second part. It may be foreshadowed in the attitude in which David finds Saul:—

> He stood as erect as that tent-prop, both arms stretched out wide
> On the great cross-support of the centre, that goes to each side ;
> He relaxed not a muscle, but hung there as, caught in his pangs
> And waiting his change, the king-serpent all heavily hangs,
> Far away from his kind, in the pine, till deliverance come
> With the spring-time,—so agonized Saul, drear and stark, blind and dumb (vi. p. 100).

But if this was meant to be symbolical, the hint remained, so far as the outer world was concerned, for ten years undeveloped.

But this hint, then undeveloped, becomes the very essence of the second part. All that is won by the previous songs is the mere beginning of revival. "Death was past, life not come." The problem becomes,

> What next should I urge
> To sustain him where song had restored him? (*Ibid.*, p. 108.)

To find an answer the poet takes the psalmist back to the fancies he had cherished as he watched his grazing flocks in solitude. He offers Saul the spirit-wine drawn from these solitary musings. The lesson is the superiority of soul to flesh, and the incalculable worth of what the spirit impels such a man as Saul to do.

> Each ray of thy will,
> Every flash of thy passion and prowess, long over, shall thrill
> Thy whole people, the countless, with ardour, till they too give forth
> A like cheer to their sons, who in turn, fill the South and the North
> With the radiance thy deed was the germ of (*Ibid.*, p. 112).

And even when life ends all is not over. The "mountain of marble" is piled up for Saul's tomb, his deeds are graven in gold on the cedar and sung by the poet.

The promise still is only of a life abounding during its continuance, transmitting its influence to others and transmitted to memory by the records men frame. There is no hint of a life continued beyond death. The full truth bursts out in the closing sections, without the aid of harp or song. The speaker has "gone the whole round of creation," and has found perfection everywhere in it. There is only one faculty, love, in which for a moment he is tempted to think the creature may surpass

FAITH AND DOUBT.

the creator. It is the absurdity of this that gives point to the argument. It would never have entered his mind, "the bare will, much less power," to dower Saul as he is dowered,

> To make such a soul,
> Such a body, and then such an earth for insphering the whole
> (vi., p. 120).

But it does enter his mind that these things, once given, should continue, and hence he concludes the Creator must

> Interpose at the difficult minute, snatch Saul the mistake,
> Saul the failure, the ruin he seems now,—and bid him awake
> From the dream, the probation, the prelude, to find himself set
> Clear and safe in new light and new life,—a new harmony yet
> To be run, and continued, and ended—who knows?—or endure!
> The man taught enough, by life's dream, of the rest to make sure;
> By the pain-throb, triumphantly winning intensified bliss,
> And the next world's reward and repose, by the struggles of this
> (*Ibid.*, pp. 120-121).

Here is clearly the promise of a second life. In the section following we are shown more fully what is to be its relation to the Universal Life. David's argument here is that as he would sacrifice himself for Saul, so would the power which made Saul; and the end is a prophecy of Christ:—

> He who did most, shall bear most; the strongest shall stand the most weak.
> 'Tis the weakness in strength, that I cry for! my flesh, that I seek
> In the Godhead! I seek and I find it. O Saul, it shall be
> A Face like my face that receives thee; a Man like to me
> Thou shalt love and be loved by, for ever: a Hand like this hand
> Shall throw open the gates of new life to thee! See the Christ stand!
> (*Ibid.*, pp. 122-123.)

This later development of *Saul* by no means stands alone in Browning's middle period. *Christmas Eve* and *Easter Day* have been already mentioned and partly discussed. The former is a vision, the latter an argumentative dialogue embodying a vision, and both deal as a historical reality with that Christianity which *Saul* prophesies.

If we take these poems as in their broad features reflecting Browning's own mind, his position may be defined as one of faith in the more important teachings of Christianity, combined with free criticism and frequent rejection of details. And the vital points of Christianity, as he understood it, would seem to be that it teaches a universal love, and that this love was embodied in a divine Man, the pattern for all who succeed him. Thus, notwithstanding much that is intellectually repellent in the extreme doctrines both of Nonconformity and of Romanism, Browning—or at least the speaker in *Christmas Eve*—finds the essential truth to exist in both. In his picture of the dissenting chapel the poet leaves the feeling that there is a kind of necessity for the very absurdities of the doctrine taught within. After his manner (for he rarely refers to external things except with the purpose of throwing light upon the mind), he brings the squalid surroundings of the chapel, and the very state of the weather, into connexion with the teaching. Something is clearly necessary to lift from the dirt those who live amidst such surroundings, and anything high would apparently be impossible, for they have not been prepared. The doctrine taught certainly does not err on the side of undue intellectual elevation. The poet is deeply impressed with "the preaching man's immense stupidity"; and even where the matter he preaches is sound, the truths seem unfamiliar,

> Grown double their size
> In the natural fog of the good man's mind (v. 218).

The stupid doctrine is received by the congregation with such a provoking contentment that the spectator's gorge rises at "the nonsense and stuff of it". He leaves the little chapel in an impatience soon lessened by reflection. The same weary thing is taking place in so many different ways,

> Each method abundantly convincing,
> As I say, to those convinced before,
> But scarce to be swallowed without wincing
> By the not-as-yet-convinced (v. 220).

The speaker among the rest has his own church:—

> In youth I looked to these very skies,
> And probing their immensities,
> I found God there, his visible power;
> Yet felt in my heart, amid all its sense
> Of the power, an equal evidence
> That his love, there too, was the nobler dower.
> For the loving worm within its clod,
> Were diviner than a loveless God
> Amid his worlds, I will dare to say (*Ibid.*).

This paves the way for the return of sympathy with the congregation he has just left, and for the vision which breaks upon him,—the vision of Christ, who has been present there too, and whose face is not seen till confession has been made that the scorn of the humble worshippers had sprung from folly and pride. For after all the vital thing is love, and that "the preaching man" and his flock possess. Their intellectual aberrations are in comparison trivial. Their tendency to take "God's word under wise protection" and "correct its tendency to diffusiveness" is indeed a mistake; but all are free to worship in their own way, provided only the one thing needful, the spirit of love, be present.

Under the guidance of the vision the speaker passes from the dingy chapel and its dismal surroundings to St. Peter's in Rome. There too his guide enters, for there too the vital thing is to be found. He himself sits awhile outside, but resolves at last to follow. He cannot feed his whole nature there, for intellect rebels against "Rome's gross yoke". Still, there is partial sympathy,

> And where the intellect devolves
>   Its function on love exclusively,
> I, a man who possesses both,
> Will accept the provision, nothing loth,
> —Will feast my love, then depart elsewhere,
> That my intellect may find its share (v. 238).

And the place to which his intellect is transported for its nourishment is the German Professor's lecture-room, the subject of the discourse being the Myth of Christ. The poet, though, as we have elsewhere seen, he depicts the Professor with admirable vividness and insight, has far less sympathy with him than with either the dissenting or the Romish congregation. Browning, or the figure he creates, is left at the entrance door of the college, with nothing but "the garment's extreme fold" to bless him, and he leaves at the first break, sanctioned by the vision, which still guides him:—

> I could interpret its command.
> This time he would not bid me enter
> The exhausted air-bell of the Critic.
> Truth's atmosphere may grow mephitic
> When Papist struggles with Dissenter,
> Impregnating its pristine clarity,
> —One, by his daily fare's vulgarity,
>   Its gust of broken meat and garlic;

> —One, by his soul's too-much presuming
> To turn the frankincense's fuming
>   And vapours of the candle starlike
> Into the cloud her wings she buoys on.
>   Each, that thus sets the pure air seething,
>   May poison it for healthy breathing—
> But the Critic leaves no air to poison ;
> Pumps out with ruthless ingenuity
> Atom by atom, and leaves you—vacuity (v. 245).

It is with difficulty that the poet summons up any sympathy with the Professor's doctrine ; and his sympathy with the man himself is largely due to the fact that he believes him to be inconsistent with his own logic and superior to it. The Professor empties the Myth of Christ of meaning, and yet enjoins his hearers to revere it.

> Unlearned love was safe from spurning—
> Can't we respect your loveless learning? (v. 253.)

The question has to be asked, and is answered with a grudge all the more significant when we remember how full and complete, as we see in *A Grammarian's Funeral*, can be Browning's sympathy with even the driest forms of learning, if only it be thorough :—

> He settled *Hoti's* business—let it be !—
>   Properly based *Oun*—
> Gave us the doctrine of the enclitic *De*,
>   Dead from the waist down.

It is of this man and for such exploits that we are told (dramatically of course, but still with the sympathy of the poet),

> Our low life was the level's and the night's :
>   He's for the morning.

Learning is good when it is developing a theory of the Middle Verb : it is more questionable when

> A tricksy demon
> (Sets her at Titus or Philemon.

The element of love is so all-important to Browning that while he can forgive everything else he cannot quite forgive the absence of it, or even the putting it in the background.

There is meaning in the fact that the speaker in *Christmas Eve* loses hold of the vesture's hem in a fit of general tolerance, valuing religion for itself and careless about sect, enjoying his own conviction and leaving his neighbour's faith uncensured. There must be some limit to that, there must be some "one way, our chief best way of worship"; and the great problem is to discover this, and having discovered it to share it with others. There is hope for the Pope, for all his "buffoonery of posturings and petticoatings". There is hope too for the Professor should his cough increase and the world darken around him. The man who is really in danger is he who, while attacking the choice of his neighbours, is found in the end with no choice made; and to evade this danger the speaker throws in his lot with the sect among whom, after his vision, he finds himself once more, and joins chorus in "the seventeenth hymn of Whitfield's Collection".

There is evidence here of a spirit strongly predisposed to the acceptance of a large element of the supernatural. It is indeed an acceptance after examination and inquiry; but the result has something of the character of a foregone conclusion. The German Professor gets hard measure. The two opposing forms of faith are, it is true, keenly criticised; but the solidity of the foundation ✓ on which they rest is presupposed; and it is clear that, while the poet is conscious of the faults and the intellectual weakness of both forms of faith, he would nevertheless hold himself to be in substantial harmony with them. Towards the Professor his attitude is quite different. It is that of intellectual comprehension, and, doubtless, partial sympathy, combined with complete emotional disagreement. It is remarkable that we find the evidence for the partial sympathy with the critical attitude rather in the early parts of the poem, and in other poems altogether, than in the place where we might naturally look for it. Browning's dislike is so great that he slurs over his sympathy. In this perhaps we see the germ of that unfortunate division between thought and feeling which becomes so prominent in his later poems.

Easter Day, the companion piece to *Christmas Eve*, written about the same time and from a similar point of view, confirms the impression drawn from the latter poem. It turns principally upon the same question of the relation between love and knowledge which plays so large a part in *Christmas Eve*, and it drives home the lesson, taught in that poem too, of the fatal effects of irresolution with regard to questions of ultimate human destiny.

Easter Day opens with a discussion of the difficulties of Christian belief, and issues, like the preceding poem, in a vision, wherein the speaker sees himself judged and condemned as one who has chosen the world, who in his doubts will not let slip the joys of sense to seize upon the promise of the spirit fitfully perceived by the human eye. It is only the Judgment Day itself that burns away all darkness from his spirit, and reveals what his choice has really been. His sentence is that he shall have for ever the earth he has chosen, and his first impulse is one of rapturous amazement and delight to think he may enjoy to the full all he has found so wonderful and so beautiful. But the feeling changes to despair when he realises that this means exclusion from all the higher beauty and greater destiny for which the world is a preparation. He prays for leave to love only. The wrathful reply comes that the choice is late. Love has been inextricably woven in with everything in the world, and yet the soul thus judged has set aside the love of the Maker of all. The last prayer, which is listened to, is that he may take once more all the limitations of his former life, only going on hoping "to reach one eve the Better Land".

It seems plain that this piece is not to the same degree, or perhaps rather not in the same way, as *Christmas Eve*, a reflection of Browning's own mind. There are two interlocutors instead of a single narrator, and it is certain Browning is not to be identified with either, but to be found, if at all, in both. He characteristically gives the lion's share of the discussion, and apparently the better part of his own regard, to the man of faith; but unquestionably he would decline to accept for himself this speaker's antithesis between the world and the spirit. He would at least express it differently, and insist, not upon "renouncing" the world, either wholly, or in the half-hearted way of the character he imagines; but upon seeing beyond it, and of rising, not despite it, but by means of it, to that of which it is the promise. Browning himself appears, not in this speaker, but in the criticism of his judge; and the idea of the world implied in his words is that of a stage in preparation for something beyond. It is not to be renounced, but to be used with reference to a further end.

> All partial beauty was a pledge
> Of beauty in its plenitude.

And the plenitude is theirs who, while using the pledge, looked above.

Of the numerous other poems of this period in which religion is an important element, it will be sufficient here to notice *A Death in the Desert* and *The Pope*; for though both have been mentioned previously, it has been with other ends in view.

Reasons have already been given for the belief that the St. John of *A Death in the Desert* must be regarded as largely the mouthpiece of Browning's own thought. What he says coheres too closely with what Browning says in many other places and under many names to be taken otherwise. The prevailing thought of *A Death in the Desert* is the necessity of doubt—another aspect of that which is elsewhere expressed as the necessity of evil. It was not expressed in this poem for the first time. It is to be found already in *Easter Day*, and also in *Bishop Blougram's Apology*. "With me," says the Bishop,

> "With me, faith means perpetual unbelief
> Kept quiet like the snake 'neath Michael's foot
> Who stands calm just because he feels it writhe" (iv. 265);

and whatever the degree of Browning's sympathy with Blougram in other respects, it is beyond question that he agreed with him that faith contained, potentially at least, an element of doubt, whether the individual was conscious of it or not. So in *A Death in the Desert* a contrast is drawn between bodily good, which is weighed and measured once for all, and accepted at its value ever after, and the soul's gain, which has to be won again and again. Were spiritual truth as indisputable as truth physical, once experienced, then

> Man's probation would conclude, his earth
> Crumble; for he both reasons and decides,
> Weighs first, then chooses: will he give up fire
> For gold or purple once he knows its worth?
> Could he give Christ up were His worth as plain
> Therefore, I say, to test man, the proofs shift,
> Nor may he grasp that fact like other fact,
> And straightway in his life acknowledge it,
> As, say, the indubitable bliss of fire (vii. 132).

There is perhaps only one expression in this passage that may not be ascribed to Browning himself. The theological idea of a test is foreign to his thought, he prefers to look upon it as an education, and indeed so states it in a later passage of this very poem. Man, he explains there through the lips of St. John, is

> Lower than God who knows all and can all,
> Higher than beasts which know and can so far
> As each beast's limit, perfect to an end,
> Nor conscious that they know, nor craving more;
> While man knows partly but conceives beside,
> Creeps ever on from fancies to the fact,
> And in this striving, this converting air
> Into a solid he may grasp and use,
> Finds progress, man's distinctive mark alone,
> Not God's, and not the beasts': God is, they are,
> Man partly is, and wholly hopes to be.
> Such progress could no more attend his soul
> Were all its struggles after found at first
> And guesses changed to knowledge absolute,
> Than motion wait his body, were all else
> Than it the solid earth on every side,
> Where now through space he moves from rest to rest
>
> (vii. 144).

Thus truth to man is ever a process. At no point is it absolute, at no point is it permanently safe; but, on the other hand, if he will only use his faculties aright, it is always sufficient for his needs. This explains at once the difficulty in every age of fidelity to Christ, and the possibility of it. St. John supposes that even those who converse with him in his old age may plead that faith was easier to those who saw. For answer he appeals to his own history :—

> Sigh ye, "It had been easier once than now"?
> To give you answer I am left alive;
> Look at me who was present from the first!
> Ye know what things I saw; then came a test,
> My first, befitting me who so had seen:
> "Forsake the Christ thou sawest transfigured, Him
> Who trod the sea and brought the dead to life?
> What should wring this from thee!"—ye laugh and ask.
> What wrung it? Even a torchlight and a noise,
> The sudden Roman faces, violent hands,
> And fear of what the Jews might do! Just that,
> And it is written, "I forsook and fled" (vii. 132-133).

Nevertheless, his "soul had gained its truth, could grow"; and soon little children and tender women who had not seen the wonders, but only heard them told, could laugh at the dangers from which he had shrunk, and welcome torture. But even then truth was not safe; and when John, the last of all who had seen with their own eyes, lay at the point of death, it seemed to be beset with new and more formidable dangers.

It is important to notice that the final forms of scepticism are not met here; the argument rather is that in their nature they cannot be met. They are like diseases that spring from repletion, with the difference, of course, that whereas it is easy to withdraw the redundant nourishment from the body, there is no process by which the mind can be so treated.

> I say, this is death and the sole death,
> When a man's loss comes to him from his gain,
> Darkness from light, from knowledge ignorance,
> And lack of love from love made manifest;
> A lamp's death when, replete with oil, it chokes;
> A stomach's when, surcharged with food, it starves (vii. 140).

So, when man reasons that since

> "Love is everywhere,
> And since ourselves can love and would be loved,
> We ourselves make the love, and Christ was not,"—
> How shall ye help this man who knows himself,
> That he must love and would be loved again,
> Yet, owning his own love that proveth Christ,
> Rejecteth Christ through very need of Him?
> The lamp o'erswims with oil, the stomach flags
> Loaded with nurture, and that man's soul dies (vii. 141).

Many of the same thoughts re-appear, expressed with a power never surpassed, in *The Pope*. "This life is training and a passage," we are told; and the fact explains much that would otherwise be perplexing. It explains the difficulties and the drawbacks of life:—

> Is this our ultimate stage, or starting-place
> To try man's foot, if it will creep or climb,
> 'Mid obstacles in seeming, points that prove
> Advantage for who vaults from low to high
> And makes the stumbling-block a stepping-stone?
> (*The Ring and the Book*: *The Pope*, 409-413.)

This furnishes the answer to those who would plead for Guido that he is poor and straitened and lacks the food his appetites demand. It is true, but these defects are only the fair counterpoise to his noble birth and culture and ancient name, which else would have set him unfairly above his fellows. Besides, it would be consistent with Browning's thought to add, though he does not here say so explicitly, that Guido had a *right* to these drawbacks, in order that he might turn the stumbling-blocks into stepping-stones.

Again, just as difficulty has a necessary place in the scheme of nature, so it has in faith :—

> What but the weakness in a faith supplies
> The incentive to humanity, no strength
> Absolute, irresistible, comports?
> How can man love but what he yearns to help?
> And that which men think weakness within strength,
> But angels know for strength and stronger yet—
> What were it else but the first thing made new,
> But repetition of the miracle,
> The divine instance of self-sacrifice
> That never ends and aye begins for man? (*Ibid.* 1649-1658.)

Reflections such as these may be found elsewhere in Browning; but the special significance of *The Pope* lies in the expression of doubts which go deeper, and which are rendered all the more telling by the lips that utter them. In the remarkable passage beginning at line 1308, the Pope first expresses his belief in God, known to man not absolutely, but in the scale adapted to his faculties. He goes on to declare his faith in the Incarnation. It is not only credible on the evidence, but it seems demanded by analogy to complete the conception of God. Man falls short of his own ideal in strength, intelligence and goodness. If he looks beyond himself to the world and conjectures "of the worker by the work," he finds there ample strength and intelligence to satisfy his conception of a God, but by no means "goodness in a like degree". The universe is "an isosceles deficient in the base". As the strength and the intelligence are limitless,

> Let love be so,
> Unlimited in its self-sacrifice,
> Then is the tale true and God shows complete
> (*Ibid.*, 1370-1372).

But what compels doubt is the sense of the vast gulf between the actual state of the world and that which might be expected as the result of the "transcendent act". The Power which made man ordained salvation for both body and soul, "and yet .... well, is the thing we see salvation?" The puzzling thing is not that some men doubt and declare their doubts; it is rather that those who profess belief act in a way that shows their faith to be unreal. The Aretine Archbishop, "champion of the faith," throws back the fawn, Pompilia, to the wolf, Guido. The monk, whom penance and asceticism should have braced, if luxury may have enervated his superior, shelters himself under the plea that where the great will not help it would be foolish for the small to run risk. "I break my promise: let her break her heart." The Monastery of the Convertites, having proclaimed Pompilia a saint, no sooner learns that wealth may be got by proving her the opposite, than they set about doing it.

> A title-deed to filch, a corpse
> To slander, and an infant-heir to cheat (*Ibid.*, 1521-1522),

are temptations irresistible.

The comfortable and easy explanation that it is all due to the hardness of human nature is contradicted by facts. It is vain to call man's heart ice or stone, for the ice can melt, the stone bloom. Human nature responds readily now, as it has always responded, to the proper stimulus. Caponsacchi himself, the mere dilettante priest, at the call for honour's sake to pity the oppressed, springs up at once to "right wrong at any risk,"—"all blindness, bravery and obedience". How is it that a mere "uncommissioned meteor" should thus in a moment cause to bud and bloom and bear fruit a nature upon which "the light of the world" had shone for years without effect? This is the question the Pope asks, and he is not content with the easy reply :—

> What, we monks,
> We friars, of such an order, such a rule,
> Have not we fought, bled, left our martyr-mark
> At every point along the boundary-line
> 'Twixt true and false, religion and the world,
> Where this or the other dogma of our Church
> Called for defence ? (*Ibid.*, 1572-1578.)

The retort is that even these publicans do the same. "Or better than the best, or nothing serves"; and all the stories of martyr-sacrifice can be capped and crowned with others "done at an instinct of the natural man". It is as if a Rosicrucian should spend his life in an attempt to transmute base metal into gold, and in the end gain

> Not a grain more than the vulgar got
> By the old smelting-process years ago (*Ibid.*, 1622-1623).

This is the Pope's impressive presentment of doubts all must have felt at times. It is true that, in spite of all, he says, "I have light nor fear the dark at all ". It is true he attempts to account for the difficulties, by urging the thought already spoken of, that some weakness is a condition of faith, and also by the suggestion that "we have got too familiar with the light". The Christian act was easy "when in the way stood Nero's cross and stake"; it is hard now when the world applauds, yet goes its worldly way, in the "ignoble confidence" that however much of the wheat may be trampled under foot and wasted in the effort to get at some poppy-flower, there will still remain enough for the comfortable loaf, if not the undiminished prize.

But there is obviously a great gap between the fact and the reasons assigned to account for it; and the suggestion thrown out by way of helping to bridge it is the most striking of all :—

> Unless . . . what whispers me of times to come?
> What if it be the mission of that age
> My death will usher into life, to shake
> This torpor of assurance from our creed,
> Re-introduce the doubt discarded, bring
> That formidable danger back, we drove
> Long ago to the distance and the dark?
> No wild beast now prowls round the infant camp:
> We have built wall and sleep in city safe:
> But if some earthquake try the towers, that laugh
> To think they once saw lions rule outside,
> And man stand out again, pale, resolute,
> Prepared to die,—which means, alive at last?
> As we broke up that old faith of the world,
> Have we, next age, to break up this the new—
> Faith, in the thing, grown faith in the report—
> Whence need to bravely disbelieve report
> Through increased faith i' the thing reports belie?
>
> (*The Pope*, 1851-1868.)

Such, in the Pope's view (which may with considerable confidence be interpreted as Browning's), is the possible function of doubt and of that criticism of old beliefs by reason which he felt just beginning. There is danger in it, the danger always attendant upon the transition from a traditionally-accepted view to a new one necessitated by the growth of knowledge. Here and there a Pompilia may "know the right place by foot's feel". Here and there a Canon Caponsacchi, who stands in place of "the Augustin that was once," may by his own mere impulse tread in the main "the right step through the maze we bade him foot". He may even repeat the prodigy a second time; but how should he teach others? He can only bid them ask their own hearts as he asked his, and then the Abate's answer is final. What he chooses is, to Caponsacchi, "the lowest of life's appetites,"

> But the very truth of joy
> To my own apprehension which decides
>
> (*The Pope*, 1935-1936).

There is no final solution of the difficulty. The old world of faith is dead—that seems clearly the poet's meaning. It has not fulfilled its promise. The new world dawns in tempest; but the tempest may, and he clearly believes it will, prove necessary to clear the ground for a fresh growth, and when that growth springs the world will be once more a world of faith.

In the closing period of his work Browning seems as it were to set free that flood of criticism which he foreshadows in *The Pope*. He never again treats these questions more profoundly, never so inspiringly as he does through his impressive figure of Innocent XII., never even in such a truly critical spirit, but he does it still more directly. For the present purpose, the most instructive poem of this period is beyond doubt *La Saisiaz;* but before we proceed to it *The Inn Album* demands some attention; for there Browning has given the most powerful expression to his negative criticism of some forms of popular belief. They are far less important than those which come under examination in *The Ring and the Book*, where it is rather Christianity that is in question than the particular views of any school of theologians. Still, they have played a large part in the life of England, and it is evident that Browning considered them by no means insignificant. Moreover, the fact that he comparatively seldom gives rein to this negative criticism makes it all the more noteworthy when he does so.

In *The Inn Album* the nameless heroine, driven by the wrong which clouds her life to marry an obscure and narrow-minded country clergyman, describes her existence with him. The description is a faithful picture of life from which all interests, except the interest of evangelical Christianity, have withered away. It is not, and is not meant to be, a picture of the greater and larger-spirited evangelicals; for the larger spirits of all sects and parties invariably overleap their boundaries. But it is true to evangelicalism as seen by a small mind some fifty years ago. The limits of the husband's powers and attainments are carefully defined. He is a drudge—not harmless, for to describe him so would be to do him at once injustice and more than justice. Life, for him, has been constantly narrowing. Any scholarship he ever had is " gone—dropt or flung behind ". He has had no youth, his January joins December. Experience, or rather that which he has put in place of experience and which has rendered it fruitless, has been since birth more and more cramping him :—

> Limited every way, a perfect man
> Within the bounds built up and up since birth
> Breast-high about him till the outside world
> Was blank save o'erhead one blue bit of sky—
> Faith : he had faith in dogma, small or great,
> As in the fact that if he clave his skull
> He'd find a brain there   (xii. 250).

The influence of an unenlightened theology on a nature small to begin with is easily conceived. It breeds in the first place selfishness, on the side both of the preacher and of the listeners. He is

> Bent
> On saving his own soul by saving theirs,—
> They, bent on being saved if saving soul
> Included body's getting bread and cheese
> Somehow in life and somehow after death   (xii. 253).

And this naturally reacts upon and degrades still further a doctrine degraded enough already. Heaven becomes " a vulgar bribe " and hell " a vulgar threat ". The former he " left wisely undescribed " :—

> But Hell he made explicit. After death,
> Life : man created new, ingeniously
> Perfect for a vindictive purpose now
> That man, first fashioned in beneficence
> Was proved a failure ; intellect at length
> Replacing old obtuseness, memory
> Made mindful of deliquent's bygone deeds
> Now that remorse was vain, which life-long lay
> Dormant when lesson might be laid to heart ;
> New gift of observation up and down
> And round man's self, new power to apprehend
> Each necessary consequence of act
> In man for well or ill—things obsolete—
> Just granted to supplant the idiocy
> Man's only guide while act was yet to choose,

FAITH AND DOUBT.

> With ill or well momentously its fruit ;
> A faculty of immense suffering
> Conferred on mind and body,—mind, erewhile
> Unvisited by one compunctious dream
> During sin's drunken slumber, startled up,
> Stung through and through by sin's significance
> Now that the holy was abolished—just
> As body which, alive, broke down beneath
> Knowledge, lay helpless in the path to good,
> Failed to accomplish aught legitimate,
> Achieve aught worthy,—which grew old in youth,
> And at its longest fell a cut-down flower,—
> Dying, this too revived by miracle
> To bear no end of burthen now that back
> Supported torture to no use at all,
> And live imperishably potent—since
> Life's potency was impotent to ward
> One plague off which made earth a hell before (xii. 255-256).

There is probably nowhere a more powerful exposure of beliefs which, though inherently absurd, have been gravely taught and widely believed. The nearest parallel is perhaps the satires of Burns, with their merciless exposure of the extreme forms of Calvinism. An important practical difference is that Burns's satires reached those for whom they were meant and who stood in need of them, while Browning appeals almost wholly to those who, on such matters, are already convinced. Browning seems to have made the mistake of his own dissenting preacher in *Christmas Eve*.

In *La Saisiaz* Browning made a deliberate attempt to state the fundamental principles of his religion after a fashion rather philosophical than poetic. It is true there is much in *La Saisiaz* of highly poetic beauty, as for instance the fine descriptions in the beginning. Still, the ground-work of the poem is a philosophical discussion of the question of immortality. The story how it took its rise from the sudden death of a dear friend is well known. This in the first place induced Browning to examine again the grounds whereon the faith rested which had supported his whole life; and in the second place to drop for once that dramatic disguise which, in dealing with such subjects, he had always worn more or less loosely.

Thus impelled, the poet starts by assuming the existence of two things, the soul and God.

> Prove them facts ? that they o'erpass my power of proving, proves
> them such (xiv. 174),

an argument which, if it convinced the poet, has probably convinced no one else. Sure thus of his own existence and of a power which placed him where he is, he finds himself strangely limited in knowledge, and surrounded by puzzles and even by seeming contradictions. He is limited in knowledge, for "knowledge stands on my experience," and the pronoun is emphatic. The experience may be valid to no other. The grass I call green, another pronounces red; and had earth no other tenants there would be no means of determining which was right and which wrong. In the same way, different men's conceptions of pain and pleasure may be equally inconsistent. Thus the whole argument is valid only for the writer, and for those, if any, whose experience tallies with his.

On this highly sceptical foundation the poet builds his system of faith. Within the "narrow hem" of his experience he beholds a wild dance of phenomena, love and hatred, goodness and evil, power and impotence. But he is convinced that, on the whole, so far as regards the existence he knows, evil outweighs good. "Sorrow did and joy did nowise,—life well weighed—preponderate." This, it may be remarked in passing, can only be accepted as true to his feeling for the time, when life was darkened by his recent loss: the whole tone of his poetry contradicts it. Further, he cannot reconcile "wisdom with a world distraught" unless he be allowed to make another assumption,—that earth is a school wherein he is a pupil, and time a "probation-space". This thought is deep-rooted in Browning's mind: we have met with it more than once already. It is this that turns failure to success, and explains what were else the insoluble contradictions of the world. For otherwise, he pronounces, life *is* failure. It may be ordained by necessity, in which case it must be borne; but "by a cause all-good, all-wise, all-potent? No, as I am man!" A second life is then a necessary postulate to balance the evils of the present, and to justify the fundamental assumption of God:—

> Only grant a second life, I acquiesce
> In this present life as failure, count misfortune's worse assaults
> Triumph, not defeat, assured that loss so much the more exalts
> Gain about to be (xiv. 184).

The concluding part of the poem, the dialogue between Fancy and Reason, is a development of the principles here laid down. There are now the three fundamental facts of God, the Soul and Immortality. The subsequent question is, what conduct will result from them? The first pronouncement of Reason is for suicide—why live on in a world where evil admittedly preponderates? Fancy replies that the living out the life here is a condition of the hope beyond; and, in face of that, the advice of Reason is to "take the joys and bear the sorrows—neither with extreme concern". Then Fancy adds the final condition, that not only must man live through his life, but that he shall " become aware life has worth incalculable," because every act involves gain or loss for that next life which depends on this. The answer is curious and most characteristic. It is given elsewhere too, but nowhere, perhaps, as explicitly as here. It is that through the promulgation of this decree good and evil cease to exist. What Browning means is that moral good and evil imply a struggle, and a liberty of choice; whereas what is really and authentically a law gets itself obeyed automatically. It is a "law" that we must breathe in order to live, but a law which need not be stated, because it enforces itself. Once make it as certain that "heaven or hell depends upon man's earthly deed," and the deed becomes as inevitable as the drawing breath. It is not yet as inevitable, because the connexion of action and consequence has never been made as indisputable as the connexion of cause and effect in nature. This is the weakness in which faith finds its strength.

Such is the poet's religion, expounded when he was over sixty. He held it all his life, and it reappears without substantial change in *Rephan* and in the *Reverie* of *Asolando*. It may seem limited beside what appears the larger faith of the earlier poems. It is not however probable that it indicates any considerable change on the poet's part, though some change was inevitable in the process of threshing out his beliefs through which he passed in his old age. The difference is rather to be explained by a consideration of the difference, on the one hand, between what is mentally accepted, and what can be, in a measure, proved; and, on the other, of the fact that Browning is speaking here in his own person. Every rag of the dramatic disguise is gone; there is no addition here, such as he no doubt thought necessary in the earlier poems, to adapt them to the characters. And what he has given us is not necessarily all that he believed, but only what he thought he could give a rational account of, satisfactory at least to himself; for it is always within his own experience that the arguments hold. In the very attempt he shows the influence of the time upon him. He is trying, after that revel of impulse in the new order of things which the old Pope foresaw, after that break-up of the old world which Arnold ceaselessly laments, to reconstruct law afresh. For his limitation of the argument to his own experience is rather dialectical than real. He knows that there is more evidence for the substantial agreement of experience in all men, than there is for the personal immortality he seeks to establish; and that therefore it is a ὕστερον πρότερον to set down the latter as a fundamental and the former as a contingent truth.

Browning and Arnold then agree as to the basis of their method. They are both seekers after truth, and both are convinced that truth must somehow or other commend itself to reason. Browning is convinced, notwithstanding the fact of his ultimate denial of knowledge. He uses reason to dethrone reason; and he has no sooner done so than he sets reason to work again to test his results. The fact is significant that in *La Saisiaz* it is with Reason, not with Fancy, that the ultimate truth lies. But the two poets, while agreeing in the fundamental process, differ widely in the results reached. Arnold is throughout, as we have seen, the poet of doubt, stretching his hands through the dark towards a faint far-away glimmer. Browning definitely states a faith which may be fairly called large, and he implies one larger still.

Tennyson stands nearer Browning in the proportions of his faith, but differs from both his contemporaries in the manner in which it is stated, and apparently also in the manner in which it is reached. In the important place such questions hold in his verse Tennyson, like the others, implicitly acknowledges himself the child of an age of doubt. He too, like them, has to reconstruct a religion from the shattered fragments borne down to him by time. In results and, superficially, in method, he partly agrees with Browning; but in both he stands in strong contrast to Arnold. Arnold's result is chiefly negative; Tennyson's is positive. Arnold's method is ruled wholly by reason; his faith, so far as faith comes in at all, is faith in reason. He finds himself led by reason to a certain point, to a view of the universe in which good, on the whole, prevails over evil; and on this ground he can believe many things he cannot prove. His faith in reason is shown further where many professed advocates of faith have been singularly weak. He has faith to follow wherever reason leads him, "to follow knowledge like a sinking star," even though it may seem to sink into the pit. Needless to say, the contrast with Tennyson is in this respect not complete. The influence of the century is too strong to permit the dethronement of reason even in matters of religion. Still, we find in Tennyson what we do not find in Arnold, the sort of opposition made by theologians between faith and reason, and the inclination to accept the former rather than the latter.

A great poet's theory of life is all-pervasive, like the soul as described by the philosophers, "all in the whole and all in every part". Tennyson's views of the fundamental relations of man to the universe are no doubt implicit in his earliest work; and in part they were soon made explicit. Still, it was *In Memoriam* that first fully and elaborately dealt, in poetic form, with such questions. Among the earlier poems we must look chiefly to *The Two Voices*, the *Supposed Confessions* and *The Vision of Sin*, though hints may be found also in *The Palace of Art*, *Sir Galahad*, *Ulysses*, and in fact in all the more thoughtful poems.

These poems have been already noticed, and it is unnecessary to dwell upon them here. The point now calling for attention is that either no conclusion is reached, or it is reached by a leap. The *Supposed Confessions* is an aspiration after a faith which is not attained.

> How sweet to have a common faith!
> To hold a common scorn of death!
> And at a burial to hear
> The creaking cords which wound and eat
> Into my human heart, whene'er
> Earth goes to earth, with grief, not fear,
> With hopeful grief, were passing sweet!

But the end is, instead of this trust, a "damned vacillating state" between faith and scepticism. It is probably not without meaning that the "sensitive mind" to which these reflections are attributed is described as "second-rate". In the other poems the positive conclusion is either suggested, as in *The Vision of Sin*, *The Palace of Art* and *Ulysses*, or, as I have said, reached by a leap, as in *The Two Voices*. It is suggested in *The Palace of Art* by the failure to find happiness in a life devoted to the selfish and solitary pursuit of beauty alone; and in *Ulysses* by that strenuous persistence of effort, "strong in will to strive, to seek, to find, and not to yield," and the courageous hope that

> It may be we shall touch the Happy Isles,
> And see the great Achilles, whom we knew.

It is moreover very carefully and deliberately suggested in *The Vision of Sin*. There, before the appearance of the grim spectre, the speaker tells us that he looked towards a mountain-tract, and

> Saw that every morning, far withdrawn
> Beyond the darkness and the cataract,
> God made Himself an awful rose of dawn,
> Unheeded: and detaching, fold by fold,
> From those still heights, and, slowly drawing near,
> A vapour heavy, hueless, formless, cold,
> Came floating on for many a month and year,
> Unheeded.

Thus the human fate and the hope behind it are alike unheeded by the reveller in the mad dance of pleasure. But fate fulfils itself, and in the vision "the mystic mountain-range" once more appears, while

> Below were men and horses pierced with worms,
> And slowly quickening into lower forms.

Even from decay and dissolution wrought by sin hope re-emerges:—

> At last I heard a voice upon the slope
> Cry to the summit, "Is there any hope?"
> To which an answer peal'd from that high land,
> But in a tongue no man could understand;
> And on the glimmering limit far withdrawn
> God made Himself an awful rose of dawn.

It is impossible to miss the meaning of the suggestion. The doubt yet entwined with it, indicated by the fact that the answer is in a tongue no man can understand, is suggestive of Arnold rather than Tennyson. But behind all is the "awful rose of dawn" still glowing.

In *The Two Voices* the conclusion is more than suggested, but there is a gap between it and the argument which fills the earlier part of the poem. The argument ends, certainly not with the victory of the opponent of the voice of doubt :—

> I ceased, and sat as one forlorn.
> Then said the voice, in quiet scorn,
> "Behold, it is the Sabbath morn".

But what is not achieved by argument is accomplished by feeling. The answer to the fundamental question is found in a spirit similar to that suggested in *The Palace of Art*, when the poet passes beyond himself, to contemplate the picture of family affection, husband, wife and child walking in the peal of "sweet church bells" to worship :—

> These three made unity so sweet,
> My frozen heart began to beat,
> Remembering its ancient heat.
>
> I blest them, and they wander'd on:
> I spoke, but answer came there none :
> The dull and bitter voice was gone.
>
> A second voice was at mine ear,
> A little whisper silver-clear,
> A murmur, " Be of better cheer ".
>
> As from some blissful neighbourhood,
> A notice faintly understood,
> " I see the end and know the good ".

By such influences the doubter is brought

> To feel, altho' no tongue can prove,
> That every cloud, that spreads above
> And veileth love, itself is love.

He wanders abroad into the fields, and finds the woods

> Fill'd so full with song,
> There seem'd no room for sense of wrong.

Still, the veil is nowhere lifted from the mystery. It is "a hidden hope" the voice of comfort proclaims. "I may not speak of what I know," it says. This is quite consonant with that faith which in later days we find still trusting that "somehow good will be the final goal of ill"; but it is obvious how widely different in spirit it is from Browning, and still more from Arnold, who deals with the future and the unseen on the same principles as he deals with the visible and the present.

The vital difference is that whereas Browning and Arnold give us intellectual convictions, Tennyson gives us emotions. The form taken by the convictions of the two first-named is indeed poetic; but the fact that it is so does not alter their substance. But Tennyson does not face and solve problems after the manner of his two contemporaries, he cuts the knot. As we have just seen, in *The Two Voices*, the voice of despair is not reasoned down, it yields to a picture, and to a tradition justifiable perhaps, but unjustified. The spirit of *In Memoriam* is exactly the same. The passages in that great poem which have passed into common use are passages which appeal from the head to the heart :—

> If e'er when faith had fall'n asleep,
> I heard a voice, "believe no more,"
> And heard an ever-breaking shore
> That tumbled in the Godless deep;
>
> A warmth within the breast would melt
> The freezing reason's colder part,
> And like a man in wrath the heart
> Stood up and answered "I have felt" (cxxiv.).

Browning, as we have seen, does something similar when he is in difficulty; but it is only at the close of a process of reasoning, and only to give a foundation for another process.

Tennyson moreover accepts the limitation of knowledge without question and without uneasiness:—

> We have but faith: we cannot know;
> For knowledge is of things we see.
>   (*In Memoriam : Introduction.*)

Or, again :—

> Behold, we know not anything;
> I can but trust that good shall fall
> At last—far off—at last, to all,
> And every winter change to spring.
>
> So runs my dream : but what am I ?
> An infant crying in the night :
> An infant crying for the light :
> And with no language but a cry (liv.).

In the same spirit are the justly celebrated stanzas in which the poet pictures himself as

> Falling with his weight of cares
> Upon the great world's altar-stairs
> That slope thro' darkness up to God (lv.).

And under the surface it is likewise apparent in his sense of the insufficiency of nature:—

> And all the phantom, Nature, stands—
> With all the music in her tone,
> A hollow echo of my own,—
> A hollow form with empty hands (iii.).

So is it also in the equally well-known passage where he pictures nature so careful of the type and so careless of the single life, with the further doubt suggested:—

> "So careful of the type?" but no.
> From scarped cliff and quarried stone
> She cries "A thousand types are gone:
> I care for nothing, all shall go.
>
> Thou makest thine appeal to me:
> I bring to life, I bring to death:
> The spirit does but mean the breath:
> I know no more" (lvi.).

There is an impassable barrier then between nature and that higher life the human spirit imperatively demands. There is always behind Tennyson's utterances the feeling expressed by a more recent poet:—

> We are too young to fall to dust
> And too unsatisfied to die.

He demands eternity, as Browning demands it; for otherwise human life is as futile as it is frail. But for warrant of his faith he points to nothing that comes within the scope of reason; the warrant lies "behind the veil".

Contrast this with Arnold. In a remarkable passage in *Empedocles on Etna* he shows that now, as long ago, man is driven by his own weakness to imagine strength elsewhere, and by the disappointments of a finite life and finite powers to imagine a life and powers freed from limit. But now, as never before, the unsubstantial character of the cloudy visions is evident:—

> Fools! That in man's brief term
> He cannot all things view,
> Affords no ground to affirm
> That there are Gods who do;
> Nor does being weary prove that he has where to rest.

But while Arnold decisively rejects this argument he modifies the view of the absolute severance between nature and morality which in Tennyson leads up to it. In the striking poem, *Morality*, he presents a view of nature in some respects similar to Tennyson's, but with a most characteristic and instructive difference. He pictures "struggling, task'd morality," bearing "the burden and the heat of the long day," and afterwards asking of nature with her "free, light, cheerful air," how *she* viewed this self-control:—

> And she, whose censure thou dost dread,
> Whose eye thou wast afraid to seek,
> See, on her face a glow is spread,
> A strong emotion on her cheek !
>   "Ah, child ! " she cries, " that strife divine,
>   Whence was it, for it is not mine ?
>
> "There is no effort on *my* brow—
> I do not strive, I do not weep ;
> I rush with the swift spheres and glow
> In joy, and when I will, I sleep.
>   Yet that severe, that earnest air,
>   I saw, I felt it once—but where ?
>
> "I knew not yet the gauge of time,
> Nor wore the manacles of space ;
> I felt it in some other clime,
> I saw it in some other place.
>   'Twas when the heavenly house I trod,
>   And lay upon the breast of God."

The gulf between nature and morality is fully acknowledged here, but not as impassable. There is continuity: in nature herself there is the suggestion of morality.

It is plain from the extracts which have been given that Tennyson was incomparably more the poet of faith than Arnold. That he had more of the spirit of religion than either of his contemporaries is very doubtful ; for that spirit is a thing which cannot be measured by the capacity to accept propositions. A man may believe the whole Athanasian creed, and yet have very little religion ; he may reject nearly everything in it, and yet have a great deal. But Tennyson had this spirit of religion in a different way from the others, in a way which made it easier for him to adapt his beliefs to existing creeds. There can be little doubt that of the three he was the one who accepted with least change the ordinary religious doctrines. He was in the main orthodox. He had sympathy with doubt, for he had felt it himself, and he has given honourable expression to his belief in the value, as faith, of "honest doubt".[1] But he had never felt it in that imperious form in which it demands a solution satisfactory to the reason. After some degree of hesitation and difficulty he was able to put it aside. The something amiss "will be unriddled by and by".

This conclusion sufficed not only for the time but for life. We have already seen how in his later years Tennyson's optimism was dashed with doubts deeper in some respects than any that touched his youth or his prime. But the indictment which, in poems like *Locksley Hall Sixty Years After*, he brings against the age, never touches the fundamental question. That, for Tennyson, was settled long ago. The cure for the numerous social evils, if there is any cure at all, lies in a very distant future, but that raises no doubts as to the goodness of the power which rules the world; it rather suggests that evil may be a condition of good—"no ill, no good". Deep-reaching scepticism is expressed by Tennyson dramatically, not in his own voice,—by the speaker in *Despair*, not by himself; and it is significant that the scepticism here is begotten equally of the "knowing and know-nothing books," and of the "know-all chapel," whose members, in the phrase of Matthew Arnold, are as familiar with the Deity as with the "man in the next street". But where Tennyson speaks for himself, it is rather as the "Ancient Sage" with his advice to "cleave ever to the sunnier side of doubt," or, without any disguise, in the celebrated lines, *Crossing the Bar*, wherein at eighty he proclaimed how steadfast was his faith.

We have now passed three great poets in review, and have interrogated them specially with reference to all the leading interests of humanity. We have found everywhere at the core of their work the thought and life of the time in which they live. The landscape is indeed seen from the vantage-ground of lofty intellect which gives a wider outlook and juster proportion to the parts; but still it is the same as that which, in smaller

---

[1] There is a curious similarity in thought between the familiar lines in which Tennyson affirms this belief, and some lines, much less widely known, in Browning's *Rabbi Ben Ezra*:—

> Rather I prize the doubt
> Low kinds exist without,
> Finished and finite clods, untroubled by a spark.

portions and therefore with greater tendency to exaggerate the minute, the ordinary eye has looked upon. The great practical task of the century has been the reconstruction of society after the upheaval of the French Revolution; and we find each of the three poets in his own way engaging in the task; Arnold insisting over and over again on its magnitude and difficulty, and on the need of lucidity and a wide outlook to accomplish it; Tennyson on his belief in ordered progress and his desire to "conserve the hopes of man"[1]; Browning proclaiming his own debt to freedom and his wish therefore that everyone should enjoy it. The dominant thought of the century has been, all are agreed, evolution; and we find it running through poetry from *Paracelsus* to *Demeter*. In religion, the need has been for a reconstruction of the fabric shaken by the negative thought of the eighteenth century, and for harmonising it with the new ideas of the nineteenth. At this task all the three poets have toiled, each in his own way, unremittingly.

It is true that if we measure their contribution to these subjects by the test, What do they prove? it is small enough. But then, if we insist upon a demonstration after the manner of Euclid, what can be proved that is worth proving? "The intellectual interest of a truth is gone the moment it becomes a fact." It is the truth towards which we reach through darkness, that which the prophet's eye sees glimmering in the distance, that gives life to the soul; and of such truth we shall nowhere, in recent times, find more than in the three great Victorian poets. The student of them becomes convinced that the great poet is indeed what Browning called him:—

> The general-in-chief,
> Thro' a whole campaign of the world's life and death,
> Doing the King's work all the dim day long.
> (*How it strikes a Contemporary*, iv. 180.)

[1] Mr. Arthur Waugh in his valuable book on Tennyson tells an interesting story about the poet:—"Aubrey de Vere asked him whether he were a Conservative. 'I believe in progress,' said Tennyson, 'and I would conserve the hopes of man.' It is," adds Mr. Waugh, "the very keynote of his poetry."

INDEX.

A.

Andrea del Sarto, 104.
Any Wife to Any Husband, 99.
Aristophanes' Apology, 157.
Arnold, Matthew, his relation to the Victorian period, 4; his conception of poetry, 12, 21; his view of the results of the French Revolution, 18, 273; Thyrsis, 72 sqq.; his first volume of poems, 122, 124 sqq.; not popular, 122; his artistic qualities, compared with those of Tennyson, 123; his changes of mind, 124, 129; his sense of thwarting destiny, 125; his view of Nature, 126, 201, 220, sqq.; the lesson of resignation, 126 sqq.; his handling of passion, 130 sqq.; his criticisms in verse, 133; these compared with Browning's poems on art, 134; his criticism of life, 134; Poems of 1853, 135 sqq.; his blank verse, 136; evidences of the classical spirit in him, 137, 141 sqq.; his self-revelation, 138, 148, 172; Poems of 1855, 138; New Poems of 1867, 138 sqq.; his sonnets, 139; his elegiacs, 139; his stoicism, 140; his restraint, 142; his sureness of taste, 146; his sense of the complexity of life, 147; as a dramatist, 172; deficient in action, 174; self-centred, 221; the sculptor of poetry, 221, 228; compared with Browning, 222; his love of subdued colours, 223; and sounds, 224; his sense of the loneliness of humanity, 224; his contrast of nature and man, 227; does not complain against nature, 229; what he adopted from science, 241, 244; his sense of the insufficiency of science, 242; his intellectual sincerity, 243, 299; accepts the spiritual interpretation of the universe, 244; his note social rather than political, 270; his distrust of panaceas, 271; his affinity to Senancour, 272; "wandering between two worlds," 273; on the intellectual leader, 275; on inability to "possess our soul," 276; his sense of the need of society, 276; his hope for the future, 279; his religious doubt, 294, 320; his fidelity to reason, 295, 325; an unwilling sceptic, 296; on the influence of early Christianity, 297; its decay, 298; his disbelief in immorality, 298; his negations account for his melancholy, 299; represents nature as leading up to morality, 326.
At the Mermaid, 158.

B.

Bacon, Lord, 231, 236.
Balaustion's Adventure, 157.
Balder Dead, 136, 137, 138, 143.
Ballads and other Poems, 268.
Bean Stripe, A, 160.
Beckett, 72, 168 sqq.
Bishop Blougram's Apology, 101, 102, 109, 309.
Bishop Orders his Tomb at St. Praxed's Church, The, 288.
Blot in the 'Scutcheon, A, 187, 190, 199, 286.
"Break, break, break," 32.
Brooke, Mr. Stopford A., 84n, 174, 262n.
Browning, E. B., 91, 98, 195.
Browning, Robert, his relation to the Victorian period, 3; on the revival of religious feeling, 9; on the character of the poet, 13, 52; his early works, 17; Pauline, 35 sqq.; Paracelsus, 37 sqq.; his monodramatic poetry, 38; his doctrine of a good inherent in evil, 42, 161, 166, 218, 255, 256, 309, 311; like the Germans, 42; period of experiment after Paracelsus, 44; Sordello, 46, 48 sqq.; causes of its difficulty, 48; its poetic beauties, 51; Pippa Passes, 56 sqq.; the sketch of Ottima and Sebald and Macbeth, 59; Dramatic Lyrics and Dramatic Romances, 63 sqq.; his use of the grotesque, 67; his love of Italy, 68, 103; Christmas Eve and Easter Day, 91 sqq.; influence of Mrs. Browning, 91, 98; his handling of religious questions, 92 sqq., 101 sqq., 108 sqq., 300 sqq.; culmination of his genius, 95; its causes, 96 sqq.; Men and Women, 101 sqq.; poems on art, 108, 134; Dramatis Personæ, 105 sqq.; poems on love, 105; The Ring and the Book, 115 sqq.; plan of it, 116; unevenness, 117; prin-

cipal characters, 117 sqq.; his want of restraint, 142; his later development, 155; decline of the dramatic spirit, 158 sqq.; his critical method illustrated from various poems, 161 sqq., 196; full development of his later characteristics in *La Saisiaz*, 169; his dramas, 186 sqq.; their deficiency in action, 188, 198; single-character plays, 188, 197; his inflexibility of style, 191; his treatment of nature, 212 sqq.; determined by his view of man, 213; influenced by his optimism, 214, 219; and by science, 237, 240; his need of humanity as a centre, 214; his pictorial power, 217; is an evolutionist, 247, 251; his doctrine of necessary ignorance, 255; not deeply interested in politics, 281; more concerned with social facts, 283; believes in men rather than in institutions, 283; hence the social element merges in the human, 284; considers all peculiarly human qualities as originating in society, 284; view of society implied in the dramas, 285; and in various poems, 288; his treatment of monasticism, 286; the religious element in the three periods, 300; difference between the earlier and the later parts of *Saul*, 301; the religious significance of *Christmas Eve and Easter Day*, 303 sqq.; his dislike of scepticism, 305; on the necessity of doubt, 309, 312; does not meet the final forms of scepticism, 311; on the older Evangelical Christianity, 315; his discussion of immortality, 317; his ultimate belief in reason, 320.
Burns, Robert, 47, 317.
Byron, Lord, 3, 27, 71, 148, 270, 293.

C.

Caliban upon Setebos, 109.
Campbell, Thomas, 263.
Carlyle, Jane Welsh, quoted, 3.
Carlyle, Thomas, 20, 232, 239, 245, 293.
Cavalier poets, The, 15.
Charge of the Light Brigade, The, 144, 155.
Charge of the Heavy Brigade, The, 151, 155.
Childe Roland, 66, 147.
Christmas Eve and Easter Day, 91 sqq., 298, 303 sqq.
Church of Brou, The, 135, 229.
Church-Warden and the Curate, The, 154.
Cleon, 102.
Clive, 159.
Colombe's Birthday, 188, 189, 198, 286.
Columbus, 152.

Cristina and Monaldeschi, 157.
Crossing the Bar, 327.
Cup, The, 176.

D.

Daisy, The, 203.
Darwin, Charles, 233, 246.
Deaf and Dumb, 105.
Death in the Desert, A, 111, 113, 309.
Death of Œnone, The, 176.
Demeter, 176.
De Profundis, 250.
De Quincey, quoted, 61.
Despair, 155, 327.
Dis aliter Visum, 106.
Dora, 29, 268.
Dramatic Lyrics, 63 sqq.
Dramatic Romances and Lyrics, 63 sqq.
Dramatis Personæ, 105 sqq.
Dream of Fair Women, A, 24.
Drummond of Hawthornden, 234.

E.

Empedocles on Etna, 129, 137, 165, 172, 242, 325.
Englishman in Italy, The, 214, 282.
Enoch Arden, 80, 85, 145, 268.
Epilogue to Lessing's Laocoön, 134.
Epilogue to Pacchiarotto, 158.
Epistle of Karshish, 101.
Euphrosyne, 132.

F.

Faded Leaves, 130.
Falcon, The, 175.
Ferishtah's Fancies, 160.
Fifine at the Fair, 53, 54, 165.
Fitzgerald, Edward, quoted, 126.
Fleet, The, 267.
Flight of the Duchess, The, 65.
Foresters, The, 176.
Forgiveness, A, 157.
Forsaken Merman, The, 145.
Fra Lippo Lippi, 103, 288.
Francis Furini, 254.
Future, The, 278.

G.

Gardener's Daughter, The, 29, 203.
Geist's Grave, 298.
Giuseppe Caponsacchi, 119.
Goethe, 14, 88, 222, 241, 264, 293, 295.
Grandmother, The, 88.
Guido, 117.

H.

Harold, 72, 176, 177.
Heine's Grave, 140, 270.
Holy-Cross Day, 66.
Homer, 13.

INDEX. 331

House, 158.
How it strikes a Contemporary, 96.
Hutton, Mr. R. H., 129, 228.

I.

Idylls of the King, 81 sqq., 248, 267.
In a Gondola, 64.
In Harmony with Nature, 134, 229.
In Memoriam, 76 sqq., 86, 87, 123, 210, 248, 249, 324.
Inn Album, The, 72, 158, 162, 289, 314.
In Utrumque Paratus, 129.
Iván Ivánovitch, 159.
Ixion, 157.

J.

James Lee's Wife, 107.
Jones, Professor Henry, 37, 300.

K.

King Victor and King Charles, 189, 286.

L.

Lady of Shalott, The, 22.
Landor, W. S., 47.
La Saisiaz, 156, 169, 317, 320.
Last Word, The, 140.
Locksley Hall, 29, 143, 151, 237, 239, 248, 269.
Locksley Hall Sixty Years After, 29, 151, 155, 250, 251, 269.
Lost Leader, The, 281, 283.
Lotos-Eaters, The, 22, 23, 207.
Luria, 188, 189, 283.
"*Lyric Love,*" 99.

M.

Macaulay, Lord, 231.
Making of Man, The, 250.
Maud, 30, 72, 80, 86, 87, 248, 267.
May Queen, The, 85, 145.
Memorabilia, 105.
Memorial Verses, 133.
Men and Women, 101 sqq.
Merope, 137, 172, 174.
Mihrab Shah, 255.
Mill, John Stuart, 239.
Miller's Daughter The, 23, 26.
Milton, 14, 77, 141, 248, 260.
Morality, 134, 326.
Morte d'Arthur, 31.
Mycerinus, 128.
My Last Duchess, 65.

N.

Nationality in Drinks, 282.
Northern Cobbler, The, 153.
Northern Farmer, The, 88, 153.
Numpholeptos, 156.

O.

Obermann Once More, 123, 139, 228, 279, 297.
Ode on the Death of the Duke of Wellington, 264.
Œnone, 152.
One Word More, 99.
Orr, Mrs. Sutherland, 44, 49, 142, 187, 282.

P.

Palace of Art, The, 24, 26, 205, 322.
Paracelsus, 37 sqq., 237, 240, 251, 285.
Parleyings with certain People, 156, 161.
Passing of Arthur, The, 208.
Pauline, 17, 35, 53, 54, 148, 300.
Pietro of Abano, 159.
Pillar at Sebzevar, A, 160.
Pippa Passes, 56 sqq., 219.
Poems by Two Brothers, 16.
Poet, The, 53.
Poet's Mind, The, 53.
Pompilia, 119, 192.
Poor Matthias, 225.
Pope, The, 111, 113, 120, 311.
Popularity, 105.
Porphyria's Lover, 64.
Prince Hohenstiel-Schwangau, 163, 254, 289.
Princess, The, 72 sqq., 87, 261, 265, 267.
Promise of May, The, 176.
Prospice, 108.

Q.

Queen Mary, 175, 176.

R.

Rabbi Ben Ezra, 113, 327 n.
Rachel, 147.
Red Cotton Nightcap Country, 161, 216.
Rephan, 256, 319.
Resignation, 125, 222, 226, 227.
Return of the Druses, The, 68, 189, 286.
Reverie, 319.
Ring and the Book, The, 66, 115 sqq., 289.
Rizpah, 150.
Rugby Chapel, 145, 277.

S.

Saul, 214, 217, 301.
Scherer, Edmond, 142.
Scholar, Gipsy, The, 135, 229, 275.
Senancour, Étienne Pivert de, 272.
Shakespeare, 4, 14, 59 sqq., 67, 196, 199, 260.
Shelley, 292.
Sibrandus Schafnaburgensis, 287.
Sick King in Bokhara, The, 128.
Sir John Oldcastle, 150, 152.

INDEX.

Socrates, his dissuasion from physical investigation, 238.
Sohrab and Rustum, 136, 137, 145, 228.
Soliloquy of the Spanish Cloister, 65, 67, 287.
Sordello, 46, 48 sqq.
Southern Night, A, 139, 145, 274.
Spinster's Sweet-Arts, The, 154.
Stanzas from the Grande Chartreuse, 138, 139, 243, 272, 273.
Stanzas in Memory of the Author of "Obermann," 133, 272.
Statue and the Bust, The, 106, 161.
Strafford, 188, 189, 286.
Strayed Reveller, The, 124, 125, 275.
Summer Night, A, 134, 227.
Supposed Confessions of a Second-rate Sensitive Mind, 22, 24, 26, 321.
Swift, Jonathan, 285.
Switzerland, 130.

T.

Tennyson, Alfred, Lord, his early admiration of Byron, 3, 16; his relation to the Victorian period, 3; on the character of the poet, 13, 53; his first publication, 16; his early works, 17; his "lollipops," 19; elements of reality in the poems of 1830 and 1833, 22 sqq.; his power of self-criticism, 22; his early interest in the Arthurian legends, 23, 31; relation of the more serious poems to the time, 25 sqq.; his patriotic poetry, 25, 87, 154, 259, 261 sqq.; *Poems* of 1842, 28 sqq.; his humour, 28, 154; his manner of modernising ancient subjects, 32; his imitation of earlier poets, 33; transition to long poems, 70; *The Princess*, 72 sqq.; difficulties of a modern subject, 72; question of his power of construction, 72, 84; his treatment of "the woman question," 74; *In Memoriam*, 76 sqq.; *Maud*, 80; *Enoch Arden*, 80; *Idylls of the King*, 81 sqq.: how far allegorical, 84; his view of war, 87, 135, 263; growth of a dramatic element, 88, 151 sqq.; his artistic qualities compared with Arnold's, 123; less restrained than Arnold, 143; his pathos occasionally false, 145; his later development, 150; his use of dialect, 153; his treatment of social problems, 155, 267; as dramatist, 174 sqq.; cause of his resort to the drama, 184; his treatment of nature, 201 sqq.; pictorial, 203, 205; contrasted with Wordsworth, 204; sometimes purposely vague, 207; his later manner, 208; objective and subjective views, 211; his observation of nature influenced by science, 237; an evolutionist, 247, 249, 250; what he took from science, 248; in his political pieces speaks for Englishmen, 259; comparatively narrow, 260; on English stability, 261; and French instability, 262; on the function of England, 263; his sense that rights involve duties, 263; sees the spirit of England embodied in Wellington, 264; his attitude with regard to religion, 320; his conclusions not reasoned out, 321; different in this respect from Browning and Arnold, 324; puts an impassable barrier between nature and morality, 325; more orthodox than the other poets, 326; had felt doubt, but put it aside, 327.
Third of February, The, 263, 266.
Thomson, James, 234.
Thyrsis, 72, 74, 77 sqq., 136, 229.
Timbuctoo, 16.
Tithonus, 89.
To a Gipsy Child, 127.
Tolstoi, Count Lyof N., 88.
"*Transcendentalism*," 105.
Tristram and Iseult, 130, 131.
Turner, J. M. W., 235.
Two Camels, 160, 288.
Two Voices, The, 322, 324.

U.

Ulysses, 31, 32, 322.
Urania, 132,

V.

Vastness, 269.
Vision of Sin, The, 30, 322.

W.

Waugh, Mr. Arthur, 328 n.
Westminster Abbey, 146.
Wilbye, John, his *Second Set of English Madrigals*, quoted, 195.
Will Waterproof's Lyrical Monologue, 28.
Wish, A., 227.
Wordsworth, W., 2, 26, 204, 213, 221, 234, 260.
Worst of It, The, 106.

Y.

Youth and Art, 105.

www.ingramcontent.com/pod-product-compliance
Lightning Source LLC
Chambersburg PA
CBHW032050220426
43664CB00008B/938